Paddy and Mr Punch

Also by R. F. Foster

Charles Stewart Parnell: The Man and His Family

Lord Randolph Churchill: A Political Life

Modern Ireland 1600–1972

The Oxford Illustrated History of Ireland

(ed.) The Sub-Prefect Should Have Held His Tongue:
Selected Essays of Hubert Butler

Paddy and Mr Punch
Connections in Irish and English History

R. F. FOSTER

ALLEN LANE
THE PENGUIN PRESS

ALLEN LANE
THE PENGUIN PRESS

Published by the Penguin Group
Penguin Books Ltd, 27 Wrights Lane, London W8 5TZ, England
Penguin Books USA Inc., 375 Hudson Street, New York, New York 10014, USA
Penguin Books Australia Ltd, Ringwood, Victoria, Australia
Penguin Books Canada Ltd, 10 Alcorn Avenue, Toronto, Ontario, Canada M4V 3B2
Penguin Books (NZ) Ltd, 182–190 Wairau Road, Auckland 10, New Zealand

Penguin Books Ltd, Registered Offices: Harmondsworth, Middlesex, England

First published 1993
1 3 5 7 9 10 8 6 4 2
First edition

The acknowledgements on pp. ix–x constitute an extension of this copyright page

Filmset in 11/13 pt Monophoto Bembo
Typeset by Datix International Limited, Bungay, Suffolk
Printed in Great Britain by Clays, St Ives plc

A CIP catalogue record for this book is available from the British Library

ISBN 0-713-99095-3

Contents

For

Tom Paulin

Acknowledgements

I owe thanks to many people for encouragement and advice in producing this book: Peter Carson and Paul Keegan at Penguin; Valerie Kemp, for her scrupulous care in producing the text; Giles Gordon; and for various criticisms and suggestions, Tom Dunne, Lynne Foster, Victoria Glendinning, Warwick Gould, Michael Ignatieff, the late Brian Inglis, Hermione Lee, Mary-Lou Legg, Edna Longley, Thaddeus O'Sullivan, Donna Poppy, Michael Slater, Deirdre Toomey, Mary-Kay Wilmers, and, above all, Aisling Foster, my most perceptive critic for many years. The dedication to Tom Paulin is both a tribute to an Irish poet and critic of the first rank, and a celebration of a long friendship, much of it spent discussing the themes considered in this book.

Versions of, or extracts from, some of these essays have appeared in the following: No. 1: *Transactions of the Royal Historical Society*, fifth series, vol. 33 (1983). No. 2: M. Crozier (ed.), *Cultural Traditions in Ireland* (Belfast, 1989). No. 3: *Studies*, vol. 80, no. 320 (Dublin, 1991). No. 4: D. Macartney (ed.), *Parnell: The Politics of Power* (Dublin, 1991). No. 8: *Contexts and Connections: Winchester Research Papers in the Humanities No. 10* (Winchester, 1981). No. 9: *Journal of Newspaper and Periodical History*, vol. 7, no. 2 (1991). No. 11: *Proceedings of the British Academy*, vol. 75 (1989). No. 12: F.S.L. Lyons and R.A.J. Hawkins (eds.), *Ireland under the Union: Varieties of Tension* (Oxford, 1980). No. 13: J. M. W. Bean (ed.), *The Political Culture of Modern Britain: Studies in Memory of Stephen Koss* (London, 1987) and Lord Blake (ed.), *Ireland after the Union* (British Academy, 1989). Numbers

5, 6, 7, 10 and 14 have not been published before, but a version of No. 5 was presented to a Wilson Center conference in 1990, No. 10 was delivered to the Synge Summer School at Rathdrum in 1992, and No. 14 to the Hewitt Summer School in the same year. I am grateful to the organizers and participants at these gatherings for comments and suggestions.

The extracts from Elizabeth Bowen's reports for the Ministry of Information in the Public Record Office are crown copyright, reproduced with the permission of the Controller of Her Majesty's Stationery Office.

Introduction

These essays deal with the historical and contemporary inheritance of the relationship between Ireland and Britain, reflected through various lives, incidents and crises. They often focus upon people who lived, or were in some sense 'caught', between the two countries; the last essay in the book explores that general theme. Such people are most readily identified simply as the emigrant millions who left Ireland to make a living; but they could also be writers (Bowen, Trollope, Yeats) or politicians (Parnell, Randolph Churchill) or neither (Katharine O'Shea). Most importantly, they could be British as well as Irish. What they have in common is that their lives and their work were shaped by that awkward relationship: described by one of my subjects as 'a mixture of showing-off and suspicion, nearly as bad as sex'.[1]

The same authority, Elizabeth Bowen, also declared her wish that the English would keep history in mind more, and the Irish, less. Britain and Ireland impinge on each other in a manner embarrassing to both: large areas are left unexplored by both sides, for reasons of bad conscience, good manners and convenient amnesia. Some of the pieces in this book also deal with general themes which reflect the Irish–British intersection, like emigration, education, the operation of the Act of Union and various cultural borrowings – which may have affected Irish history no less decisively than the more obvious cataclysms of rebellion and sacrifice. This is not, therefore, an attempt to engage Irish historical experience in anything like its totality; it is restricted to particular intersections in the modern period. After all, the unique Irish polity as we know it today was not just the outcome of a complex and sophisticated national culture; it was also shaped by what happened between Ireland and Britain.

Yet that polity and that culture have sometimes been seen as created apart from Britain, and in deliberate defiance of British values and British influence. On one level, this is quite true; on another, it is impossible. But it is a sensitive question: and unsureness in this area is indicated (as elsewhere in Irish history and politics) by uncertainty about what name to use. Elizabeth Bowen, it will have been noted, writes 'England' where 'Britain' might be more logical. Many Irish people do the same, myself among them – not least in the title of this book. This does not indicate cavalier disregard of Scotland and Wales; rather, that 'England' carries a historical charge, an implication of attempted cultural dominance, an assertion of power, which is not conveyed to an Irish ear by 'Britain'. It is the word we expect, and find, in Fenian ballads or Yeats's nationalist poetry. And Scotland's or Wales's relationship to Ireland is on many levels a different entity from that of 'England'. Interesting though their cases are, it is the Irish–English relationship that preoccupies me here, particularly at points where apparent weakness or disadvantage is turned into strength. The aspects of Irish history looked at here may not be those most congenial to people who believe the 'real' Irish experience is that of unrelieved pain (though there is plenty of painful experience surveyed in the following pages). Living between Ireland and Britain may be seen as the historical consequence of exploitation; it could, in one way, create confusion; but it was sometimes an enabling experience. This phenomenon is illustrated by the extraordinary record of Irish literature in the English language; its more obscure social aspects are interrogated at length in a little-known masterpiece of autobiography, Donall Mac Amhlaigh's *An Irish Navvy* (*Dialann Deoraí*), whose hero eloquently reflects cultural displacement, wide-eyed innocence and saturnine irony. Through his eyes, the English universe appears at once uncomprehending, well-meaning and unsatisfyingly two-dimensional. Materially necessary but astoundingly philistine, the English market-place only achieves meaning in relation to his visits home, to Kilkenny, where life suddenly assumes its full proportion, shape and colour. But he is inevitably reminded why he had to leave in the first place; and gradually the ironies of a life spent between the two countries appeals to him. At Hyde Park one Sunday he listens to 'a Sinn Féin speaker denouncing England and holding forth about her evil deeds. This annoyed an Englishman who happened to be listening. "As an Englishman," he said, "I should go up and sock you." Right then a big constable, with a strong Kerry accent, said to the Englishman: "Move along there now and don't be disrupting a lawful meeting!"'[2] By the end of Mac Amhlaigh's apprenticeship, life in England is a necessary part of life itself, and the perils of nostalgia are cannily evaded.

Not everyone sees it this way. When Irish historians in the last generation began to examine the received truths of conventional Irish historiography, it is significant that some of the most agonized responses to this iconoclasm came from *émigrés*. With emigrant communities everywhere, the memory of homeland has to be kept in aspic. The perspective over one's shoulder must remain identical to that recorded by the parting glance – even if that moment happened two (or more) generations back, and even if the remembered impression is spectacularly contradicted by the mother country itself as experienced on return visits. In a similar way, ownership of received historical memory is fiercely guarded. Historians raising questions about the accepted version aroused an agonized resentment; they were, it was alleged, attempting to assert 'a perspective on Irish history which would depopulate it of heroic figures, struggling in the cause of national liberation'.[3] In a sense, this reflects the cultural insecurity expressed by some of the subjects of this book. They may not be presented as plaster icons, but ambivalence does not preclude empathy.

This is not always understood by those who have decided that exploration of its complexities and ambiguities simply 'depopulates' Irish history of 'an immemorial native race'.[4] The word 'revisionism' has become shorthand for the kind of historical exploration unacceptable to those clinging to the shattered rock of the received version; it is further discussed in some of the essays that follow. It has also become fashionable to allege that there is a school or conspiracy of 'revisionism' among contemporary Irish historians, but this holds no water at all. Polemicists – not, usually, practising historians – have broadened the term to mean (crudely) anti-nationalist – in itself a fairly meaningless concept. If revisionism means the replacement of old pieties with new certainties, or, even worse, using selective history to underpin current political policies, no self-respecting historian could subscribe to it. Where the notion has vitality and relevance in the Irish historiographical context, in fact, is outside the traditional confines of 'political history'. A perceptive historian has pointed out that the most fundamental revisionism is now being forced by revaluation of hitherto undervalued areas, like the history of women and of locality.[5] On the other hand, when self-appointed scourges of revisionism call openly for 'the abandonment of the value-free principle' in order to reassert the exclusive teleology of faith-and-fatherland history,[6] one is given cause for thought.

In such manifestos words like 'scepticism' and 'iconoclasm' have also been levelled at the recent generation of professional Irish historians, who allegedly lack 'a sense of piety towards our nationalist past';[7] and these accusations may be more readily acknowledged, and defended. Though revisionism has been too heavily loaded for safe usage (since it now stands duty for 'anti-nationalist'), it remains true that historians any good at their job are 'revisers', because that is what they are trained to do; and this applies to Irish historians too. The more sinister charge of deliberately representing ill-defined but anti-national interests is sometimes raised; but *soi-disant* revisionism need not be (and often is not) incompatible with sympathy towards nationalist politics. (There is a significant confusion in anti-revisionist polemic as to whether the supposed revisionists are propping up the political system of the contemporary Irish Republic, or chipping away at its foundations.) The historical profession in Ireland has not been much riven by the *Kulturkampf* which some ideologues have tried to erect between revisionists and anti-revisionists; for one thing, the credibility of such polemicists has not been enhanced by their close identification with the highly politicized movement against full Irish membership of the European Community, based on a distinctively *passé* blend of old-style communism and older-style xenophobia.

Moreover, historians are well aware of ideology's input into historical narrative: they spend an increasing amount of time teaching and researching this very angle. But this is not to say that they are therefore either so simple-minded as to believe it does not apply in their own case or machiavellian enough to conceal a deliberate agenda. Generally, they know their limitations, and the provisional nature of most verdicts. It is true that one Irish historian (not a modernist) has recently argued that commentary ought to be bent for 'patriotic' and hagiographical purposes, reverting to an evangelical and even confessional approach.[8] This is regrettable, since Irish historiography has a fine tradition of scholars (and clerics) from a variety of backgrounds attempting to write as impartially as they can on inflammable subjects. From outside academe crude attempts have been made to equate revisionist history with what is scathingly called a 'liberal agenda'. The Gaelic Athletic Association has long been identified with cultural defensiveness, so it may not be surprising to find its President attacking revisionist historians for 'denouncing Irishness and nationalism, refusing to distinguish between that which we should cherish and that which cannot be condoned, opposing traditional values, the family, the Church and Christian values, and, not least, rural Ireland'.[9] Simultaneously, a sophisticated but essentially similar version has been promulgated by some cultural commentators calling for a return to 'nation, nationality and tradition': 'if Ireland could afford pluralism, it would not be the Ireland we know'.[10] This has been accompanied by less coherent attacks on the 'liberal humanist ethic' as 'a cultural fantasy' when applied to Ireland.[11]

Is this a new *trahison des clercs*, or an old wheel coming round full circle? It is significant that some of these denunciations come from literary critics, because the effect of critical theory on historical discourse is worth noting – in Ireland as in America, in the age of Hayden White and Paul Ricoeur. Some accompanying concepts have added much enlightenment to Irish history, notably the analysis of colonial collusions elsewhere in the Empire. But the recently fashionable idea that the historian/writer is in corrupt and unconscious collusion with the text, and that reference to an ascertainable body of fact is a delusion of the late bourgeois world, leads quickly to the useful position that all history is suspect and all readings questionable. By an easy elision, this sanctions a turning back to the old verities and the old, atavistic antipathies.

In fact, it is curious how old-fashioned the conclusions of modernism tend to be; as cultural commentators turn their attention to history, perfidious Albion and betrayed Hibernia take the stage once more, along with a rhetoric which (as the bewildered George Orwell pointed out fifty years ago) would be denounced as unacceptably chauvinist if spoken in any other accent than Irish. It is time to look at the implications of some anti-revisionist assertions. When reference is made to the 'national community' being betrayed and insulted by the questioning of heroic traditions,[12] what (or which) community is referred to? When the Gaelic Athletic Association President claims that modern historians 'denounce Irishness',[13] what kind of Irishness is he thinking of? When a journalist calls for historians to be 'sympathetically respectful' of 'the people's value-systems',[14] whose value systems are being erected beyond criticism? When a literary critic rails against pluralism, who is he trying to exclude?

All these examples repeat the stance taken up by exclusivist brokers of a supposedly threatened 'Irishness' at the beginning of this century; whatever the window-dressing about respecting other traditions, their logical implication is that Irish cultural diversity ought not to exist, and where it does exist, could be overthrown only by forced conversions or by violence. It was notable at the time that those who most vociferously advanced a purely Catholic–Gaelic notion of Irishness were also those who would claim the most unconditional jurisdiction over a million non-Catholic, non-Gaelic Irish people – upon whom 'sympathetic respect' towards the Catholic–Gaelic value systems would presumably have been enforced. One does not have to be a supporter of Partition, then or now, to find in this an enduring irony.

But the credentials of a pluralist Ireland are not only the preserve of beleaguered historians; they are also being displayed, without bravado, by an increasing number of figures in Irish public life. It is a theme of these essays that cultural diversity and cross-channel borrowings are implicit in Irish history, and cannot be denied by piety or suppressed by violence. The way people saw themselves as Irish deserves more attention than the awarding or denying of Irishness as a mark of good conduct, or embarking on self-justifying searches for uncorrupted 'roots', or taking refuge in self-congratulatory conspiracy theories.

None the less, one version of Irish history stood for many years as an important component in political state-building and in religiously dominated education: any mild attempt to review it arouses a disproportionately vehement reaction from vested interests. What is essentially at issue is possessiveness, and this partly explains the temperature of some Irish cultural debate, as well as the insecurity evinced in one neo-traditionalist's revealing admission that 'the received version of Irish history' is a beneficent legacy, '*its wrongness notwithstanding*'.[15] Modern Ireland has surely come further than that. Ownership of Irish history is claimed from all sides; the idea of a common stock, much less a universal scepticism, is not popular in all quarters. No one is exempt from this possessiveness; but we need not give up our own claims on Irishness in order to conceive of it as a flexible identification. And in an age of exclusivist jihads to east and west, the notion that people can reconcile more than one cultural identity with their individual selves may have much to recommend it. These essays, taken together, form a kind of commentary on the process as it has appeared at certain intersections in modern Irish and English history.

I

History and the Irish Question

'History is more backward in Ireland than in any other country,' wrote the historian J.R. Green's Anglo-Irish widow fiercely in 1912.

> Here alone there is a public opinion which resents its being freely written, and there is an opinion, public or official, I scarcely know which to call it, which prevents its being freely taught. And between the two, history has a hard fight for life. Take the question of writing. History may conceivably be treated as a science. Or it may be interpreted as a majestic natural drama or poem. Either way has much to be said for it. Both ways have been nobly attempted in other countries. But neither of these courses has been thought of in Ireland. Here history has a peculiar doom. It is enslaved in the chains of the Moral Tale – the good man (English) who prospered, and the bad man (Irish) who came to a shocking end.[1]

Through her own works on early Irish society, Mrs Green had set herself, not to produce a scientific or a poetic history, but simply to reverse the moral of the story; and, with the establishment of the Irish Free State ten years after this outburst, events seemed gratifyingly to show that the good had come into their kingdom. The rewriting of history after this consummation, following the practice of most irredentist states, is part of the subject of this essay; but more important, perhaps, is the intention to establish such a process in a wider framework, stretching back over a longer period.

The use of history by politicians and intellectuals provides a theme which will recur: the frequent personification of 'Ireland' in nationalist writing is matched by the personal identification on the part of a long line of Irish activists of their country's history with their own identity.

'The general history of a nation may fitly preface the personal memoranda of a solitary captive,' wrote John Mitchel in his *Jail Journal*; 'for it was strictly and logically a *consequence* of the dreary story here epitomized, that I came to be a prisoner.'[2] Time and again national history is presented as an actor in personal autobiography; by the same token, Irish leaders emphasized the apostolic succession of nationalism by identifying themselves with specific evangelists from the country's past.[3]

This was just one way in which past history was made to serve a legitimizing function for present commitment. In a wider sense, moral attitudes could be inferred from ideas of 'Gaelic' or even 'Celtic' practice and traditions, overlaid and corrupted by conquest. In late nineteenth-century Ireland, egalitarianism was held to have flowered in the Celtic mists, much as in England democracy was supposed to have flourished in the Teutonic forests. Professional historians can ignore both myths; Irish scholars have gone so far as to dismiss most of the canon of Irish history as conceived by the generation of 1916. However, this can itself be seen as part of the pattern whereby the study of Irish history registers, like a seismograph, the waves of politics; and the whole process can only be elucidated by considering the roots of the Irish discovery of their past, and the resulting interpretations of that past, on both sides of St George's Channel. It must also involve, at the conclusion, some consideration of very recent history, trenching upon politics. In so doing, this essay exposes itself to most of the criticisms it levels at history's treatment of the Irish question – and thus becomes part of the process.

The concept of nationalism has been defined and analysed with increasing rigour in recent years; the history of the Irish case, for obvious and pressing reasons, has been the subject of a spate of recent inquiry.[4] But when did the writing of Irish history come to have an effective political function in public discourse? The background to this is not to be found in the series of explanatory histories from the time of Giraldus Cambrensis, and including Elizabethan–Jacobean apologists like Fynes Moryson, Edmund Spenser, Edmund Campion, Sir John Davies and company.[5] The didactic nature of their work was self-confessed, and obvious to contemporaries; their function can only be understood in terms of their time. In some quarters, much emphasis is put on the fact that these works represent English manipulation of early Irish history in order to excuse the Conquest.[6] So indeed they do; but to expect otherwise is to require a detached historical sense exercised on behalf of Irish history, at a time when it was not applied to English history, or to any other. The more sophisticated tradition which concerns us begins with antiquarian explorations in the late eighteenth century, compounded with the various senses of nationalism – colonial, Gaelic and revolutionary – stirring in Ireland at the time.

The coherent effort to establish an Irish past did, of course, rely on some of the material in the earlier histories just mentioned; but the work of the Royal Irish Academy (founded in 1786) and other learned institutions of the time was far more directly inspired by the exploration of bardic tradition, the archaeological evidence scattered profusely throughout the island, and the exploration of indigenous folk culture.[7] As elsewhere in Europe, those most enthused by the process were rarely themselves of the 'indigenous folk'; as so often in Irish history, they were largely the Anglo-Irish middle classes, and the sociological explanations for this (especially in the age of surviving, if largely ignored, penal legislation against Catholics) are obvious. But antiquarianism reacted with the discovery of folk tradition and the Ossianic cult to produce history-writing which attempted to use evidence in place of hearsay, and to present a history of the land and its various peoples, rather than a rationalization of administrative or religious policies in the guise of history.[8] Liberal nationalism both used and was reinforced by the antiquarian and romantic view of early Irish history; the capacity of the land to assimilate its invaders, a matter for censure in earlier commentaries, was implicitly now approved of.

A number of caveats should be established early on. For one thing, the scholarship of these polite enthusiasts was far from impeccable and remained prone to wishful thinking; the seductive spirit of Ossian beckoned them down false trails like a will-o'-the-wisp.[9] The real importance of the Royal Irish Academy in collecting Irish antiquities did not come until later, with George Petrie's advent to the Council in the 1830s. And a certain amount of hokum was inseparable from the fashion: the philology of Charles Vallancey, obsessed with the Punic root of the Gaelic language and culture, is one example;[10] the later controversy over the origins of the round towers another;[11] the work of Thomas Comerford, who attempted to relate Gaelic culture to that of ancient Greece, might also be instanced.[12] Nor should 'liberal nationalism' be anachronistically defined: Petrie, Caesar Otway, Frederick Burton and other enthusiasts could still be of Unionist beliefs as well as of Protestant stock;[13] and while it is always remembered that the Patriot politician Henry Flood left a celebrated bequest to encourage study of the Irish language, it is often forgotten that he did so for antiquarian, not revivalist, purposes.[14] But artistic and literary evidence shows that it was from this time that the currency of thought, running on antiquarian and historiographical lines, familiarized the Irish mind with shamrocks, wolfhounds, round towers, the cult of Brian Boru, and the image of an ecumenical St Patrick. And the historical work of Thomas Leland and John Curry combined a repudiation of the old propagandists with the discoveries of the new antiquarians, to produce detailed and fairly scholarly interpretations of Irish history.[15]

By 1800 political developments in America and France as well as in Ireland itself infused a new direction into the current of historical thought; but even after the trauma of rebellion and Union, the political uses of antiquarianism and of early Irish history continued. An improving Ascendancy landlord like William Parnell-Hayes produced amateur histories with titles like *Inquiry into the Causes of the Popular Discontents in Ireland* (1805) and *Historical Apology for the Irish Catholics* (1807), in between prospecting for antiquities and restoring a seventh-century church at Glendalough.[16] The Gaelic Society of Dublin was founded in 1807, declaring that 'an opportunity is now, at length, offered to the learned of Ireland, to retrieve their character among the Nations of Europe, and shew that their History and Antiquities are not fitted to be consigned to eternal oblivion'; other societies followed.[17] In fact, the heyday of patriotic antiquarianism was nearly past; but the heyday of patriotic historiography was at hand.

The nature of the 'patriotism', however, was not yet exclusive. From the 1830s Church of Ireland scholars devoted themselves to research into early Irish ecclesiastical history; their findings had a forum in Petrie's *Irish Penny Journal*, founded in 1840 to explore 'the history, biography, poetry, antiquities, natural history, legends and traditions of the country'. Irish Anglicans had an apologetic and propagandist motivation, besides a patriotic one; their preoccupation, then and later, was to establish their Church as the true 'Ancient, Catholick and Apostolic Church of Ireland', the uncorrupted continuation of early

Irish Christianity rather than the offshoot of Tudor statecraft. This aim vitiated much of their research. None the less, a tradition of restoration, fieldwork and the recording of antiquities helped towards the understanding of the past. This was greatly reinforced by editions of early Irish texts prepared by the Irish Record Commission (1810–30) and the Irish Historical Manuscripts Commission (founded in 1869), and by the facsimile edition of medieval codices issued by the Royal Irish Academy; if commentaries tended to apologetics, texts remained relatively uncorrupt. And some Irish historians at least had already been impressed by the sceptical spirit of Henri Bayle, and were determined to doubt all testimony and tradition; notably Edward Ledwich, whose *Antiquities of Ireland* consciously attempted to demolish 'bardic fictions'.[18]

These developments were accompanied by a new wave of predictable but sound histories of Ireland, too long to detail here, but vitally important in considering the early nineteenth-century background to intellectual patriotism in the age of Young Ireland. Many used original records, critically analysed; many attempted to distance themselves from contemporary political preoccupations. But the overall impression was to show early Ireland as bright with culture, not dark with barbarism. The Celt was no longer considered congenitally addicted to massacre; the methods of conquest employed by England in Ireland were generally deprecated. Such reassessments did not percolate through to the English public; but, aided by Thomas Moore and the fashion for Irish ballads, they helped to reinforce the sense of Irishness which the ideologues of Young Ireland exploited so astutely in the 1830s and 1840s. On the neutral ground of 'ancient history and native art,' wrote Sir Charles Gavan Duffy long afterwards, 'Unionist and nationalist could meet without alarm.'[19] This was not, however, the case; and it is a disingenuous statement, reflecting the position of Gavan Duffy the federalist and ex-colonial governor in 1880, not of Gavan Duffy the ardent Young Irelander in 1840. Ancient history and native art could be easily manipulated (either to prove native sophistication or to indicate Gaelic propensities for unreliability and exaggeration). And even the membership cards of Young Ireland made their own statement – these were embossed with images from Irish history, thus establishing the iconography of sustained struggle which was to characterize the nationalist version of events. The figures of Brian Boru, Owen Roe O'Neill, Patrick Sarsfield and Henry Grattan were posed against harps, sunbursts and the Parliament House in College Green, wreathed by shamrocks. Young Ireland politicians like Thomas Davis graduated into politics by writing historical studies – in Davis's case a vigorous but tendentious rehabilitation of the 'Patriot Parliament' of James II.[20] And though Davis combined this with a belief in 'learning history to forget quarrels',[21] his successors took a directly contrary approach.

For even as the materials for studying Irish history were slowly being collected and arranged in a way that might facilitate dispassionate analysis, a biased and political priority was taking over. It is doubtful if the great antiquarians John O'Donovan, Eugene O'Curry and Petrie would have recognized themselves under the title given by the Reverend Patrick McSweeney to his study of their historical work in 1913: *A Group of Nation-builders*. But that is what constituted their importance to retrospective opinion. And history-writing after the Union, even under titles which trumpeted themselves as impartial, very often directed itself at a political moral.[22] In the campaign for Catholic Emancipation both sides used history to prove and disprove massacres and disloyalty over the centuries; during parliamentary debates 1641 and the Treaty of Limerick were as bitterly contested as the actual issue of Catholic rights in 1829, rather to the bewilderment of English Members.[23] This was emblematic of what was to come.

Ironically, in the early nineteenth century a composite – one might almost dare to say interdisciplinary – approach to the Irish past was just becoming possible. It was represented by the epic effort put into the early work of the Ordnance Survey, which was contemporarily described as associating geography with 'the history, the statistics, and the structure, physical and social, of the country'.[24] Thomas Larcom recruited scholars of the quality of O'Donovan, Petrie and O'Curry, and furnished his researchers with demanding and densely written instructions about discovering the traditions of their designated areas.[25] To explore the history of place-names alone meant embarking on something very like the history of a locality. But the finished result of this magnificent conception stopped at one parish study, finally produced in November 1837, and so loaded with accretions and detail that the original idea of accompanying every map with a similar study was abandoned.[26] The controversy over this has been long-lived and need not be disinterred here; Alice Stopford Green, who grandiloquently interpreted the Ordnance Survey team as 'a kind of peripatetic university, in the very spirit of the older Irish life', believed that their work magically 'revealed the soul of Irish Nationality and the might of its repression', and was accordingly suppressed by the government.[27] The Survey's most recent historian, in a classic study, points out the injudiciousness and impracticality of the original concept, and the shapelessness attendant upon interpreting 'modern topography' as 'ancient history'.[28] The politics of the report irrepressibly assert themselves; but its historiographical background is of at least equal significance, for here can be seen archaeology, geography and a cautious sense of historical inquiry working together.

However, as Gavan Duffy cheerfully admitted, that 'cautious and sober strain' of learning was chiefly the province of middle-class scholars, some of the gentry and dilettante Protestant clergy;[29] and the future was with Young Ireland's Library of Ireland series of pocket histories, the street ballad, the pious cliché and the historical novel (to write one of which was Davis's great unfulfilled ambition).[30] The revival of Irish historiography, which was built upon by Young Ireland, by Celtic Revivalism, and even by an impeccable Unionist like W.E.H. Lecky, was dominated by this consciousness – evident in the assumptions of learned pamphlets as in those of hedge-schools. A history lesson delivered by a teacher in a Munster hedge-school in the early nineteenth century was described by a contemporary:

> He praises the Milesians, he curses 'the betrayer Dermod' – abuses 'the Saxon stranger' – lauds Brian Boru – utters one sweeping invective against the Danes, Henry VIII, Elizabeth, Cromwell, 'the Bloody' William of the Boyne, and Anne; he denies the legality of the criminal code, deprecates and disclaims the Union; dwells with enthusiasm on the memories of Curran, Grattan, 'Lord Edward', and young Emmet; insists on Catholic Emancipation; attacks the Peelers, horse and foot; protests against tithes, and threatens a separation from the United Kingdom . . .[31]

This vividly depicts history being elided into politics, and into the sense of national identity built upon a powerfully articulated consciousness of past grievances as much as present discontents.

And this was the historical consciousness displayed at popular levels by the Irish to countless Victorian travellers, who, on fact-finding missions, were constantly exposed – half fascinated and half appalled – to the rhetoric of Irish nationalist history. Sometimes, indeed, they seem to have been unconsciously subjected to the Irish taste for guying their own image; the experiences of innocents like Mr and

Mrs S.C. Hall, as well as those of the hard-headed Thackeray and Carlyle, record many ironies enjoyed at their unwitting expense by the cynical natives.[32] Travellers from the Continent, like de Tocqueville and de Beaumont, may not have been exempt either.[33] But de Beaumont, though he did not originate it, popularized the genocidal theory of England's historical policy towards Ireland; and the same note of vehement moralizing enters the history of his compatriot Augustin Thierry, warmly praised by Gavan Duffy.[34] Other foreign publicists entered the field, including Karl Marx.[35] And, finally, the demotic view of Irish history found its way by unlikely channels into the English consciousness.

This was not always acknowledged, at the time or since; and some of those responsible tried later to cover their tracks. Macaulay's *History* is notable for its scathing remarks on Irish barbarianism, Robert Southey's Toryism was notoriously unreconstructed, and Lord Lytton became the rabidly anti-Irish hymnologist of the Primrose League. But in youth Macaulay wrote epic poetry about the Gaelic resistance to Strongbow, Southey eulogized Robert Emmet, and Lytton produced verses commemorating Hugh O'Neill's war against Elizabeth.[36] Even as unlikely a figure as Samuel Smiles was inspired to write the history of a people whom many Victorians condemned as more opposed to self-help than any in the world. 'It is necessary that Irish history should be known and studied, for we are persuaded that *there* only is the true key to the present situation to be found – *there* only are the secret springs of Irish discontent to be traced.'[37]

Other Victorian intellectuals felt that this was so, though the argument is not self-evidently true, and in terms of economic policy at least it may be strongly contested. But every Victorian pundit dipped into Irish history and whatever panacea they were manufacturing emerged subtly altered.[38] 'I know tolerably well what Ireland was,' confessed John Stuart Mill to an Irish economist, 'but have a very imperfect idea of what Ireland *is*.'[39] This could stand as an epigraph for the ruminations of others as well as himself; and it was reflected in the lacunae and contradictions so evident in Mill's own writings on Ireland.[40] It has been shown how untypical was his pamphlet *England and Ireland*, when viewed in the canon of his work; but it is with this strident piece, subjecting economics to a moral and political approach to landholding, that his views on Ireland are identified. And though the pamphlet argued – as he himself reiterated afterwards – *for* the Union, its effect was to reinforce the nationalist opposition to the measure. On a different level but in a similar manner, Matthew Arnold's belief in Celtic qualities, though part of an argument for bringing Celtic culture fully into the Anglo-Saxon cultural and political system, reinforced a view of early Irish history and an interpretation of Celticism which strengthened irreconcilable ideas of separatism.[41] The most influentially misinterpreted authority, however, in this unintentional *trahison des clercs* was the historian W.E.H. Lecky.

Sitting down to write his *History of England in the Eighteenth Century* (1878–90), Lecky was increasingly preoccupied by the history of Ireland: both as an Anglo-Irishman and as a rather troubled liberal. He knew the dangers, seeing Irish history as 'so steeped in party and sectarian animosity that a writer who has done his utmost to clear his mind from prejudice, and bring together with impartiality the conflicting statements of partisans, will still, if he is a wise man, always doubt whether he has succeeded in painting with perfect fidelity the delicate gradations of provocation, palliation and guilt'.[42] His *History of Ireland*, extracted from the original production for a special edition in 1892, remains a classic of liberal historiography; but despite his commitment to rationality and cool scepticism, it was dictated as much by topical preoccupations as guided by the pure light of research.[43] For one thing, he was writing *contra* James Anthony Froude, whose study of *The English in Ireland*[44] had maligned and belaboured the native Irish in a manner not to be seen again for a hundred years.[45] Lecky wrote against Froude, not for nationalist reasons, but because, as an Anglo-Irish Unionist, he feared that Froude's distortions by their very exaggeration would support the case being made by the nationalists for Home Rule. (He also worried deeply about the unintended effect of his own early *Leaders of Public Opinion in Ireland*, and opposed what would have been a very profitable reprint.) Both Froude and Lecky, in the context of the 1880s, saw their histories as relevant to the contemporary struggle for Home Rule. Froude argued, in Salisburian terms, the 'Hottentot' case of Celtic incapacity for self-government. Irish criminality 'originated out of' Irish Catholicism; Protestant virtues were commercial and social as much as religious. (This is not an anticipation of Weber and Tawney, but reflects the more exotic fact that Froude had regained his lost faith through a sojourn in a Wicklow rectory.) Culture as well as worship could be defined in religious terms, and 'Irish ideas' were a debased set of beliefs which should have been socialized out of the natives. Moreover, Anglo-Irish colonial nationalism was equally corrupt; Irish declarations that they would fight for nationhood should, then and now, be seen as bluff.

In contradicting the former statements, Lecky came near to implicitly refuting the latter: notably in his use of 'Grattan's Parliament' of 1782 to rehabilitate the Ascendancy class under siege in his own lifetime. He treated Orangeism and Protestant evangelicalism with faint distaste; this was not only a reaction against Froude, but also a reflection of the fact that he was the historian of the rise of rationalism. The exclusion of the Catholic gentry from political rights, and the ensuing development of the priest in politics, distressed him; he believed 'the secularization of politics is the chief measure and condition of political progress',[46] by which criterion Irish politics were regressing back to infinity. But this was precisely the lesson which many of his readers did *not* learn from his book; they came away from it imbued with ideas of Irish nobility, English pusillanimity, the missed chance of 'Grattan's Parliament', and the perfidiousness of the Act of Union. Lecky himself, by this stage of his life, did not want to see 'Grattan's Parliament' restored; an opinion with which he believed Henry Grattan would concur.[47] But the immorality of Union seemed to many the moral of his book.

It was, moreover, a moral drawn by politicians. 'I read for the History School at Oxford in the "seventies",' recalled Herbert Gladstone, 'and subsequently lectured on history. Froude, Lecky, Matthew Arnold, Goldwin Smith and John Bright brought me to conviction on Irish affairs. Four of my guides lived to be distinguished Unionists. Nevertheless, their facts and arguments led me to an opposite conclusion.'[48] Politicians of all colours had this nodding familiarity with Irish history (the most dangerous kind of acquaintance); and in private correspondence as well as public exchanges they wrangled good-naturedly about recondite issues. Thus Sir William Harcourt and Lord Randolph Churchill beguiled their time in 1889 with letters detailing the arguments for and against the honesty of Irish politicians in the eighteenth century.[49] The effect on W.E. Gladstone of his readings in Irish history was more cataclysmic. He had Gavan Duffy's word for it that Carew's campaign in sixteenth-century Munster was the closest historical parallel to the Bulgarian atrocities;[50] he had Lecky's authority for the iniquity of the Act of Union. 'He talked of the Union,' recorded Lord Derby,

> called it a frightful and absurd mistake, thought Pitt had been persuaded into it by the King, who believed it would act as a check upon the Catholics, said that every Irish man 'who was worth a farthing' had opposed it, and if he had been an Irishman he would have done so to the utmost . . . quoted as I have heard him do before, a saying of Grattan about 'the Channel forbidding Union, the Ocean forbidding separation' – which he considered as one of the wisest sayings ever uttered by man – then dwelt on the length of time during which Ireland had possessed an independent, or even a separate legislature.[51]

Gladstone, as so many others, was dazzled by the historians' notions of 'Grattan's Parliament': the acceptable face of Irish nationalism. The Irish pamphlet literature of the 1860s and 1870s, much of it written by insecure or improving landlords, adverted constantly to this; it had been much in the minds of those who initially supported Isaac Butt.[52] Samuel Ferguson, despite Ulster and Tory associations, had once called for the restoration of 'Grattan's Parliament' (though the 'plebeianizing' nature of the Home Rule movement, and the Phoenix Park Murders, later moderated his ardour); it was a reaction shared by an important element of the gentry before the political polarization of the 1880s. The idealization of the late eighteenth century, a direct result of the way history had been written, remained.

Among those politicians who idealized 1782, the prime example was a Wicklow gentleman whose ancestors included both a famous anti-Union patriot and the improving pamphleteer quoted earlier: Charles Stewart Parnell. He was not a reader of the literature discussed above; his strength as an Irish politician lay in his *not* knowing Irish history.[53] But his preoccupation with 'Grattan's Parliament', as invented by popular history, irritated those of his followers who had thought Home Rule through. 'There is no subject about which Mr Parnell is so ignorant as that of Irish history,' wrote Thomas O'Connor Power,

> and his contempt for books is strikingly shown in his reference to Grattan's Parliament. Mr Parnell deceives himself, through sheer indifference to history and a dislike of the trouble of inquiry into facts, when he tells us he wants

Grattan's Parliament. Does Mr Parnell want a parliament in Dublin controlled by a few nominees of the British Cabinet who, under the Viceroy, constitute an Irish government in no way responsible to the Irish House of Commons? If not, then it is not Grattan's Parliament he wants, and it is not Grattan's Parliament he should ask for.[54]

But 'Grattan's Parliament', as legitimized by historians, remained the objective to be cited, for most of Parnell's audience. The idealization was based on Sir Jonah Barrington's account of an Irish nation that never was,[55] on Thomas Newenham's erroneous ideas of Irish prosperity as created by the parliament of 1782,[56] on Lecky's misplaced faith in the influence of Foster's Corn Law,[57] and in the general prescription of nationalist historians that prosperity was automatically induced by native government and poverty by alien rule.

By the end of the nineteenth century, given that many such assumptions had become articles of faith for the English intelligentsia as well as the Irish people, it need not surprise us to find them governing the popular mind. What Lecky did for readers of the journals, A.M. Sullivan's *Story of Ireland* did for the general reader.[58] While Irish literacy seems to have been remarkably high in the late nineteenth century, the Irish literature which preoccupied the populace still awaits its historian; but a pioneering impressionist survey carried out in 1884 is of some interest in showing the hegemony enjoyed by Davisite poetry and history in one Cork parish. The list of histories most often borrowed from the Catholic Young Men's Society Reading-room told its own tale.[59] A popular conception of history facilitated the general view that saw the Home Rule movement as 'the heirs of all the ages that have fought the good fight after their several ways':[60] a notion which, while enabling Parnell to walk the political tightrope, was very far from the truth. And when Parnellism collapsed, the popular conception of history instantly located the catastrophe in the context of a long succession of Saxon (rather than Anglo-Irish) betrayals.

Sinn Féin was to prove the successor movement to the Irish Parliamentary Party, but in everyday ways which were strategically underplayed at the time;[61] its emphasis was rather upon a specific reading of history. The founder Arthur Griffith's ideas of autarky in economics and Gaelic purity in politics fused an idealization of 'Grattan's Parliament' with a belief in Celticism which brought together the teachings of nineteenth-century historians, ancient and modern: the very name of his first weekly, *United Irishman*, was a reference to Mitchel and Tone, and the politics of Sinn Féin synthesized constitutionalism with implicit violence.[62] Griffith's 'Hungarian policy' of boycotting institutions in order to win separate but equal status under the crown was itself based upon misapplied historical parallels: as George Birmingham acidly pointed out, if Griffith was really following the Hungarian model, he should have seen that the equivalent of the Magyars were the Anglo-Irish.[63] But Griffith, and still more his contemporaries among nationalist ideologues, defined 'Irish' in a way that implied, or even stated, its congruence with 'Gaelic' and 'Catholic'. And this sectional reading, the result of sectional history, set the tone of twentieth-century nationalism.

It was an identification which contradicted the official spirit of Young Ireland, but which had achieved dominance in the late nineteenth century, for political and educational as well as intellectual reasons.[64] Its articulation by the Gaelic Revival has been ably analysed, though there were elements of pluralism and inclusivism present which have sometimes been underestimated.[65]

Shaw remarked that 'there is no Irish race any more than there is an English race or a Yankee race [but] there *is* an Irish climate which will stamp an immigrant more deeply and durably in two years, apparently, than the English climate will in two hundred';[66] but this reading of Irish history went as unheard as the expostulations of John Eglinton, George Russell, W.B. Yeats and others who saw themselves as no less Irish for being of identifiably settler descent. What happened instead was that the period of nationalist irredentism saw the culmination of historical writing which mined the past for political continuities and extrapolations.

Patrick Pearse was the prime mover in this process, and in recent years much has been done to clarify the bases upon which he built his view of history: a visionary world of early Celtic traditions where racial identification was automatic, a national sense was the paramount priority, and the sacrificial image of the ancient hero Cuchulainn was inextricably tangled with that of Christ.[67] Not only Pearse's youthful *Three Lectures on Gaelic Topics* (1897–8), but all he wrote and taught up to his execution in 1916 owed far more to John Mitchel and the Library of Ireland than to the researches of Eoin MacNeill, whose path-breaking lectures on early Irish society were delivered in 1904 and published two years later.[68] Pearse's use of Irish history was that of a calculatedly disingenuous propagandist; it was this that enabled him, for instance, so thoroughly to misinterpret Thomas Davis.[69] But if it is argued – as it might be – that the importance of Pearse's distortions is diminished by the fact that he was very far from being an accepted historian, it is instructive to turn back to Alice Stopford Green.

Daughter of an archdeacon in County Meath, and wife of the greatest popular historian of the age, Mrs Green moved from revising her husband's works to writing medieval history on her own account, and ended as a formidable and partisan advocate of Irish nationalism. This identification was reflected in works like *The Making of Ireland and Its Undoing* (1908), *Irish Nationality* (1911) and *A History of the Irish State to 1014* (1925). A Freudian, or a seeker after symbols, might note that from the age of seventeen she spent seven years in semi-blindness, and during the ordeal relied upon an already well-stocked mind and a remarkable memory; for her view of Irish history represented a similarly restricted vision, and an ability to feed omnivorously on preconceptions. The concept of 'the Irish national memory', indeed, recurs obsessively in her works;[70] she may be seen as a representative of those Ascendancy Irish whose insecurity drove them to extremes of identification, much as the urban nationalist intellectuals of the era embarked upon a *narodnik* search for 'the West'. Mrs Green's pre-invasion Ireland was a classless, egalitarian 'Commonwealth', where 'the earliest and the most passionate conception of "nationality" flourished';[71] 'democratic' continuities were asserted, the purity of 'Gaelic' culture emphasized, and the moral as well as aesthetic superiority of 'Gaelic civilization' trumpeted.[72] Despite her declarations in introductions and footnotes of indebtedness to Eoin MacNeill, the scholarly subtlety and tentativeness of his approach to the early Irish past had no part in Mrs Green's productions; and probably for that reason they entered the mainstream of Free State culture.

Here they remained, despite the accumulated findings of historians who showed that land patterns in early Christian Ireland argue for a landholding system very far from her version of Gaelic society,[73] that the so-called High-Kingship of Ireland did not exist before the middle of the ninth century,[74] and that – as MacNeill indicated in 1904 – the received framework of early Irish history was an invention of chroniclers from the ninth century and later, working assiduously for the glorification of their patrons. If, however, Mrs Green was fooled by what a later historian has crisply called 'the concoctions of the Annals',[75] she had a real and immediate reason for being thus fooled: the desire to establish a legitimate continuity for Irish separatism. George Russell, on the other hand, knew and accepted that his view of early Ireland was legendary and symbolic, and thus 'more potent than history'.[76] But the spirit of the Free State was more in accord with Mrs Green's literalism. Thus the *Catholic Bulletin*, bemoaning modern times in 1925, reflected Mrs Green's vision when it remarked, 'It is very different in Ireland now to those old days when the poorest Catholic family would, on assembling in the evenings, discuss scholastic philosophy and such subjects.' And in the same year the same journal recommended Daniel Corkery's *Hidden Ireland* to 'G.W. Russell and his clique . . . they will there see how the Gael, the one Irish nation with the Irish literature, regards and dealt with and will deal with that mongrel upstart called Anglo-Irish tradition and culture.'[77]

What followed was the institutionalization of a certain view of history in the Free State, as instructed by the Department of Education from 1922, and memorialized in textbooks that did duty for the next forty years. Teachers were informed that 'the continuity of the separatist idea from Tone to Pearse should be stressed'; pupils should be 'imbued with the ideals and aspirations of such men as Thomas Davis and Patrick Pearse'.[78] Thus history was debased into a two-dimensional, linear development, and the function of its teaching interpreted as 'undoing the conquest'; even the architecture of the Irish eighteenth century was stigmatized as ideologically degenerate. One must be wary of falling into the same trap as those who, by condemning the sixteenth- and seventeenth-century historians, imply that scientific objectivity was possible at that time; textbooks in British schools in the 1920s and 1930s were hardly models of fairminded detachment. Moreover, in the new state of Northern Ireland, the recommendations of the Lynn Committee (established in 1921) reflect an equally strong sense of history as a tool, or weapon, to be manipulated through the schools.[79] But the popularization of invented tradition in the Free State and the Republic served a directly political function important enough to bear analysis; and it came about as the result of a longer process than is sometimes assumed.

Moreover, the process itself created some contradictions and paradoxes. One is that the exclusive glorification of one strain in Ireland's complex history caused as a reaction the equally tendentious glorification of another. Thus the record of the 'Anglo-Irish' was equally idealized in different quarters, sentimentalizing the Bourbon spirit of a class notable in the main for its philistinism and bigotry, which, when the testing time came, failed in everything – social duty, political imagination and nerve.[80] More important for our purpose is the major paradox: the fact that the institutionalized debasement of popular history was accompanied from the 1940s by a historiographical revolution in academic circles which, within twenty-five years, reversed nearly every assumption still being made by the textbooks. The foundation under Eoin MacNeill of the Irish Manuscripts Commission in 1929 had something to do with this; so did the formation of the Ulster Society for Irish Historical Studies, and the Irish Historical Society, a few years later. Bureaucratic philistinism, and an idiosyncratic attitude to the availability of government records, provided obstacles in North and South – as they still do. But a school of Irish history evolved at the research level which transcended traditional divides within Southern society and culture, as well as across the new border.[81]

By the 1960s the work of a whole generation of scholars had exploded the basis for popular assumptions about early Irish society, the conquest, the plantations, the eighteenth-century parliament, the record of landlordism, and most of all the continuities between the various manifestations of nationalism: in some cases, reverting to ideas held in the past by minority opinion but contemptuously dismissed.[82] By the mid-1960s, coinciding with signs of realism and adaptation in Irish politics, a number of indications presaged the establishment of a new interpretation of Irish history as a complex and ambivalent process rather than a morality tale. The Institute of Irish Studies was founded in Belfast in 1965, with the object of co-ordinating research in different disciplines. An important report on the teaching of history in Irish schools appeared in 1966.[83] The next year, a new Irish history school textbook was launched which at last replaced the didactic tracts that had done duty for decades.[84]

Most symbolically, the commemoration of the 1916 rising produced some unexpected historiographical results. One was a work by an impeccably nationalist scholar which portrayed Dublin Castle in 1916 as characterized by well-meaning muddle and a vague acceptance of the desirability of Home Rule.[85] More strikingly, a Jesuit historian, commissioned to write an article on Patrick Pearse to celebrate the anniversary, produced an intemperate and violent attack on Pearse's preference for striking a rhetorical blow against an England that had put Home Rule on the statute book, instead of taking on the Ulster Volunteers who had prevented its implementation; and went on to denounce Pearse's falsification of past history in the interests of present politics.[86]

Not the least significant thing about this outburst, however, was the fact that the article was deemed unsuitable for publication in 1966, and saw the light of day six years later, only after its author's death. By then, the results of simplistic historical hero-cults had become obvious in the carnage of Northern Ireland. When the seventy-fifth anniversary of 1916 arrived in 1991, it was treated by the Irish government as a sensitive issue, to be approached in a deliberately restrained way – very different from the unequivocal celebrations of 1966. This caused a small-scale but vociferous old-Republican reaction – featuring not historians but out-of-office politicians, freelance journalists, ex-1960s activists (including, quaintly, a Pop Art painter), and the members of the Short Strand Martyrs Memorial Flute Band.

And this points up the paradox mentioned earlier. It would be tedious as well as time-consuming to detail the areas of Irish history where old stereotypes have been questioned. This has been done with the aid of sociology, geography, economics, and most of all a new approach to statistics. Mentalities, Protestant as well as Catholic, have been examined. In the early period the Irish Sea has been reinterpreted as the centre, not the frontier, of a cultural area. In the plantation era, patterns of settlement and the very framework of dispossession have been revised. Divergent local socio-economic and political cultures have been analysed; our sheer ignorance about, for instance, the effects of the Famine have been stringently exposed. In recent years Irish historians have presented their readers with a version of ancient Ireland where some estates were worked by slaves,[87] and of early Christian Ireland where much of the damage to churches was done not by invaders but by marauding rival abbots;[88] we have even been shown a Dermot MacMurrough who is not the villain of the piece.[89] To take another period, the Fenians have been presented as 'easily recognizable and fairly typical mid-Victorians', using the movement as a vehicle for leisure activities and not particularly committed to

Republicanism;[90] the emigrating Irish have been defined as 'among the greatest supporters of the second British Empire and the Commonwealth'.[91] Sinn Féin has appeared as a similarly utilitarian and ideologically uncommitted machine for the brokerage of local power politics;[92] the Land War has been seen as 'sacrificing economic progress on the altar of Irish nationalism';[93] and 'traditional Ireland', so far from a frugal rural community exempt from the taint of materialism and modernization, has been explosively derided by an Irish economic historian as 'full of rats who just did not know how to race'.[94]

It might be assumed that the point had been reached for which Shaw hoped in the 1920s, when he wrote of the national history:

> There are formidable vested interests in our huge national stock of junk and bilge, glowing with the phosphorescence of romance. Heroes and heroines have risked their lives to force England to drop Ireland like a hot potato. England, after a final paroxysm of doing her worst, has dropped Ireland accordingly. But in doing so she has destroyed the whole stock-in-trade of the heroes and heroines . . . We are now citizens of the world; and the man who divides the race into elect Irishmen and reprobate foreign devils (especially Englishmen) had better live on the Blaskets where he can admire himself without disturbance. Perhaps, after all, our late troubles were not so purposeless as they seemed. They were probably ordained to prove to us that we are no better than other people; and when Ireland is once forced to accept this stupendous new idea, goodbye to the old patriotism.[95]

What happened, at least until very recently, seemed a contrary process: academic revisionism has coincided with popular revivalism. The version of Irish history presented in P.S. O'Hegarty's influential *Ireland under the Union* persisted: 'the story of a people coming out of captivity, out of the underground, finding every artery of national life occupied by the enemy, recovering them one by one, and coming out at last into the full blaze of the sun . . .'[96] This version long remained in vogue among politicians and popular historians (and *a fortiori* television historians). The simplified notions have their own resilience: they are buried deep in the core of popular consciousness, as recent analysis of folk attitudes in rural Ireland has shown.[97] The point should also be made that the triumph of revisionism in Irish academic historiography is a particularly exact instance of the owl of Minerva flying only in the shades of nightfall: events in the island since 1969 have both emphasized the power of ideas of history, and the time it takes for scholarly revolutions to affect everyday attitudes. Nor have Irish readers always been particularly anxious to explore the historical analysis offered by scholars from other countries.[98] But the discrepancy between beliefs in the university and outside it raises some questions. The transition from piety to iconoclasm may have been too abrupt for the change to percolate through immediately. Still the depressing lesson is probably that history as conceived by scholars is different to what it is understood to be at large, where 'myth' is probably the correct, if over-used, anthropological term. And historians may overrate their own importance in considering that their work is in any way relevant to these popular conceptions – especially in Ireland. The habit of mind which preferred a visionary Republic to any number of birds in the hand is reflected in a disposition to search for an Irish past in theories of historical descent as bizarre as that of 'the Cruthin people' today,[99] the Eskimo settlement of Ireland postulated by Pokorny in the 1920s,[100] the Hiberno-Carthaginians of Vallancey, or the Gaelic Greeks of Comerford.

Such an attitude goes with the disposition to legitimize, to praise and to blame, conspicuously evinced by the old traditions of Irish history-writing. The same pieties are still reiterated by self-appointed 'anti-revisionists', but it is noteworthy that they restrict themselves to delivering the same generalizing lecture in different places, or concentrating on small theological disputations based on highly selective readings: whereas the general histories published in the last decade have begun to reflect the interrogations of academic research. Not only do these now reach a wide market, in a country which reads about itself obsessively; there is also every sign that a new generation finds the old disputes and obsessions less and less relevant to immediate problems. In this, like much recent scholarship, they incline towards the line of Goldwin Smith, articulated by his study of *Irish History and Irish Character* in 1861: 'There is no part of all this which may not be numbered with the general calamities of Europe during the last two centuries, and with the rest of these calamities buried in oblivion.' Elsewhere in his rather weary and acerbic, but essentially sympathetic, study, the same author remarked that the 'popular writer on Irish history' should 'pay more attention than writers on that subject have generally paid to general causes, [should] cultivate the charities of history, and in the case of the rulers as well as the people, [should] take fair account of misfortunes as well as crimes'.[101] Professional Irish historiography has turned this corner; but the question which may interest future historians is why the 'popular Irish history' took so long to follow.

2

Varieties of Irishness: Cultures and Anarchy in Ireland

I

The idea of cultural diversity in Ireland has advanced hesitantly into focus, not before its time: though this does not make it a development welcomed in all quarters. Partly the result of questioning the monolithic received view of a purely Gaelic nation, it is also, obviously, a result of forced reconsiderations since the detonation of the Ulster crisis. Another manifestation of historiographical reassessment has been the search for parallels with previous eras of crisis: the guiding principle in works like Oliver MacDonagh's *States of Mind* (1983). And when considering the inheritance of cultural diversity, it is tempting to look back to the last juncture in Irish history when this concept was at the forefront of public debate: at the turn of this century, among the generation before the revolution.

Any such consideration has to be inspired by the mingled admiration and reservations aroused by Leland Lyons's tremendously influential book *Culture and Anarchy in Ireland 1890–1939*, which began life as a series of lectures delivered at Oxford in the Hilary Term of 1978. I was in the audience, and still remember the impact of the concluding words. Our Irish diversity, Lyons said,

> has been a diversity of ways of life which are deeply embedded in the past and of which the much advertised political differences are but the outward and visible sign. This was the true anarchy that beset the country. During the period from the fall of Parnell to the death of Yeats, it was not primarily an anarchy of violence in the streets, of contempt for law and order such as to

make the island, or any part of it, permanently ungovernable. It was rather an anarchy in the mind and in the heart, an anarchy which forbade not just unity of territories, but also 'unity of being', an anarchy that sprang from the collision within a small and intimate island of seemingly irreconcilable cultures, unable to live together or to live apart, caught inextricably in the web of their tragic history.

> Out of Ireland have we come.
> Great hatred, little room,
> Maimed us at the start.[1]

The sardonic tone was not entirely new for Lyons, but the bleak pessimism was. It also, in a sense, ran counter to the school of liberal, synthesizing historiography which he had come to embody. The lectures, published, went on to tremendous and deserved success. In many respects, *Culture and Anarchy* was Lyons's best book. But the doubts I felt while listening, along with the exhilaration, have remained.

The premise of the lectures, and a phrase whose derivation Lyons carefully examined, involved what was called 'the battle of two civilizations' – crudely, an Anglo-Irish, pluralist, essentially secular culture arrayed against the heady resurgence of Gaelic, Catholic, separatist values. (Lyons had already discussed this opposition under the same title, in a brilliant chapter of his *Ireland since the Famine*.) His development of the theme at once raised some questions. His chosen representatives of the Anglo-Irish culture, like Horace Plunkett and George Russell, maybe expressed a certain version of secularism, but hardly answered for the Irish Protestant consciousness at large. (Lyons partly evaded this difficulty by partitioning off Ulster into a chapter of its own.) More seriously, the retrospective angle of his historical view gave cause for some doubts. This was particularly notable when he dealt with the ferment of ideas unleashed in the very early 1900s, because many of these might be as easily identified with reconciliation between cultural traditions as with confrontation. Lyons admitted: 'Superficially, it seemed, as the nineteenth century ended, that a new era was opening, an era of constructive thinking and doing in which men and women of different cultures might join in friendly collaboration.'[2] Anyone who reads the journalism and literature of the period must agree. But, he goes on to say, beneath this the old fissures remained, and the battle of the two civilizations was drawing up its lines, to culminate in the real battle of 1916.

It might be argued that this runs the risk of reading the story backwards – over the shoulder, in a sense, across the gulf created by the events of 1914–18. That brief period saw not only the span of the Great War, but the shelving of Home Rule, the British government's tacit acceptance of Ulster's secession, the takeover of the Gaelic League by the Irish Republican Brotherhood, the Easter rising and subsequent executions, the Irish Convention, the conscription crisis, and the Sinn Féin election victory. Lyons's view, however, implies that the lines of development were laid out independently of all this. It is, in fact, the Yeatsian reading of the period since Parnell's death. 'A disillusioned and embittered Ireland turned from parliamentary politics; an event was conceived; and the race began, as I think, to be troubled by that event's long gestation.'[3]

The reasoning behind this is discussed elsewhere in this book.[4] But when Yeats and others pressed this argument, as they began doing early on, it was in order to state a larger thesis: the idea that cultural revivalism, in the Irish context, deterministically produced extremist politics and set up a zero-sum game which eliminated all middle ground. Douglas Hyde and other 'non-political' brokers of the early Gaelic League innocently opened a Pandora's Box. This idea, incidentally, rather ignores the fact that before his adoption of the Gaelic League, Hyde had already gone through his extremist political phase, and come out the other side; his youthful Fenianism and Anglophobia, revealed by Dominic Daly,[5] had given way to what he (rightly) saw as the more mature politics of cultural autonomy. The Gaelic League, he later remarked, was 'charming until it became powerful'. Whether or not Hyde was proved wrong, he certainly was no innocent.

Yeats, however, possessed an astounding ability to sense 'the way things would look to people later on', and his version of inevitability took hold. It is no coincidence that Lyons was immersed in Yeats while preparing his 'Culture and Anarchy' lectures; the dichotomy set up by his argument fits tightly into the Yeatsian scheme of things, and has a satisfying coherence and symmetry. But it is also over-determined and reductionist – always a danger with Yeats, whose over-compensation as a marginalized Irish Protestant often led him into rigid and declamatory attitudes.

Personal anecdotes may obscure these issues as much as illuminate them. But it is perhaps relevant to recall the reaction at a Dublin dinner table when I described Yeats as a marginalized Irish Protestant. 'You can't talk about Yeats like that!' retorted a fellow guest indignantly. '*He was as Irish as I am*.' Protestantism, in this automatic reaction, negated Irishness. This was a latter-day echo of D.P. Moran's conclusion round the turn of the century, that 'the Gael must be the element that absorbs'. Lyons had picked out this phrase, presenting it as the inevitable outcome of Gaelic cultural revivalism, culminating in political separatism. But it is worth remembering that elsewhere in the same text (*The Philosophy of Irish Ireland*) Moran was scathing about 'prating mock-rebels . . . whining on about England stealing our woollen industries some hundreds of years ago'; that he queried the notion of the spirit of nationality as eternal; and that he mocked the idea of military assault on England as pointless. 'All we can do, and it should be enough for us, is remain Irish in spite of her, and work out our destiny in the very many fields in which we are free to do so.'

Moran's paper, the *Leader*, also remarked: 'Perhaps the greatest of all difficulties which underlie the whole of what is known as the Irish Revival is the length of time we are obliged to go back before we arrive at any mode of life that may with truth be termed distinctively Irish.'[6] This now seems like the kind of realistic reflection associated with the sane and balanced inquiries of a modern scholar like Estyn Evans. It is worth noting, too, the moderation and lack of Anglophobia in Hyde's early Gaelic League manifestos at the same period. Even without invoking Plunkett, Russell, Synge and Yeats, there are arguments for seeing cultural diversity at the turn of the century in terms which are *not* necessarily confrontational – leaving aside what happened to Irish politics with the precipitation of crisis by unforeseen contingencies from 1912 on.

II

Why, then, the prevalence of the opposing view? Who were the brokers of the idea of *inevitable* confrontation? It is significant that, when looking back at the extraordinary upheavals of the early twentieth century, both 'sides' had their reasons for presenting the same historical argument. There were the survivors among those who had been cultural entrepreneurs in the pre-revolutionary period – notably Yeats, tracing 1916 back to the influence of *Cathleen Ni*

Houlihan rather than to the logic of Liberal pusillanimity over the Ulster Volunteer Force and (more importantly) the knee-jerk Fenian reaction to England's involvement in an external war. There was also Hyde, victim of a *putsch* on the Gaelic League committee in 1915, and anxious to assert the inevitability of politics driving out cultural revolution. There were the new generation of political irreconcilables, of the Ernie O'Malley stamp, who left their own literary testaments – though they, significantly, had *not* been active in the cultural initiatives of the 1890s and early 1900s. All this lent credence as well as potency to the next generation of Gaelic League and Gaelic Athletic Association chauvinists, defining cultural identity as a matter of negation and exclusiveness rather than as an affirmation of pluralism. This often meant deliberately embracing illogic – what Moran had contemptuously called 'thinking from hand to mouth'. There is a good example in a reminiscence by the old Belfast republican Denis McCullough:

> We lived in dreams always; we never enjoyed them. I dreamed of an Ireland that never existed and never could exist. I dreamt of the people of Ireland as a heroic people, a Gaelic people; I dreamt of Ireland as different from what I see now – *not that I think I was wrong in this . . .*[7]

These elements represented, in a sense, the winning side convincing themselves that their myopia had been vindicated by history. But the losers, in post-revolutionary terms, also had a vested interest in asserting the inevitability of cultural diversity producing political confrontation. Augustine Birrell is one example: as his memoirs more or less argue, what *could* Dublin Castle do to stop the rising, with the inevitable onset of an oppositional Gaelic culture predicating a nationalist revolution? (This argument had the added advantage of giving Liberals like Birrell a chance to imply that the Tory initiatives of 'constructive Unionism' had been irrelevant and doomed from the start.) But others among the losers also seized the same point. The middle-class Irish parliamentarians, rhetorically as well as electorally trumped by Sinn Féin in 1919, went along with the determinist version rather than analysing the way they lost control of the commanding political heights apparently gained by 1914. (Until very recently, historians have tended to follow them in this evasion.) Looking back over the early years of the twentieth century, the work of the Recess Committee, the two million acres redistributed by the Congested Districts Board and the Land Acts, the creation of committees which could accommodate not only warring nationalists like John Redmond and Timothy Healy sitting together, but even the Unionist Colonel Saunderson – all this seemed to weigh little in the scale. Nowadays those of us who also long for unspectacular but real steps, taken forward together, may be less easily impressed by that apparent logic.

What might be queried is the view that cultural diversity was inevitably confrontational; and in this context one might look briefly at the nineteenth-century background. The idea of a revived 'Irish culture' and an Irish-Gaelic identity is in its modern form firmly rooted in nineteenth-century developments – historiographical, antiquarian, archaeological, as well as political and polemical. As outlined in the last essay, the moving spirits in this intellectual exploration were initially often Protestant Unionists. There are some obvious reasons for this, grounded on social advantage, university education and the amount of free time available to clerics of the Established Church. But to see their researches into Gaelic Ireland as necessarily sawing off the branch upon which they were sitting, is again rather a retrospective view. They had their own psychological identification with Ireland, which was not threatened by an interest and a pride in the evidently ancient origins of Irish settlement and Irish culture. 'Victorian Ireland' could be middle class, English-speaking and non-separatist in its politics, but no less 'Irish' for that. Samuel Ferguson is the figure most often instanced here; but his friend and colleague on the *Dublin University Magazine*, Isaac Butt, might be taken as another example. Recent research into Butt's early writings and career[8] has brilliantly queried the idea that defending the Fenians in 1867 somehow converted him to his peculiar and (to some of us) sympathetic brand of nationalism. It is a presumption that assumes the pure milk of the separatist tradition is the only sustenance that can produce an Irish nationalist worthy of the name. Actually, the preconditions of Butt's nationalism were set long before, in the 'national' preoccupations of the student-journalist cliques of the 1830s, stimulated by their impatience with the shortcomings and incompetence of the British government, and most of all by the experience of the mismanagement of the Famine (Butt was, after all, also a political economist who swam against the current of the day). David Thornley's supposedly definitive study of Butt, *Isaac Butt and Home Rule* (1964), assumes throughout that he was somehow destined to miss the nationalist boat; however well meaning, his background left him stranded on the shore. He might equally be seen as someone with a Protestant, even Orange, pedigree who shared in and helped create a sense of Irishness that accepted historic English influence while claiming realistic autonomy, and required no apology for its credentials at all.

Gaelic sympathies, Celtic researches, irritation with many of the actions of British government and Anglicized educations could all coexist, and often did, among the Irish Victorian middle-class intelligentsia. (Yeats, pioneer of Irish folklore and Celtic legends, was first influenced by Scott and Macaulay.) The great antiquarian George Petrie was also to be the great artistic memorialist of the early nineteenth-century Irish landscape, and he derived his highly personalized approach to his native countryside from Wordsworth. The personification and highly charged nature of the Irish response to the land of Ireland is, of course, a tradition in Gaelic literature too; and it can, poetically speaking, be used to express conflicting and aggressive claims to the land, as in *aisling* poetry, or in Seamus Heaney's 'Act of Union'. But it does not belong to that tradition alone. The Irish identification with the land, its unique appearance, its light and shade, also owes much to English-derived romanticism (a sensation which one paradoxically receives even through texts like Ernie O'Malley's lyrical descriptions of bivouacs in the Tipperary mountains in *On Another Man's Wound*). It has inspired masterpieces by Lloyd Praeger and Estyn Evans. And this might indicate that such perceptions can be reconciling and unifying too. In 1976 the historian J.C. Beckett, addressing the first Conference of Irish Historians in Britain, talked about those who live outside Ireland, and recalled a meeting with a fellow Ulsterman, a student, on a long-distance bus journey in Canada. They talked, as he remembered, enthusiastically about *the Irish land*: the uniquely varied landscape of Ulster, its super-charged quality of beauty. It never, as he thought afterwards, occurred to either of them to consider, let alone investigate, what background or which 'tradition' each came from. Though historic claims to the land might have separated them *within* Ulster, when they went abroad their common identification with it acted as a uniting factor. This cannot be a unique experience for Ulster people abroad, and carries a particular resonance.

To indicate this is not, perhaps, to draw attention to so very much.

But in a similar way it is worth remembering that the very fact of inhabiting Ireland imposes its own common bonds, and that these coexist with different cultural, religious and even political traditions. It has been pointed out by Professor Buchanan that in most of the fundamental characteristics of day-to-day living, the settlers of Ulster were quickly homogenized with the natives. Folk belief about deeply opposed ways of life are described by Buchanan as 'a homely mixture of learned fact and heard tradition', and should be queried.

> In his homeland the Scottish Planter had a way of life little different from his Irish neighbour. They lived in similar houses, used similar tools and implements, and marked the changing seasons with the same festivals and customs. In no sense can their settlement among the Irish in Ulster be regarded as a confrontation between alien cultures, for the bonds developed during the first millennium AD and sustained through the medieval period provided a common basis in folklife.[9]

It is true that the religious and linguistic divisions of the early modern and modern periods imposed new barriers. But even modern surveys (the classic studies by Rosemary Harris and Richard Rose, as well as later surveys by Hickey and Whyte) show that supposedly diverse cultural and religious traditions are compatible with similar value systems and social practices. And similarly, the social subcultures of nineteenth-century Ireland were subtler, more flexible and more interwoven than used to be admitted. Men like Samuel Ferguson, preaching pluralism (and a sort of embryonic Home Rule) in 1834, believed that joint study of Irish origins and Ireland's history would have a reconciliatory effect. The tragedy is that he was wrong, and over the ensuing century the effect of studying Irish history, mediated through contemporary political preconceptions, tended to have exactly the opposite result.[10]

This is where the over-used conception of historiographical revisionism comes in. In the last generation, path-breaking work like that of Theo Hoppen, Tom Garvin, Vincent Comerford, David Fitzpatrick and many others has delineated a political map far less neatly demarcated than the landlord-versus-tenant, orange-versus-green patterns of the old textbooks (now adhered to mostly by wishful-thinking English and American observers). But 'revisionism' may be the wrong term here, because contemporary fiction indicated a similarly varied universe at the time: elsewhere in this book there are references to the surreal view of Dublin's middle-class and Bohemian worlds after the Union in forgotten novels by John Banim, Gerald Griffin, and even Isaac Butt (again), or the surprisingly subtle social gradations and interconnections in Trollope's *The Kellys and the O'Kellys*, or the variations of rural Galway Catholics in George Moore's *Drama in Muslin*, or the anatomy of Protestant County Cork in Somerville's and Ross's *The Real Charlotte*. Can it be a coincidence that all these texts were banished from the supposedly authentic canon of Irish literature by the exclusivist version of Irish culture peddled by Daniel Corkery? But their credentials as Irish literature have now been reasserted and so must the Irishness of the kind of subcultures they portray.

If Irish historians and literary critics now realize the viability of cultural diversity, their agenda remains (as Lyons indicated in *Culture and Anarchy*) the study of mentalities – not only those of the separatist nationalist persuasion (where Tom Garvin has made a start), but of Castle Catholicism also, and *a fortiori* of Presbyterian Ulster. In the process, unexpected overlaps may appear, and definitions of nationalism may have to be broadened, and made inclusive rather than exclusive.

At the same time, it is worth reconsidering recurrent characteristics in Irish nationalism as normally conceived, which impose their own patterns and work against an acceptance of diversity. One might instance Thomas Davis's use of anti-materialism as a strategy of distinguishing Irish against English values, and asserting moral superiority thereby – a line later adopted by Yeats as well as by de Valera.[11] This vein of argument should be investigated; on the one hand, to describe Ireland in 1903 as 'a place where men plough and sow and reap, not a place where there are great wheels turning and great chimneys vomiting smoke' clearly indicated that Belfast did not enter into this vision of Ireland. On the other hand, there *is* an analogous anti-materialism in Ulster Protestant ideology, and one cliché that has now mercifully been despatched is the notion of the 'hard-headed Ulsterman' whose political orientation is supposedly dictated by the interests of his pocket. The woeful inadequacy of the wishful thinking behind such an analysis is beginning to come into focus. It is possible that in studying anti-materialism, and the religious habit of mind, as well as confessional and sectarian modes of social organization, a certain unity behind our diversities of culture would become surprisingly apparent. (Whether the implications are very cheerful for the secularists among us is another matter.)

III

This raises the question of the various forms of Protestant commitment to Irish identity. We are all used to the disingenuous litany of Protestant names invoked in the extremist nationalist tradition – Tone, Emmet, Mitchel, Parnell (the Parnell of 1890–91) and Childers. It is an argument used *ad nauseam* by de Valera, and still adverted to. The implication triumphantly drawn from it is that present-day Protestants have, therefore, nothing to fear from Irish nationalism. This is hardly logical, since all the figures in the extremist-nationalist-Protestant pantheon reacted diametrically against the general Protestant background; they are exceptions, not representatives of a latent syndrome. Those who argue the case for platonic Protestant nationalism do not mention one of the silent subjects of twentieth-century history, tacitly ignored by both sides for their own purposes: the victimization, murder and banishment of 'ordinary' Protestants (not landowners or British army figures) in places like Limerick and Cork *after* the Treaty, in 1922.[12] Here, thinking from hand to mouth approaches selective amnesia.

But this should not negate some other kinds of Protestant identity that are unequivocally Irish. Lyons, for instance, describes Colonel George O'Callaghan Westropp (one of the lost heroes resurrected by David Fitzpatrick's *Politics and Irish Life*) as 'an Anglo-Irish type still too little noticed by historians – the man or woman in whom love of place transcended divisions based on origins, religion or politics'.[13] The same characteristic is striking when one focuses on a family like the Yeatses. The background and ethos was invincibly clerical, professional, middle-class Irish Protestant. But all of them – John Butler Yeats, his daughters Lily and Lolly, his sons Willie and Jack – were absolutely and unquestionably certain of their Irishness. Politically, this existed alongside opinions that ranged from unreconstructed Buttism in John Butler Yeats and increasing ambivalence about Irish nationalism in W.B., to out-and-out Republicanism in Jack. Religiously, it was not inconsistent with the robust suspicion of Catholic mores displayed in Lily's letters, a note also found (more surprisingly) in her brother's correspondence with Lady Gregory. But their ethos cannot be seen as objectively British–Imperialist, though that is how Sinn Féin (past and present) choose to define more or less every Irish Protestant. There was nothing English about their accents. And even at his most pretentious, W.B. Yeats was never accused of wanting to appear *British*.

The Yeatses were an extraordinary family in terms of genius, but unexceptional for their religion and class in terms of their instinctive national identification. At the same time, they were never shy – or bogus – about admitting that much in their cultural conditioning came from English intellectual sources. (An equally self-confident and well-educated American would have had no difficulty in making a similar admission.) It is possible that Yeats's reliance on the idea of an *Anima Mundi*, a common repository of world memories to which all mankind has potential access, was partly directed by his experience of a common cultural pool of identification in things Irish, which united him not only with Davis, Mangan, Ferguson, but also with Allingham and O'Leary: as broad a political spectrum as could be wished but all, in terms of cultural identity, absolutely Irish and all educated in, and expressing themselves through, cultural norms heavily influenced by English literature and English thought.

This leads on to consideration of another disingenuous argument, which must be clarified: the notion that 'we Irish' are more influenced by Europe than by Britain. It was briefly, for obvious reasons, very popular in the Republic in the early 1970s, but has a much longer pedigree. It is satirized gently (I think) in Brian Friel's *Translations*, where the hedge-school master tells the English surveyor: 'Wordsworth? . . . no. I'm afraid we're not familiar with your literature, Lieutenant. We feel closer to the warm Mediterranean. We tend to overlook your island.'[14]

This is grandiose self-delusion. But one can still be told in all seriousness that the process whereby some Irish school-leavers are claiming EC rights to apply to British universities will be replaced by a flood of intellectual emigration to the Continent when they discover how much better off they will be at colleges in France and Germany. This betrays a touching if hilarious nostalgia for the days when Irish missionaries dominated Louvain and Salamanca; but it bears no resemblance to the realities of the cultural and educational profile in Irish schools, nor – even more importantly – does it admit the

Anglophone reality of modern Irish society. What it represents (like the Scots emphasis on the Auld Alliance with France) is a desire to grasp at any argument that might support the idea of intellectual independence from a powerful and culturally aggressive neighbour – at the expense of facing up to the more interesting reality of a culturally diverse inheritance within the polity. In a sense, the pan-Celtic subgroup within late nineteenth-century Gaelic Revivalism adopted the same wishful-thinking argument when it emphasized Irish links with Scotland, Wales and Brittany; Yeats in 1897 claimed Renan, Lamennais, Chateaubriand and Villiers de l'Isle-Adam as Bretons rather than Frenchmen, and William Morris as a great Welshman.

All this is laudably ingenious, but fantastical. Tom Garvin has written with characteristic percipience about cultural insecurity in late nineteenth-century Ireland as an 'emotion in disguise'. Extreme and exclusivist attitudes were a compensatory reaction to contempt, anti-Catholicism and separation from the establishment; the educational system mobilized a class of the discontented, up to schoolteacher and minor civil servant level, who formed the avant-garde of the alienated. 'They projected their personal quandaries on to the social system in general, typically in the form of a noisy and romantic anti-British nationalism constructed from a mixture of traditional elements and new radical ideologies coming in from outside Ireland.'[15] This sounds strikingly familiar (as it is perhaps meant to). But the idea of an Irish culture affected more by Europe than by Britain is as unrealistic as the late nineteenth-century notion that a world of prelapsarian innocence survived on the western seaboard. Nor is the interaction of European influence with Irish nationalism, where it *does* occur, automatically a good thing. The anti-Semitic ravings of Arthur Griffith's *United Irishman* in the early 1900s make chilling reading ('The Three Evil Influences of the century are the Pirate, the Freemason and the Jew'[16]). And these obsessions, like Maud Gonne's similar opinions, derived directly from the anti-Dreyfus campaign in France, to which Griffith was violently committed. J.J. O'Kelly and J.J. Walsh, other brokers of Gaelicism and Anglophobia, were more virulent anti-Semites still. The influence of Germany on the careers of Frank Ryan or Francis Stuart cannot be seen as a particularly encouraging precedent. A genuine Irish Europeanism, or European Irishness, is devoutly to be wished. But it cannot be achieved simply as an adroit diversionary reaction conditioned by atavistic Anglophobia. In that case, it must produce, yet again, a rancid and self-congratulatory form of nativism. This characteristic, mercifully moderated in the South, persists in certain areas of cultural propaganda in the North. It needs to be opened up to an acceptance of the mixed cultural polity which so much of Ireland – like it or not – has inherited.

IV

It is time, then, to return to the views posited by *Culture and Anarchy*. Essentially a view from the disillusioned South, Lyons's text presents the outcome of variations in Irishness as, inevitably, a monolithic confrontation:

> Political solutions are indeed urgently needed, but they will continue to be as unavailing in the future as in the past if they go on ignoring the essence of the Irish situation, which is the collision of a variety of cultures within an island whose very smallness makes their juxtaposition potentially, and often actually, lethal. Recent events in Northern Ireland have certainly shown us that two very different communities are at death-grips with each other, but the fact that this conflict is so often described in religious terms has still further confounded confusion, leaving many observers convinced that a people so inveterately addicted to its ancient, obscure quarrels is best left to its own murderous devices.[17]

Such a view has since become, in a sense, entrenched – partly because of the persuasive and authoritative nature of Lyons's writing, and his own stature as a historian. His subsequent, more optimistic statement that the 'roots of difference' were at last beginning to be explored was sidelined. The bleak implication of *Culture and Anarchy* was given further credence by the miseries of day-to-day politics, and day-to-day murder, in Ireland over the decade since Lyons first lectured at Oxford. There is also a thought-provoking paradox, in that the historiographical tradition, whence Lyons came, had for forty years been resolutely breaking down the barriers imposed by pious nationalism – which was all to the good. But another, implicitly contradictory characteristic of the historiographical revolution, with its deliberately even-handed determination to give all sides their due, was a corresponding softening of certain sharp edges, and a blunting of embarrassing disjunctions. In Ireland, political aspirations and social thought, for Protestants as well as Catholics, often derive from ethics, theology and emotion rather than from economics or politics. The sectarian conflict and confessional identification present in every walk of Irish life were underplayed by modern liberal historiography (including Lyons's own *Ireland since the Famine*), perhaps because they were temperamentally distasteful.

One of the interesting things about *Culture and Anarchy* was that it confronted this phenomenon, reassessed it and extended it – possibly to excess. Lyons's roping off of Ulster into one chapter is a symptom of this. So is his virtual ignoring of the First World War as a necessary precondition for 1916 (and much else). So, perhaps, is his choice of the eccentric Standish O'Grady as an emblematically doomed figure of the Protestant Anglo-Irish attempt at *rapprochement*. (Here, again, Lyons's inspiration was Yeats.) At the same time, Lyons underrated the influence (and efforts) of less spectacular non-Catholic, non-separatist nationalists such as Hubert Oldham of the *Dublin University Review*, perhaps because he assumed their loss of influence after the polarization of 1912–14 was inevitable. Similarly, he saw the Gaelic League early on as a nursery of political separatism: an interpretation which fitted certain cells within the organization, like the celebrated Keating Branch in Parnell Square, but not true universally until a late stage of the game. In fact the Keating Branch, a coven of *émigré* Munstermen conspiring against their Dublin colleagues, were seen by fellow Leaguers as 'footpads'. In the end, the Gaelic League had to be taken over forcibly by the strategy of handing out proxy votes to non-Irish-speaking IRB men (fifty in Dundalk alone). By 1913 Pearse was declaring, 'I have come to the conclusion that the Gaelic League, as the Gaelic League, is a spent force; and I am glad of it.'[18]

In terms of allowing for cultural diversity, the League had initially enabled Protestants to be Irish without being Catholic or separatist, and to annoy English-speaking Catholic Irishmen by being more 'Irish' than they. And this particular vision was another casualty of political polarization after 1912. But whether this was inevitable from the 1890s is a very different question. Lyons's treatment makes little of Hyde's development, and his increasing political moderation: except as yet another Irish Protestant inevitably retreating into the laager after playing with nationalist fire. And this may be a misinterpretation.

There is also the question of the brilliantly entertaining but highly selective range of sources from which Lyons intuited Catholic and Protestant mentalities. Father Timothy Corcoran and the *Catholic Bulletin* may not have expressed the whole Catholic view; and at the same time, George Russell and the *Irish Statesman* represent a pretty idealized version of the Irish Protestant mind.[19] Lyons's last work was innovative, elegant and deeply exciting; what its influence should now be doing is sending other scholars in a similar direction of cultural exploration, but with their nets cast more widely.

And, if one dare say it, more speculatively and more optimistically. If A.T.Q. Stewart's belief that to the Irish all history is applied history is true, maybe it can be 'applied' to break down old ideas instead of reasserting old prejudices. If there is one single unalloyed good that has come out of the overdone debates about historical revisionism, it is the idea of the historian as subversive. We should be seeking out the interactions, paradoxes and subcultures – not only Oldham, with his *Dublin University Review* and his Contemporary Club bringing in Theosophists, Fenians and Trinity dons, but also speculative theories of origins, if only to rearrange the pieces in more surprising patterns. A new history could show that varieties of Irishness can be complementary rather than competing. Another key quote from Lyons: 'Perhaps the most important consequence of the 1921 settlement was that by concentrating attention on physical boundaries and questions of political sovereignty, it postponed almost till our own day any serious consideration of the cultural differences that underlay the partition of the country.' Elsewhere, though, he pessimistically remarked: 'the old argument for cultural fusion [revived by AE in the *Irish Statesman* during the 1920s] as usual went unregarded save by the few who were already converted'.[20] The implication is that this was as true for the 1970s as for half a century earlier. But there are alternatives to fusion which need not necessarily be confrontation.

Perhaps, towards the end of the twentieth century, it is time to investigate definitions of nationalism that could be inclusive rather than exclusive. At the end of the nineteenth century, an energetic cultural debate was apparently opening up between brokers of the different cultural traditions in Ireland – Plunkett, Griffith, Father Tom Finlay, Alice Milligan, Moore, O'Grady, Yeats, Synge, Moran. Reading their journals brings home the fact that they were not operating in several states of solipsistic isolation: they were engaging in dialogue with each other, however angrily. Sometimes it seems that a similar process has been evolving in the columns of *Crane Bag*, *Fortnight*, the *Irish Review*, the Field Day pamphlets, *Krino*, *Making Sense* – and this is only an off-the-cuff list of the proliferating publications noticed by a periodically returning emigrant. There is also the theatre of Friel, Parker, McGuinness, Murphy, Kilroy; and various initiatives on other levels from Belfast and Dublin. Along with this efflorescence there is, perhaps, a Europeanization which is less bogus than the kind previously mentioned, and which may be able to teach us more.

It might, for instance, look at the political history of 'transfrontier' areas within the EC – in which case, the supposed inroads made by the Anglo-Irish Accord into 'sovereignty' might look rather different. (In these areas, including regions like Alsace–Lorraine, Lichtenstein, and a *département* of the Pyrenees, external powers exercise authority on behalf of marooned minorities, through bipartisan commissions of governmental representatives of local and regional authorities of the countries concerned.) The very notion of indivisible sovereignty is now being questioned;[21] feasible or not, the concepts of dual allegiance and cultural diversity are surely associated. Other areas where comparative historical study might open up new perspectives involve the practice of jurisdiction over designated individuals rather than specific territories: allegiance, in a sense, as an option rather than an imposition. Already it is being suggested that ethnic identification might be interpreted in a more flexible and contingent way, which might query the old zero-sum game, and break up some of the supposed congruences. We might even be beginning to question whether nationalism need imply the politics of old-fashioned separatist republicanism. (Especially since extremist Northern Republicans are now faced with the prospect of a Southern state which no longer represents anything they want to unify with, and will therefore have to be destabilized and reconstructed in its turn.) A 'new nationalism', bearing in mind these subversive notions, might take many forms. Cultural self-confidence can exist without being yoked to a determinist and ideologically redundant notion of unilaterally declared nation–statehood; political and cultural credentials have for too long been identified together. The slate of required qualifications for being Irish was beginning to be redefined a century ago, in the period Lyons wrote about; but the process was, in a sense, hijacked by a percussion of political upheavals. Might we not be coming back to a similar juncture now?

And as for cultural nationalism: need it be reactionary? Or exclusive? Or anti-modern? It is seen by many scholars as, historically, a defensive response to widespread social change, economic dislocation and sectional decline, even as 'a disease of development'. But just as Unionism cannot continue to define itself only by negatives, an inclusive national ideal cannot look to Anglophobia as its cement without becoming automatically negative. It is remarkable how long the inheritance of the turn-of-the-century formulations has lasted. The cultural roots of that nationalist revival stressed a perceived conflict between the values of the 'city' (English) and the 'country' (Irish). Despite a half-century of cultural imposition in independent Ireland, the values of the city may have won out. But that is no reason not to make the city Irish too. Looking back once more to some unexpected aspects of turn-of-the-century nationalism, we find the *Leader* in 1901 defining the 'real Irish people' not as pampootie-wearing Aran fishermen, but as *petit bourgeois* artisans living in provincial towns in the south of Ireland. This is the beginning of realism; but the reference to the *south* of Ireland should be noted. It is significant that when analysing the revolutionary elite of the 1913–22 period, Tom Garvin found a striking under-representation of Ulster, even of Catholic Ulster. This is reminiscent of an exchange in Stewart Parker's play *Northern Star*, where Henry Joy McCracken tells Jemmy Hope that Ireland is perceived by nationalists as 'a field with two men fighting over it, Cain and Abel. The bitterest fight in the history of man on this earth. We were city boys. What did we know about two men fighting over a field?' What official identity has lacked up to now is the sceptical perspective of the city boys.[22]

And the need to modernize nationalism has tremendous relevance for cultural diversity and its acceptance in the North, as well as for a relaxation of attitudes in the South. Cannot a secular ethic now be taken as a reasonable aspiration in both parts of the island? With unconscious irony, Sean Cronin wrote a few years ago of how Pearse 'purified' Tone's politics of their irreligion. We could do with some of that impurity again. It may have been apparent in the fact that the city vote went against religious dictation in the recent referenda in the Republic. But we live with the results of the strategy whereby first Parnell in 1884–5, and then Sinn Féin in the First and Second Dáil, made huge concessions to the Church in the field of education. It may have been in line with Irish historical precedent, but it utterly negated the pluralist, one-nation rhetoric of official nationalism. If the idea that antagonistic attitudes and cultural apartness are sustained by separate schooling is a liberal cliché, it is a liberal cliché because it is true. One of the few unequivocally cheering pieces of news to come out of Ireland in recent years was a statement by those promoting integrated education that they hope to be educating a third of the children of Northern Ireland by the year 2000. Cannot integrated education be presented, not as an anodyne and deracinating mish-mash, but as an affirmation of differences which might lead to mutual acceptance?

The question has been raised whether cultural nationalism, in the revival of the late nineteenth and early twentieth centuries, appealed to 'young religious and political intellectuals at times of national crisis, when the dominant ecclesiastical and political institutions of their society seemed powerless against an alien state'.[23] This seems, to a historian at least, unnecessarily schematic. But there may be grounds for hope that the discovery of an outward-looking and inclusive cultural nationalism, not predicated upon political and religious differences, will be the salient business of young and not so young intellectuals and educators at this current crisis of both Irish states. If such a process, teamed with economic optimism, achieved its own momentum, hopes of vague 'political movement' might be left for later. More importantly, the message that cultural diversity need not imply political confrontation might get through to the rockface of attitudes in the housing estates of Belfast and Derry. Kevin Boyle and Tom Hadden have trenchantly pointed out that the simple solutions do not work.[24] If this means concentrating on education at all levels, rather than politics, it may still be a step forward. And eventually, perhaps that is the kind of oxygen required to revive what in Northern Ireland Tom Paulin has caustically called the 'cadaver politic'. Here, too, the implicit 'cultural revolution' of attitudes which some observers have discerned in the South may be relevant.[25] To paraphrase a recent formulation, if a solution is a political mirage, one should turn to irrigating the cultural and social desert.[26] In terms of direction, Irish history contains encouraging signposts as well as depressing culs-de-sac.

It remains true that abstract academic nostrums, condescendingly dictated from an outside vantage, are the last thing Northern Ireland needs. There is a line in Stewart Parker's play *Spokesong* about 'buzzards flocking in' to the North with notebooks and tape-recorders, and any 'commentator' should keep it humbly in mind. However, another Ulster writer's name might be invoked – someone who, like Stewart Parker, provided a voice Northern Ireland could ill afford to lose. This is the poet John Hewitt, who articulated that quintessential combination of Protestant scepticism and commitment, linked with a sense of place that was absolutely Irish. Hewitt's poetry tour with John Montague in 1970, 'The Planter and the Gael', was a landmark affirmation of creative cultural diversity. He once visualized himself as a Planter's Gothic church, like the one at Kilmore, with an ancient round tower encased inside, 'needled through every sentence I utter'.[27] Like his own tough-minded poetry, the image faced up to allegiances that might have been formally divided, but could be personally reconciled. It is a cautious ambition; but it could be a beginning.

3

Interpretations of Parnell: The Importance of Locale

I

In 1922 the pioneer psychoanalyst and Freudian disciple Ernest Jones delivered a paper entitled 'The Island of Ireland: A Psychoanalytical Contribution to Political Psychology'.[1] A year after the Anglo-Irish Treaty, Jones was impelled to consider Ireland's severance from Britain; not unexpectedly, he dealt with the notion of Ireland as animating mother-figure. Most of all, he concentrated upon that enigmatic nationalist, Charles Stewart Parnell. Jones demonstrated the importance to Parnell's development of the police raid on his mother's house in the 1860s. Seeking Fenians, the police penetrated her bedroom; they then took away a sword belonging to Charles. Symbolic violation of the mother and castration of the son, Jones concluded triumphantly, focused Parnell's implacable Oedipal hatred upon the British government and helped change Irish history.

Unfortunately for Jones's theory, this incident is probably apocryphal, and certainly exaggerated.[2] But his essay takes its place in a long tradition of attempts to decode the motivation behind Parnell. Part of the point of preserving a pantheon of national heroes is that its denizens be endlessly adaptable. Tone, Davis and O'Connell can be altered to suit the needs of the age and of the people commemorating them. Parnell (like de Valera) is less tractable. Yet the discussions continue, and the enigma remains – partly because of what Henry Labouchère called the Irish 'fetishism' for Parnell, which 'placed him on a higher level than common humanity'.[3] Parnell's later career demonstrates the drawback of pantheons, especially when their inhabitants take up premature residence before they are safely dead. The process of putting him there involved analysis and interpretation in off-the-peg biographies from very early in his career; a century after his death, it continues still. Back in 1946, the anniversary of his birth, J.J. Horgan called for a definitive biography as 'our centenary tribute to Parnell';[4] despite F.S.L. Lyons's attempt to fill the gap in 1974, many questions of interpretation remain.

Parnell haunts his biographers, much as he haunts the memoirs of his contemporaries. As his ageing lieutenants like William O'Brien, T.P. O'Connor, T.M. Healy and Michael Davitt wrote their autobiographies in the decades after his death, the baleful eye of the dead Chief seemed to look over their shoulders; he remains oddly distanced from their accounts of the great struggle they had lived through together. Barry O'Brien, in his two-volume biography of 1898, was one celebrated exception; another, less well known, is the journalist M.M. O'Hara, whose comparative study of Parnell and Davitt (*Chief and Tribune*, 1919) was more analytical and more perceptive than many others. O'Brien, however, established the orthodox interpretation. Horgan, reviewing his achievement, said that O'Brien had 'many of the characteristics of Boswell', which may have been intended as a rather backhanded compliment. But O'Brien's belief, for instance, that Parnell's mother inculcated the anti-British feelings in her children was rapidly accepted, despite a scornful rebuttal from Parnell's sister Anna, who might be supposed to know. Other interpretations of the Parnell enigma were firmly engraved by O'Brien. He was an aristocratic rebel who took up nationalism like Fitzgerald, Tone and Emmet, turning his back on class, caste and fortune. He solved the land question in 1882. The O'Sheas had little intrinsic importance in his life until the bombshell of 1890. He was all-powerful until his fall. Home Rule was the great missed chance of Irish history.

There were some contradictory noises early on. Anti-Parnellites like T.M. Healy, Frank Hugh O'Donnell and Jasper Tully claimed that Parnell was a cardboard figure: the creature of the men around him.[5] Anna Parnell attacked the Land League as a 'Great Sham', never prepared to go the length of its rhetoric, which sold the smaller tenantry down the river; but her account remained buried for decades in a long-lost manuscript.[6] Others, who could have told a great deal, remained silent – like Parnell's secretary, Henry Campbell, generally discreet to the point of invisibility. (Where he did reveal himself, as in his libel suit against the *Cork Herald* in June 1891, he showed that he knew a great deal.) And the enigma remained fuelled by uncertainty – about everything from the circumstances of Parnell's childhood to the cause of his fatal illness and even the whereabouts of his body after his death.[7] (Giving a lecture in Waterford in the early 1970s, I was told categorically from the audience, 'Parnell was never in that box!')

Moreover, finding the Chief's opinions on almost any question is nearly as elusive an undertaking. His own resolute anti-intellectualism has something to do with this, and his refusal to engage in analysis or even arrive at an intellectually argued position, at least in public. His thought processes, unlike those of his garrulous lieutenants, are shrouded in silence. T.P. O'Connor expressed their bemusement at this: 'It is one of the strongest and most curious peculiarities of Mr Parnell not merely that he rarely, if ever, speaks of himself but that he rarely, if ever, gives any indication of having studied himself . . . It is a joke among his intimates that to Mr Parnell the being Parnell does not exist.'[8] It is difficult to form an intellectual profile of him, or even to try and imagine his mental world; his ideology seems to have been as instinctual as his politics.

There are clues, however, in his personal background: scraps of information in his brother's patchy memoir,[9] inferences from the Avondale library catalogue,[10] throw-away remarks in his oddly stilted speeches. And there is his haphazard family life, the constant absences of mother and sisters, the coolness of relations between family members, the sense of disassociation from much of Irish life. In some ways Parnell is a classic instance of marginalized Irishness; he reflects the dislocation of his class and his caste in the late nineteenth century. It is symbolic that the few new Parnellite records to come to light over the last decade or so have to do with finances: letters extending loans or meeting overdue bills, bundles of worthless share certificates. The relative poverty of the Parnells and the hopeless position of the Avondale estate cast implicit doubts on O'Brien's picture of Parnell's background. His precarious position as a landlord was mirrored by his ambivalence about the direction of the land struggle. Michael Davitt's memoir, *The Fall of Feudalism in Ireland* (1904), pointed up the tension between the two charismatic Land League leaders on the question of land nationalization. Mrs (O'Shea) Parnell's explosive memoir in 1914 contained even more traumatic shocks, enshrined in her late husband's love letters. 'I cannot describe to you the disgust I always felt with those [Land League] meetings, knowing as I did how hollow and wanting in solidity everything connected with the movement was. When I was arrested I did not think the movement would have survived a month, but this wretched Government have such a fashion for doing things by halves that it has managed to keep things going in several of the counties up till now.'[11]

The chilly attitude towards those 'keeping it going' – in actual fact, the Ladies' Land League led by his sister Anna – is breathtaking. Parnell's conservatism on the land issue has since come into increasingly clear focus – a process begun by Davitt's memoir in 1904. The date is significant: as with O'Hara's *Chief and Tribune* in 1919, contemporary events at that time were demonstrating the limitations of the 1879–82 revolution, exposed by a new surge of radical land agitation and the application of current left-wing social theory to the Irish situation. None the less, any interpretation of Parnell must put his ideas into the context of their own times, not ours. Lyons's judgement that as late as 1878 Parnell still saw the land question as incidental to the political struggle[12] is open to question. Certainly, opinions and writings attributed to him at this time seem to have actually been those of his sister Fanny.[13] But his great contribution remains the confluence of the Home Rule and the land campaigns, and the audacious political strategy that enabled him to accomplish one revolution and to advance another. Parnell's tactical genius was the necessary precondition of Gladstone's 1886 manoeuvre, where land reform and Home Rule were attempted (misguidedly) in one package. Paul Bew, radically differing from Lyons, believes that Parnell's priority was land reform, as a strategy to lead landlords into the nationalist camp;[14] he was certainly preoccupied by the extent to which a peasant proprietary could develop through government aid and how far this could be reconciled with the pursuit of political autonomy. In the last year of his life, when projected arrangements for Home Rule might have been expected to preoccupy him since his astounding repudiation of Gladstone's plan, he seems to have been far more obsessed with a laborious scheme of land purchase – the fruit of ten years' thinking, or so he said.[15] It is tempting to reverse Lyons's order of priorities and see him as a land reformer who deviated into politics, rather than the other way round.

What kind of politics he really espoused remains equally debatable. O'Brien believed that 'he saw as if by instinct that Fenianism was the key of Irish nationality,' and that his extremist American speeches of 1880 'came from his heart'.[16] Others are less sure. O'Brien stressed the importance of Fenian sympathies during the 1860s among members of Parnell's family, but Anna Parnell's little-noticed testimony about Fanny's girlish poetry for the *Irish People* at this time adds a sceptical note (and characteristically provides an economic analysis):

Now, Fanny's writing for that paper had nothing to do with politics whatever. She knew nothing of the existence of the Fenians when she went to that office, and the only purpose she had was to see if she could make a little money to supply some of the necessaries of life of which we were deprived. This was the only paper that would pay for poetry, though others were willing to publish it without paying. It is true that she went there very often, because it was very hard to get money out of the people at the office. She was obliged to dun them. The editor told her the objects of the Fenians, and she told me, which set me wondering what obstacle there would be to the Government stopping the accomplishment of those objects, and also why the Fenians 'told everybody' that way. Her poetry had nothing to do with Ireland. The editor asked her to write something national but she tried and found she couldn't. In the autumn of '64 we got a new governess, and she found she could not study and write poetry at the same time. So she left off going to the office and abandoned the attempt to get the balance of the money still owing to her.[17]

Again, it was the polarizing conditions of the late 1870s, and the radicalization of Anna and Fanny themselves, which created a different scenario. Parnell was capable of working the Fenian interest in his first election campaigns – at a time when Butt's Home Rule party was still 'on trial' as far as the Irish Republican Brotherhood were concerned, and several figures like Patrick Egan, Thomas O'Connor Power and J.J. O'Kelly sustained parallel connections with the two movements. During his last campaign in 1891 Parnell rhetorically came round full circle, paying his respects to James Stephens, as he had done to John Mitchel sixteen years before. And the celebrated Gaelic Athletic Association guard of honour at his funeral apparently linked him to the Phoenix flame revived. But he kept the Fenians at arm's length, and the remarkable thing is how little direct connection was decisively proved between Parnell and IRB emissaries – even in the testimony of informers and enemies during the hearings of the *Times* Special Commission.

II

Here again, historiography reflects contemporary circumstances. When O'Brien wrote his biography of Parnell, Fenianism seemed a romantic memory. By the time the old Parnellites wrote their memoirs in the 1920s, the IRB had revived, and helped to generate an armed struggle for independence; the stock of the movement was high, and an association with it conferred national respectability. By the 1960s and 1970s, when Lyons was publishing his books on Parnell, T.W. Moody was running his influential research seminar on the Home Rule movement at Trinity College, and Brian Farrell was organizing the lectures and papers published as *The Irish Parliamentary Tradition*, connections between constitutional and extremist agitation in Irish politics were considered more problematic, and the assertion of a viable non-violent tradition was much in people's minds. This necessarily affected interpretations of Parnell's relations to Fenianism.

At the same time, the actual effectiveness of Parnell's brand of constitutional politics was being queried, and not only by extreme nationalists. In 1974 A.B. Cooke's and J.R. Vincent's saturnine exposure of Gladstonian pretensions, *The Governing Passion: Cabinet Government and Party Politics in Britain 1885–1886*, provoked impassioned historiographical debate. They claimed that the Home Rule Bill was never meant to amount to anything; possibly just a stalking horse for the land bill, it was unworkable in the real world and epitomized the opportunist and cynical approach to Home Rule of all contemporary politicians, preoccupied by short-term power struggles, not long-term strategies. More recently, in the centenary year of the first Home Rule Bill, Alan O'Day and James Loughlin analysed the shortcomings and evasions of the Gladstone–Parnell Union of Hearts.[18] It is certainly odd that issues such as the Irish presence at Westminster remained up in the air until such a late stage, that Ulster was effectively ignored, and that financial and economic implications stayed open questions. But what is undeniable is the achievement of converting one of the British parties of government to accepting autonomy for Ireland – even taking into account the Cooke–

Vincent view of Gladstone's cynical priorities (itself questioned by recent Gladstonian research). And Parnell must take the credit. This is vividly illustrated in Gladstone's interview with O'Brien, shortly before his death, where the retired Prime Minister reiterated that the Union of Great Britain and Ireland had no moral force.[19] Consciously or unconsciously, he was repeating word for word the phrase employed by Parnell in a speech at Wexford sixteen eventful years before: the speech for which Gladstone then had Parnell consigned to Kilmainham Jail.[20]

Notwithstanding this obvious achievement, recent interpretations of Parnell have reassessed issues like his commitment to land reform, the practicability of Home Rule as drafted, and his relations to Fenianism – often in the light of current preoccupations. In such a process, another issue inevitably comes into focus: his attitude to Ulster. How far did he realize the strength and distribution of Ulster Unionism? He certainly underestimated its populist roots, though in this he was hardly unusual. Bew's revaluation puts Ulster at the centre of Parnell's political preoccupations towards the end of his career – imaginatively, if not always convincingly. Certainly, at Belfast in May 1891 Parnell expressed a belated recognition that Unionism was not restricted to landlords and Dublin professional Protestants; he emphasized the need to conciliate the religious prejudices of the minority and to prove that Home Rule could accommodate a pluralist Irish identity. By then, his own hostile relations with the organization of the Catholic Church made it easier to embrace such a line, though there were more Parnellite priests than the general picture allows. In any case, at this stage the political realities of the Irish situation seemed to contradict him. Parnell's celebrated and self-confessed ignorance of Irish history[21] may be relevant here. He is often pictured as riding the tiger of Fenian flirtations while remaining a constitutionalist. But perhaps the real tiger, which helped consume him, was the confessional basis of Irish politics. His establishment of the National League in 1882–5, with its clerically dominated constituency organization, together with his long-standing public commitment to denominational education, probably alienated Ulster opinion as much as anything (with the exception of economic protectionism, another particular inspiration of Parnell's). Conservative and Unionist polemicists affected to see the National League as simply the Land League *redivivus* – assuming that it was O'Connellite quick-change artistry in operation again, where political organizations succeeded each other with bewildering rapidity, altering names but not underlying forms. But this was not, in fact, accurate. The National League was a new political organization, not an agrarian one. And it accepted and reinforced the divide in political and religious culture between the north-east and the rest of the island.

Interpretations of Parnell, then, rely as much on the climate of the times and the needs of the interpreter as on the charismatic central figure himself. Even in his own lifetime, the Parnell image owed much to contemporary journalists with an interest in dramatizing politics – Henry Lucy's 'Diary of Politics' in *Punch* no less than William O'Brien's *United Ireland*. Accounts of strange, almost supernatural meetings became a set-piece of contemporary memoirs: William O'Brien's disguised encounter in a fog at Greenwich Observatory, Standish O'Grady's meeting on a Wicklow mountainside in a mounting storm, Lord Ribblesdale's surreal railway journey where Parnell talked intensely the whole time but never once looked at his face.[22] He carefully preserved the theatrical apartness of his manner towards most people, even on occasion members of his family. He treated many of his political associates as if they were troublesome tenants; they for their part sometimes spoke of him as if he were their eccentric landlord. In an effort to describe him, so many images and comparisons have been employed that cataloguing them has formed the basis of at least one rather bizarre book.[23] Perhaps Parnell's own off-beat humour deserves more analysis. Was it a joke when he remarked to his brother that he was thinking of raising another Tribute, as politics was the only thing that ever made him any money? Or when he told Davitt that his first action as President of an independent Irish government would be to lock him up? Or when he told the gushing Mary Gladstone that the greatest actor he had seen in London was her father? Or when he dismissively remarked to Elizabeth Mathew that Ireland was a delightful country from June to October?[24] He liked to say the unexpected, in a deadpan way; some of his more mysterious answers at the Special Commission hearings may have been in the same vein. Like W.B. Yeats, he probably became impatient at the reverence accorded his lightest remarks, and weary of constantly being taken seriously.

If we respond by trying to rid ourselves of the romantic myth, Parnell makes a certain partial logic in various unromantic contexts:

as a tenant-reform landlord fallen on hard times; as an industrialist *manqué* and closet protectionist; as a throwback to Grattanism; as a Buttite conservative who in essence continued Butt's policies; even as an American Irishman (half American himself, he was more sensitive to playing on the nuances of American opinion than many Irish orators; his brother thought that it was neither land reform nor Fenianism that awoke his interest in politics, but the American Civil War).[25] Even his strange personal life makes sense, when he is seen as an abandoned child, emotionally immature and repressed, who became late in life utterly dependent on the mother-figure of Katharine O'Shea.

III

Above all, one context in which he deserves attention is that of native locality. F.S.L. Lyons's biography recurs to the image of a figure hewn from Wicklow granite, and Parnell's connections with Wicklow have been the subject of continuing interest – most recently evidenced in the development of a lively and stimulating annual symposium at Avondale, which was inaugurated in 1991 as a fully fledged summer school.[26] This reflects the growing realization of a vital theme in Irish history: the importance of place. On one level, the analysis of large subjects and issues, like the 1798 rising or the Famine or the War of Independence, more and more stresses local aspects and local variations; on another, historical initiatives are increasingly taken from the localities too. This is not a recent development; the anniversary year of Parnell's death was also the centenary of the foundation of the Cork Archaeological and Historical Society, while other local historical societies originated over fifty years before that. Parnell's connections with his native county are symbolized in Avondale, his family's house, perched in an idyllic setting in one of the loveliest parts of the county. The situation of the house, too, is emblematic: close to Rathdrum but not dominating it; one of a number of fine houses in that part of Wicklow, built between the mid-eighteenth and mid-nineteenth centuries; not aggressively large, or cordoned off by miles of avenues and barriers of gate-lodges. Its great glory is its planting rather than its architecture: those unique stands of trees planned by the house's builder Samuel Hayes and continued by the Forestry

Commission.[27] In this, Avondale is fairly representative of those houses scattered through east Wicklow (such as Westaston, Clonbraney, Clonmannin, Inchinappa, Glendalough) which, unlike the great Italianate *palazzi* of Kildare, have a certain integral relationship to their surroundings. This might be taken to symbolize the existence of middling gentry-families like the Humes, Actons, Tottenhams, Howards, Synges, Tighes, Westbys, Grattans, Truells, Brookes, Bayleys, Probys and Parnells.[28] Several of these families had prominent eighteenth-century ancestors who had been active in politics and were retrospectively claimed for the Patriot tradition: notably the Grattans, the Tighes and – again – the Parnells. These families, and the world they inherited, formed the background to Parnell's early life; and it was a background with which he kept up connections, though those connections naturally altered as his extraordinary political career distanced him from them.

The fact that his career was so extraordinary means that Parnell tends to be seen very much as a figure who stands alone: 'glamorously unique, as well as uniquely glamorous'.[29] But there were tissues and threads which bound him to Rathdrum and continued to do so. Some were personal and disappeared into obscurity, like the closest friend of Parnell's youth, Major Bookey of Derrybawn. The two young men experimented on their sawmills together, played cricket together, socialized together; when the youthful Parnell and his drunken brother-in-law Arthur Dickinson were prosecuted for rowdy behaviour in the hotel at Glendalough in 1869,[30] Bookey was, fortunately, the magistrate in the case. With Bookey's death by drowning off Algiers in 1875, a link to Parnell's Wicklow life was lost.[31] It is possible, even likely, that had he lived, their friendship would have been threatened by politics, as happened with Parnell's other great friend among his neighbours, his exact contemporary John Barton.

The Parnells were, however, closely linked into the cousinage of the local county. Many of their local relationships stemmed from the Howard family connection, created when Parnell's grandfather William Parnell-Hayes married Frances Howard. This brought relationships to the Powerscourts and Carysforts, since Frances's two sisters married into these families. Sir Ralph Howard of Castle Howard, Member for the county in Parnell's youth and a great local magnate, was a powerful presence in the Parnell children's lives, especially after their father's premature death; he became guardian for many of their financial interests and was involved in litigation against Mrs Parnell over them.[32] The huge Fitzwilliam estate at Coolattin near Shillelagh, whose agent Robert Chaloner was a key figure in local life, was also important in Parnell's world; Chaloner was a friend of his father's, and had co-operated with him in Famine relief measures in 1846–7. Years afterwards, at the height of the Land War in 1881, Parnell would uncharacteristically defend the administration of Coolattin: 'As to the Fitzwilliam estate in Wicklow, I know a great deal about it; it is so well managed that the tenants up to the present refused to join the Land League.'[33] In fact, a great deal of material relating to the Fitzwilliam estate has survived and does show a complex and ambitious scheme of management: free schools, widows' pensions, a carefully structured approach to aided emigration, a Poor Shop, and well-meaning but probably infuriating attempts to regulate hostile relationships between tenants ('Edward Kelly is not to beat his wife Johanna any more and his wife is not again either to keep company with the Kirwans of Ballyconnell or to go into their house').[34] The estate also paid a half of all improvement expenses and limited rent increases to five per cent. This may seem whistling against the wind, and the attempts at social control equally hopeless and misplaced: the tone of landlord benevolence is grating at best nowadays, and often seems objectively self-interested. What is interesting, however, is that the evidence for nineteenth-century estate management in Wicklow does present a picture of involvement and amelioration on the landlords' part which was hardly typical, and more closely resembles the English norm. The Fitzwilliams may have been unusual; they were certainly unusually rich. And a squirearchical approach might be expected on their estate, since the owners were English Whig grandees rather than local Anglo-Irish (or Irish) Tories.

This could also explain their committed resistance to sectarian education. The estate paid grants to schoolmasters who founded hedge-schools, for instance,[35] and opposed the attempts made by a bigoted local Protestant clergyman to institute religiously separate schooling. Lord Fitzwilliam had already alienated Protestant foundations like the Erasmus Smith Board by opening his school to Catholics as well as Protestants, and appointing Roman Catholic priests to his Schools Committee.[36] Schools on the Grattan estate were similarly 'open to all'.[37] An exceptionally good relationship with local Catholics was also evident on the Powerscourt estate (and not only because of

Lord Powerscourt's friendship with the famous Father Healy of Little Bray[38]). Another estate instanced during the Land War in 1881 as being managed 'on the English model' was the Carysfort holding, practically next door to Avondale, where before 1870 free sale prevailed, and tenants were given incentives to reclaim, fence and drain. Even in 1881 rents were paid without reduction.

Wicklow had its bad landlords too (there were terrible evictions at Crony Byrne during the Famine); and before the Parnellite revolution it was not overwhelmingly Liberal in political terms, generally returning Conservative Members. The family interest of Lord Wicklow, notorious for political dictation to tenants, was Tory.[39] However, the impressive figure of James Grattan represented the Radical Whig interest between 1827 and 1841; Lord Monck was a prominent Liberal MP in the 1850s; and Sir Ralph Howard was described by Chaloner in 1848 as representing 'the Liberal cause'.[40] Where Orangeism appeared in the county, it was not among the gentry, and local JPs were opposed to its manifestations.

Was mid-Victorian Wicklow 'special' – with the 'English' character of estate administrations, implied by names like Humewood, Belmont, Woodstock and Avondale, producing an ethos that differed from the norm? Certainly there was prosperity outside the model estates, to go by the records of the savings banks, the type of crime recurring at assizes, the speed of agricultural recovery after the Famine, the low illiteracy figures. Individual estate records show wages well above the average. Grandees like the Powerscourts, in between acclimatizing Japanese deer and afforesting the landscape, took good care to keep in with local opinion.[41] At least in the east of the county there was a dominant 'estate culture'; one recent authority, discussing the way that estates 'landscaped' both physical and social geography in Ireland, refers to Wicklow for many of his examples.[42] And while in control, the Wicklow gentry bent themselves to making their mark on the population, often through education. School accounts are prominent in estate records: Robert Truell of Clonmannin and Mrs Smith of Baltiboys were preoccupied by educational initiatives; the Halls were impressed by the Putlands' school at Bray and the Latouches' at Delgany.

If a tradition of good local relationships in nineteenth-century Wicklow existed, it may have been because of the prevalence of secondary residences in the county; many houses like Avondale were owned by people who drew their major income from larger estates elsewhere in Ireland but preferred to live in Wicklow and could therefore, in a sense, afford a more liberal and relaxed attitude to their holdings there.[43] For instance, the Tighe family came to Rossanna because an ancestor was ordered by his doctor to live in the country; his estates were in Carlow, but he so disliked that county that he bought the Wicklow holding as well.[44] Parnell's father not only possessed another estate in Armagh, but also bought a far larger holding in Carlow just before he died.

At the same time, the liberal attitudes of local gentry went deeper than this, and were represented in the attitudes and writings of Parnell's grandfather: campaigner against English exploitation of Ireland, enemy of bad landlords and early advocate of Catholic Emancipation. In his *Inquiry into the Causes of the Popular Discontents in Ireland* (1805), William Parnell-Hayes violently attacked the Union:

> You tell us to interest ourselves in the glory of the English government; we tell you we cannot. Why? Because we cannot love our stepmother as our mother . . . Give us, then, back our independence; hunt our trade from your ports; that national spirit which lightened our shackles can assert its freedom; leave us to our rebellions, the courage that repressed them once can repress them again; take back the lenitives you would apply to our religious distinctions, we shall not always be bigots but shall one day acknowledge the maxim that by removing religious distinctions we remove religious animosities. These are evils that time and experience will remedy and we might yet be a happy and wealthy people; but if you destroy the principle of national honour you destroy the very principle of wealth and happiness and our misery will be such as our baseness deserves, our poverty as complete as your narrow jealousy could desire.[45]

The language derives from late eighteenth-century Patriotism, but it also anticipates the rhetoric of early Home Rule. In a sense both William Parnell-Hayes and his neighbour James Grattan, another liberal pro-Catholic, were attempting the impossible: the situation of an Irish landlord in the early nineteenth century made liberal initiatives effectively unviable. History, and the prejudices of their neighbours, were too strong for them. None the less, they tried; and William Parnell-Hayes found his own niche in history, since it has recently been established that it was he who first hit on the subscription idea which funded Daniel O'Connell's Catholic Association.[46]

William Parnell-Hayes's ideas were in many other ways ahead of his time, if less immediately influential. He propagandized for educational reform and agricultural innovation; he worked long and hard for a reversal of landlord attitudes towards 'those unfortunate beings who are placed at the extremity of the scale of degradation, the Irish Peasantry',[47] and constantly reverted to this preoccupation in his writings. The surrounding miseries of the tenantry, he said, made a landlord's existence almost unbearable.

What is striking here is the sense of an interdependent connection between a reforming landlord and his dependants; and, even more remarkable for the time, the fact that religious differentiation did not enter into this. It is the kind of scenario conjured up by the didactic novelists of the early nineteenth century (among whom William Parnell-Hayes must himself be numbered) but which bore little resemblance to normal reality. Himself a liberal Protestant, close to Catholic activists, he dedicated his one novel to 'the Priests of Ireland'. His son John Henry Parnell during his short life achieved a similar reputation for good relationships with his Catholic neighbours, and the record of his activity on the Rathdrum Poor Law Union Board of Guardians bears this out; he also campaigned for the building of a Catholic church at Rathdrum and warmly praised the good work done by orders of nuns.[48] And this also bears upon an aspect of Charles Stewart Parnell which is not often paid attention, but which has direct relevance to his Wicklow background.

IV

Parnell was a Protestant; a member of the Synod of the Church of Ireland; and dutifully took some part in local parish organizations like the Select Vestry when he was living at Rathdrum. His private religious feelings appear to have been agnostic, with an inclination (like others of his family) towards the Plymouth Brethren. But from the first stirrings of his political career, it is notable that he sustained extremely good relationships with local Catholic clerics. His early endorsement of denominational education indicates that he looked more favourably on the social agenda of Catholicism than many Protestant politicians. The parish priest at Rathdrum in 1875, Father Galvin, gave him influential backing in his first political contest; Father Galvin's brother, also a priest, befriended Parnell and his brother John on their American tour in 1872. The Reverend James Redmond of Arklow was another local priest who brought heavy pressure to bear on Parnell's behalf in the 1875 Meath election. A later parish priest at Rathdrum, Father Dunphy, was an even closer friend and associate; when he moved to Arklow he worked closely with Parnell not only in political organization, but also in his development of quarries at Big Rock, and in campaigns to develop Arklow Harbour. More surprisingly, these local clerical friends remained friends, even during the terrible days of the Split (there were more Parnellite priests than one might think[49]). After the Kilkenny election of December 1890, when Parnell had quicklime thrown in his eyes, he spent Christmas Day with Father Dunphy, now based in Waterford. Father Dunphy told him he would always have something to eat and drink from him and asked him, reasonably enough, 'Where was your brain? Why did you not get three sensible men to advise you?' Parnell said that he was getting old, like Father Dunphy, and would accordingly get sense.[50] Not many people could talk to Parnell like that, especially at that stage of his life. Like Major Bookey at Derrybawn or John Barton at Glendalough or the Gaffney family at Avondale, Father Dunphy knew Parnell as a Wicklow neighbour: and his testimony, were it available to us, might accordingly clarify several aspects of the enigma.

Parnell, of course, was a Wicklow gentleman and conscious of it; his brother's memoir emphasizes this, and stresses his irritation at foreigners (American as well as English) who did not recognize 'an Irish gentleman' when they saw one.[51] This identification as 'an Irish gentleman' was not as inimical to support for Home Rule as might be supposed – at least in the 1870s. It is interesting to note that Wicklow's first Home Rule MP, Andrew O'Byrne, who was returned in 1874, was a landlord, owner of Cabinteely House, a JP, and High Sheriff for the county; he had been a close ally of Parnell's father on the Rathdrum Poor Law Union Board of Guardians. Many of Isaac Butt's early supporters were from a similar background.[52] As a general rule, this ceases to be true from 1880. But, significantly, one of Parnell's closest friends in the party was another obscure and forgotten figure: the Wicklow MP and Parnell's neighbour at home, W.J. Corbet. Corbet, a regular guest at Aughavannagh shooting-parties and a frequent visitor to Avondale, remained a firm supporter of Parnell to the end, as a Wicklow neighbour as well as a political ally.

Indeed, the support in Wicklow for Parnell could sometimes come from unexpected quarters: here again, neighbourliness may have counted for more than political affiliation. When the practice of 'ploughing matches' at Avondale was instituted (originally to work Parnell's land when he was imprisoned in Kilmainham), several of those who contributed help were not Home Rulers. And the local newspaper, the *Wicklow Newsletter*, owned and edited by the firmly Unionist William McPhail (who had bought the press from the Tighes at Rossanna), sustained an odd relationship with Parnell: at once antagonistic and affectionate. Parnell's politics were consistently attacked by the paper; but his Wicklow identification was seen as a cause for pride, and the paper warmly endorsed his campaigns for improving the harbour facilities at Wicklow and Arklow, and his creation of local employment in mines and quarries. In the terrible last year of his life, the *Newsletter* took a Parnellite rather than anti-Parnellite line, while every now and then reminding itself and its readers that its politics were officially Unionist. Its leader on Parnell's death was genuinely grief-stricken and memorialized him as a great son of Wicklow as well as a magnanimous employer and good landlord:

> In one connection particularly do we desire to speak of his sad demise, and that is as it regards Wicklow itself. In the death of Mr Parnell we have lost a benefactor in the true sense of the word. What he has done for the people of the county, and what he intended to do, will never be adequately realized. How much his heart was centred here, and how deep an interest he displayed in the home of his childhood, was little thought of. It was absorbed in the whirl of political excitement, but we are now beginning to faintly see the inmost recesses of his heart. The walls of his study at Brighton were hung with engravings of Avondale, for which he ever retained an abiding love . . . Mr Parnell's life was sacrificed for Ireland. No matter how we may condemn his policy, he lived to aid her progress. When the Archbishop of Dublin taunted him with the money he received from the Irish people, he replied that the inhabitants of Arklow could explain how he employed it. And well they might. It was in the recent speech he delivered in Wicklow he made use of those words; and to the minds of those who were aware of his interest in the county, they carried emphatic conviction.[53]

These identities meant more to Parnell than is often realized, and can help explain some of the anomalies mentioned earlier, such as his conservatism on the land issue. He was a conspicuously good landlord: building cottages for his tenantry (one of whom went to great lengths to conceal from him the fact that the chimney smoked, for fear of disappointing him[54]); letting rents run for long periods and keeping them below recommended valuation levels; remaining deeply preoccupied with his experimental sawmills on the estate, which at their height employed twenty-five people (the buildings are still there, on the left of the avenue as one approaches the house); engaging in turf production for various purposes at Aughavannagh. (Ahead of his time in this as in much else, he also started a peat-litter industry in Kildare.) The estate overall employed more than a hundred and fifty people. The efforts of many hostile journalists to prove the Land League President a bad landlord in private life all failed. They very often confused him with his brother Henry, who was an absentee, managing his Carlow estates purely as land speculations and quite prepared to evict non-paying tenants. Parnell, however, was uniformly praised by his tenants and never made money from his rent-rolls – already declining when he took over the estate.

This strengthens the argument that tenant right and the general agricultural position brought him into politics, rather than the inspiration of the Fenian ideal, whatever that came to mean later. Avondale must have demonstrated to him the logic of land reform, for all concerned. He was the archetypal encumbered landlord; the estate was burdened with mortgages, inherited and acquired.[55] Parnell was, unlike many of his colleagues, a genuine farmer; T.P. O'Connor merrily recalled that most of the agrarian leaders could not tell a cow from a horse, or a field of oats from a field of potatoes, and Parnell had to explain these mysteries to his followers.[56] His early and consistent embrace of the land purchase ideal – peasant proprietary – was probably encouraged by the realization that the traditional system had not worked at Avondale.

And this also helped inspire the non-political activities for which his neighbours knew him best, and which brought him back into contact with them: stone quarrying and mineral explorations. In 1882 he had been excited to discover granite stone quarries, '*on my own land*', at Ballyknockan: in fact, these quarries had been drawn attention to by the Ordnance Survey in 1838, when they had been exploited by another owner.[57] From producing beechwood paving-setts in his sawmills, he progressed to turning out granite setts from his stone quarries, with the major ones at Big Rock, Arklow, and minor efforts elsewhere. We think of Parnell's monument as the Gaudens statue at the top of O'Connell Street in Dublin; he might prefer it to be the paving stones at the other end, on O'Connell Bridge, which were supplied to Dublin Corporation (against Welsh competition) from Parnell's quarries at Arklow. Parnell's preoccupation with his quarries, and his developments at Arklow, brought him back into the mainstream of local politics. His relationship with his relative, Lord Carysfort, had turned sour over politics, and bitter mutual criticism had been exchanged over their respective espousal of the Wicklow and Arklow harbour schemes. However, the development of Big Rock, and Parnell's subsequent support of the Arklow Harbour scheme meant that they began to co-operate again.[58] His political biographers tend to express surprise at Parnell's obsession with these matters – at the fact, for instance, that his first inquiry of a visitor to him in Kilmainham Jail in 1881 was about the progress of the Wicklow Harbour works.[59] Similarly, during his highly controversial interview with Lord Carnarvon in 1885, on which so many speculations about a Tory Home Rule initiative were based, Parnell devoted much valuable time to expounding the success of his quarries and the significance of the Dublin Corporation contract, as earnests of the industrial resources of Ireland.[60] His preoccupation with his mines and quarries during 1891 struck some people as evidence of delusion.[61] But considered in the context of Parnell's local identity, such obsessiveness comes as no surprise. Even when he was strategically lying low during the high political fever of 1885, he emerged to give an eagerly awaited address on St Patrick's Day in London. Most of it was devoted to the Arklow and Wicklow harbour schemes. Political analysts might interpret this as a machiavellian red herring dragged across the tracks, or as a deliberate exhibition of impassiveness. But it is more easily explained merely as a genuine expression of what meant most to him at the time.[62] The oracle appears less Delphic when his words are simply taken to mean what they say.

These priorities bear out his economic ideas, which increasingly tended towards protectionism for Irish industry; and significantly, he first endorsed the principle openly in a speech at Arklow. In the world of political calculation, this was read as a deliberate snub to Joseph Chamberlain, at the time pressing his own schemes for Ireland. In historical terms, as has been noted, it alienated Ulster yet further from any association with Home Rule. But the point of the speech is surely that an encouragement was being expressed to local Wicklow industry and that this was Parnell's genuine preoccupation. Sharply focused as always, he seems not to have been juggling the larger implications.

In his first reported political speech (during the 1874 Dublin election campaign), he gave his reasons for wanting Home Rule. It would encourage manufactures, develop fisheries and stimulate a resident gentry, who would be socially and politically responsible.[63] These were sentiments spoken from platforms where he was accompanied by warmly supportive Catholic priests, and where Fenian influence had been brought into play on his behalf behind the scenes. In a sense, all the elements of his future career are there; and it is possible that their order of priorities, and relative weighting, did not alter as dramatically as might be assumed.

And these priorities should be related not only to his family background (they closely echo William Parnell-Hayes), but also to the ethos of nineteenth-century Wicklow. Even in the Land War, local Land League priests like Parnell's friend Father Dunphy found themselves rather grudgingly praising the record of local landlords for reducing rents below Griffith's Valuation and keeping up the 'kind and considerate traditions of their families'.[64] The *Wicklow Newsletter*, though Tory, Unionist and pro-landlord, called on local landlords to grant rent abatements, and approvingly published lists of those that did. Corbet, one of the new Home Rule MPs for the county, was himself a landowner and a popular one; he also denounced advocates of violent methods. Even a lashing from Michael Davitt failed to rouse the supine tenantry of Blessington in December 1880.[65] Unpopular landlords like Lord Brabazon rapidly reduced their rents by fifty per cent; the general level of agitation in the county was very low, a phenomenon remarked with varying degrees of disapproval by visiting politicians.[66] The focus of most of the local criticism was the Fitzwilliam estate, but this tended to concentrate on the interventionist practices of recropping, reallocation, drainage and so forth rather than evictions; in the words of one tenant, 'introducing English ideas, contrary to the feelings and views of the Irish people'.[67] Relationships with landlords were more fraught in the less prosperous west of the county, as local opinion admitted; this was a tradition of long standing, at least to judge by the diary of Mrs Smith of Baltiboys, who lacerated her landlord neighbours with a fine Scots impartiality in the 1840s.[68] Even she, however, had felt that 'the Irish gentleman is at last waking from his dream of idle pleasure, which never satisfied, which deteriorated his character, impoverished his resources, spread distress round him, and left him to drown religion in the bottle'. Neighbours of hers in west Wicklow, like Lord Downshire, Lord Milltown and Hugh Henry, may have approximated to the type; the interesting thing is that they seem to have been fewer on Parnell's side of the county. Reading between the lines of Mrs Smith's diary, which ends in the early 1870s, it is clear that she felt the whole structure of landlordism was doomed. And by the 1880s it was increasingly clear to far-sighted people that the Irish land system had run its exploitative course, and a new world was looming.

Some of Parnell's neighbours saw this development as apocalyptic; we need only look at the publications of the local Irish Loyal and Patriotic Union (a pro-landlord ramp, dominated by Lord Meath and his cronies). Yet Parnell's neighbours, like himself, came from a tradition where landlords maintained good relations with tenants, even if the system's *raison d'être* was increasingly doomed; where opposition to the Union had been a deeply felt commitment among families like the Tighes, Ponsonbys, Grattans and Parnells; where estates had been given more attention than was the norm (though this may have been at the expense of a larger holding elsewhere, which met the bills); and where modern initiatives and productivity plans featured with surprising frequency. Here, too, relationships between Catholics and Protestants were easier than in many other areas; and, possibly, relationships across social divides as well (Anna Parnell's evolution towards radical politics and feminism was probably aided by her friendship with the Comerford family, millers at Rathdrum). And, despite the conventional Unionism of run-of-the-mill gentry politics, it is worth remembering that at the end of her life Mrs Smith of Baltiboys supported Isaac Butt's Home Government Association, since she gave up all hope of Britain running Ireland effectively after the Famine; and that not only James Grattan and William Parnell, but later local gentry like Andrew O'Byrne and Viscount Monck embraced liberal politics. Ged Martin, indeed, has pointed out that Monck by the 1860s was overseeing in Canada the kind of extension of devolved government which Parnell would press for in Ireland a decade later.[69]

The dramatic convulsions of politics in the 1880s, and the revolutions of the subsequent period, jolted these complacent continuities out of existence. And where they did exist, the reformist ideas of the Wicklow gentry probably depended on old-style deference politics – one of the first casualties of the new order. But they have great relevance to the conditions of the early 1870s, when Parnell entered politics; and the influence of his background and conditioning in Wicklow stayed with him all his life. As with his father and grandfather, the idea of appropriate behaviour on the landed gentry's part was central to his thinking. No one who has read the memoirs of those who knew him, or the accounts of newspaper reporters who tracked him round Avondale, can doubt that he was most at ease in that role. Paul Bew, indeed, has put at the very centre of Parnell's motivation his belief in the necessity of regenerating the landlord class and constructing a political and social order where they could play a viable national role; at key points in his career he certainly recurred to this.[70]

Considering Parnell's Wicklow life also restores to the centre of the picture his preoccupation with developing and protecting the mineral and industrial resources of the country: to him Wicklow, with its uniquely varied geology and topography, was a potential microcosm of what an industrially developed Ireland might be under Home Rule. And we are also reminded of something rarely stressed enough about Parnell himself, perhaps because we view his career backwards, through the clericalized politics of the Split: that is, his easy friendships with Catholics and his lack of bigotry. He represented a belief in the possibilities of a future pluralist Irish identity – unrealistic as that may have been in contemporary terms. But it probably reflected the variety, tolerance and depth of relationships to be found around his part of Wicklow: a syndrome which might well apply to any rural Irish community when explored in detail. It is certainly witnessed by any number of individual memoirs, though often lost sight of in the cut-and-dried overall picture of confrontational monoliths.

In conclusion one might return to the question of place, locality and identity, and the ethos of neighbourhood. Over at Glendalough House lived John Barton, an exact contemporary of Parnell and like him a fanatical cricketer; he also had a sawmill, the largest in the area, and possibly inspired Parnell to emulate him. They were close friends as young men, but politics sundered the friendship completely; Barton was a strict Unionist. However in 1888, during a storm, a great tree came down in front of Glendalough House, and Parnell asked permission to test his sawmill on it. This was granted, and Parnell rode over to inspect the tree. Barton's seven-year-old son was lifted up to the window by his nurse, to see the great man arriving by permission at the house where he had once been a frequent and casual guest. That son, Robert, like Parnell, went on to follow a predictable course early in life: Rugby, Oxford, the army. But like his Childers relations, after 1916 he took another path: resigning his commission, joining Sinn Féin, commencing a career as a nationalist which took him into Portland Prison, the first Dáil cabinet, and the Treaty negotiating chamber. Shortly before the end of his life, well over ninety, he talked to me about Parnell: the inspiration of that glimpse from the window remained. It is in its way a Carlylean moment: a sudden conjunction of the personal and the 'world-historical'. But it also puts back in focus the world of Parnell and his neighbours, the symbiotic way in which his life reacted upon theirs, and theirs upon him.

4

Parnell and His People: The Ascendancy and Home Rule

The last essay attempted to address the question of what made Parnell the kind of politician he was – by establishing the dimensions of the world he came from, rather than seeing him retrospectively through the operatic tragedy of his last year, or even through the very high profile of the 1880s. This might be extended, arguing that he can be located in a strain, which might be called the hard-headed landlord tradition: a minority, but still an influential one. And this raises the question: was there a tradition of conservative, propertied, politically Protestant landlords who formed a potential constituency for moderate nationalism in the 1870s, precisely the time Parnell entered politics?

Their ideological background is probably to be found, indirectly, in the ideas and writings of the people around the *Dublin University Magazine* in the 1830s, whose guru was the brilliant young Isaac Butt.[1] This group was, politically speaking, dispersed by the Famine, but a certain continuity might be discerned; and Butt became the leader of the party to which Parnell attached himself in the 1870s. When we see Parnell simply as the man who displaced Butt, we forget that he was, before that, the man who followed Butt.

Throughout the development of articulate Irish nationalism in the later nineteenth century, there is a minor procession of unlikely figures: Conservatives, Protestants, often landlords, who were interested in the potentialities of devolution, antagonistic towards English party politics, disposed towards education and land reform. Allegiances could be curiously confused, 'interests' hard to define, the circle often squared. Some of the unexpected identifications of Irish

Protestants after 1868 may have been electoral red herrings.[2] But before the great divide of 1885–6, when Gladstone went for Home Rule, Conservative politics were not invariably 'anti-Irish'. The Catholic clergy always tended to prefer to work with Conservatives; and after Disestablishment the Tories, with no Irish Church to defend, were freer to become a more 'Irish' party – as several of them saw in the late 1870s.

It is too often forgotten that Parnell entered politics at the same time as the element of Conservative Home Rulers whose sincerity has been trenchantly questioned by David Thornley. And even after Irish politics had been clericalized and radicalized under Parnell's direction, the recurring guests at his shooting-lodge, Aughavannagh – Thomas Esmonde, John Redmond, W.J. Corbet – represented something closer to this strain than to the new men. It is tempting to wonder whether he felt politically as well as socially closer to this tradition.

Nor were Irish Toryism and Irish proto-nationalism incompatible. The Home Government Association was strongly Tory and Protestant in its origins,[3] being, in many ways, a reaction to Disestablishment. Moreover, one should continue to beware of thinking 'Conservative', 'Protestant' and 'Unionist' synonymous, at least before the mid-eighties; Tories held out far more hope to the Catholics on the education issue, for one thing. By the early 1870s, however, the Tory Home Rulers are generally seen as headed for the dust-heap of history. They were, according to their severe historian, 'divorced from the main sources of Irish political energy',[4] and paid the penalty. Conservative 'taints' had to be purged; identification with popular liberal elements had to be made. Certainly, the body of Conservative Home Rulers withdrew soon enough, with Sir John Barrington, a founder of the HGA, declaring that the initial 'efficiency' motivation and the desire for federalism had been swamped by repealers and agitation. Thornley castigated such attitudes as representative of the 'shallowness of conservative nationalism'.[5] He has shown how the issues of land and education, cautiously embraced after Disestablishment, came to worry other landlords and Conservatives, and put them off the HGA. But they were to accept both, if only tacitly, in ten years' time. Meanwhile, however, events had pressed the movement in a Catholic and anti-Conservative direction: while Gladstone's treatment of the hierarchy over education drove them into the arms of the Home Rulers.

A case can still be made for the fluidity of constitutional nationalist ideology in the mid-1870s, when Parnell entered politics. It was an era when the middle ground in politics was supposedly opened up.[6] Was the adoption of the Home Rule League's programme by politicians like Chichester Fortescue (a supposed model of Trollope's Phineas Finn) necessarily insincere? Were the sprigs of the gentry who were returned in 1874, like Lord Francis Conyingham, C.M. Vandeleur, Wilfrid O'Callaghan, representative of a more thoroughgoing, if still idiosyncratic, nationalism than they were accused of? Thornley analysed the landed element and found a lack of 'genuine nationalist zeal' in their statements about 'not injuring the integrity of empire'.[7] But the point surely is, that Home Rule at this time did not imply anything to injure 'the integrity of empire'. For many nationalists in the mid-eighties the same still held true. Devolution was the order of the day. Nor did it imply hard-line political discipline: the landed element objected to the whip, but this did not necessarily coincide with lukewarmness about the Home Rule principle.[8] A refusal to follow a pledged party line was part of the political culture of these Members. And this argument against an imposed party discipline was repeated by another aristocratic young recruit three years later, when Butt tried to bring him to heel: if it strikes us as ironic that this Member was Charles Stewart Parnell, the irony is largely retrospective.

To evaluate the upper-class Home Rulers by their lack of 'genuine nationalism' seems a little off-beam. They would not have disagreed with Butt that their object was 'to make honest and intelligent Englishmen realize to themselves the deficiencies of their Irish government and Irish legislation'. Parnell, as history would show, took things further. He joined them for reasons of personality and ambition, as well as political principle; he was less well adjusted to the easy traffic between England and Ireland than were his peers in Anglo-Irish society. And he used the opportunity of public debates over what Home Rule meant to emphasize that it entailed Repeal (and, in time, to imply Fenian sympathies). But he still used the archetypical Anglo-Irish weapon of arrogance in his wrangles with Butt, and we hear the authentic tone of the Big House in his cold dismissal of those who aimed at *rapprochement* with England as representing 'Irish snobbery, compelling some Irishmen to worship at the shrine of English prejudice'. And in his line against Butt he was supported by an improving landlord like Mitchell Henry and an aristocrat like Lord Francis Conyingham.

There was widespread fear that Parnell's victory over Butt would mean the end of an important preoccupation of the early HGA: the desire to represent as wide a spectrum of Irish society as possible.[9] And certainly when Butt went, so did 'all-Irelandism', as well as federalism. With Butt went much of the landed and Protestant support for the movement. It had always represented a minority element in the party. But such men remained as a suppressed strain in the Irish political culture. And in some ways Parnell, who is usually seen as having rooted out this growth, can be seen (with typical Anglo-Irish ambivalence) as continuing to represent the kind of 'efficiency Home Rule' that had brought landlords like Rowland Blennerhasset, Sir John Esmonde, Sir George Bowyer, Edward King Harman and the O'Conor Don into the party before him. He was also an 'improving landlord' (by his own lights), whose politics suited his position.

In the wider context, his attitude becomes in many ways a logical one. For the attitudes that brought some landlords to Home Rule in the latter part of the nineteenth century were widely diffused. The more one reads in the rich literature of memoirs and letters, the more this appears to be the case. Examples abound, like John Hamilton, the good landlord of Donegal: born an ultra-Tory but progressing during his long life to favouring local provincial councils, a peasant proprietary, joint-stock farming and sweeping land reform.[10] It was the same attitude, strongly laced with self-preservation, that fuelled the later devolution initiative on the part of Conservative landlords in the early 1900s and the notion of federalism so warmly propounded by Erskine Childers round the same time: Home Rule as 'an indispensable preliminary to the closer union of the various parts of the Empire'. Butt and *his* contemporaries were articulating a 'responsible government' claim which was in tune with contemporary developments elsewhere.

And in these counsels, we can hear the voices of those (few) landlords who saw the way things were going: the doom of the Irish land system, as spelled out by land values, agricultural price movements and uneconomic rents. For all the recent argument on the issue, many contemporary landlords anticipated James Donnelly's judgement that by 1879 it was 'as clear as the shine on their best-polished silver' that without reorganization their time had come.[11] Pamphlets from the 1850s on had been reiterating that the landlord system was doomed. 'Their day is nearly gone; the Encumbered Estates Act has sealed their doom,' wrote 'An English Clergyman' in 1851. Five years later a different kind of visitor, Friedrich Engels, described the Anglo-Irish in a much quoted letter to his friend Marx:

> These fellows are droll enough to make your sides burst with laughing; of mixed blood, mostly tall, strong, handsome chaps, they all wear enormous moustaches under colossal Roman noses, give themselves the false military air of retired colonels, travel round the country after all sorts of pleasures, and if one makes an inquiry, they haven't a penny, are laden with debts, and live in dread of the encumbered estates court.[12]

Such impressions describe only an element of the landowner class; on other levels, the Famine 'acted as a Darwinian selector of the fittest' landlords.[13] But some of the more astute among them began to see that land reform, and land purchase, might be their only hope. This realization could have led them into the Home Rule movement in droves. One reason why it did not was the altering and broadening of Irish political organization at this very time. Another was rapid identification of the movement with a revanchist Roman Catholic Church and with the drive for denominational education. Another was the rhetorical form that land reform took when it came, in the wake of the Land War: the language of social revolution and expropriation (though not their realization).

To view the Land War as a revolution of rising expectations, concealed by the rhetoric of destitution, is no longer novel, and indeed is already up for reassessment: Paul Bew and Cormac Ó Gráda have recently dealt the *simpliste* version a swingeing blow, and drawn out the various conflicts of interest which 'the tenantry' embodied. Nor was the 'rising expectations' theory completely new: it was articulated by some observers as early as 1880. One journalist saw the Land War as an adroit takeover by the middling tenantry, manipulating a credit squeeze; Clifford Lloyd repeated (from the opposite political angle) Anna Parnell's analysis, that the tenant farmers never acted up to the letter of the Land League because they never needed to; Samuel Hussey noted how the Church was worried by the Land War because they held mortgages on so many landlords' properties.[14]

Probing back into the intervening years, between the 1850s and the Land War, the pamphlet literature of the late 1860s includes many broadsides from enlightened landlords, calling on Gladstone to do the right thing and help the landlords out with a sweeping plan of land purchase. Implicit in many of these productions is a curious sense of angry apartness which suggests an anticipation of nationalism. One writer appeals to the Italian example of Cavour; another remarks:

> I write and will speak as one of those Irish classes which England has scarcely seen or heard of for seventy years – namely, the descendants of the Irish patriots of 1800, and the great body of the middle classes of all creeds. England for the last seventy years has only known and seen those who sold their country (and were glad to have a country to sell), and the labouring population, who went to earn a scanty livelihood; but she will now find, having bided our time, quite a different class of Irish to deal with.[15]

This author was a landlord, ex-High Sheriff, millowner; a defender of resident landlords; the subject of threats from Ribbonmen. And we find him calling for 'an Irish independent vote and voice', at least in local affairs, and – like so many of his kind, and like Parnell himself – constantly invoking the hallowed date of 1782. Another pamphleteer of the time, producing a 'Dialogue' on *Fixity of Tenure* and signing himself 'An Irish Landlord', moved easily from tenurial questions to a plea for financial Home Rule.[16]

Such men, whether or not they ever reached Parliament, were representative of the original element so marked in the HGA. They were largely replaced by the 'new' Home Rulers, typical of the much analysed party of the 1880s: professional men of lower middle-class origin. This new element, partly through brilliant oratory, did much to obscure the tradition of the old landlord Home Government men; the rhetoric of the Land War created a great divide. Even more potent propagandists entered the picture too, including Karl Marx. On a different level, popular Irish novelists anatomized a society which was certainly bizarre, but which subsisted on exaggeration. One sometimes feels that each side of the landlord–peasant equation did its best to live up to the formidable literary tradition created for it by Maria Edgeworth, Lady Morgan, Samuel Lover, Charles James Lever, John Banim, Gerald Griffin, William Carleton, et al. Mr and Mrs S.C. Hall, indefatigably touring Ireland and as indefatigably finding themselves sent up by people enthusiastically responding to their own stereotypes, recorded this painstakingly in three volumes. Samuel Hussey, in his memoirs, deliberately represented himself, according to literary convention, as the absolute type of feckless half-mounted gentry: 'I thought farming was the idlest occupation and suggested it should be my profession – an idea hailed with rapture, principally because it saved everybody the trouble of racking their brains about me.'[17] Yet the facts show him a hard-working and flinty steward of his talent, obsessed with farming on the Scotch model.

In every contemporary account from the landlords' side, a lost Golden Age of good relations between landlord and tenant, Protestant and Catholic, is attributed to some stage of the recent past. W.R. Le Fanu, as befitted a clergyman's son, identified it as pre-1831 – 'before the Tithe War'.[18] Others looked back to the days before O'Connell; others, before the new landlords set up by the Encumbered Estates Act. Arthur MacMurrough Kavanagh spoke of it as being before the 1870 Land Act: a critical betrayal of the old sanctity of landlord–tenant relations. Finally and irrevocably, it was to be 'before the Land War'.

But there had always been 'improving landlords' – a feature of every nineteenth-century Irish novel, if only as an exception to point up the general rule. Contemporary observers frequently pointed out that it was in the landlord's own interest to help his tenants. The stereotypical landlord–tenant relationship often has to be modified.[19] Even in a county like Donegal, a parish priest declared at the height of the Land War that several of the local landlords were the reverse of oppressive; and their lands covered a good deal of the county.[20] And Wicklow embarrassed its local Land Leaguers by the readiness of its landlords to swim with the tide.

Wicklow (as outlined in the last essay), with its notable tradition of model estates and improving landlords, confounds the stereotype; at mid-century, before the Famine, every visitor eulogized the 'improvements', the 'cultivation', the well-built houses at all levels of society. In the 'numberless fine residences and handsome family mansions' were to be found some figures who appear at an odd angle to the accepted landscape of nineteenth-century Ireland. The same thing was hopefully noted by the Halls. 'Of late a decided improvement has taken place among all classes throughout Ireland . . . the country is on the eve of a new era – from the one side jealousy and suspicion are rapidly removing, and from the other, prejudice is rapidly departing.'[21]

This, of course, did not happen; all these blithe prognostications were interrupted by the Famine. And there was in both judgements a certain lack of realism, compounded by the kind of deliberate delusion necessary for self-preservation (and self-respect). But, though a novel like Carleton's *Valentine McClutchy* shows things necessarily black and white, and Maria Edgeworth's Lady Dashfort remarks that 'you must live with the people of the country or be torn to pieces, and for my part I should prefer being torn to pieces', the diaries and records of the gentry culture imply a more varied and subtle pattern of relationships – at least in Wicklow. Mrs Elizabeth Smith's diary discusses questions like the elastic social position of the land agent.[22] She also recorded what historians have inferred from statistics, the fact that an eviction notice did not necessarily impose any necessity to leave. And even Carleton, at the close of the 1860s, remarked that 'the lower Irish *until a comparatively recent period* were treated with apathy and gross neglect by the only class to whom they could or ought to look up to for sympathy or probation',[23] but things were better now. After the trauma of the Famine, some of these themes re-emerged in strengthened form.

Change was on the way by the 1870s, only dimly perceived and analysed in a number of ways. Searching for reasons, observers uneasily noted that the landlord system could not be sustained *ad infinitum*. Another more specific revelation concerned the new, home-grown variety of parish priest since the growth of Maynooth's influence. This was seized upon as the most obvious reason for the change in social relations in post-Famine Ireland.[24] The terrain was changing. The bitter criticisms of a Wicklow landlord and politician, James Grattan of Tinnehinch, had been poured into his diary throughout the 1830s. Irish society was 'ignorant, prejudiced, vulgar, brutal', 'bad education and bad company', 'a gentry embodying the character of a military without the discipline'. The people in many places are 'insufficiently civilized', he had written,

> pursued by tithes, habituated to see a great military force and to think that the law depended upon them; for the most part unacquainted with an active magistracy or an efficient police, kind or indulgent landlords, or a respectable clergy, they are what they have been and will continue to be until a milder government and system changes their character and education changes their habits.[25]

This was a rationalist belief shared by his neighbours like William Parnell-Hayes (grandfather of Charles Stewart) and Lord Fitzwilliam:

the sons of those who had prominently opposed the Union, believers in 'education open to all', critics of the effects of the Union on Ireland; all owning estates abutting on to each other in Wicklow. The reasonable reaction of such people was to attempt to change the system, gearing it for more efficiency and speedier reform. William Parnell-Hayes and James Grattan had entered liberal politics (and had been opposed by their more predictable neighbours for doing so). The horrific lessons of the Famine only amplified the reaction. However, especially after the 1860s, those landlords who opted for progressivism often tended to be marked down for local criticism, because too often such attitudes went with consolidation of holdings, modernization of farming methods and other changes that disturbed the traditional integument of Irish country life. Though these developments were conveniently aided by demographic decline, threats of eviction were not necessarily part of such strategy; recropping, migration, reallocation and drainage were. These were generally summed up as 'English ideas', and resentment against them was articulated in the Land War. Staying with Wicklow, we find one of Lord Fitzwilliam's tenants telling the Land Commission in 1881: 'He has without a doubt introduced English ideas, contrary to the feelings and views of the Irish people. I do not know any landlord who has with greater determination attempted to carry out English ideas than he has.'[26] This was evidently something to be resented. And yet Parnell, as discussed above, defended the Fitzwilliam estate: it is one of the instances where the improving Wicklow landlord speaks more clearly than the nationalist politician. In Wicklow, at any rate, we can isolate a gentry subculture: once past the preoccupation of letters and diaries with religion, illness, visiting and the weather, we find a vein of analytical criticism of the stereotypical Irish landlords, generally coming from landlords who have *not* adopted the status quo. They may view their tenantry as mean, foolish, demanding and unreasonable with a condescension that makes our blood run cold. But they tend to argue that the *system* has produced this effect. Self-delusion and self-preservation, again: but it should be noted that these critics are as anti-British as any colonials. James Grattan criticized his and William Parnell-Hayes's friend Tom Moore 'for eulogizing the English character and institutions overmuch – a fault very usually found with those who have lived long abroad'.[27] The same mentality was taken up with Irish history and tradition, and irritated by their undervaluation in comparison to fashionable Scots preoccupations. Antiquities and restoration became an obsession from the 1830s on. But 'Irishness' for these critical gentry was carefully defined. Grattan and Mrs Smith felt equal repugnance for violent Orangemen and violent Catholics, and were suspicious of the Repeal movement's associations.

How, then, to defuse dangerous passions and ensure social stability? A 'resident gentry' was the safer, recurring panacea. Men like Parnell's father tried to live up to this. Such attempts were often uphill work, not only struggling against a system that was already outmoded, but also against the expansive cynicism of local opinion. And this predisposition to good works often went with an aggressive Protestantism which negated their effect, in Wicklow no less than elsewhere. At the same time, Wicklow grandees like Powerscourt, Meath, Monck and Proby clubbed together to buy a house for the celebrated Father Healy of Little Bray, who appeared regularly at their dinner-parties, and they at his.[28]

Where, then, does Charles Stewart Parnell fit into this tapestry? The researcher feels an attractive glow in reading Lady Alice Howard's diary for 1873 and finding Charlie and Fanny Parnell, the future President of the Land League and the future muse of Irish American nationalism, playing tennis at Shelton Abbey. Once again, the retrospective irony is worth savouring. But it is also an indication of the variety and ambivalence of the gentry culture. Schizophrenia, as a concept if not a word, recurs in contemporary descriptions of Parnell's position. But he certainly makes sense as a pragmatic, Tory-inclined landlord, just as much as a figure in the tradition of Lord Edward Fitzgerald, Erskine Childers, Maud Gonne or Bridget Rose Dugdale; the zeal of the convert is not appropriate. Carson is nearer the type, or Bismarck (whom he admired). Sometimes he has the air of an arrogant colonial, fighting to preserve something. This ties in too with the anti-Union tradition. As F.S.L. Lyons has shown, Parnell's identifiable preoccupation, up to 1886 at any rate, was with 1782: to the irritation of those who had thought Home Rule through to its logical conclusion.[29] And 1782 had been the apotheosis of the gentry culture.

This brings us back to the connection between nationalism and Toryism, which was far warmer than Liberals could understand. The Land War identified Home Rule with Radicalism, but this was an erroneous connection. Even while it was dominant, the nationalists were engaged in elaborate parliamentary games with the Conservative Fourth Party, a ginger-group of MPs who more often took up ultra-Tory than neo-Liberal positions. (We find the Irish Parliamentary Party, with obvious pleasure, supporting an obstructive move made by their allies on behalf of the owners of foxhound packs; Parnell speaking 'in the interests of the dogs themselves'.[30]) In November 1881 the maverick nationalist Frank Hugh O'Donnell, with characteristic ineptitude, attempted to form an Irish–Conservative alliance while Parnell was in jail; it might have stood more chance with him out of it. Wilfrid Scawen Blunt and others found to their sorrow that the Irish were more potentially conservative and imperialist than a people supposedly breaking the bonds of colonialism had any right to be; Labouchère used this very phenomenon as an argument to persuade wavering right-wing Liberals in 1885–6. In Terence McGrath's *Pictures from Ireland* (1880), nearly all his selected stereotypes – agent, attorney, gentleman farmer, parish priest, distressed landlord – are basically Conservatives in politics. In the same year J.G. Swift MacNeill, a Home Ruler with a Conservative background, emphasized how the policy of Home Rule could be taken up by either party. And a certain element of British Conservatives were quite ready to speculate privately about the possibilities inherent in the Home Rule card during the early 1880s.[31] One thinks of the phenomenon of the Conservative Roman Catholic in Irish politics; of the success the Marlborough viceroyalty had in winning over influential Catholic opinion to the Conservative Party in the late 1870s. In the early 1880s Conservatives like Gorst, Wolff and Blandford all favoured versions of Home Rule from their various angles: in 1885 the Viceroy, Lord Carnarvon, not unreasonably believed that he was widely supported by other Conservatives in his bid for a Home Rule initiative. It was fear of Conservative *rapprochement* with Home Rulers in 1886 that produced the organized Ulster bloc in Parliament.

This remained a minority trend. By the mid-1880s a Conservative Catholic priest like Father Healy seemed an anomaly; a landlord like King Harman (old HGA man, instrumental in Famine relief, proud of his 'good landlord' reputation) was pitilessly attacked in the *Freeman's Journal* as the whitest of sepulchres. Samuel Ferguson, a key figure in the Irish rediscovery of the past, had originally moved from fervent

Tory associations and an Ulster gentry background to founding the Protestant Repeal Association in 1848; but first the 'plebeianizing' nature of the Home Rule movement, and then the Phoenix Park Murders (which moved him to lengthy poems in the Browning mode) stopped him going further. He had once called for 'a restoration of Grattan's Parliament', as did Lecky, who then became the Unionists' intellectual champion, and as did Parnell.

And Parnell remained archetypically Anglo-Irish – a fact greatly appreciated by his party. The characteristic arrogance persisted, and was found in his sister Anna too. He could address the electorate in the tones of a landowner demanding his due.[32] There was also the archetypical hard-upness; Dublin opinion decided that Parnell's trip to America in 1879 was undertaken in order to pay his bill to his tailor, and his perilous financial position comes more clearly into focus with every scrap of Parnell family material that comes to light. It is amusing to find the family solicitor writing in 1882 that he well understands Captain Boycott, since he has to collect Parnell's brother's rents protected by two armed constables. The Parnells, however, considered that they needed their rents; they were as reduced in circumstances as many other Wicklow gentry. Up to 1882, it is true, Parnell pursued a line in politics marked by Fenian flirtations and a well-publicized (and probably genuine) rejection of English mores and English politics. But at the same time, he remained firmly identified with his background. It is apposite to find – though not in Barry O'Brien's biography – that, on a visit to Waterford in December 1880, the joy-bells of the *Protestant* cathedral were rung for him; and that he subsequently hunted with the Marquess of Waterford's hounds. Or that, at a dinner with Victor Hugo in Paris in February 1881, Parnell was the only Irishman in evening dress. It is possible to see him as believing that land reform would bring the landlords into the nationalist ranks. Ambivalence dogs his image throughout. Parnell may profitably be connected back to the Home Ruler landlords, Tory and Protestant, who had 'joined up' in the 1870s, and whom he had supported in classic Tory Home Rule issues like Grand Jury reform.[33] Times, and politics, changed; and he helped change them. As early as 1876 Richard Bagwell, the historian, could write a choleric article violently indicting any landlords who were associated with the Home Rulers; and, as for Protestant Home Rulers, Bagwell wrote, 'let all imagine that can, what sort of Protestants would support Mr Parnell'.[34]

But why did more landlords *not* follow Parnell's example, and accept the radicalization of the Home Rule demand as something that might work in their long-term interests? Certainly, the rhetoric of the Land War, and the general polarization of attitudes (religious as well as social) by 1886, worked against this: subsequently cultural revivalism and the revolutionizing effect of the First World War transformed everything. By 1919 that attractive novelist and incomparable observer, George A. Birmingham, could write that 'the most striking feature of Irish politics is the stability of parties': the lack of dialogue and fluidity between nationalists and unionists. Yet, Birmingham correctly surmised, before the 1880s there had not been this rigidity. There had once been the strain of nationalism that believed in independence for the increased efficiency of Ireland and of the Empire, and had been closely associated with the British Conservatives. But the new nationalism had to exclude it.[35]

Elsewhere, Birmingham mused about the failure of the Anglo-Irish to take up nationalism. He could not see them as a 'garrison', as Sinn Féin claimed; and if Griffith had thought through his Hungarian parallel, he would have seen that *they* were the Magyars. From 1800 the English had consistently sold the Anglo-Irish down the river; why then adhere to the Union?

Largely, Birmingham answered himself, because they were distrustful of 'ideas' and 'enthusiasms', in the tradition of the eighteenth century which they still represented. It is an inadequate answer, but the question remains valid. An obsessive and misplaced fear for property had more to do with it; Birmingham himself was allegedly told by a local nationalist 'Damn Home Rule! What we're out for is the land. The land matters. All the rest is tall talk.'[36] By 1919, in any case, snobbery, social superiority, deference and Unionism had fused; since long before, the connection of a Unionist ideology with the gentry had been taken for granted. But, as Birmingham pointed out with characteristic percipience, it had not always been so.

The hardening and fixing of gentry attitudes is more immediately reflected in George Moore's haunting novel of the 1880s, *A Drama in Muslin.* Written from contemporary notes taken by Moore's brother, it reflects Moore's own ambivalence as a landlord and a hater of Gladstone, who still realized the exploitative basis of the Irish rural economy. And in this book, Parnell looms in the background: all the more threatening to the insecure gentry since he was once the kind of eligible young landlord who obsesses the scheming county ladies.[37] He is a baleful figure to the whispering girls, who belong to a class already doomed; he spells the end of what they have known. The news of the Phoenix Park Murders interrupts a county picnic. 'I think they ought to hang Mr Parnell,' says one of the girls; 'I believe it was he who drove the car.' Lord Kilcarney, the encumbered landlord, explaining his dislike of Dublin society, says of the Castle: 'I used to hate it; I was as bad as Parnell, but not for the same reasons, of course. Now I am only afraid he will have his way, and they will shut the whole place up.'[38]

In fact, Parnell had once much enjoyed Castle society. But by the mid-1880s no one would believe that. And by then, too, the vast majority of Irish landlords had retreated into fear. The threat to property and a failure of imagination had led to a fear of displacement: of *no place being left to them*. It is no accident that a favourite story in Unionist memoirs dealt with the apocryphal jarvey who answered John Morley's remark that Home Rule would bring him 'great times': 'Yes, *for a week*: driving the quality to the steamers.'[39]

The 1880s, like the 1840s, occasioned a great spate of 'Irish observations' literature, in which the threatened landlord is a recurring figure. The hysterical note of the Irish Loyal and Patriotic Union tracts from the mid-1880s is an eloquent reflection: it also solidified, and made (more or less) coherent, a party line. And this attitude had spread to Wicklow. Symbolically, an ILPU pamphlet in 1886 forecast that under Home Rule, 'there would be nothing in the world, except the cowardice of the Parnellites, to prevent the loyalists of a secluded spot like *Delgany* from being massacred on any Sunday afternoon'.[40] And the loyalists of Delgany – the archetypical retreat of retired clergymen and half-pay colonels, tucked comfortably between the Wicklow hills and the sea – agreed.

Twenty years later the mother of the playwright John Synge used to rent houses in Wicklow for the summer, including Casino, the dower house on the Avondale estate. Wandering around Wicklow, Synge found 'a curious affection for the landed classes' lasting on among those who remembered them in their heyday; the older country people saw them as the losers, though the younger felt differently. This may have reflected the difference between the nationalism of the Irish Parliamentary Party and of Sinn Féin. Exploring a ruined garden in the vicinity (probably at Castle Kevin), he mused:

Everyone is used in Ireland to the tragedy that is bound up with the lives of farmers and fishing people; but in this garden one seemed to feel the tragedy of the landlord class also, and of the innumerable old families that are quickly dwindling away. These owners of the land are not much pitied at the present day, or much deserving of pity; and yet one cannot quite forget that they are the descendants of what was, at one time, in the eighteenth century, a high-spirited and highly cultivated aristocracy. The broken greenhouses and mouse-eaten libraries, that were designed and collected by men who voted with Grattan, are perhaps as mournful in the end as the four mud walls that are so often left in Wicklow as the only remnants of a farmhouse.[41]

The note is, apparently, one of elegy rather than of whining: which often obtrudes on the memoirs of those gentry who simply could not understand how rapidly they had come to be seen as dispensable. Parnell had been a product of this very background; the rupture of his career makes us forget that in many ways it was originally set on a course entirely consonant with this.

Of course, this leaves out his sense of practical politics: his use of the Fenians, his American background. All this set him far apart from gentry culture. And it leaves out the imponderable effect on him of the vivid Wicklow traditions of 1798, and the later influence of his sisters and – possibly – his mother. This is vitally important in the formation of the phenomenon. But so is that tradition of anti-Union gentry families. Parnell, seen in this tradition, helps illustrate a continuity in Irish history, from the (self-interested) opponents of the Union, through the improving county gentry, to the Tory and landlord supporters of early Home Rule.

And there the continuity ends. The pieces of the jigsaw were jolted and reshuffled, first by Catholic *revanche*, then the sudden and violent, if temporary, agricultural crisis of the late 1870s, and then by the identification of Liberalism, Radicalism, Catholicism and Home Rule from the 1880s. Perhaps most of all the social map of Irish politics was redrawn by the introduction of the secret ballot, and the franchise and redistribution reforms of 1884–5, which put paid to deference politics in the old style. Irish society did not provide a political party staffed by Parnells instead of Healys and O'Briens, though Parnell stayed on to lead it.

He broke and shaped moulds; he remains uniquely glamorous, and glamorously unique. But in some ways he was originally a representative figure too. From the time he emerges into the spotlight in the 1870s he appears, as Yeats wrote, to be schooled in solitude. But some at least of what lay behind him involved the experience of a rationally minded gentry, putting – as they had always done – their instinct for survival first, realizing the land system would no longer support them, cautiously attempting an initiative towards devolutionary independence, strongly conscious that things had to change in order to remain the same. This strain should equally be borne in mind – and not only because it had such a formative part to play in the making of Parnell.

5

Knowing Your Place: Words and Boundaries in Anglo-Irish Relations

I

Even to a historian, it is surprising how consistently history is produced as an argument, or a witness, regarding Anglo-Irish relations: at junctures when the discourse should – one might think – be concentrating upon affairs more immediately at hand. Daniel O'Connell, introducing his motion for Repeal of the Union in the House of Commons on 22 April 1834, remarked bitterly, 'I shall be as brief as I can upon this subject, for it is quite clear, that no man ever yet rose to address a more unwilling audience.'[1] But he implacably entered upon a disquisition about Irish history from the year 1172, which takes forty-six columns of Hansard before coming anywhere near the present. In just the same way thirty years later, Isaac Butt, introducing a motion for Home Rule, paid comparatively little attention to contemporary arguments for the measure, but devoted most of his speech to a learned expatiation on the late eighteenth-century Irish economy.[2]

The tradition continued. Lloyd George, opening negotiations with de Valera, was told that the problem lay rooted in the recent great dispossessions of land perpetrated in Ireland, which turned out to have been 'in the time of Cromwell'. In the Treaty debates of December 1921, the same syndrome recurs, as speeches by Mary MacSwiney, Austin Stack, Seán MacEntee and others demonstrate.[3] And the proceedings of the debates in the House of Commons on the Anglo-Irish Accord of 1985 carry it on; the strongest speeches, John Hume's supporting the agreement and the late Harold McCusker's attacking it, are equally devoted to the argument from history.[4] It is striking, though, that in the debate of 1921 practically all who relied heavily on historical exposition were arguing against the Treaty. Those arguing for it, notably the powerful speech by Desmond FitzGerald,[5] tended to stick to the question in hand. And in the preceding era, the politician who perhaps came nearest to bringing about a *modus vivendi* between Britain and Ireland, Charles Stewart Parnell, was the one who knew least about Irish history.[6]

Those who quote history do so because they believe history – or their version of it – is on their side. A great deal of ink has been spilt on the question of the uses of Irish history, and the angle of perspective employed. The word 'revisionist' has been adopted by the orthodox for those who see certain aspects of Irish history in a manner that is different to theirs, or who have reinterpreted certain key junctures. It is an irrelevant tag in its way, because there are no professional historians who are not revisionists; and many essays in this book argue that the concept is intellectually meaningless.[7] In the very nature of the business, the latest publications of research are now querying the findings of those judged to have been revisionist twenty years ago, when they 'revised' received versions of the Famine or the Land War.[8] This does not make their new-wave critics anti-revisionist. They may be reasserting some of the judgements held by an earlier generation still. But they are not reasserting the imposed political view which Irish history necessarily represented in the irredentist period, when an official national identity had to be constructed from the 1920s. For a historian, the politics do not automatically follow the historical critique.

Subliminally or not, politics often remain inextricably involved in the assessment of historical evidence; and a political 'sense' is an essential ingredient in interpreting it.[9] But this is different from (for instance) taking a deliberate decision to exclude *soi-disant* revisionist conclusions, because they are deemed politically unsound – as has happened to the study of 'Irish history' in certain circles in Britain. It may sound chauvinist to say so, but such crude manoeuvres are rarely nowadays found in Ireland, north or south. And revisionist historians are listened to far more dispassionately by the Irish in Ireland than by their sundered brethren in Britain or America, for psychological and social reasons which are probably obvious.

What I want to outline here is neither a revisionist agenda nor a chronological reinterpretation; more, a discussion of historical perspectives on certain recurrent themes. The topic of Anglo-Irish relations is subject to certain specific preoccupations which come up again and again. One, for instance, is the idea of a turning-point, after which nothing would be quite the same again. 1885–6 provided such an occasion, when Gladstone took up Home Rule and made it respectable. Another was 1914, when it became clear that the Liberal government was not going to impose Home Rule on Ulster by force. Another was 1920–21, when the state of Northern Ireland was set up, and subsequently the Treaty signed which established the 26-county Irish Free State, with the powers of an implicitly autonomous dominion. Another was 1972, when the Heath government suspended Stormont and Northern Ireland returned to direct rule from London. But the nearer one approaches the present, the more risky such assertions become. The Maze hunger strikes of 1981 seemed a turning-point, at least regarding support for the IRA in the island at large. But so did the European election of June 1984, when John Hume decisively beat Danny Morrison, the Sinn Féin candidate, and called Sinn Féin's bluff that the time had come when their popular support would supplant that of the SDLP. 1985, and the Anglo-Irish Accord signed at Hillsborough, may seem an indisputable turning-point. But can we tell yet whether it will be like that of 1920–21, a fundamental reordering of the relationship between the two countries? Or might it resemble the Irish Convention of 1917, which clarified only that goodwill, desperate urgency and constitutional imagination were not enough, faced with the implacable opposition of extremists on both sides?

Other recurrent themes involve an obsession with forms of words, and the discovery of a winning constitutional formula which will somehow reconcile the opposites. Here, as always, British self-deception and wishful thinking is every bit as marked as the Irish variety, and with less historical excuse. Thus much of the negotiation around the Treaty of 1921 concerned the form of the oath to be taken, and ignored the meaning and implications of the Boundary Commission on Northern Ireland. Similar ingenuities preoccupied those who drew up the Anglo-Irish Accord, notably regarding any implication that the Irish government accepted the constitutional basis of Northern Ireland.[10] From the 1880s much effort was spent on discovering variants of the 'Home Rule' formula – 'National Boards',

'Home Rule All Round' and so on – which would enable constitutional virtue to be preserved. Nor is this merely a pedantic preserve of constitutionalists. The new words to deal with Irish antipathies and oppositions now tend to be 'traditions', 'communities', 'identities', 'exclusions' and (cautiously) 'inclusions'. There is a danger of euphemism here; some phrases like 'community worker' have achieved a very distinct meaning in certain Ulster contexts. And when the ostensibly innocent word 'tradition' is adopted, it might be worth remembering that historians are increasingly preoccupied by the idea of 'the invention of tradition':[11] the artificiality and recentness of many world-views and identifications which are assumed to be venerable and therefore unchangeable. In this context, the British capacity for reassuring themselves about their own providentialist history is, once more, every bit as striking as the Irish variety: the academic analysis of British nationalism is only just beginning, and not before time.[12] But at the same time, the search for new words as tools with which to approach the Irish past must be encouraging, if it enables the kaleidoscope to be shaken around a little, and the shapes and colours to be disposed in potentially new patterns.

There is room, to begin with, for some new thinking on the idea of the Union – the concept so central to the history of Ireland's relations with Britain over the last two hundred years. At the moment, unions are much in the mind; one enormous experiment in the union of states is proceeding in Western Europe, while in the East another is crumbling. Looking at Scandinavia, the Netherlands, Finland and other examples, one is struck by the disparateness of the conditions and factors which create a union, and dissolve it. In the case of Ireland and Britain, several sensitive elements were there from the beginning and helped to jeopardize it at the end.

Theoretical or metaphorical descriptions of this relationship tend to be brutally simple: colonization as rape, union as shotgun marriage. At the same time, though, eccentricity and ambiguity are inseparable parts of the Union. The nature of the legislation, in principle so logical, was convoluted and contradictory in practice. The theory was to amalgamate the nations – taking 'nation' in its eighteenth-century sense, always closely defined in Ireland. 'If we understand [by nation] a compass of land, or an extent of land, our notions are too narrow and material,' wrote one eighteenth-century theorist. 'We must understand by it that system of law and polity by which we are kept together in peace and order, and preserved in security from our enemies and ourselves. And this is the civil sense of the word.'[13] In this sense several claims could be made on the 'nation' of Ireland – Presbyterian, Anglican and Catholic. But the developing nineteenth-century sense of 'nation' brought in ideas of language, race and supposed organic tradition which ended that earlier, more abstract scenario. These modern ideas were themselves transmitted and facilitated in Ireland by processes which were, paradoxically, inseparable from the Union with Britain. Ironically, in many unintended ways, the fabric of Union and the process of Anglicization were the necessary antecedents of modern Irish nationalism.

Misgovernment, poverty and alienation fit into this structure too, of course. So do the eccentricities and ambiguities of the Unionist style of government. If the Westminster theory said that Ireland was as British as Yorkshire (or Finchley), the Whitehall and Dublin Castle practice brazenly admitted the opposite; and in numerous areas of administration and policy, innovations were made and special practices preserved. When the dissonance between the theory and the practice of the British–Irish connection was brutally clarified, the political results could be explosive. This usually required the irruption of an outside crisis – like the First World War. Another instance was the potato famine of the 1840s. Here, the theory of Union should have worked to the Irish advantage: by spreading the burden and the cost on to the private rates and public revenues of the largest possible unit, the United Kingdom. But the practice was exactly the opposite: Ireland paid, or did not pay, county by county – and people died like flies. This cruel paradox affected at least one Orange Tory Unionist economist, Isaac Butt, and set him on the path which ended by his founding the Home Rule movement. Rather than being led towards the nationalist light by the Fenian trials of 1867, or merely acting as John the Baptist to Parnell's Messiah, his enlightenment came through an economic analysis of the Union's paradox.

Economic and political exploitation formed the basis of its operation, whether that had been the original intention or not; this was clearly demonstrated by the Famine. But there was always the question of contested legitimacy: an argument stated at the outset by the Opposition in the old Irish parliament, later adapted by O'Connell, and finally accepted by Gladstone. There was the argument that the mechanism of the Union held the ring against warring local factions;

though this assertion could be turned on its head by the nationalist opposition, who claimed that the Union actually fomented rather than inhibited those warring factions. And there was the fact that throughout its 120-year history, the Union, so constitutionally rigid, actually changed its nature all the time. Another way in which the terms of the Union changed on the ground, so to speak, was the simple fact that so many Irish people came to live in Britain, or lived between the two islands. And both of these factors still remain, complicating the Irish–British relationship and affecting the situation of those on the island of Ireland who still subscribe to the Union of Great Britain.

Partly because of the way the situation kept changing, adapting the Union was always a tortuous process. Home Rule itself was, in a sense, a developing aspiration rather than a set and unshakeable blueprint. By the time of its passing, in 1914, it was a refined and complex version of the 'simple demand' of Butt's and even Parnell's day – probably because it was now in the real world at last. The freedoms conferred by the Treaty of 1921 were wider than those envisaged by Home Rule, but the opposition took care to claim that it embodied nothing different: Cathal Brugha, for instance, made the point that the 'freedom to achieve freedom' argument had been pressed by John Redmond; and this, to him, was an immoral compromise.[14] It also indicated a belief in Britain's fundamental untrustworthiness, which was quite rational in 1921, given the events of the previous decade, but which the subsequent period did not vindicate. For their part, the proponents of the Treaty had to claim that they had extracted something qualitatively different from, and better than, the Home Rule which had been on the table in 1914. If they had not, the implications were too devastating to contemplate: making nonsense of the heroics of the War of Independence. Behind all these arguments lay the question of how far, through oaths of fidelity and commitments to the Commonwealth, the Union could be allowed a sort of prolonged, if progressively enfeebled, life.

II

There is a left-wing or vulgar-Marxist approach to Ireland which sees today's problem simply as 'the Irish Question' *tout court*: tacitly assuming the Republic to be under effective British rule, a colony continued by other means – principally the means of finance capitalism. (Why this shadowy structure should be so closely connected with Britain, rather than making part of the European or international scene, is never clarified; perhaps a clue comes in the way that such rhetoric quickly shifts to the old-fashioned personifications of 'England' and 'Ireland'.) As with the repudiation by many Irish emigrants of sceptical views of Irish history, the psychological reasons for this determined evasion are easy to find: it is difficult, if not morally impossible, for the left to admit that an independent Irish state has become so decisively different from the left's vision of what it should be. As part of this process of compensation, it is important for such advocates to argue that James Connolly, the single Marxist ideologue among the revolutionary leaders of 1916, has somehow been betrayed; they consequently fail to investigate the ways in which he may himself have adapted the socialist analysis of Irish history, to the point of abandoning it.

This kind of Green-Marxist view of the Union shades easily into the Old Republican view of Ireland's unfinished revolution, which puts any shortcomings in independent Ireland down to the fact that it is not really independent at all. From the 1960s, particularly with the Anglo-Irish Free Trade agreement of 1965, the Republican argument has stressed that the Act of Union has been, in a sense, brought in again by the back door, an argument adverted to even more strongly in the aftermath of 1969.[15] The failure of the Northern Ireland state threw into sharp relief the disasters and negligence apparently inseparable from British conduct of Irish affairs. It was probably inevitable that the development which has really altered the parameters of Irish sovereignty, involvement in the European Community, is more or less ignored in favour of the ancient historical enemy. The idea of a British masterplan to regain Ireland for the Union was subscribed to by both wings of the IRA in the early 1970s, though they never quite explained why this should be so earnestly desired. The notion of Stormont as a 'puppet regime', manipulated by the British, was also adhered to, against all the evidence: if anything, the opposite was the case. The only way the British government could manipulate Stormont was to abolish it.

This was not incompatible with the maintenance of unruffled complacency and deliberate ignorance on the part of British politicians, where Northern Ireland was concerned – vividly demonstrated in diaries like Crossman's as well as apologias like Callaghan's. The Ulster Unionist approach to the Union is equally unrealistic, to the point of evasion. As in the nineteenth century, it is for them a psychological necessity rather than a constitutional arrangement. And here the historian has a role: to try to uncover the instincts and expectations which have led to this attitude, and possibly to analyse the deep-level trauma that lies behind (though this makes the profession sound rather like Hollywood's idea of psychiatrists, operating as detectives in the underworld of the subconscious). Certainly one historical perspective which can be brought to bear in explaining this is the study of religion; and significantly, much interesting work is beginning to appear on religion and society in nineteenth-century Ireland, abandoning the superior attitude of the old positivist approach and examining the mechanisms which reinforce communal identifications and group solidarities.[16]

This makes it all the more important to look at what – occasionally – united Orange and Green together against the British state in the years of the Union. Money was important, with campaigns against over-taxation uniting unlikely allies. So was the demand for local government reform. And so, most of all, was the opposition of both Catholic and Protestant ideologues to any idea of non-sectarian education, from Edward George Stanley's Irish Education Act of 1831 right up to the present. (One of the most depressing recent developments has been the anathema delivered by both Churches against the initiatives taken towards integrated education in Northern Ireland.) In general, however, what kept the Orange and Green sides apart was far more potent than what united them – politically speaking. Politics are not the sum of humanity's social experience, and there are cultural levels upon which the two traditions were less divided, and more intuitively aware of a common Irishness, than is often allowed.[17] But the question of the Union was political, and focused powerful feelings. Even if there were some administrative and even economic arguments to be made for it, these stood for nothing against the often irrational potency of the separatist ideal.

III

The continuity of this ideal is one of the most thoroughly kicked footballs in historical debates. Most historians would now accept that, while there were recurrent calls for total separation from Britain, usually on the part of an elite minority, the idea of a continuous and representative nationalist wish for independence on the part of 'the Irish people' is an anachronism before the nineteenth century (at the earliest). In Ireland, classically, there are problems regarding the borders of state and nation, and overlaps between the two. The questions we are left with today concern knotty questions such as whether the borders of a 'state' can contain 'nations' – in a federal, or other, arrangement.

In Ireland the development of nationalism, or nationalisms, precipitated a situation of incongruence: 'bad fit' between the state as conceived by Britain, and the historic nation as conceived or reinvented by nationalist Ireland. The further complication of how Unionist Ireland perceived the relationship of state to nation is the part of the border question that endures most obviously today. These questions of incongruence are at the centre of Irish history through the nineteenth and twentieth centuries, but their origins go back very far indeed. In the supposed age of the nation-state, from the end of the sixteenth century, Ireland was undergoing a process of conquest and colonization – which meant being technically subsumed into the theoretical borders of the British state, at a time when that state itself was in the process of formation and definition. This interaction made for a development different from that of other colonies. There was a strong, vital and culturally sophisticated native culture, as well as a native class of notables who were not exterminated; the arrival of the Normans and the pre-Tudor kingship meant that Ireland had claims to joint sovereignty and its own parliament; and finally, Irish identity was, from the sixteenth century, indissolubly linked with the Catholic religion.

All this, after the great conflicts and dispossessions of the seventeenth century, made Ireland's position, as a kind of metropolitan colony, unique; and this is evident when modern nationalism began its formation in the early nineteenth century. The historical frame of reference, and the assertion of continuity with earlier forms of resistance to the British state, complicated the picture; and so did the tradition of colonization in one particular part of the island, the north-east. Here, not only a different religious configuration but a different economic development meant that relationship to the British state would inevitably be viewed differently.

Two questions recur. First, how far were historicist claims realistic, in the face of the historical influence of the British connection since the twelth century? And, second, how far could a delimited national territory be claimed in the face of such a large element (concentrated in Ulster but distributed throughout the island) who were irreconcilable to the claims of nationalism and Catholicism, and who saw their own survival as indissolubly linked to a connection with the British state? The nationalist idea presupposed a nation within a natural island border, and an immemorial sense of nationhood reinforced by 800 years of struggle against the oppressor. (The nationalist historian Alice Stopford Green published a book early this century called *A History of the Irish State to 1014*.) This interpretation presupposed a highly coherent notion of 'the Irish people', a closely defined border, and a tightly coherent policy on the part of the oppressors.

As to the idea of a bordered state, it is perhaps worth pointing out that many historians view the Irish medieval period as characterized by an archipelago, rather than an island, consciousness, taking in western Scotland and the northern half of the Irish island; while within that island, the reality seems to have been a patchwork of regions, up to the incursions of the British administration in the seventeenth century. Another dislocated border was represented by communities of colonists in, for instance, Munster during the sixteenth century, who retained a connection with the west of England whence they came, the sea between acting as a bridge rather than a boundary. Then there is the question as to how far boundaries existed between native and colonist. The evidence of literature, notably that of bardic poetry, implies a culture where praise-poems were produced for English settler patrons almost as easily as for Gaelic lords, and where bonds were perceived along lines of caste solidarity or client relationships rather than territorially, much less nationally. Borders existed more obviously *within* the island. (In a way this accords with Ernst Gellner's idea of the situation pre-dating national identity: pre-modern agro-literate communities, with an elite culture divided from that of the food-producing masses.)

Nor is the record of the government as consistent as traditionally supposed. Even the notion of how far the Irish came within the English law fluctuates in the late medieval period, varying between open admission and a form of cultural apartheid. By the early modern period, it seems clear that Irish people could enter the state if they Anglicized themselves and (eventually) protestantized themselves; and many did. Against this was the persistent notion, gathering force from Tudor times, that the Irish were barbarous and therefore unassimilable; this was reinforced by their stubborn identification with Roman Catholicism. The fact that the island of Ireland had never really been unified or centralized until the imposition of English law created a difficulty for nationalist theoreticians, who argued that 'the Irish people' possessed a platonic ideal of Irish unity within sacrosanct borders, but were continually and inexplicably betrayed by traitors when on the point of achieving liberation.

It seems that the idea of a racially common people inhabiting an internationally delimited territory is an anachronism in the Irish context until the eighteenth century. Supposed warriors of 'national' liberation in the late sixteenth century, like Hugh O'Neill, prove on closer examination to have been fighting for Ulster autonomy and a local clan power-base, though he was sophisticated enough to use Continental contacts and the rhetoric of religious solidarity against the infidel, when it suited him. By the late seventeenth century, the idea of a Catholic Irish nation outside the state, by its own election, and a Protestant Irish nation which actually represented the state, had developed; and this would characterize Irish history in the eighteenth century. But it raises nice questions about borders.

The other traditional nationalist definition of the parameters of national territory also raised problems, because it involved the language; and for all the efforts of the Gaelic Revival, this was a headache for theoreticians of Irish nationalism from the early nineteenth century onwards. The gospel of European nationalism as preached by Herder, von Humboldt and Mazzini had insisted on the primacy of a national language; movements like Young Ireland had lent this lip-service, but rapidly discovered that if they agitated through this medium there was no one to listen. It also raised problems in defining the national territory – the North, again. Perhaps this is why Arthur Griffith and other Sinn Féin theorists, inspired by Georg Friedrich List, laid such emphasis on creating an economic border between Ireland and Britain. Autarky and a wall of tariffs would enable a pure nationalist form of economy to be constructed. This could include Belfast; it was also very relevant to the ideas of James Connolly.

This idea of invasion as corruption raises another problematic issue for Irish nationalism, if it relies upon the concept of a homogeneous people within a set natural frontier. In a country continually invaded and settled, who qualifies as 'Irish'? The assimilationist option had been crudely offered in the colonial period, producing by reaction the subsequent identification of Irishness, Gaelic descent and Catholicism. This lay behind the historic slate of qualifications for being Irish, variously interpreted: for old Jacobites, legitimacy rested on the Stuart monarchy and the Catholic religion; for Protestant Ascendancy, their monopoly of state religion and parliamentary representation allowed them to describe themselves as 'the Irish nation'. Nationalist rhetoric and historiography of the nineteenth and twentieth centuries established an image of uncorrupted native Irishness, guarding a flame of nationality within the sacred borders. This required a good deal of historical sleight of hand, and some selective amnesia about the tangled racial origins of most inhabitants of the island. But modern Irish nationalism increasingly decided upon qualifications for Irishness which required Gaelic descent and the Catholic religion as signifiers; proof of Gaelic race was necessary to be a member of Arthur Griffith's nationalist organization Cumann na nGaedheal in the early 1900s, and what hurt the nationalist revolutionary Maud Gonne most during her scandalous legal separation proceedings from John MacBride in 1905 was the allegation that she was not racially Irish. The insistent emphasis on these criteria arose from insecurity: insecurity about the language as a legitimate qualifier (because so few Gaels would speak it), insecurity about descent (because so many of the revolutionaries were of partially British ancestry), and insecurity about the limitations of the national territory, because the record of nearly a million Ulster Protestants of all classes was so blatantly and implacably anti-nationalist.

Again in reaction, the separatist rhetoric imposed its own reality. Patrick Pearse, in his propagandist essays 'Ghosts' and 'The Separatist Idea', invented a coherent political tradition of separatism, brilliantly weaving together disparate strands in Irish history into a common fabric of Anglophobia; most conspicuously, he reinvented the eighteenth-century radical Theobald Wolfe Tone.[18] Pearse was not the only one to take him out of context, for Tone had made several memorable statements that lent themselves to adoption. 'Our freedom must be held at all hazards; if the men of property will not help us they must fall; we will free ourselves by the aid of that large and respectable class of the community – the men of no property.'[19] This has been taken by twentieth-century radicals as a call to the working class; at least one such has proudly claimed it as the title of his autobiography.[20] But what Tone meant by 'men of no property' was the non-parliamentary classes, who were, in the 1790s, literally a 'respectable class of the community'. He was, as so often, throwing a line to the radical middle classes, especially the Belfast merchants and journalists who shared his political faith. His attitudes towards the proletariat and to the Catholic peasantry were a great deal more fearful; and his idealistic crusade came to grief on the rocks of sectarianism. The other great Tone phrase, enshrined by Pearse, recorded his admirable and inspiring wish 'to unite the whole people of Ireland, to abolish the memory of all past dissensions and to substitute the common name of Irishman in place of the denominations of Protestant, Catholic and Dissenter'.[21] But what mattered here is not that he was morally right, but that he was politically obtuse.

Still Tone re-emerged, a hundred years after his death, as the inspirational icon of the 1798 centenary celebrations arranged by James Connolly, Maud Gonne and others; while Pearse apostrophized him as the holiest of the apostles who preached the gospel of Irish separatism. What is interesting for our purposes is that the idea of dissolution of the Union was related closely to the idea of purity, and of a regained soul. Oddly enough James Connolly, Pearse's contemporary, and eventual unlikely companion in arms, used the same implicit imagery in his idea of the 'Reconquest' of Ireland.[22] Economically and politically, the British connection had polluted Ireland. Connolly was a Marxist; but rather than completing capitalism's contradictions, he wanted Ireland to revert to the purity of a pre-capitalist order and to rediscover the potential of communal organization which was, in his opinion, part of the Irish national psyche. A rupture with Britain would entail the rediscovery of social and economic innocence. Thus Connolly's socialism is very closely linked to Gaelic Revivalism, enabling him to see the peasants of the west as future soldiers in an economic class war – an unlikely prospect, looked at from any other angle.

IV

It is worth instancing these two examples of separatist ideology because they indicate the power of the images and motivations built into the wish to dissolve the Union. The wish to reclaim a golden past, fantasized through 'history', is not at all a distinctively Irish quirk, especially in the late nineteenth century; it is, in many countries and cultures, a classic response to dislocation and modernization.[23] But ironically the dissolution of the Union was enabled and in a sense precipitated by nineteenth-century processes which were introduced and facilitated by the Union itself; and which transcended the simple fact of Britain's apparent inability to govern Ireland with sensitivity or even good sense. For instance, the loss of the Irish language through commercialization and modernization was seen by Irish ideologues as a trauma that must be reversed: the language had to be revived in order to gain independence. But this much decried process itself had helped to create nationalism. 'Anglicization', in the loosest sense, brought about increased literacy; revolutionized communications; a spreading culture of highly politicized provincial newspapers; and a revolutionary though peaceful distribution of land through the Land Acts from the 1880s on. The creation of what Joseph Lee has called a 'possessor class'[24] made for an implacably conservative and *petit bourgeois* base to Irish society.

The process was aided by emigration. What would have happened if the most energetic and alienated elements of society, with the least to lose, had stayed at home instead of leaving? (It could be said that we can see what would have happened – since they stayed at home during the First World War, helping to bring about a period of sustained revolution in Ireland.) Emigration fostered that search for a golden past which I have mentioned: a nation on the move has to affirm a spiritual home.[25] And emigration also underpinned the *embourgeoisement* of Irish rural society. The possession of land, achieved by successive Land Acts up to 1909, had a political implication too, well put by Henry Patterson: 'It was precisely because the Irish programme on the land question had been largely met by the British Parliament that an Irish constitutional party at Westminster became irrelevant.'[26] It was pointed out at the time that 'until land purchase was peacefully completed the man who would suggest the withdrawal of the Irish Party from London would make himself the laughing stock of Irish politics'.[27] In a sense, where the Union actually worked, it also helped to prepare the way for its dissolution.

Moreover, the form which dissolution of the Union took was characteristically idiosyncratic. After 1921 an implicit acceptance of special links and peculiar conditions remained. Special commercial relationships were sustained; Britain's defence and strategic interests in the area were tacitly allowed. Irish residents in Britain had a special constitutional status (an arrangement only recently reciprocated in the Republic). But for good historical reasons, the Irish line on constitutional abstractions continued tough, and often determinedly, idealist. Uncomfortable facts – the majority vote for the Treaty, the actuality of Partition – were not admitted. When de Valera brought the process of dissolving the Union a few stages further in the 1930s, he was thus enabled to legislate platonically for the six north-eastern counties, 'pending the reintegration of the national territory'. Yet in practical matters the process of dissolution was gentle and rather ambiguous. Reformist and mildly autarkical economic policies gave way to a series of important commercial agreements in the late 1930s. The gradualist constitutional evolution of the Anglo-Irish relationship into the new-look Commonwealth seemed a viable and not unpopular option. The Irish approach to phased disengagement was, in retrospect, both sophisticated and effective. Certainly de Valera's policy of rhetorical separatism but practical caution was extremely popular – far more so than the perfectionist exhortations of the Republican left like Saor Éire, still trying to 'achieve the Reconquest'.[28]

It should be remembered, though, that the gradualist policies which led eventually to an Irish republic externally associated with Britain would not have been possible had not Partition preceded the creation of the 26-county state. It removed the huge stumbling-block of the Protestant presence, leaving an exceptionally homogeneous Catholic and rural state where social and cultural differences to the perceived English norm could be, in a sense, reinforced. What was left to the South was the abstract idea of an ideal 32-county republic, cherished by the opponents of the Treaty, who followed de Valera: the dream of a national community uncorrupted by any lingering associations with the British state. The tightly coherent nature of the 26-county unit, in terms of religion, economics and social structure, facilitated this fantasy. Official policy tried to demonstrate that a new border had been erected between Ireland and Britain by its policies of education, compulsory Gaelicization, social policy (or denial of it) and censorship. The symbolism of the national being, the inculcation of shared myths and memories, the construction of what Antony Smith calls a 'civil religion', was central to this. The fact that over ninety per cent of the new state subscribed to the same actual religion helped to create a remarkable stability: a stability dependent on the myth of a common ethnic descent or memory, more convincing in the Irish case than in many other post-colonial countries (especially in Africa, where a territorial demarcation often contained several ethnic identities and no shared political memory). Equally important in creating the ideal boundaries of a stable state was the fact that the Catholic Church could claim (or had contrived to create) a history of popular identification; it was not tainted with pre-revolutionary elitism or collaborationism. Finally, the long history of highly disciplined popular organizations was celebrated as representing a suppressed 'national' history.

However, a paradox must be noted. All these traditions were made much of, 'the national being' continually celebrated, the national language compulsorily introduced into schools, Civil Service, government and so on, to emphasize that a new order was being created and a new national border established. But it was also done in large part to conceal the extent to which the new order replicated the forms of the old colonial state. Words like 'Dáil' and 'Cathaoirleach' helped obscure the fact that these terms meant 'parliament' and 'speaker' in an obstinately two-party system. The necessity to speak Irish in order to get a job in the Civil Service concealed the fact that it represented an independent mandarin officialdom in the Whitehall tradition. And the strong line taken by the Free State government on matters of censorship, social policy and Gaelic purity distracted attention from their past, as the party that had made terms with the British to stay within the borders of the Commonwealth on the basis of something very like dominion Home Rule.

When de Valera entered power and began dismantling Ireland's connection to the Commonwealth, he saw it as a redefinition of boundaries on all sorts of spiritual as well as geopolitical levels. But even when the political opposition jumped the gun by declaring Ireland a republic in 1948, a special relationship was sustained with the Commonwealth – whose boundaries of citizenship extended to special rights for the Irish, whether they wanted them or not. Yet again, the question was raised of incongruence between theoretical national identity and the effective borders of the state.

There was also the fact that British perceptions reliably failed to realize that the world actually contained and accommodated other norms than their own. John Stuart Mill's remark that Ireland was in the mainstream of general European developments, and England in an eccentric tributary, has never been registered by his countrymen. The essential cultural difference bedevilled, and continues to bedevil, Anglo-Irish relationships. Shaw's play *John Bull's Other Island* is still one of the best commentaries on it; the most recent reactions to, for instance, certain Irish legal decisions offer a continuing illustration. One of the most irreducible differences, and something which English opinion continues to find incomprehensible, is the close relationship of religion to politics. Even the socialist–republican Saor Éire, after all, began their 1931 congress with a religious invocation; and the close involvement of priests with extremist nationalism runs from the Fenian period right through to arms-buying activities in 1969[29] and the 1981 hunger strikes.[30] It is not just an eccentric historic hangover or, as some British opinion has it, an obscure Irish delusion; it should not be forgotten that the unrest of 1969 and the slow collapse of the Northern Ireland state began, not with a campaign for nationalist liberation, but with a movement claiming civil rights for Catholics.

There were also continuing differences of social structure and practice which made Ireland deeply foreign to the British mind. (If the judge and jury who sentenced the Birmingham Six had read, for instance, Conrad Arensberg's anthropological work on rural Irish society, they might have taken a different view of the defendants' fatal insistence on returning to Belfast for a funeral: in the culture whence they came, it was a simple social obligation.) From the Irish side, the proximity of Britain allowed the luxury of absolute moral standards in questions of sexual morality – since these too could be exported to the abortion clinics and divorce courts of the larger island. Meanwhile, statements about Irish social ideals in the twentieth century continued to be ostentatiously bizarre to the English mind; the *Manchester Guardian* was told by de Valera in 1928 that he hoped 'to free Ireland from the domination of the grosser appetites and induce a mood of spiritual exaltation for a return to Spartan standards'.[31] The point here is not whether this was feasible or even, really, representative; Joseph Lee has remarked that if Irish values were to be deemed spiritual, then spiritualism must be redefined as covetousness tempered by sloth.[32] But the point is that it was considered an appropriate way to frame a political agenda; and that such statements helped to reinforce the British view of the Irish as a race apart. That the British themselves were perceived by most of Europe as a race apart rarely entered the question.

This is reminiscent of Connolly's preoccupation with differentiating Ireland socially and economically from Britain, as well as politically. If you were a Marxist or a Gaelic Revivalist, some sort of blueprint for this was at hand. If you were neither, however, you silently assented to some kind of continuing relationship with Britain; accepted that the Irish agricultural economy would be conditioned by the proximity of British markets; and saw many of your family established in London and Manchester, even if they always came, as they put it, 'home' for Christmas. The firm imposition of a distinctively Irish cultural ethos, in education and religion, met the psychological and political needs of nationhood; the social and religious coherence of the country made for an enviable stability, reinforced, as before independence, by emigration. Neutrality in the Second World War affirmed the reality of Irish autonomy. Yet economic links continued to be extremely close; the legislation of 1965, establishing a free trade area, just slipped through, though some far-left Republican prophets fulminated against it. The special Anglo-Irish relationship, as subtle and persistent in its way as the impulse to national independence, somehow sustained itself. It was inevitable that this should be so; but it also sustained traditional British attitudes to Ireland, usually obtuse as well as condescending.

And from the Irish side, some double-think was strategically necessary. From the days of the Irish Free State on, the need to compensate for inevitable Anglicization was demonstrated by the formal effort to emphasize Irishness. (The official *Guide to the Irish Free State*, edited by Bulmer Hobson, is a particularly vivid example.[33]) Again, this is by no means an exclusively Irish phenomenon; all states which achieve independence disappoint their nationalists, and the efforts of, for instance, the Finnish government in national image-building during the 1930s carry a very familiar note for an Irish reader.[34] But this is where Northern Ireland played a vital part in the difficult tissue of Anglo-Irish misunderstandings: its very existence could provide a convenient reason why Utopia had not been attained. 'Pending the reintegration of the national territory', life must necessarily be imperfect. The aspiration of unity provided a reason for present failings, in addition to an idealist policy for the future. But in the face of the rank impossibility of a political 'solution', the purist Republican ethos essentially had to rely on violence.

V

Violence, the strategy for cutting the Gordian knot, is a response to conditions of psychological rather than actual desperation; and, once more, it raises the vexed question of the argument from history. Nor should the legitimization of violence be seen as the sole responsibility of the Irish. British policy often implicitly endorsed it, officially as well as unofficially. And it could be articulated in other ways than the manipulation of 'law and order'. Gladstone characteristically outraged many contemporaries when he stated that it was the Fenian outrages such as the bomb attack on Clerkenwell Jail that made him turn his mind to seeking remedies for Ireland. This did not, in fact, reflect accurately the chronology of his interest in Ireland.[35] But the admission was rapidly seized upon as the necessary justification for the use of violence, and not only by Irish nationalists. The suffragettes in 1912 used the parallel and quoted Gladstone approvingly: 'Sir, is it not the case that in all great movements in human affairs even the just cause is marked and spotted with much that is to be regretted?' Elsewhere he had remarked that without violence, 'the liberties of this country would never have been attained'. This was much more to the suffragettes' taste than being told sharply by Lloyd George that 'the Irish never had a chance of succeeding until Mr Parnell engaged in constitutional agitation'.[36] Parnell was a frequent if careful user of the argument that the British would listen only to violence, or the threat of it. So, less expectedly, was Redmond.[37] And so have been the apologists for colonial resistance movements all over the world, notably Kenya.[38]

The case for proving that violence is counter-productive is difficult to make, largely because it relies on counterfactual speculation. Without 1916, and with the Irish Parliamentary Party involved in drafting the Home Rule legislation of 1920, how far would its terms have approximated to the 1921 Treaty achieved by violence? And how far would Labour governments in the 1920s, and Chamberlain in the 1930s, have accepted the evolution of Ireland's relationship to Britain in any case? And was Partition reinforced by the events of

1916–21, whereas it might have been muted by a federal Home-Rule-within-the-Empire arrangement like that drafted in 1920? No one can answer these questions; violence in this period changed the terms and created the structure for political action. In fact, the way it came about was partly a deliberate short-circuiting of the drift towards non-violent action. Dan Breen, who led the attack on the Royal Irish Constabulary at Soloheadbeg that traditionally 'began' the War of Independence, recounted frankly in the first edition of his autobiography why he took this action. It was, he said, because his companions were taking to politics – a development which he dismisses with contempt. This telling observation went missing in later editions of his book, but it remains enlightening.[39]

As Dan Breen realized, the state would have to meet violence with violence. By some reckonings, the government had already shown in its reaction to Edward Carson's rebellion that it would listen to force, and indeed back down in front of it. The ineptness with which it gave in to violent threats on one side, and responded to them by employing its own underhand violence on the other, characterized policy until the withdrawal of the army garrison in 1922. Both elements have, it might be said, often been equally noticeable in policy towards Northern Ireland since 1969.

This is one of the factors which conditions the Republican mind against political negotiation or compromise: 'the Republic' stands for the negation of politics. It is striking how clearly this is affirmed by the guardians of the pure Republican flame in the Treaty debates.[40] Similarly, the debate of the General Army Convention of the IRA in November 1925 provided many tirades against 'mere politics'. And the vote which went against the abstention policy at another IRA convention in December 1969 aroused a similar reaction. The theological adherence to the Second Dáil, refusing to admit the legitimacy of anything that had happened since, enforced a repudiation of all politics as corrupt and corrupting. The corollary of this was a commitment to violent tactics until they magically stopped being necessary with the 'reintegration of the national territory'.

It should be noted, once again, that the record of British government policy in 1916–21 and its covert approach to Northern Ireland in the ensuing period add some historical weight to the argument. But the idea that violence is the realistic response to the situation is fundamentally unhistorical, and indeed unrealistic. The easy solutions posited, by their very nature, deny the real conflicts and ignore the basic conundrum. As in the nineteenth century, those who embrace solutions which rely on violence merely shift the ground and identify an easier enemy than the one who really constitutes the problem. This remains the case, whether the slogan is 'Clear out the troublemakers' or 'Drive the oppressor into the sea': it applies just as much to draconian British governments as to visionary Republican nationalists. It is equally true of Gladstone invoking martial law against the supposed 'village ruffians' who provoked land agitation in the 1880s; and of the 1916 rebels preferring to attack a British government that had put Home Rule on the statute book, rather than take on the Ulster Volunteer Force who were actually blocking its way. As the sterility of the extremist option becomes clearer, and intellectual opinion in the Republic and the North is more and more prepared to see the ambiguities, difficulties and obstacles that bedevil the traditional versions of our histories, it is interesting to notice unfashionable subjects coming back into the historical spotlight – among them Redmond, and the political era between the fall of Parnell in 1891 and the Easter rising in 1916. This is beginning to be seen, not as a necessarily demoralized and sterile landscape, redeemed by the Easter sacrifice, but as a period when new options were tried, new alliances cautiously tested out, and traditional identities debated and examined.[41]

This brings us back to historical perspectives on Anglo-Irish relations, and indeed to questions of historical revision. In some ways, historical reinterpretations in Ireland over the last generation gave a number of hostages to fortune. Perhaps too much faith was put in the brave-new-world expectations of the 1960s, and later in the *bien-pensant* bias of many of the practitioners of the art, who tended to elide some of the more awkward confrontations of Irish history. It is interesting that the most rebarbative questioning of historical pieties tends to come from the traditionally Catholic and nationalist ethos of University College Dublin, University College Cork and even from Maynooth, whereas the most graceful smoothing over of jagged outlines originally came from traditionally Protestant and Unionist Trinity and Queens: perhaps another sign that old identities have been interrogated. It should also be pointed out that initial examination of the geographic, social and religious basis of Irish nationalism tended to come at first from scholars working outside Ireland altogether.[42]

We have arrived, however, at a point when historical perspectives on Anglo-Irish relations, and on Irish history in general, have thrown some interesting light from new angles and asserted some provocative parallels. Oliver MacDonagh has written a brilliant book on Britain and Ireland, in which he compares the 1970s to the 1790s – that era of recurrent crises, missed chances and reactionary obtuseness on both sides.[43] Liam de Paor has recently noted parallels in the politics of Ireland during the 1980s with the Redmond era, and has compared the current Irish constitutional relationship to Britain with the situation of flux following 1916.[44] Elsewhere I have likened the atmosphere of cultural activity and the potential for a cross-cultural debate currently opening up in Ireland to the ferments of early twentieth-century Ireland, when many of the most interesting developments were taking place outside the formal arena of politics.

In Ireland the study of history might ideally be used for such 'non-political' explorations: but it remains resolutely a political issue. I was struck recently by reading a reflection on national history:

> We need history that promises signposts to identity, moorings in the rapids of progress . . . History holds for [us] the chance to find ourselves again . . . Today the issue is the salvation of our intellectual personality . . . the calculability of our policy, the inner good sense of our political culture, and last of all the continuity of our fatally threatened constitution of freedom . . . The cultural politics of the sixties sowed the storm, and today we are reaping the whirlwind. If we fail to agree on an elemental cultural curriculum, which can prepare the way for continuity and consensus in our country, and which can prepare once again the measure and mode of patriotism, then [this country] may well find that the best part of its history is behind it.[45]

This plea for a politically acceptable history, nurtured for state-building purposes, might be the manifesto of an Irish anti-revisionist; or possibly a conservative critique of the National Curriculum in British schools. As it happens, it is neither; it comes from a plea by a prominent German historian, Michael Sturmer, who believes that too much examination of the German past is leading to national demoralization, and who reacts against those German revisionists who have brought the forbidden subject of Nazism into the foreground of general treatments of German history in the nineteenth and twentieth centuries. And the question of historical interpretation in Germany is so highly politicized that it has affected federal elections since the early 1980s. It is worth remembering that controversy over the legitimate use of the national past, and over who has the right to reinterpret it, is not a peculiarly Irish phenomenon. And to fully possess your history, you may have to give some of it up.

It is also worth noting that, despite fashionable nostrums to the contrary, there is no such thing as an 'end' to history; even if one form of struggle ends, or changes its mode, a static millennium does not automatically arrive. This is as unrealistic as the idea of a past Golden Age, mentioned earlier as bedevilling received notions of Irish and Anglo-Irish history: the belief that social, political and economic relationships were rightly and happily ordered before someone came along from outside and spoiled everything. We have seen how this lies behind the apparently socialist analysis of Connolly (who was much influenced by Alice Stopford Green's resolutely unhistorical tract of 1908, *The Making of Ireland and Its Undoing*); but it is a fantasy indulged in by both sides. The Golden Age has been variously perceived as before the Normans, before the plantations, before O'Connell, before the Land War, before 1916, before the civil rights marches of 1968, or before the British troops arrived in 1969. And those who try to recapture the supposed Golden Age spirit are condemned to recreate an artificially exclusive environment: whether it is the Victorian landlord's idea of a model estate without any 'land agitators' living on it, the Gaelic Revivalists' fantasy of life in the west of Ireland, the idealized version sometimes presented of social relations in Northern Ireland under the old Stormont regime, or the romantic accounts already appearing of the 1989 West Belfast Festival. Again, the judgement holds good against British and Irish, Unionist and nationalist, alike. And it is the denial of plurality, variousness and ambiguity that seems unrealistic; by contrast, acceptance of the complex strata of identities laid down by the irreversible accumulations of history seems a pragmatic response, not just a well-meaning liberal cliché.

It is at least mildly encouraging that in Derry in 1989, 12 August and the traditionally Protestant celebration of the Apprentice Boys anniversary was presented as a shared event in the history of the city, with the support of the nationalist-controlled city council; and that in 1990 the centenary of the Battle of the Boyne was organized at Drogheda with the local Fianna Fáil councillors taking a leading part. But that same year a commemoration of the Siege of Derry, organized by the SDLP, was boycotted by Unionist councillors; and the popular view of the history of Anglo-Irish relations, Northern Ireland and much else will not accommodate ambiguities and paradox. Once more we confront the fact that professional history-writing will remain too tentative and too specialized to please those who demand history as a tonic for the national soul, like the German professor quoted above. Historical perspectives can obscure as well as illuminate. If this is the case, maybe political brokers should – unlike Daniel O'Connell, Isaac Butt, Mary MacSwiney et al. – forget 'historical perspectives' and concentrate on the present and the future. More profoundly, though, deliberate refocusing might lead us out of imprisoning historical perspectives. Another way of approaching that residual 'border problem' formally created in 1920, but standing for much more, might be to radicalize thinking about the nature of borders and communities: allegiance might be seen as an option, not an inheritance. The idea of immutable and impermeable borders for an Irish national state is fraught with difficulties and contradictions, historical and political. The acceptance of ambiguity might expand the frontiers of the historical impasse that remains.

6

The Irishness of Elizabeth Bowen

> Few people questioning me about my novels, or my short stories, show curiosity as to the places in them. Thesis-writers, interviewers or people I encounter at parties all, but all, stick to the same track, which by-passes locality. On the subject of my symbology, if any, or psychology (whether my own or my characters'), I have occasionally been run ragged; but as to the *where* of my stories, its importance in them and for me, and the reasons for that, a negative apathy persists.
>
> Why? Am I not manifestly a writer for whom places loom large?
>
> . . .
>
> Permanence, where it occurs, and it does occur, stands out the more strongly in an otherwise ephemeral world. Permanence is an attribute of recalled places.
>
> – 'Places' from *Pictures and Conversations* (1975)

I

'Placing' Elizabeth Bowen remains difficult: reasonably enough, since she was never quite able to place herself. Here, the *œuvre* tangles inseparably with the biography. She lived ambivalently between two worlds. One was that of the Anglo-Irish gentry in the post-independence dispensation, long bereft of *raison d'être*, bound to a history which was a matter of mingled pride and bad conscience. The other was literary London and Oxford, with forays into America, a new world dashingly explored in her last novel, *Eva Trout* (1969). This universe revolved around effusive literary friendships in the milieu of Cyril Connolly, Rosamond Lehmann, Virginia Woolf: the drawing-room battles of early novels like *Friends and Relations* (1931) and *To the North* (1932) derive from this, with their upper-class dragons and gorgons, conversing in elliptical dialogue out of Henry James via Ivy Compton-Burnett. And she is probably best known for the novel she liked least, *The Death of the Heart* (1938), which describes with terrible thoroughness the disillusionment of an awkward sixteen-year-old at the hands of her smart London relations and their friends.

But even in this world there is another voice, a vein of uncompromising brutality, and an alien humour. Her friends remember her as presenting a 'tough' face to the world, disliking literary coteries and 'muffishness', jeering at 'the Fortnum & Mason sorrows of the rich';[1] Virginia Woolf saw the young Bowen as 'a very honourable horse faced, upper class hard constricted mind'.[2] This is a myopically narrow characterization. Like Yeats, Bowen longed for order, abstraction, classical symmetry, yet wrote most brilliantly at times of dislocation and conveyed in her best writing a sense of chaos: her style is, in itself, a subversion. In one of her vivid, slangy phrases she spoke of a taste for 'life with the lid on'. But she put it more precisely in a radio interview where she explained her artistic intention as 'aiming to give the effect of fortuity, of a smashed-up pattern with its fragments impacting on one another, drifting and cracking . . . [because of] the horror beneath the surface, the maintenance of the surface of a subject fascinates me. In fact, the more the surface seems to heave or threaten to crack, the more its actual pattern fascinates *me*.'[3]

Her real themes are dispossession, double-crossing, cruelty, betrayal. It annoyed Bowen that the heroine of *The Death of the Heart* was interpreted as a victim; she saw Portia as a sensationalist, a deliberate wrecker, and she approved of this. Portia's life, another character remarks, is actually dominated by the lunatic giant who is knocking away inside all of us, but whom most of us try to ignore. That mad giant knocks away beneath the glittering surface of the Bowen style; it indicates an underworld of uncertainty and fragmentation. And there is a dimension here missed even by those critics who proceed beyond simply seeing her as a link between Virginia Woolf and Iris

Murdoch: because it derives from the Irish world which underpinned her life and her sense of history, and the Irish sensibility which runs as an undercurrent through nearly all her best fiction.

II

In biographical commentary about Bowen, the Irish element is prominent but usually kept firmly in its place.[4] Conventionally, her place is Bowen's Court, the tall Georgian family house in County Cork: 'merely a great stone box', Virginia Woolf reported to her sister, 'but full of Italian mantelpieces and decayed eighteenth-century furniture and carpets all in holes'.[5] The time is high summer (or an impossibly sunny and extended September), when Bowen entertained literary friends there from the 1930s until the early 1950s – purely on the exiguous income she earned from writing and her husband's small salary, though few of her guests realized this at the time. Her Irish associations are usually thought of in those lofty terms, though Bowen's friends emphasize the variety of engaged and enthusiastic relationships she sustained with the neighbourhood: Charles Ritchie remembered endless visiting around Kildorrery, interminable chatting, 'a very Irish sort of relationship'.[6] The house and its history obsessed her: an obsession given full rein in *Bowen's Court* (1942), a composite portrait of Anglo-Irish culture (or lack of it), social history and family autobiography. Hermione Lee has placed Bowen in a Burkean tradition of history-mindedness, and she was always conscious of the presence of a defeated history in Ireland. Visiting England as a child, she was struck by the accessible, 'dramatizable', triumphalist mode of 'English history' – Good Queen Bess, Martello towers, pageants.[7] This contrasted with where she came from, with its dispossessions, evasions, unspoken antagonisms. In other contexts, too, there is an implicitly Irish agenda behind her observations on the subject:

> We must not shy at the fact that we cull the past from fiction rather than history, and that art, out of the very necessity to compose a picture, cannot but eliminate, edit – and so, falsify. Raw history, in its implications, is unnerving; and, even so, it only chronicles the survivors. A defeat accompanied every victory; faiths failed; millions went under leaving behind no trace. If the greater part of the past had not been, mercifully, forgotten, the effect upon our modern sensibility would be unbearable; it would not be

only injustice and bloodshed that we should have to remember but the dismay, the apathy, the brutalizing humiliations of people for whom there was no break.[8]

After *Bowen's Court* the other text usually invoked to illustrate her Irishness is *The Last September* (1929). It is sometimes treated as historical evidence, though it was really written as a historical novel – recording events of a (just) previous era, when she had, in fact, been living abroad. The novel records Irish country-house life in 1920, as guerrilla war rumbles around like thunder. Two passages have become almost canonical, and are often used to illustrate the supposed mentality of that milieu. The first describes the feelings of the young girl, Lois, at seeing a mysterious trench-coated figure flit past Danielstown, her uncle's house:

It must be because of Ireland he was in such a hurry; down from the mountains, making a short cut through their demesne. Here was something else that she could not share. She could not conceive of her country emotionally: it was a way of living, an abstract of several landscapes, or an oblique frayed island, moored at the north but with an air of being detached and washed out west from the British coast.

Quite still, she let him go past in contemptuous unawareness. His intentions burnt on the dark an almost invisible trail; he might well have been a murderer he seemed so inspired. The crowd of trees, straining up from passive disputed earth, each sucking up and exhaling the country's essence – swallowed him finally.[9]

The second familiar quotation comes from the concluding passage of the book, which describes the ultimate destiny of the house at the hands of the IRA, a fate she dreaded for Bowen's Court.

For in February, before those leaves had visibly budded, the death – execution rather – of the three houses, Danielstown, Castle Trent, Mount Isabel, occurred in the same night. A fearful scarlet ate up the hard spring darkness; indeed, it seemed that an extra day, unreckoned, had come to abortive birth that these things might happen. It seemed, looking from east to west at the sky tall with scarlet, that the country itself was burning; while to the north the neck of mountains before Mount Isabel was frightfully outlined. The roads in unnatural dusk ran dark with movement, secretive or terrified; not a tree, brushed pale by wind from the flames, not a cabin pressed in despair to the bosom of night, not a gate too starkly visible but had its place in the design of order and panic. At Danielstown, halfway up the avenue under the beeches, the thin iron gate twanged (missed its latch, remained swinging aghast) as the last unlit car slid out with the executioners bland from accomplished duty. The sound of the last car widened, gave itself to the open and empty country and was demolished. Then the first wave of a silence that was to be ultimate flowed back, confident, to the steps. Above the steps, the door stood open hospitably upon a furnace.[10]

These two extracts are often taken to encapsulate Bowen's Irishness – or Anglo-Irishness, since they are quintessential views from inside the demesne wall.[11] Even *The Last September*, however, contains another dimension. The scene just before the final conflagration is worth considering: a visit to Danielstown by a county neighbour, who has come over specifically to complain about how bored she has recently been on a visit to the North (which Lois, it will be remembered, sees as the part of Ireland still 'moored' to the real world). The two women talk in idiom and cadences deliberately 'Irish' ('Come in now', 'Ah, don't mind the time'), and the covert theme of their conversation is one that surfaces throughout the book: the insufficiency of the English, and their inability to understand the complexity of Irish relationships. The owner of Danielstown, informed earlier in the story that the army have arrested a local Republican, bewilders the soldiers by his reaction of regret; the English concepts of war and civilization appear alien, unsubtle, very possibly uncivilized. And the Anglo-Irish contempt for them comes ironically close to national pride in their own revolutionaries: at least they are *intelligent*. Lady Naylor recalls with satisfaction her put-down of English friends, whose local tenantry she had found stupid and phlegmatic. To their landlords' retort that 'at least they were loyal . . . I said they hadn't got any alternative, and if they had an alternative I didn't suppose they'd see it.'[12]

As a child, Bowen recalled believing that 'our politeness to England must be a form of pity'. This is the attitude of the Irish in *The Last September* towards the English whom the local garrison has deposited in their midst. The army wives talk too much about their insides; to the Irish, the opinions of the soldiers are at once appallingly literal and totally bizarre. This makes for comedy, but also for something more. Bowen's adherence to Irish modes of manners was a recognition of the historical difficulties and social antipathies evaded and negotiated by codes of politeness and other collusive stratagems. In this, her fictional universe has obvious affinities not only with that of Somerville and Ross, but also with Sheridan Le Fanu and Maria Edgeworth; and seen from this angle, the elliptical dialogue of her characters derives from Edgeworth rather than Henry Green or Ivy Compton-Burnett. It was Edgeworth, after all, who declared that 'it is from men's careless conversations, their half-finished sentences, that we may hope with the greatest probability of success to discover their real characters'.[13]

Irish perspectives are inserted obliquely into far more of her fiction than simply *The Last September*, or even the often-forgotten *A World of Love* (1955). *The House in Paris*, for instance, published in 1935, deals with two children being temporarily taken care of for a day in Paris; its time-structure slowly reveals a background of betrayal, tragedy, illegitimacy, cruelty, desire, often expressed obliquely through the children's conversation. 'Nobody tells the truth when there's something they must have,' Leopold tells Henrietta. However, the novel has a biographical subtext (Bowen's love affair with the critic Humphry House), and a key scene involves a long-ago visit to Cork by Leopold's mother, secretly pregnant and involved in a mesh of deception. Her visit to relations, burned out of their Big House, is all about not telling the truth – for a variety of reasons. It anticipates a much more celebrated novel, *The Heat of the Day* (1949), where a famous evocation of wartime England is brought into focus by a journey to Ireland, defining the questions of patriotism and allegiance around which the story revolves.

Bowen characters, as she said herself, are always in transit;[14] she felt most at home in mid-Irish Sea. The transit from Ireland to England and back again dominates her work as it did her life. Here, too, there was a skewed perception:

> . . . my most endemic pride in my own country was, for some years, founded on a mistake: my failing to have a nice ear for vowel sounds, and the Anglo-Irish slurried, hurried way of speaking, made me take the words 'Ireland' and 'island' to be synonymous. Thus, all other countries quite surrounded by water took (it appeared) their generic name from ours. It seemed fine to live in a country that was a prototype. England, for instance, was 'an ireland' (or, a sub-Ireland) – an imitation. Then I learned that England was not even 'an ireland', having failed to detach herself from the

flanks of Scotland and Wales. Vaguely, as a Unionist child, I conceived that our politeness to England must be a form of pity.[15]

Her own Irishness, therefore, made her 'a naturally separated person'; her early novels bristle with barbs aimed at English obliviousness and parochialism, much as the cosmopolitan Leopold of *The House in Paris* is astounded by the *Strand* magazine's 'rigid symbolism and Martian ideology'. She herself brought a loftily extraterrestrial view to bear on suburban south-east England, in which she affected to discern an Arabian Nights exoticism. She recalled this, with irony and love, in describing her migrations with her widowed mother from County Cork to the Kent coast.

As it was, where we *were* stood out in absolute contrast to where we came from. Gone was the changing blue of mountains: instead, bleached blond in summer, the bald downs showed exciting great gashes of white chalk. Everything, including the geological formation, struck me as having been recently put together. Trees were smaller in size, having not yet, one could imagine, had time for growth. 'Thunderbolts' – meteorites? – to be collected along the slippery dogpaths of the Warren might have rained down from the heavens the night before. And this *newness* of England, manifest in the brightness, occasionally the crudity, of its colouring, had about it something of the precarious. *Would* it last? The edifices lining the tilted streets or gummed at differing levels above the Channel seemed engaged in just not sliding about. How much *would* this brittle fabric stand up to? My thoughts dallied with landslides, subsidences and tidal waves.[16]

The villas of this landscape occur throughout her work – 'a paradise of white balconies, ornate porches, verandahs festooned with Dorothy Perkins roses, bow windows protuberant as balloons, dream-childish attic bedrooms with tentlike ceilings, sublimated ivory-fretwork ingle-nooks inset with jujubes of tinted glass'. From 'Waikiki' in *The Death of the Heart* to 'Cathay' in *Eva Trout*, they provide the essence of Bowen grotesque. It is an Irish perception, not only in its Ascendancy snobbishness (they are the correct habitats for those suburban army wives talking about their insides), but also because it constructs a house into an expression of personality. Bowen, like many Anglo-Irish writers, treated houses as personifications. Those houses at the end of *The Last September* are named with the names of people, and are 'executed'; and in her pioneering discussion of

Sheridan Le Fanu's *Uncle Silas* she targeted his houses as really Irish houses, and their symbolic terrain as essentially Irish.[17]

Le Fanu's appeal for her is significant on other levels too. 'It is not the last belated gothic romance,' she wrote of *Uncle Silas*, 'but the first (or among the first) of the psychological thrillers. And it has, as terror-writing, a voluptuousness not approached since.' She was to approach that same voluptuousness in some of her own supernatural short stories. Le Fanu's displacement, his supernaturalism, his acutely observed childish vision, all appealed to her as an Ascendancy genre; so did the world of sensation which, she said, 'I have never fought shy of or done anything to restrain'.[18] It went with the aura of brilliant limitations which she thought characteristic of Anglo-Irish achievements in literature.

> Accommodating ourselves to a tamer day, we interchanged sword-play for word-play. Repartee, with its thrusts, opened alternative possibilities of mastery. Given rein to, creative imagination ran to the tensed-up, to extreme situations, to confrontations. Bravado characterizes much Irish, all Anglo-Irish writing: gloriously it is sublimated by Yeats. Nationally, we have an undertow to the showy. It follows that primarily we have produced dramatists, the novel being too life-like, humdrum, to do us justice. We do not do badly with the short story, 'that, in a spleen, unfolds both heaven and earth' – or should. There is this about us: to most of the rest of the world we are semi-strangers, for whom existence has something of the trance-like quality of a spectacle. As beings, we are at once brilliant and limited; our unbeatables, up to now, accordingly, have been those who best profited by that: Goldsmith, Sheridan, Wilde, Shaw, Beckett. Art is for us inseparable from artifice: of that, the theatre is the home.[19]

This self-conscious bravado, born of multiple insecurities, persists in her work. Again like Somerville and Ross, beneath an elaborate surface of manners the will fights through. This goes with strokes of savage comedy, and an ability to dislocate genres: ghost story, thriller, comedy of manners succeed each other within the same covers. By 1939 she had already marked out a certain territory for herself, and sustained (with very little money) a life between England and Ireland.

III

The war cast this into relief. Rightly, she has taken her place as one of the dominant voices in the literature of the Second World War: less often considered is the way that this catharsis enforced an examination of her own Irishness, and the effect of this process on her work.[20] Wartime England fully met her need for sensation; she wrote later that her usual sense of the abnormal was suspended.

I felt one with, and just like, everyone else. Sometimes I hardly knew where I stopped and somebody else began. The violent destruction of solid things, the explosion of the illusion that prestige, power and permanence attach to bulk and weight, left all of us, equally, heady and disembodied. Walls went down; and we felt, if not knew, each other. We all lived in a state of lucid abnormality.[21]

She stayed in Regent's Park, working as an air-raid warden, refusing to leave her house until it was bombed around her in 1944. The atmosphere of bright autumn mornings in 1940, with the charred smell in the damp air, the tinkle of glass being swept up, the levelled landscape, the odd survivals, is preserved in her wartime fiction. But she also continued to travel to Ireland; and Ireland was neutral.

The concept of neutrality was central to de Valera's gradual redefinition of Ireland's constitutional and diplomatic relationship to England; though there were also utilitarian considerations, like the fear of repeating Redmond's mistake in 1914 of committing Ireland to an unpopular war, and the suspicion (common in Ireland up to 1941) that Britain would lose. But, above all, technical neutrality was an assertion of sovereignty within the Commonwealth – whatever about implicit and unpublicized support for the British war effort, evident in individual and even government gestures. 'To abandon neutrality,' remarked Joseph Walshe, head of the Irish Department of External Affairs, 'is to accept Britain's conception of our place in the world.'[22] This was a point missed by many British observers, and the whole question of neutrality was resented by many Anglo-Irish, especially those with army connections. Where would Bowen stand on this question, deeply committed to the British war effort as she was?

She emerged as a strong defender of neutrality, and an acute observer of the Irish mentality during the early 1940s: preserved in her confidential reports on Ireland compiled for the Ministry of Information and now accessible in the Public Record Office.[23] Before examining these, it is worth considering the special atmosphere of Ireland during the war, and the sensitivities aroused by the very idea of neutrality. F.S.L. Lyons famously and controversially described

Ireland during 'The Emergency' as an existence in Plato's Cave: watching flickering shadows of the real world projected exaggeratedly or obscurely in front of a people who lived with their backs to the light. This, as has been frostily pointed out by other historians, makes the assumption that Irish reactions ought to be defined by the 'real' world of British experience.[24] Bowen was careful not to make this mistake – though some of her assumptions were condescending enough. And her reactions to Ireland in 1940–42 should be seen, not only against her own ambiguous background, but in the light of her close friendship with another Cork writer, Sean O'Faolain, who was at that very time mounting the cultural offensive which produced, in 1940, the first issue of the *Bell*.

A Republican activist in the 1920s, O'Faolain had by the later 1930s become a sceptical interrogator of many of the purist assumptions behind hard-line Irish nationalism. For his new periodical he borrowed the name of a great Russian journal of the previous century; and the *Bell* published many of the short stories which gave Irish writers a good claim to stand in the Russian tradition. It also involved writers and thinkers from various shades of the Irish political spectrum, and from different historical and religious traditions within the island; it raised many of the issues of pluralism, secularism and Irishness which the *Irish Statesman* had tried to advance in the 1920s.[25] Under O'Faolain's editorship, the *Bell* advanced the uncomfortable and often unwelcome case that Ireland's unique cultural inheritance was inescapably affected by traffickings with Britain as well as the Gaelic legacy; and that this commerce, tragic and exploitative in so many ways, could be culturally enriching in others. Through this process, an 'Irish' sensibility emerged which was both more complex and more intellectually liberating than realized by those obsessed either by colonial imitativeness or purist *narodnik* Irish-Irelandism.

O'Faolain and Bowen became close friends in 1937; a brief love affair developed on a visit to the Salzburg Festival that year. He stayed at Bowen's Court, where he met the holidaying English literati; while from him she learned a new vocabulary of Irishness. 'Do for God's sake write a book about Ireland,' he wrote to her in April 1937.[26] For the first number of the *Bell* in 1940, she produced a deliberate manifesto on behalf of reconciliation of Irish and Anglo-Irish traditions, called 'The Big House'.

From the point of view of the outside Irish world, does the Big House justify its existence? I believe it could do so now as never before. As I said, the idea from which these houses sprang was, before everything, a social one. That idea, although lofty, was at first rigid and narrow – but it could extend itself, and it must if the Big House is to play an alive part in the alive Ireland of today . . . 'Can we not,' big, half-empty rooms seem to ask, 'be, as never before, sociable? Cannot we scrap the past, with its bitternesses and barriers, and all meet, throwing in what we have?'[27]

This reverses the irony of the conclusion to *The Last September*, where Danielstown's door 'stood open hospitably upon a furnace'. The language in this essay is deliberately 'Irish': refracted and inverted, rather like the conversations in that novel, with phrases like 'making a poor mouth'. Since its publication, her work had largely been set in England, though the image of the Big House burning persists inside the St John's Wood setting of *To the North*. But the war, and her first-hand experience of it, meant she had to confront the question of British and Irish allegiances, at the very time when her friendship with O'Faolain and involvement with the *Bell* were imposing another kind of reconsideration.

She was writing with a heightened sensibility, especially notable in her two collections of wartime short stories, *Look at All Those Roses* and *The Demon Lover*. Audacity is their keynote, as in her transposition of blitzed London on a moonlit night to 'Mysterious Kôr', the great ruined city of H. Rider Haggard's *She*. She took risks – so much so that her English literary friends thought she was departing into vulgarity. And one particularly audacious story, 'Summer Night', is about neutral Ireland: emphatically not Anglo-Ireland. It begins with a woman on the run, speeding through the night in an empty car, a suitcase sliding around on the back seat. She has given her family the slip in order to keep an assignation with her lover, an enigmatic businessman in a provincial Irish town. When she reaches him, he is entertaining two people: a neurotic young man and his deaf sister. Their fractured, off-key conversation revolves around neutrality – and it eventually sputters into confrontation. When they part, everyone's behaviour is odd, jarred, unsynchronized: war is the obliquely mentioned but ever-present condition of everything.

In work like this 1941 story the genesis can be traced of *The Heat of the Day*. She began it in 1944, sending chapters out of

London for safekeeping, and eventually published it (to great acclaim) in 1949. But the novel was also inspired by an aspect of her visits to Ireland which was not known at the time: the reports which she was furnishing to the Ministry of Information, who passed them on to the Dominions Office and, eventually, the Foreign Secretary.[28] (They were also studied by John Betjeman, currently press attaché to the UK representative in Dublin, where he indulged in a camp Hibernian High Church fantasy: writing to his opposite number, Richard Hope, as 'Brother Hope' and signing himself 'Seán Ó betjemeán, attaché na press'.[29]) Bowen recycled some of her impressions for a *New Statesman* article,[30] but the original reports are more outspoken and personal; they also confront, much more clearly, the lack of understanding between Ireland and Britain which she had already exploited fruitfully in her fiction. She is even-handed, if condescending, about a tactless speech by Churchill on the Treaty ports and the 'childishness and obtuseness' of many Irish attitudes; she allows that in Ireland genuine 'spirituality' bolsters up official smugness and Pharisaism; there is a certain colonial impatience with the obtuseness of the natives which she was careful to excise from more public writings. On neutrality, however, she is perfectly clear; Joseph Walshe could not have put it better.

> It may be felt in England that Eire is making a fetish of her neutrality. But this assertion of her neutrality is Eire's first *free* self-assertion; as such alone it would mean a great deal to her. Eire (and I think rightly) sees her neutrality as positive, not merely negative. She has invested her self-respect in it. It is typical of her intense and narrow view of herself that she cannot see that her attitude must appear to England an affair of blindness, egotism, escapism or sheer funk.
>
> In fact, there is truth in Mr de Valera's contention. It would be more than hardship, it would be sheer disaster for this country, in its present growing stages and with its uncertain morale, to be involved in war . . .
>
> I could wish some factions in England showed less anti-Irish feeling. I have noticed an I suppose inevitable increase of this in England during the last year. The charge of 'disloyalty' against the Irish has always, given the plain facts of history, irritated me. I could wish that the English kept history in mind more, that the Irish kept it in mind less.[31]

Her view of Dublin public opinion, writing in November 1940, is striking: the claustrophobia, the restlessness, the intelligence and lack of 'stereotyping' in conversation, but also the lack of influence of intellectuals on government and politics.

> The literary people sequester themselves, or are sequestered. With the death of Mr Yeats and the departure of Dr Gogarty Dublin seems to have lost her only two social-literary figures. No view expressed by an Irish writer (novelist or poet) on the European situation, on Irish politics, seemed to be much listened to, or cut much ice. In fact, Dublin in general holds the Platonic view of the poet. The writer as propagandist in any sense seems to be ineffective in this country. This may or may not be a pity; in view of any psychological approach that Britain might wish to make to Eire it seems to me worth noting.[32]

For the purposes of gleaning information and impressions, her own contacts were not primarily 'literary', but included people like the Republican journalist Frank Gallagher, the UCD economist George O'Brien and the Fine Gael politician James Dillon (who fascinated her).

> In the material sense he is in the position to be disinterested: he is well-off (owing to a business in the West of Ireland), unmarried (and therefore clear of the domestic influences that count for so much in the middle-class Irishman's life) and shows a contempt for 'society'. His nature seems to me concentrated, and his intellect powerful and precise. I give this note on Mr Dillon at some length because both as a person and as a factor in Ireland he struck me as important. He is important now, if only as a counterpoise to Mr de Valera. In any dealings with Eire he is a man with whom one would have to reckon; he might become the man with whom one would have to deal.
>
> He may, on the other hand, be a man who is better in Opposition. This time may or may not show.
>
> I have heard Mr Dillon labelled a Fascist – which is I am afraid at least partly true. I have also heard him accused of pro-Germanism – which is, I think, 'wild'. He showed a truer sense than most Irishmen of the British mentality: his attitude towards England struck me as guarded, calculating, satirical-respectful, not hostile in even the oblique sense.[33]

She was detached from *Gaeilgóir* revivalist circles, though no more so than many Irish urban intellectuals:

The Gaelic gathering and festival was in full swing in Dublin last week while I was there; it lasted a week and took place in the Mansion House. Plays, singing and conferences appeared to compose the programme. I say 'appeared' because all reports were printed in Irish, which I cannot read. For the same reason (not knowing Irish) and because I was busy, I did not attend any of the sessions. As a gathering of people (largely teachers) from all over Ireland, they would have been interesting to *see*.[34]

However, she found 'the worst defeatism, on behalf of Britain' among the Protestant Anglo-Irish, and she rather bitingly related this to self-interest and the fears for a West Briton future. 'If the Anglo-Irish would merge their identity with Eire's, they could make – from the point of view of England – a very much more solid and *possible* Eire with which to deal.' Here, the message of the *Bell* was used for a purpose that might not have pleased all her new literary friends in Dublin.

This was in 1940. There is a gap in her reports until 1942, possibly because the Foreign Office destroyed them or passed them on. In 1942 her 'Notes from Ireland' for the Dominions Office stress a generalized nervousness: 'a nebulous feeling that war is *infectious*'[35] and a prevalence of exaggerated delusions about conditions in Britain. Anti-Americanism, focused against the Ambassador and the activities of GIs and journalists in Northern Ireland, had reactively produced some pro-British feeling. She also forecast (correctly) the emergence of a third party in politics after the war, which would reap the benefit of public impatience with the established parties' unconstructive approach to domestic social policy; and she was present in the Mansion House for Dillon's speech at the Fine Gael Ard-Fheis which precipitated his resignation from the party.[36] She found the standard of Irish political debate in general unimpressive, 'at once cagey and muddled', with a worrying 'crypto-fascist' element. For herself, impatience was setting in. After two years' war experience in London, Irish neutrality seemed less defensible. She thought there was a sense of 'moral deterioration' since 1940; people seemed to have 'lost face' with themselves and with each other. (Dublin, in this mood, is recorded in short stories like 'Sunday Afternoon'.) By July her reports show yet more asperity: criticizing the influence of disaffected 'returned emigrants' in Dublin, noting the lack of animus towards black-marketeers, recording the apathy of Dublin opinion and politics, though accepting the 'considerable common sense' of de Valera's government. Her description of de Valera in the Dáil is memorable. Dillon told her that, during a speech he (Dillon) made against neutrality, de Valera 'made no reply or comment and did not once, while Mr Dillon was speaking, raise his head from his hands'. Bowen added:

> I must observe, however, that from my own attendance at the Dail I formed the impression that this attitude of Mr de Valera's, during *any* debate, is habitual. He remains with his head supported inside his hands, his fingers laced over his forehead. The attitude implies intellectual weariness, and the very barest degree of tolerance exercised towards most of the speakers.[37]

In the countryside she found a 'passionate interest' in war news on the radio, though a 'dispassionate tone to discussions, as few people are willing to declare themselves *parti pris* on either side'.[38] A classic Bowen interpretation followed:

> One psychological explanation of this interest in the war is that it is a form of escapism. With regard to Eire's domestic affairs the country people are at once bored and depressed. A sense of immediate dullness, fretted by deprivations, seems to cloud life here. 'The war' stands for drama, events in a big way, excitement. All this appeals to the Irish temperament.

There is a certain self-identification here. At the same time, she appreciated the Irish facility for self-criticism and nuance, and continued to explore Irish opinion on every level available. One notable instance was an afternoon spent tête-à-tête with Archbishop McQuaid of Dublin – an unlikely conjunction, set up by Constantia Maxwell of Trinity College on the pretext that her friend was interested in social work. This created a scenario worthy of a Bowen novel, with enthusiastic discussion of the Municipal School of Cookery, and elaborate regret expressed by Bowen (under normal circumstances resolutely undomestic) that she could not observe their classes at work. From this unpromising subject they proceeded to discussing life in France, for which they both shared an attachment, the Archbishop defending both Pétain and Laval. Courtesy and diplomacy were preserved throughout; Bowen obviously relished it. 'I was struck by the balance he kept in his point of view, between the mystical (we discussed visions) and the practical – belief in good cooking, intelligent domestic life, etc. . . . he made every allowance for my view in any matter we talked about.' This was evidently not her expectation of a Catholic prelate; but they both appear to have negotiated delicate areas with a certain flair.

All this activity, however, raises more fundamental questions too. Writers, according to Bowen's friend Graham Greene, are in a sense fifth columnists; and in her position among her Irish acquaintances during wartime, this has a double application. Always fascinated by espionage, she was now a kind of spy. Her reports are headed 'Secret'; and she had proposed herself for the task.[39] Nobody in Ireland, apparently, knew of this commission; Dillon, discovering many years later that she had recorded and reported their conversations to the British government, was furious at what he saw as a betrayal of trust.[40] It is unlikely that even O'Faolain knew what she was up to. How far had she wanted to formalize the uneasy position occupied by an Ascendancy writer trying to operate outside the stockade?

Along with an exploration of the ambiguity of her stance regarding Ireland and Irishness went a more general interrogation of all that had made her the person she was. The war precipitated a vogue for precocious autobiography; in Bowen's case it was accentuated by her childish doubts about the permanence of England, which seemed suddenly vindicated. '*Would* it last?' In the early years of the war she wrote about her lonely childhood, the books that had shaped her flaring imagination, her family's connection to Ireland's past, and her own Irishness. In 1942 she published (with the Cuala Press in Dublin) a brief memoir of her early childhood called *Seven Winters*; the same year she brought out the far more substantial and ambitious *Bowen's Court*, written very fast between 1939 and 1941. In its structure, the architecture of the house bears a great weight of historical and psychological interpretation. On one level, it is a generally unsentimental threnody to the Anglo-Irish past; on another, a demonstration of the 'Versailles fantasy' which reduced them to ghosts and strangers in the country's present. In its historical analysis the influence of O'Faolain is implicit and pervasive. Intriguingly, Jonathan Cape rejected it 'on the grounds that it contained too much controversial material about Anglo-Irish relations'; Cape himself, according to Bowen, thought it 'subversive'.[41] This is doubly ironic, because in its evocation of place, family and Irishness *Bowen's Court* is, like *The Heat of the Day*, a book about allegiance.

Bowen was interviewed, on one of her wartime visits to Ireland, by the *Bell*.[42] Even that pluralist journal asked the predictable question: could she really be classed as an Irish writer, with her Ascendancy background and her London domicile? The answer was trenchant.

I regard myself as an Irish novelist. As long as I can remember I've been extremely conscious of being Irish – even when I was writing about very unIrish things such as suburban life in Paris or the English seaside. All my life I've been going backwards and forwards between Ireland and England and the Continent but that has never robbed me of any feeling of my nationality. I must say it's a highly disturbing emotion. It's not – I must emphasize – sentimentality.

And yet the Anglo-Irish ambivalence remained. By the time the war ended she had changed some of her ideas; the alteration in tone between her Irish reports in 1940 and in 1942 had progressed to impatience with much about the new Ireland. She had also developed a tough and dismissive approach to ideas of a new British post-war world; political conservatism and Ascendancy snobbery fused. Her fleeting idea that she might live permanently in Cork owed something to a flight-from-Moscow reaction after Labour's victory in 1945. 'I've been coming unstuck from England for a long time,' she wrote to William Plomer. 'I have adored England since 1940 because of the stylishness Mr Churchill gave it, but I've always felt "when Mr Churchill goes, I go". I can't stick all those little middle-class Labour wets with their Old London School of Economics ties and their women. Scratch any of these cuties and you find the governess.'[43]

In 1949 she finally published *The Heat of the Day*, the book which crystallized much of what she felt about England through those transfigured years – and about Ireland. She built into it, not only her experience as an air-raid warden, but her observations of Ireland at war. Part baroque spy story, part psychological thriller, part social comedy, it embraced a wide scope of action and experimented with the fracturing of communications and language at a time when the whole brittle structure of London itself was being shaken to its foundations. Uncertainty and dislocation characterizes every perception. ('"You are looking more like yourself." "More like myself, am I looking?" asked Roderick, with interest and curiosity. He attempted to remember what she must mean.') The novel was acclaimed for its re-creation of blitzed London, with its smells and sounds and surreal freedoms, its strange giddy underworld of fleeting liaisons in pubs and clubs. But it is also a novel about knowing where you belong, about England, and about Ireland: reflected, characteristically, through houses. Stella Rodney, the central character, has a soldier son who inherits an Irish house; in a key section of the novel, she travels to Ireland to inspect it on his behalf. She is already involved with a man suspected of spying, and the Irish interlude demonstrates, oddly, loyalty and continuance. When Stella visits Mount Morris, the local people bring the news of El Alamein (using the impressions Bowen collected on her 1942 visit and recorded in her secret 'Notes from Ireland'). This is deliberately counterpointed against her excruciating visit to her lover's mother in deepest Surrey. Their house, Holme Dene, is a 'man-eating house', one of 'a monster hatch-out all over southern England in the 1900s'. It is all fussy garden, leaded windows, dripping laurels, imitation old oak, and bedrooms arranged as if their occupants were dead. But this is not just snobbish social comedy; the point is that this scenario, completely English and completely unreal, has bred a traitor.

The sun had been going down while tea had been going on, its chemically yellowing light intensifying the boundary trees. Reflections, cast across the lawn into the lounge, gave the glossy thinness of celluloid to indoor shadow. Stella pressed her thumb against the edge of the table to assure herself this was a moment *she* was living through – as in the moment before a faint she seemed to be looking at everything down a darkening telescope. Having brought the scene back again into focus by staring at window-reflections in the glaze of the teapot, she dared look again at Robert, seated across the table, opposite her, between his nephew and niece. Late afternoon striking into the blue of his eyes made him look like a young man in Technicolor. That the current between him and her should be cut off, she had expected; dullness, numbness, even grotesquerie she had foreseen. But what could be this unexpected qualm as to the propriety of their having come to Holme Dene? The escapade, bad enough in its tastelessness and bravado, had a more deep impropriety with regard to themselves. Nothing more psychic than Mrs Kelway's tea table, with its china and eatables, interposed between them: the tea table, however, was in itself enough. The English, she could only tell herself, were extraordinary – for if this were not England she did not know what it was. You could not account for this family headed by Mrs Kelway by simply saying that it was middle class, because that left you asking, middle of what? She saw the Kelways suspended in the middle of nothing. She could envisage them so suspended when there *was* nothing more. Always without a quiver as to their state. Their economy could not be plumbed: their effect was moral.[44]

The Heat of the Day crystallized Bowen's preoccupation with what lasts in a world where people lead lives of 'canvas-like impermanence': a condition realized for her not only by wartime but by the ambiguities of her Irish background. And this in turn stimulated an interest in the supernatural which had its own Irish dimension.[45] Collections like *The Demon Lover*, as the title indicates, are peopled by ghosts; 'The Happy Autumn Fields' conflates past and present, living and dead, in the subconscious of a girl who is transported from a bombed London house to a picnic in early Victorian Ireland. Even the London ghosts of *The Heat of the Day*, orphaned by bombing, move through the streets like those Swedenborgian apparitions beloved of Le Fanu and Yeats.

Most of all the dead, from mortuaries, from under cataracts of rubble, made their anonymous presence – not as today's dead but as yesterday's living – felt through London. Uncounted, they continued to move in shoals through the city day, pervading everything to be seen or heard or felt with their torn-off senses, drawing on this tomorrow they had expected – for death cannot be so sudden as all that. Absent from the routine which had been life, they stamped upon that routine their absence – not knowing who the dead were you could not know which might be the staircase somebody for the first time was not mounting this morning, or at which street corner the newsvendor missed a face, or which trains and buses in the homegoing rush were this evening lighter by at least one passenger.

These unknown dead reproached those left living not by their death, which might any night be shared, but by their unknownness, which could not be mended now. Who had the right to mourn them, not having cared that they had lived? So, among the crowds still eating, drinking, working, travelling, halting, there began to be an instinctive movement to break down indifference while there was still time. The wall between the living and the dead thinned. In that September transparency people became transparent, only to be located by the just darker flicker of their hearts. Strangers saying 'Good night, good luck', to each other at street corners, as the sky first blanched then faded with evening, each hoped not to die that night, still more not to die unknown.[46]

This owes much to *Uncle Silas*: Bowen's introduction appeared in 1947, claiming that the novel was Irish not only in its physical terrain but also in its preoccupation with architecture and morality, its infantilism, its sexlessness, and its economical but heavily freighted theme of the hauntings of history. The same could be said of much of her own work, as she surely knew.

IV

In the post-war period Bowen's Irishness continued to shape her writing, but less intensely. *A World of Love* in 1955 was her last wholly Irish novel, and reads as a kind of *envoi* to the classical Bowen atmosphere – with its impossibly hot summer on a decaying farm, odd relationships with the surrounding locality, and a left-behind English wife, bred for the Thames Valley and hopelessly at sea in the subtleties of Irish country life. But it is notable that the collusive politenesses of trips to the town (where credit is shaky) do not cross the social divide. The Danbys inhabit a dilapidated 'small mansion' rather than a grand estate; it has an obelisk and an arch, rather like ruined Kôr. But they look to London for a Chekhovian fantasy of escape, not Dublin, and the wireless signal that galvanizes them is Big Ben, not Radio Éireann. Religious barriers are also frankly admitted; an acutely observed detail is 'the Protestant van' that collects the demonic Maud for school. In an autobiographical fragment Bowen had recalled 'taking the existence of Roman Catholics for granted . . . They were, simply, "the others", whose world lay alongside our own but never touched'[47] (rather like Swedenborgian ghosts). *A World of Love* describes something very different from the 'alive Ireland of today' which she had invoked in 1940; it is the ice-age Ireland of the 1950s, the censorship board, and the Fethard-on-Sea boycott.[48] The reconciliatory ideas of the *Bell* had receded beyond recognition.

Neither of Bowen's last two novels had an Irish content. *The Little Girls* (1964), sardonically symbolist, takes place in south-coast England during the early 1960s, with flashbacks to the lost domain of childhood before the First World War; *Eva Trout* (1969) conjured up an immense, awkward heiress-heroine and pursued sensationalism to its limits. But she left an unfinished fragment called 'The Move-In' which starts with an unwelcome visit to an Irish house, Pinteresque and menacing. And she had begun notes for an autobiography, posthumously published as *Pictures and Conversations* (1975), which contains some of her sharpest commentary on those dilemmas of Irish identity that preoccupied her all her life.

After the war, as always, the conditions of Bowen's personal life help explain the attitude towards Ireland in her work. Unlike most of her books, *The Heat of the Day* made her a good deal of money; she used it to put bathrooms into Bowen's Court. But she did not return to live permanently in Ireland. Her husband died in 1952; after some years of difficulty she sold the house very quickly in 1959 to a neighbour, who – interested only in the land – unexpectedly tore the roof off and then demolished the walls. She said deliberately tough-minded, anti-'muffish' things about its fate and continued to return to Cork and stay with friends. But she avoided the site.

The uneasy relationship between English and Irish continued to preoccupy her ('a mixture of showing-off and suspicion, nearly as bad as sex'[49]). The Anglo-Irish, she said elsewhere, were the 'only children' of Irish history – spoilt, difficult, unable to grow up. It is a striking metaphor, coming from someone who was herself an only child, and became a great novelist of unhappy childhoods. She had also written that the Anglo-Irish, born of displacement, were able to 'instantly strike a root into the intersections of any society in which they happened to find themselves, and in their own way proceed to rule the roost'.[50] In fact, many of their problems arose from their chronic inability to strike root. But true or not, she needed to believe it. O'Faolain, her old friend and mentor in Irishness, eventually judged her as 'heart-cloven and split-minded . . . consistently declaring herself born and reared Irish, residing mostly in England, writing in the full European tradition; no wonder all her serious work steams with the clash of battle between aspects of life more easy for us to feel than to define'.[51]

Shortly before her death in 1972 she astounded her friend the writer Hubert Butler and his wife Peggy by the vehemence with which she said, 'I *hate* Ireland.'[52] It had grown away from her – or away from the collusive, stylish, never-never land which she had chosen to inhabit. But that same imagined country, central to her imagination, made her see England as eccentric, peculiar, exotic. The interaction between the two, rather than 'writing in the full European tradition', produced her art: created as she lived, in a tradition distinctively if uncomfortably Irish.

7

Love, Politics and Textual Corruption: Mrs O'Shea's *Parnell*

DR YEATS: We had a good deal of trouble about Parnell when he married a woman who became thereby Mrs Parnell.

AN CATHAOIRLEACH [The Speaker]: Do you not think we might leave the dead alone?

DR YEATS: I am passing on. I would hate to leave the dead alone.

– Debate in the Irish Senate on the Divorce Bill, 1925

I

Yeats's preoccupation with Parnell developed quite late in life; and though the Chief was already a haunting presence in the poems of 1913, representing an Anglo-Irish integrity supposedly lost to modern Irish politics, Parnell's reception into the Yeatsian pantheon was given a more dramatic impetus the following year. For in May 1914 Parnell's widow Katharine, once notorious as 'Kitty O'Shea' in the 1890 divorce case which shattered Parnell's career, arrived back into the public eye with the publication of her memoir *Charles Stewart Parnell: His Love Story and Political Life*. Yeats, his father and Lady Gregory all read the book avidly;[1] it affected the poet's view of the private Parnell, of English hypocrisy, of the conflict of passion and will, and it supplied him with images which recur in *The Trembling of the Veil* and *A Vision*.[2]

Nor was the Yeats circle alone in its preoccupation. 'Everyone is reading the O'Shea revelations,' noted Wilfrid Scawen Blunt.[3] Sales of the book were gratifyingly large, running into three printings and helped by pre-publication serialization and widespread newspaper coverage. The story of Parnell's fall, and the political new world not so well lost for love, carried a particularly potent charge in 1914: the third Home Rule Bill, having been passed by the Commons, was being stymied by Ulster's resistance and the Liberals' pusillanimity. For Irish nationalists, particularly his ex-colleagues, the publication of Parnell's letters, revealing his cavalier attitude towards them and his 'disgust' at the 'hollowness' of the Land League, provided an additional traumatic shock. But beyond its immediate political relevance, the story of passion and betrayal revealed (often in an extraordinarily chatty and matter-of-fact way) a ten-year cohabitation between the Irish leader and his colleague's wife which not only defied convention but also at times defied belief. Belief, that is, in the central contention of the divorce court (unchallenged at the time because neither Parnell nor Mrs O'Shea offered evidence): that Captain O'Shea had been a deceived husband, who had neither condoned nor connived at his wife's relationship with Parnell. Yet this unlikely assertion was also the central argument of Mrs Parnell's book.

The internal contradictions of this picture, even as presented in Mrs Parnell's own treatment, were obvious enough to raise some reviewers' eyebrows;[4] the reaction of Parnell's champion Henry Harrison, who had helped Mrs Parnell in the weeks following her husband's death twenty-three years before and heard a very different story, was unequivocal. The book, he wrote, was 'no less a forgery even though the weak fingers of the authoress may have held the pen which stronger fingers guided'.[5] Yeats's father retailed a more lurid version to his old friend Rosa Butt (daughter of the man whom Parnell had supplanted in the leadership of the Irish Parliamentary Party). 'Mrs Parnell did not write that book and never saw it or even heard of it, for she was in a Lunatic Asylum where she still is. Young O'Shea wanted money so he took all the letters and made a pecuniary arrangement with Costello, and they employed a skilful literary hack who wove these into a narrative.'[6] The story of how the book came to be written deserves elucidation, and so does its composition. In the process, the three figures of the divorce-court triangle come into clearer focus: particularly the only one still alive in 1914. This was the very far from insane 69-year-old Katharine Parnell, previously O'Shea, née Wood: a strong-minded and well-bred Englishwoman, daughter of a clerical baronet and niece of a Liberal Lord Chancellor.

She had never been to Ireland, never been called 'Kitty', and (unlike nearly everybody else) pronounced her name O'Sh*ee*, not O'Sh*ay*.

II

In the case of *Charles Stewart Parnell*, gestation and composition are not completely interdependent processes. The immediate inspiration for the book was apparently an article in the *Cork Free Press* by Parnell's old colleague William O'Brien, which appeared on 6 September 1913; a mere eight months later Mrs Parnell's two stout volumes were published, copiously glossed and illustrated. Initially advertised as a collection of letters, the book is in fact a detailed autobiography up to 1891; the quantity of material and its sometimes haphazard arrangement suggest that at least part of it was written over a far longer period. Chapters like the one called 'Captain O'Shea's Letters', as well as the highly tendentious introduction, represent the forensic element in the book, marshalled to attack the case presented by William O'Brien. But there is far more to it than this; and much of Mrs Parnell's material is in implicit or explicit contradiction of the argument presented by the unnamed (though scarcely invisible) editors who doctored it in the O'Shea interest. Before separating out the voices in the chorus, what case were the O'Sheas trying to refute?

O'Brien's article, like Mrs Parnell's book, was based on hitherto unknown letters of Parnell's – particularly one dated 14 January 1890, after the divorce petition had been entered by Captain O'Shea but well before the hearing. 'If this case is ever fully gone into, a matter which is exceedingly doubtful, you may rest assured that it will be shown that the dishonour and the discredit have not been upon my side.'[7] This letter, O'Brien added, proved that 'it is now certain that if Parnell had been allowed to go into the witness box the public verdict would have been altogether revolutionized' and Parnell shown to be 'rather the victim than the destroyer of a happy home . . . and the divorce would never have taken place'. O'Brien's implication was that both the O'Sheas hunted Parnell down, and the subsequent liaison was facilitated by a 'transaction' with the Captain.

O'Shea himself had died in 1905; but his son Gerard promptly wrote to *The Times* denying this interpretation and quoting a letter sent to him by his mother:

I quite agree with you as to the insult to myself, your father's memory, and above all to my late husband, Mr Parnell. I now propose, with your consent, to publish, as soon as possible, myself the letters of my late husband which, as you know, I had left directions should be published after my death.[8]

Gerard, then aged forty-three, was an obstreperous and litigious character with an aggressive commitment to the rather forlorn cause of defending his father's character (at least, until the price was right). He had testified on his father's side and against his mother in the divorce case; now he apparently supervised the production of his mother's memoirs, and provided a preface. Bulletins started to appear in the newspapers, imaginatively recording threats to the author from 'several Irish gentlemen' if their names were mentioned; revelations were advertised about 'Salisbury, Churchill, Labouchère, Davitt . . . Constable, Landseer, Trollope, Manning, Meredith, Rhodes'. Most of these luminaries disappointingly merited a single allusion in the book when it appeared, and then as friends of Mrs Parnell's mother, the popular novelist Lady Wood. More accurately, promises were also held out of 'wire-pulling tactics in high political circles' and new material regarding the divorce proceedings.[9] From 5 May 1914 excerpts began to appear in the *Daily Sketch*, with all the accoutrements of a serial romance: the rosebud, worn by Mrs O'Shea at the lovers' first meeting and kept by Parnell until his death, appeared as a motif at the head of each instalment. Parnell's most sensational letters, larded with epithets like 'Queenie' and 'My Own Wifie', appeared in heavy type; the serial was also embellished with photographs which did not appear in the book, including a recent one of Mrs Parnell waving merrily from a bath-chair on Brighton promenade. The linking narrative was similarly breezy ('notes such as the following . . . will give an idea of the shifts we were put to when Willie was down [at Eltham]'). The concluding excerpt was followed by an advertisement for 'our next serial – "The Sacrifice of Love", by Mr Paul Urquhart'.

The general reaction by reviewers after publication date (19 May 1914) was correspondingly appalled. *The Times* denounced the 'desecration' of 'Mrs O'Shea's confessions';[10] 'lack of delicacy' was a charge often levelled, the *Bookman* remarking 'one shivers a little at the easygoing references to her unhappy husband as "Willie"'.[11] The general consensus was that she stood revealed as unworthy of Parnell:

a frequent image invoked Delilah, proclaiming to the Philistines just how she had destroyed the hero.[12] A few voices, however, were raised in defence of such a 'bravely written book': the *Pall Mall Gazette* thought its 'power and sincerity' raised it 'from the plane of scandal to that of drama'[13] and the *Standard* called it 'a most intensely interesting document . . . shameless in its proper sense, not connoting anything disgraceful . . . it talks of long years of intrigue with as little reserve as a professor describing the love affairs of a Roman Empress'.[14] These are qualities which strike a modern reader too. But the most prescient reaction of all came from an Irish suffragette journal, which robustly pointed out that Parnell's fate was 'the Nemesis of the anti-feminist . . . to fall victim to a woman of the highly sexed, unintellectual type, developed by the restriction of women's activities to the sphere euphemistically styled "the Home"'.[15]

Otherwise, the Irish reaction was an almost complete silence. This was due less to lofty disregard than to an effective boycott organized through the Dublin Vigilance Committee, a Catholic pro-censorship pressure group. The original *Cork Free Press* controversy had received much press attention, but there was very little coverage of what the *Leader* called 'this vile traffic in a fallen woman's revelations'. The *Freeman's Journal*, *Irish Times*, *Daily Express* (Dublin) and *Irish Book Lover* all ignored it. So did the *Cork Free Press* itself, despite its inspirational part in the book's genesis. Only the *Independent* owned by Parnell's (and Yeats's) old enemy William Martin Murphy, gave any prominence to this 'work of shocking character . . . giving the revolting details of a disedifying liaison . . . with an audacity and effrontery that must be repulsive to every decent man and woman'.[16] After a monster meeting of the Vigilance Committee on 14 June, British newspapers carrying notices of the book were boycotted, and country branches of the Committee imposed undertakings on Catholic booksellers not to stock it, though advertisements continued to appear in some Dublin papers. By and large, it was the most effective voluntary black-out of a scandal by the press until the Abdication crisis. It was still, however, read, even by respectable people. 'Have you read the *Life*?' Lady Gregory was asked by that model of Irish rectitude and anti-Parnellism, John Dillon. 'It is a wonderful love story. It would have been all right if it had not been made public . . .'[17]

Thus the publication inevitably set old ghosts walking; and the one surviving principal suddenly advanced from the obscurity in which she had spent the years since Parnell's death. On 18 May 1914 many newspapers carried full accounts of an interview Mrs Parnell gave to the Press Association. Though ignored by both her biographers,[18] it is full of interest – apart from proving conclusively that the author was very far from entering a lunatic asylum. She had, she said, no idea of publication until the O'Brien controversy. 'But this thing is new, this bowdlerized, excusing, current version of his character and personality; and this I cannot bear.' The book was therefore 'in no sense an apology: I have never answered our critics before'. She had not intended to include political matters but could not avoid them; in any case, she read 'newspapers of all shades of political opinion, because it is still an interest to me to deduct his views from the whole, and speculate what his probable action would be'. To the inevitable question about the contemporary impasse in Ulster, she remarked that since Parnell's death, 'the Irish are beginning once more to look for favours from England instead of rights . . . Sir Edward Carson's little army [the Ulster Volunteers] would have appealed strongly to him – only he would have tipped the Ulster rebellion into the Home Rule cauldron and directed the resulting explosion at England.'

She herself, however, was 'no longer a whole-hearted Home Ruler' since the Home Rule Bill had been 'whittled down to a glorified local government bill, and even so forbidden in Ulster'; this was a punishment of 'Ireland's blindness and England's hypocrisy'. At the time of the Parnellite split, she confided, she had longed to expose the 'hypocrisy' of English statesmen, but Parnell 'would not lift a finger to retard, to even make difficult for England that possible ultimate issue' (given Parnell's tactics in 1891, a very special piece of pleading indeed).

Most accounts of the interview emphasized her political speculations, but the *Daily Mail* recorded her statements about 'Parnell the Lover': 'for a woman of my temperament he was the ideal lover'. All interviewers described her charm, humour and intellectual alertness; even the *Cork Examiner* was struck by 'an air of *distingué* about her, and an unmistakable charm'. Significantly, her son Gerard was by her side, though Mrs Parnell confided that in the matter of answering O'Brien's allegations, 'he considers two volumes less convincing than one fist'.[19]

III

The substance of those allegations concerned Captain O'Shea's knowledge of the affair, and this preoccupied many reviewers; but there was much else to chew upon too. In Britain, attention was concentrated upon the revelation that Gladstone used the then Mrs O'Shea as an intermediary to Parnell, in many letters and several interviews, beginning nearly ten years before the divorce case. This was a godsend to the Conservative press, given that he had withdrawn support from Parnell's leadership on the moral issue. Denunciation of the 'Grand Old Humbug' was widespread and gleeful. In Ireland the chief shock-value of the book lay in Parnell's own letters, particularly those from Kilmainham Jail in 1881–2, where he not only spoke dismissively of the 'hollow' land movement which had brought him there, but offered to give up politics and run away with his 'own sweet wifie'. The nostalgic relish with which she described their various feints and evasions to avoid public attention was also deprecated. But many reviewers assumed that such steps were being taken to deceive Captain O'Shea; and this was hardly the case. For a decade Parnell lived in Mrs O'Shea's house; he returned to Eltham after late-night sittings, stabled his horses there, had a cricket-pitch constructed in the back garden and a study built on for his experiments (assaying minerals from his Wicklow estate and designing unsinkable ships). Meanwhile, 'Willie' turned up occasionally on Sundays to take his children to Mass. As Mrs Parnell had remarked to Henry Harrison in 1891, 'How could he fail to know?'[20]

Yet one theme of her complex book dutifully insisted on his ignorance; and the theory of straightforward connivance from the beginning presents some problems. As told in *Charles Stewart Parnell*, Katharine O'Shea determined to meet Parnell in order to advance her husband's career; a recent and unfashionably Whiggish adherent to the Irish Parliamentary Party, he showed no better hope of succeeding in politics than in previous disastrous involvements like Spanish banking and Hertfordshire stud-farming. They were living largely apart, he in London, she in a suburban villa at Eltham bought in her name by the rich aunt to whom she acted as companion. Well connected, decisive, attractive, Mrs O'Shea presented herself to Parnell at Palace Yard in July 1880 and commanded him to come to dinner;

love blossomed at once and (from the evidence of letters) was apparently consummated by October. In January 1881 there was a quarrel with O'Shea over Parnell's presence at Eltham; after which 'Parnell and I were one without further scruple, without fear, and without remorse'.[21]

This statement follows oddly on the previous assertion that O'Shea had been pacified by denials; she told Harrison in 1891 that a *modus vivendi* had been arrived at and 'we were on a perfectly clear basis from that onward'. In any case, it seems clear that this quarrel happened in July, not January (Parnell was in Ireland in January, and the dates of letters elsewhere indicate July). By 1882 the affair was already a staple of political gossip.[22] How long did Captain O'Shea remain in ignorance? It is tempting, and reflects better on the romantic hero and heroine, to accept Mrs Parnell's line to Henry Harrison: 'Of course he knew . . . There was no bargain; there was no discussion; people do not talk of such things. But he knew, and he actually encouraged me in it at times.'[23]

And yet there is Sophie Claude. This was the short-lived daughter born to Parnell and Katharine in February 1882, while Parnell was incarcerated in Kilmainham. She was conceived during a seaside holiday with Parnell in May 1881, and Katharine was therefore two months pregnant at the time of the quarrel in July. In *Charles Stewart Parnell* she states categorically that O'Shea thought the child was his. This is the scenario for the most extraordinary scene in the book. Parnell, on parole from jail, arrives at Eltham to work out the so-called 'Kilmainham Treaty' whereby the Irish Parliamentary Party would co-operate with the Liberal government in return for concessions on the Land Act and the release of the prisoners. In one room, husband and lover draft the historic terms; next door, the wife/mistress keeps vigil by the dying infant whom each man believes to be his. 'Willie wanted me to join them, but I would not leave my baby, and when the daylight came and they went to lie down for a few hours' rest before Parnell left for Ireland, my little one died as my lover stole in to kiss us both and say good-bye.'[24]

Unsurprisingly, this was a key scene in a recent television drama about Parnell; it mesmerized reviewers in 1914. It is rather spoiled by the fact that Parnell was still at Eltham two days after Sophie died;[25] and much of the effect would be ruined if O'Shea actually knew perfectly well that the child who carried his name was not his. This seems to have been the case with Parnell's other two daughters, Clare and Katie, born in 1883 and 1884. The London editor of the *Freeman's Journal* remembered Parnell and O'Shea visiting the office, and Parnell, after showing a piece of paper to O'Shea and receiving his assent, handing it casually over for insertion in the paper. 'It was an announcement in due and also rather curt form of the birth of a daughter to Mrs O'Shea.'[26] And Mrs Parnell's book, faced with this awkward subject, opted for the simple expedient of never mentioning the existence of Clare and Katie at all; presumably because it would make the theory of O'Shea's consistent ignorance impossible to sustain.

The romantic Parnellite case would extend this to the birth of Sophie Claude, and assume that Mrs Parnell's repeated statements that O'Shea believed he was the father were dictated by Gerard in 1914. A close reading of the key chapter adds some evidence. The language used is repetitive and clumsy; phrases like 'the deception I had to practise on Captain O'Shea' jar oddly. And one careless sentence deserves decoding. 'Willie was very good; I told him my baby was dying and I must be left alone.'[27] This hardly fits a situation where 'my' baby was his too. Other clumsy interpolations in this chapter – irrelevant letters to show the O'Shea family believed the child to be Willie's, and unsigned missives from Parnell, for which no facsimiles are given – suggest the hand of the pugilistic Gerard. In her own narrative Katharine remarks 'since my first meeting with Parnell, Willie knew *at least* that I frequently met him at the House'.[28] The qualification is suggestive. And many of the formal 'cover letters' from Parnell, instanced as evidence of the necessity to deceive O'Shea, relate to periods when the latter was out of the country.[29]

And yet for 1882 there remains an aura of doubt. All O'Shea's references to Sophie, in the divorce case and elsewhere, suggest he thought she was his; as, of course, he had to. But he never mentioned Clare and Katie, letting the case go (so to speak) by default. How much did he want to know about the convenient friendship which during 1882 gave him the political role of inept Mercury, ferrying messages to the Liberal leaders? Recent biographers of Katharine have robustly accepted the possibility that she arranged a temporary resumption of marital relations with O'Shea in 1881, when she discovered her pregnancy, in order to cover herself – an assumption which Harrison found it impossible to make.[30] In 1891, and indeed in 1914, this made her look like a loose woman; by the 1970s it fitted with the picture of a resourceful feminist heroine, trapped by divorce laws and settlements which discriminated against women, determined to keep her lover and assert a role for herself.

The interpolations on O'Shea's behalf continue unevenly throughout the book; but so does a less clumsy, more unforced strain of reference which probably reflects Katharine's own attitude towards O'Shea. By and large, this is oddly, exasperatedly affectionate. 'Willie' becomes a character; still recognizably the 'gentlemanlike adventurer' epigrammatically described by Sir Alfred Robbins, 'who makes the world his oyster and is disappointed at the size of the pearls'.[31] Irritating as he was, a certain camaraderie with Katharine remained in the early eighties, though as the decade wore on he became a cross to bear. Increasingly importunate and threatening, the subject of many of Katharine's letters to Gladstone as she sought a job for him, he was indirectly dependent (through Katharine) on hand-outs from 'Aunt Ben', whose huge fortune and unaccountable longevity preserved the shaky triangular structure far longer than its constituents had intended. Katharine's expectations from her aunt's will inspired resentment and litigation from the Woods even before she finally died; Joyce Marlow believes that O'Shea was encouraged to his spectacularly belated divorce action in 1889 not by any shadowy political cabal but by Katharine's jealous family. Yet up to this the tone of her references to 'Willie' remain quite friendly; after a coolness in 1882–4 when, possibly, an agreement was hammered out, their letters of the mid-eighties return to the affectionate nicknames of courtship days. 'Boysie' and 'Dick' alternate with 'Wifie' and 'King'. It may not be heroic, but it carries a certain psychological conviction. Her grim efforts to find him a parliamentary seat in 1885–6, leading to the Galway election when coded public references were made to the affair by everyone from Lord Randolph Churchill to the *Pall Mall Gazette*, were urgently necessary for many reasons. O'Shea was hinting, obscurely and not so obscurely, at exposure. Her machinations to avoid this constitute one of the most riveting chapters in the book. It was the culmination of many years spent trying to 'place' Willie.[32] Again, significantly, decoding her own narrative supplies a clue to the real state of affairs. She remarks that failure to land her husband a seat would endanger Home Rule by leading to action that would shatter 'the silence of years'.[33] 'Silence', not 'deception'.

IV

If Willie sings baritone in this verismo opera, the tenor part belongs to Parnell; and the portrait of him in private life constitutes one of the chief values of the book. His existence outside politics has always been cloaked in obscurity; yet there is much evidence that it meant more to him than the public life he was constrained to lead.[34] 'We will be so happy, Queenie; there are so many things happier than politics.'[35] After a haphazard and loveless childhood (parents separated, mother mostly absent, himself packed off to English schools from the age of six), he had found the perfect partner, and her picture of their partnership is essential to any biographer. There are myriad small mistakes and confusions in the sequence of events as she describes them. Letters of Parnell's, for instance, are glossed 'sent to Dublin to be posted' when he can be shown to have been there;[36] the story of his concealment for a fortnight in a room off her bedroom during 1880 (a delight to salacious-minded reviewers) simply does not fit with the record of Parnell's movements at this time. The context of his notorious letters from Kilmainham is ignored. Parnell's reassurances that he welcomed imprisonment and was leading a life of ease and luxury there must be seen in relation to the frantic letters from Katharine which can be reconstructed between the lines; she was pregnant, insecure, quarrelling with Willie, deeply worried about Parnell's health, and strained to breaking-point. Her account of his movements at junctures like the Phoenix Park Murders or the publication of the Richard Pigott forgeries in *The Times* does not always square with other sources. But often it is simply one recollection against another; and she was the person who was with him all the time.

Moreover, much of her evidence casts new light on Parnell – particularly on the psychology of a man deluded and solipsistic enough to believe that Mrs O'Shea could safely visit him in prison, passed off as one of his sisters,[37] and whose whole attitude to the world was that it had no business to question his bizarre private life. (In the *Times* Special Commission hearings of 1888, investigating the Pigott forgeries, a little-noted correction is indicative of Parnell's attitude. Asked 'Did you go to see Captain O'Shea at Eltham' in April 1882, Parnell replied, '*He came to see me.*'[38]) Mrs Parnell's book also threw light on Parnell's attitude to the divorce case, and the decision of the co-respondents not to follow up their counter-charges against Willie as petitioner – though this whole issue had to be skirted carefully, as those very counter-charges invalidated the central premise of the work. They listed connivance, unreasonable delay in instigating the suit, wilful separation, cruelty and the petitioner's own adultery. It is well established that the story O'Shea told in the divorce court was a travesty; even undefended, at least two jurors had severe doubts about it, and attempted to interrogate O'Shea on their own account. Though the British press accepted it with delight, American journalists – again, as with the Abdication – treated it very differently. On 29 December 1891, for instance, the *New York Herald* ran a long piece under the unequivocal heading 'UN MARI COMPLAISANT: Captain O'Shea at Last Objects to Mr Parnell's Liaison with Mrs O'Shea'.[39] Then as now, British libel law forced the local press to be more circumspect; and in the Parnell case, political bias also made the worst construction of events the most attractive.

More to the point, what of the contemporary belief (at least among Home Rulers) that Katharine refused to allow Parnell to contradict O'Shea's version of events, in order to facilitate their marriage? In her book she gives exactly the opposite analysis: the insistence on letting the divorce go through was his. Either way, another vital issue could not be mentioned: that they were hoping to pay O'Shea £20,000 to drop the suit, right up to the last moment.[40] And certainly, her account of keeping their lawyers in doubt up to the very morning of the trial is borne out by completely independent, unpublished evidence: a memorandum in the James Papers with an account by Sir Frank Lockwood (Katharine's counsel). This describes his attempts to persuade them to prove Willie's connivance, Katharine's excuse of 'neuralgia' for delaying a decision to the eleventh hour, and Parnell's violent quarrel with Lockwood (again at the last minute) on the grounds that he believed they had been promised custody of Clare and Katie in return for abstaining from pressing counter-charges.[41]

His desire to be married to her, at whatever cost, is undoubted. In this, and in the picture of a Parnell insulated from political reality, Katharine's account has been corroborated by recent analysis. And she provides a portrait of Parnell, the quixotic, single-minded, oddly shy man who 'hated to be hated',[42] which was a revelation. Perhaps most striking of all was her account of his threat to leap off Brighton Pier with her in a storm:

> . . . as I turned to get a fresh hold on him, for I could not stand against the wind, and the motion of the sea sickened me, the blazing fires in his eyes leapt to mine, and, crushing me roughly to himself, he picked me up and held me clear over the sea, saying, 'Oh, my wife, my wife, I believe I'll jump in with you, and we shall be free for ever.' Had I shown any fear I think he would have done it, but I only held him tight and said, 'As you will, my only love, but the children?' He turned then, and carried me to the upper deck, hiding my eyes from the horrible roll and sucking of the sea beneath our feet.[43]

In scenes like this near-*Liebestod*, she added a new dimension to a Wagnerian hero more often seen as Siegfried than Tristan.

What of Isolde? Katharine Parnell's book is essentially an autobiography, and from early on she displays certain marked characteristics: an impatience with convention, a sense of humour, a feeling of frustration with her lot, a dogged persistence and loyalty. There is also an asperity, a certain self-satisfaction, an air of the *grande dame*. She could write, on occasion, with astringency and facility (which makes the double stream of composition throughout the book all the more obvious) and possessed an individual and lively style, corroborated in her more recently released letters to Gladstone.[44] And for all her disclaimers ('I was never a "political lady"'[45]) she revelled in her activity as intermediary; the Gladstone papers do not contradict her claims to an important role, despite attempts to discredit her account.[46] Gladstone certainly soothed his colleagues about her communications, claiming he could not control them but did not encourage them;[47] equally certainly, he continued to approach Parnell through her as often as convenient, though not as often as she claimed, and frequently through the Chief Whip Lord Richard Grosvenor rather than directly. The Liberal leader's 'hypocrisy' in later abandoning Parnell is a tricky question: Katharine's constant intercessions seeking jobs for Willie may have given him the impression they were a devoted couple and, rather like Willie himself, Gladstone may have known only as much as he wanted to know. He was certainly told of the liaison at least three times in 1882, but affected incredulity.[48]

Katharine's relationship with Parnell also had its political dimension. She advised him on speeches,[49] had more opportunity to discuss day-to-day strategy with him than anyone else, and authorized a number of important communications, signing them with the name of Parnell's secretary, Henry Campbell – as Parnell himself later admitted, with breathtaking insouciance.[50] Her personal influence is emphasized by all Parnell's modern biographers; her political influence receives less analysis, though she was an intelligent and astute woman from a Whig family who prized good conversation, and her mother and sister were well-known writers much in the social world. Here, as in many other ways, the background position Katharine occupied in Parnell's public life has led to an assumption that his political decisions, as well as his political appearances, were conducted independently of her; and this seems unlikely, to say the least.[51] Between the lines, *Charles Stewart Parnell* certainly suggests otherwise. Generally, the only influence allowed is that she kept him obdurate during the leadership negotiations after the split; she was explicitly linked by *Vanity Fair* to H. Rider Haggard's sexually threatening Ayesha, as 'The Political Princess: O'Shea Who Must Be Obeyed'.[52] But this seems unlikely on every level: Parnell's decision to fight against the majority of his followers and jeopardize Home Rule may have been unbalanced, but it was his own. It is not unnatural that his colleagues should have thought otherwise. Their attitude to her was inimical, and so was hers to them. The Irish Parliamentary Party are often the butts of her malicious humour in *Charles Stewart Parnell*; ironically, they had been treated in a similar manner by her first husband. Parnell once came home to her with the diverting news that an Irish Member had threatened to kill Willie, merely because he had smiled at his colleague's pronunciation of 'Mr Speaker, Sir': 'Willie's smile is a bit of a twister sometimes.'[53] So was Katharine's, though her attitude was less grounded in otiose snobbery. She evidently enjoyed indicating over and over again how readily Parnell would have abandoned party commitments to be by her side. It was her revenge, not only for the myth of 'Kitty O'Shea' created in 1891, but also for a decade of frustration in the political shadows.

When the crash came, cupidity rather than immorality might have been an accusation more relevantly levelled at the notorious couple. Katharine had kept her unconventional *ménage* going for ten years, determined not to risk losing a financial inheritance through divorcing O'Shea; and Parnell acquiesced in this. The dual stream of composition in her memoir replicates the duality preserved through that strange decade at Eltham and Brighton: uxorious with her lover, intermittently stormy with her husband, soothing her imperious aunt across the Park. But in 1914 she was much more responsible for her book than chivalrous Parnellite champions like Henry Harrison allowed. Amid the obvious interpolations, the perfunctory tone of editorial 'ghosting', the inescapable archness and coyness of the genre, an original voice comes through.

V

Katharine Parnell lived on for seven more years, dying in poverty in 1921. After litigation, she had obtained less than half of her aunt's fortune; much had gone on legal costs, and more had been embezzled by a family solicitor. *Charles Stewart Parnell* had made her money, but that too ran out; she moved restlessly from watering-place to watering-place along the south coast of England, from Kent to Cornwall and back again. At the time of her death she was living in a small terraced house in Littlehampton: 'the space and beauty of [the] home of my youth', she had written in 1914, 'left me with a sad distaste for the little houses of many conveniences that it has been my lot to inhabit for the greater part of my life'.[54] A letter from her daughter Norah to Henry Harrison delicately hinted at a taste for the bottle and periods of nervous breakdown. In her last years someone else described her as 'a sonsy, comfortable soul not unlike the best type of theatrical landlady'.[55] This suggests an impression too much influenced by assumptions about the old age of scarlet women; but there are not many options for an Isolde or a Deirdre who survives, and perhaps Katharine became more like Rosie in Somerset Maugham's *Cakes and Ale*.

Still, the power of her story remained, and so did its potential for controversy. In 1936 there was another flurry when Elsie T. Schauffler's successful play *Parnell* was launched on Broadway, slightly based on Katharine's book, with a farrago of inaccurate embellishments. Gerard O'Shea was still active; that same year the husband of one of Parnell's daughters begged a historian not to quote him on his wife's paternity, 'as Gerard O'Shea is somewhat rough at times, and I wish to live a little longer'.[56] Gerard drummed up a campaign to prevent Schauffler's play being produced in London, but eventually he was bought off by a large fee and disappeared to America as 'script consultant' on a projected film of the story – his father's son to the last.

The revived interest in the O'Shea–Parnell triangle inspired Henry Harrison, who had published his 'vindication' of Parnell five years before, to write to Yeats, asking him to 'make it known in Dublin'. Yeats had remained haunted by the story. In *A Vision*, written in 1922, he had recurred to the *Liebestod* on Brighton Pier and placed Parnell in Phase Ten of his occult system of archetypes: the 'Image-Breaker', his Mask conferring both 'self-reliance' and 'isolation'; 'creates some code of personal conduct, which implies always "divine right"'. Private desires in this phase conflict with public restrictions, which are undermined by 'some woman's tragic love almost certainly'. Much of this was inspired by *Charles Stewart Parnell*, which also influenced some of Yeats's comments in the divorce bill controversy a few years later. So he was ready for Harrison in 1936. Reading *Parnell Vindicated* for the first time and spending an afternoon with the author induced high excitement; he was particularly delighted by Harrison's account of Parnell breaking up a tedious discussion with Willie by throwing Katharine over his shoulder and bearing her off to bed. The encounter with Harrison precipitated a relapse of ill-health and a number of ballad poems.

The Bishops and the Party
That tragic story made,
A husband that had sold his wife,
And after that betrayed . . .

Meanwhile, in Hollywood, the film of Elsie T. Schauffler's play went ahead, directed by John M. Stahl for MGM and released in 1937.[57] To Gerard O'Shea's talents were added those of Clark Gable and Myrna Loy. One scene stays in the mind: an echo of Joyce's 'Ivy Day in the Committee Room', a silver-screen personification of the Yeatsian Phase Ten, or perhaps another, indirect manifestation of Katharine's revenge? Gable and Loy arrive at a London hotel. Passing through the lobby, they glance into a room; it is inhabited by members of the Irish Party, sitting around a table well supplied with bottles of stout. An expression of distaste crosses Gable's (unmoustached) features. '*Those* fellows!' he remarks with a twang of contempt, and masterfully steers Mrs O'Shea away from them, up the stairs.

8

'Fatal Drollery': Parliamentary Novels, Outsiders and Victorian Political History

I

Critics seem unable to agree whether or not there is a tradition of political novels in English literature. In one of the very few monographs devoted to the subject, written over half a century ago, Morris Speare breathlessly revealed the genre as central to Victorian intellectual history, and described the political novel thus:

> It is a work of prose fiction which leans rather to 'ideas' than to 'emotions': which deals rather with the machinery of law-making or with a theory about public conduct than with the merits of any given piece of legislation; and where the main purpose of the writer is party propaganda, public reform or exposition of the lives of the personages who maintain government, or of the forces which constitute government.[1]

Yet the Victorians themselves were not so sure. 'Of all novels the political novel is hardest to write,' remarked *St Stephen's Review* gloomily in 1886: 'of all political novels those which deal with Radicalism present the most difficulties.'[2] The implication of a necessarily propagandist function is unnecessarily restrictive. Other critics, taking a different tack, have sweepingly referred to *Phineas Finn* as 'the only English political novel', or else altered their definition to take in novels that deal with issues which are in the widest sense 'political'. Christopher Harvie's *The Centre of Things* has recently attacked the subject with brio, but he casts his net to take in the fiction of social critique, up to the late twentieth century.[3] By this standard, the trawl enlarges to pull in works like *The Princess*

Casamassima and *The Secret Agent*. The literary standard of the work thus considered rises hearteningly, but at the cost of a central coherence in the definition.

'Political novels', for the purposes of this essay, must be taken to mean those which deal with the formal world of politics, as conceived in nineteenth-century Britain: the English 'system', or what Disraeli described in *Tancred* as 'that fatal drollery called a parliamentary government'. This at once raises another point noted by Speare: 'the drawing-room is frequently used as a medium for presenting the inside world of politics'.[4] It is this that has given the classical political novel its aura of silver-forkery, so evident in the work of authors as dissimilar as Disraeli, W.F. Rae, and Mrs Humphry Ward; and it is this which is often influential in leading the radical heroes of novels which are 'political' in the wider sense to opt out in disgust from the ritualized structures that surround them. This is explicitly true for Daniel Deronda and Alton Locke, and implicitly for many of the characters of Dickens (in whose novels the political world is treated either metaphorically or as a satirical aside[5]). It is also true, in a different way, for the hero of H.G. Wells's *The New Machiavelli*, a novel that is 'political' in both senses. Moreover, to radical critics from left or right, there appears to be more political 'meat' in the fiction of the age before Victoria's ascendancy: the set-piece *causeries* of Peacock, frantically discussing ideas, or the authentic annals of John Galt, especially *The Member* (1832).[6] Here, outsiders tend to break into the charmed political circle. What becomes of them in the Victorian world?

If there is an identifiable strain of novels dealing with the world of politics in the nineteenth century, literary critics have tended to avoid it: probably because of the generally conceived mediocrity of the individual works. An assumption has existed that Meredith or George Eliot 'tried' one specifically political novel and then, with a flawed though interesting *Felix Holt* or *Beauchamp's Career* behind them, moved on to their true destiny. Historians have also generally ignored political novels as evidence, because they considered their authors to have been excluded from a 'real' knowledge of politics – rejected candidates, like Trollope or the young Disraeli, writing from a combination of pique and wish-fulfilment. Recently, however, a change of attitude is discernible, dictated by a number of factors. Benedict Anderson and others have stressed the importance of popular and periodical literature in forming a nation's image of itself and its institutions, and even in conceiving of itself as a functioning whole.[7] Accompanying this is the rising critical stock of writers like Meredith and, much more noticeably, Trollope; the increased and increasing tolerance of interdisciplinary approaches to history and literature; and changes in the whole approach of historians to the political history of Britain in the nineteenth century. To generations imbued with the reassuring notions of Whig teleology, the story was one of peaceful evolution from oligarchy to democracy by means of Reform Bills and reasonably articulated pressure from out-of-doors: the classical issue being, how change was effected without revolution. From the late 1960s, however, the question has been posed from a different angle: the preoccupation being, not how much change was peacefully effected, but how little. The extraordinarily successful rearguard action of the landed aristocracy in defence of their influence has been emphasized, to the extent where even political reform has been interpreted as their aggrandizement rather than their weakening.[8] The great battles of Gladstonian Liberalism have been seen as calculatedly holding the gap against the forces of radical social departures in politics.[9] In the 1970s, collusiveness and manipulation were the qualities stressed most in discussions of nineteenth-century high politics: the comfortably climbing graph of Whig history was redrawn into a zigzag figure where the 1850s were seen as a decade of restabilization and class collaboration following the critical radicalization of the 1840s, and where lurches in the economy from 1870 dictated desperate shifts in political initiatives.[10] This historiography has now itself come under scrutiny, with a new generation asserting different perspectives, and a rediscovered emphasis on, for instance, idealistic imperatives in the case of Gladstone.[11] But the old verities have not been reinstated *in toto*. And the light cast on this world by political novels, even those where the silver forks flash most luridly, seems less artificial now.

The ingredients which attracted some novelists to representing politics in fiction – an aristocratic cast, the psychology of manipulation, the collusive dramas of Westminster – were in fact not far distant from the reality of the English political world. (There were different problems presented by the system in America where, according to Edith Wharton, people above a certain class simply did not consider entering politics.) In an age of sceptical inquiry, political historians have rediscovered what Trollope called 'that special set which dominates all other sets in our English world',[12] and in the process they have discovered Trollope as well. With a curious appositeness, those historians who engaged themselves most closely in the process were attacked with exactly the same criticism levelled by his contemporaries at Trollope: that of pandering to cynicism by reducing politics to the proposition that 'every man is actuated by motives of the basest self-interest'.[13]

It is none the less true that the liberal rationalizations which generally did duty for political history in the pre-Namier age (and after it) could flourish more easily by dismissing the fictional representations of high politics produced by contemporaries, and relying instead on the version of reality created by politicians' memoirs or pious family biographies. Thus both Leopold Amery, politician-cum-historian, and Bradford Booth, a historical literary critic, considered that Trollope wrote political novels 'with the politics left out'.[14] Elsewhere Booth wrote that in Trollope, political warfare appeared 'shadowboxing'; but Trollope's point is that this is exactly what it was. He also apprehended a point that historians in a later age equally emphasized: that in the democratic era, rhetoric tended to usurp reality, and the real issues of government were kept out of Parliament. 'In Downing Street and the Treasury Chambers our great men are now comparatively true. It is when they go down to the House and assume their guise as legislators that fallacy or intrigue are necessary or permitted. There they are both necessary and permitted.'[15]

Thus Plantagenet Palliser, in the (arguably) first novel of Trollope's political series, is presented as 'priding himself on being dull' and 'very careful in his language'. 'He had taught himself to believe that oratory, as oratory, was a sin against the honesty in politics by which he strove to guide himself.'[16] (This is counterpointed in the same novel by the unscrupulous George Vavasor's repetition of his meaningless mantra: 'Vote for Vavasor and the River Bank'.) And the story of Palliser, spun through the novels, is appositely that of his failure: the rhetoricians and manipulators win out. His wife begins their marriage wondering 'would it not be better to be beaten by Burgo than to have politics explained to her at one o'clock at night by such a husband as Plantagenet Palliser?' She revenges herself by treating politics solely in terms of the venality and frivolity which he abhors. Trivia takes over: the politics of social contacts lead to an exclusive political obsession with minutiae. (Lady Glencora's political preoccupations, whether concerning Lizzie Eustace's diamonds or Sir Orlando Drought's invitation, might be seen as not much more trivial than her husband's devotion to decimalization or potted peas; but the latter are at least ostensibly public issues.) And it is her vulgarization that keeps pace with the times; it is she who gets it right.

They should have made me Prime Minister, and have let him be Chancellor of the Exchequer. I begin to see the ways of Government now. I could have done all the dirty work. I could have given away garters and ribbons, and made my bargains while giving them. I could select sleek, easy bishops who wouldn't be troublesome. I could give pensions or withhold them, and make the stupid men peers. I could have the big noblemen at my feet, praying to be Lieutenants of Counties. I could dole out secretaryships and lordships, and never a one without getting something in return. I could brazen out a job and let the 'People's Banners' and the Slides make their worst of it. And I think I could make myself popular with my party, and do the high-flowing patriotic talk for the benefit of the Provinces . . . But a Prime Minister should never go beyond the generalities about commerce, agriculture, peace, and general philanthropy. Of course he should have the gift of the gab, and that Plantagenet hasn't got. He never wants to say anything unless he has got something to say. I could do a Mansion House dinner to a marvel![17]

II

It is with Trollope that a consideration of nineteenth-century political novels must begin, for the very reason that Speare more or less dismissed him: he does not write to advance an 'idea'. His acute behaviourism did not suffer from his own celebrated failure to gain a parliamentary seat; it was only in the literal sense that he researched his politics from the Strangers' Gallery.[18] Reviewers who remarked upon 'Mr Trollope's unaccountable desire to enter "Parliament"' anticipated the confession in his *Autobiography* that politics were to him 'a visionary weakness'.[19] His view of political motivation in this work is not that generally implied by the novels – being, as he said himself, 'high-falutin'. Though it is not often appreciated just how disingenuous that *Autobiography* is, the point should be noted. But in the Trollopian world actions speak louder than motivations. In his autobiography he also stated that he wanted 'to teach politicians that they can do their business better by truth than by falsehood', but the novels carry a contrary implication. The Pallisers, he averred, speak for him, 'as I have not been able to speak from the benches of the House of Commons', and, if there is the development towards pessimism which some critics have discovered in Trollope,[20] his view of politics became accordingly gloomier. But *The New Zealander*, written in 1855 though not published until 1972, shows a pessimistic and sceptical cast of mind about public life; and it seems as likely that the darkening world of Trollope's political novels represents not so much an alteration in his own views as a change in his conception of what he could get away with in fiction.

If early critics of Trollope's political novels had had the opportunity to read *The New Zealander*'s critique of hypocrisy and dishonesty in British public life, they might have read the subtext of his political novels more accurately. And it is significant that this book was written towards the end of his time in Ireland, where he lived for seventeen years on and off from 1841. There is a strong case for seeing Trollope's politicization, like so much else about him, as taking root in that country.[21] His first novel, *The Macdermots of Ballycloran* (1847), which he deprecated unnecessarily in his autobiography, presented a theme that was strongly political, if unparliamentary. The decline of Thady Macdermot into Ribbonism has been compared by Harvie to the 'politics' of Galt's earlier novels, and Owen Dudley Edwards has pointed out that the poor reception of Trollope's early Irish novels may have been affected by reactions to the Irish rebellion of 1848. In his last, unpublished novel, Trollope fell back on an Irish extremist position, after a fact-finding tour through Land League Ireland, and ended by denouncing Bright and Gladstone for letting loose the Fenian genie. But his Irish experience gave him one consistent theme in all his political fiction: a fascination with the outsider who enters a closed society.

The Kellys and the O'Kellys (1848), his best Irish novel, also prepares the way for the double plots and drawing-room politics of his Barchester and London series; his Irish fox-hunting scenes acutely indicate the different social and political context of the sport between the two countries; and Mrs Kelly is an avatar of Trollope's long line of female politicians. But above all, the idea of Phineas Finn as political tyro could not have been born without a deep knowledge of

Irish mores. Finn's career may have been suggested by Irish adventurers like William Gregory (for the precocious political advancement) and Chichester Fortescue (for the grand marriage); but his social position is based on close observation of Irish provincial society. He is the son of a Catholic doctor and his Protestant wife in Killaloe; his father, distinctly a gentleman, is on easy terms with local aristocracy; his sisters are clearly *bonnes bourgeoises*; the family is financially poor but socially secure. Finn possesses natural good manners, a way with horses, and the kind of attractiveness that charms men as well as women (everybody, apparently, likes to touch him). Victoria Glendinning has speculated on Finn as Trollope's alter ego; and it is significant that this alter ego comes from Ireland, the adopted country where Trollope discovered happiness, in order to conquer England, the mother country which broke his youthful heart.

This is not contradicted by the fact that Trollope eventually repudiated the importance of Finn's being Irish, declaring in his autobiography that this had been a mistake; as suggested above, this is in itself a significant statement, reflecting his own feeling that the new politics of Parnellite Ireland had rejected him. (Had he lived out the 1880s, he would have been given a great subject for political fiction in the Parnell divorce case; and, oddly, he had known Katharine O'Shea as a girl, through his literary friendship with her mother and sister.) Trollope's emotional ambivalence about Ireland may also be reflected in his deliberately myopic view of administration during the Famine: a crisis where the politics and prejudices of English Whiggery manifestly failed.[22] Trollope's Irish politics meant that he had to believe the Union worked – as it had triumphantly worked for him. Hence the choice of an Irish hero for his parliamentary series of novels: the implicit message was that the Irish could be insiders too. In the early drafts of the novel Phineas's mentor Joshua Monk had also been Irish, and he is coached in cynicism by a political insider with the resonantly Irish name of Fitzgibbon.

Phineas's Irishness remains a vital dimension of his politics, particularly regarding tenant right and the moral test imposed by giving a correct vote on the issue. It also affects the sexual politics which replicate so much of the political action on another plane. His human failings brought out the horrified housemaster in Morris Speare ('it would be a sad day for England if men of his weak moral fibre and mental flabbiness became samples of "an ambitious younger generation" struggling with public affairs'[23]). But Phineas is no Julien Sorel, slipping through the interstices of the elite class system; he is a more confused hero, finding as much unhappiness as happiness. Made by women, he is also unmade by them: the same ambiguity characterizes his relationship to the political world, which he conquers only after disillusionment. Had Ireland provided more opportunity for advancement than an 'Inspectorship of Poor Houses in the County of Cork', he would clearly have done better to stay there. Phineas's development through Trollope's Palliser series parallels the development of Trollope's own ideas on Ireland. In *Phineas Finn* he goes against his party by taking a radical stance on tenant right, but in *The Prime Minister* he opposes the Irish Parliamentary Party over Home Rule; in one of his last appearances he is clearly at odds with Palliser (still a worried idealist) over the principle of social equality. It is a principle which a duke has less trouble endorsing than an Irish *arriviste*.

Well before Trollope embarked upon the Palliser series, a specifically political theme was developing in the Barset novels. Since the Reform Bill, he portrayed Barsetshire as separated into two divisions, which coincide with two political cultures: Whiggish, latitudinarian West and unreconstructed Tory East. A political element enters novels like *Doctor Thorne* (1858) and *Framley Parsonage* (1861) which goes much further than simply the expectations nourished by sprigs of the gentry about being returned for the local seat. Both these novels introduce characters who move on into the Palliser series, so may be seen as transitional to the political novels proper; but even the early Barchester books are informed by metaphors of politics (much as the Chancery Court comes very near to standing in for Parliament in *Bleak House*). And in *The Warden* (1855), the celebrated debate on the 'Convent Custody Bill' is constructed around Irish issues, and the division of the Irish Parliamentary Party 'who had bound themselves together to force on the ministry a bill for compelling all men to drink Irish whiskey, and all women to wear Irish poplins'.[24] Religion and politics pervade each other. Trollope described clergymen as open to 'that subtle, selfish, ambiguous sophistry to which the minds of all men are so subject', which could lead them to believe that 'in doing much for the promotion of their own interest they were doing much also for the promotion of religion';[25] his clerical politicians are portrayed responding to the trauma of Church reforms in the 1830s and 1840s much as his secular politicians would respond to the traumas of later political reform. (The Reverend Crawley of Hogglestock, at odds with the world in every way, is his only clergyman who completely transcends such calculations.) And in the later Barchester novels, the new worlds of commercial fortunes and agricultural change are wreaking havoc on local politics, formal and informal.

This was one theme which would resurface in the Palliser series, along with another, traced out in *The Three Clerks* (1858): the question of how to reconcile personal probity with political success. After his own success with the Barsetshire novels, Trollope turned to politics 'proper' – and created his Irish hero, a young man from the provinces (or the frontier) whose function was to be exposed to temptation and to explore the mechanisms of the great British system of compromise. This would be the issue posed by the careers of Phineas Finn and Plantagenet Palliser, and refracted through the six novels generally demarcated as a 'political' series: *Can You Forgive Her?* (1864), *Phineas Finn* (1869), *The Eustace Diamonds* (1873), *Phineas Redux* (1874), *The Prime Minister* (1876) and *The Duke's Children* (1880).[26] *Ralph the Heir* (1871) has its celebrated election passage, and *The Way We Live Now* (1875) is in its mordant way a more 'political' novel than many of them; but the Palliser series contains Trollope's most consistent representation of the formal world of politics.

Ever since the time of Henry James, who pretended he found Trollope's political novels unreadable and then referred copiously to their plots and characters, their critical reception has been oddly erratic. Perhaps because of their pessimism as much as their psychology, they currently enjoy more respect and attention than any other part of Trollope's *œuvre*; but a recent study of his ideas on gentility can still obtusely declare that 'the so-called political novels disclose very little about the political set-up in nineteenth-century Britain in the sense that we might expect to discover from a constitutional history'.[27] What they do disclose is in many ways more accurate. It is a world where Parliament is the refuge of the financially embarrassed, as well as the desideratum of young men making their way in the world; the latter no less than the former, since they lacked financial independence, ran the risk of debasing its function. As with elections, the more his heroes expect of the ritual, the more brutally disabused they are. Phineas's progress is the most pointed case, but not the only one. The shibboleth of party is treated with equal ambivalence: the formula that Trollope sees Tories as 'belongers' and Liberals as 'inquirers' is too simple.[28] Party commitment is far closer to the Duke of St Bungay's conception in *Phineas Redux*: 'devotion to the side which a man conceives to be his side, and which he cannot leave without danger to himself'. Trollope disliked much about the contemporary Conservative Party, but his experience in the Beverley election showed him that the Liberals could bribe just as easily as the other side.[29] It might be said that this engagement, while excluding him from the charmed chamber, taught him more than successful entry could have done.

This raises the question of how far Trollope's novels reflect a knowledge of the real political world. The classic pseudo-insider dismissal was uttered by James Bryce in 1903, and often repeated. 'As he had no practical experience of politics either in the House of Commons or as a working member of a party organization in a city where contests are keen, the pictures of political life which are so frequent in his later tales have not much flavour of reality. They are sketches obviously taken from outside.'[30] This tells us more about Bryce's myopia than Trollope's. The idea that exclusion entailed ignorance stems from a misapprehension about the nature of nineteenth-century politics. Friendships in Whitehall and Fleet Street, the life of the clubs, the social round of drawing-rooms and country-houses, were enough to ensure that Trollope's ear was kept close to the ground, and his own brief editorial career at *St Paul's* added an important identification: the first leader stated that '*St Paul's*, if it be anything, will be political'.[31] Several pronouncements in its leading articles resurfaced in the later Palliser novels; *St Paul's* foundered, but the political commentary continued in the guise of fiction. The question of how far the figures in the political novels are portraits from life has provided a literary parlour-game for over a century.[32] Simple-minded critics, of whom Trollope has had more than his fair share, follow implicitly his own disclaimers that he had any real statesmen in mind,[33] but, to borrow a phrase from a twentieth-century political scandal as sensational as anything in Trollope, 'He would say that, wouldn't he?' Naturally he had to deny deliberate likenesses, where they were as uncomplimentary as the portrait of Bright in Turnbull. It should also be remembered that the pictures, recurring as they did, blurred with time and art. In Trollope's earlier novels, Gladstone and Disraeli appear transparently through the aliases of Finespun and Sidonia; later, the images were refined into Gresham and Daubeny, more rarefied creations but still unmistakable. The increasing subtlety of his portraits partly resulted from Trollope's own improved powers, and partly stemmed from the fact that the characters achieved an independent life as the series progressed, thus diverging inevitably from their original prototypes. The more central the character, the more this was the case; thus strenuous attempts to balance Palliser against Lord John Russell, or Finn against Chichester Fortescue, have a limited value at best.

None the less, the intention of caricature was there, amply larded with references which would not be lost on any readers with a taste for current public affairs. Sometimes the prescience was curiously accurate, a reminder that Trollope was intimate with those on the inside, like Lord James of Hereford, as well as with acute political journalists, like T.H.S. Escott. The unlikely duo of Daubeny and Turnbull connive against Mildmay, just as Disraeli and Bright did against Russell, though this was not generally known at the time. Daubeny's relationship to De Terrier is anatomized much as historians now see Disraeli's to Derby.[34] In *Framley Parsonage* (1861) Trollope forecasts how the Tories will steal the Reform issue. Reality is never far away. In the earlier novels, the transpositions are more direct: the Thornes' *fête champêtre* in *Barchester Towers* (1857) closely echoes the Eglinton Tourney.[35] Later, a kind of shorthand is adopted. The ballot stands in for the franchise in *Phineas Finn*, disestablishment of the Church of England for political reform in *Phineas Redux*.[36] Trollope's grammar of politics would have read with complete clarity to his contemporaries, though earnest critics have wasted too much time trying to explain it away ever since.

On more general levels, too, reality finds an accurate reflection: notably in the chanciness and boredom endemic to the system. Bishops leave the House *en masse* in order not to miss dinner, even though the debate is concerned with the disestablishment of the Church. Treasured issues of specialized knowledge are pushed roughly aside; frivolous trivialities engage passionate interest. The brutal insouciance of a Lord Brock (Palmerston) is preferred to the hypocritical agonizing of lesser – and later – men. Most of all, manipulation behind the scenes preoccupies the actors above all issues of principle. To the politician, 'a successful plot is as dear . . . as to the writer of plays'.[37]

'Politics' in Trollope spreads out from the House of Commons, to take over society and achieve the wider definition discussed at the beginning of this essay; it has been remarked by one of his better critics that *everything* in *Phineas Finn* has a political dimension.[38] Not only are 'all social gatherings brought together with sole reference to the state of parties',[39] but political modes are used as analogy for all areas of activity. A chapter entitled 'Madame Goesler's Politics' is about Society, not Parliament; and the great Palliser marriage is a constant reference-point for political parallels. What is conveyed by these novels is the incestuous world of a political elite: two sides composed of similar people, separated by so little of substance that they have to emphasize all possible differences, no matter how frivolous.

When two foes meet together in the same chamber, one of whom advocates the personal government of an individual ruler and the other that form of State which has come to be called a red republic, they deal no doubt weighty blows of rhetoric to each other, but blows which never hurt at the moment. They may cut each other's throats if they can find an opportunity; but they do not bite each other like dogs over a bone. But when opponents are almost in accord, as is always the case with our parliamentary gladiators, they are ever striving to give maddening little wounds through the joints of the harness. What is there with us to create the divergence necessary for debate but the pride of personal skill in the encounter? Who desires among us to put down the Queen, or to repudiate the National Debt, or to destroy religious worship, or even to disturb the ranks of society? When some small measure of reform has thoroughly commended itself to the country – so thoroughly that all men know that the country will have it – then the question arises whether its details shall be arranged by the political party which calls itself liberal – or by that which is termed conservative. The men are so near to each other in all their convictions and theories of life that nothing is left to them but personal competition for the doing of the thing that is to be done. It is the same in religion. The apostle of Christianity and the infidel can meet without the chance of a quarrel; but it is never safe to bring together two men who differ about a saint or a surplice.[40]

When the political world came to include those who did want, at least theoretically, to 'disturb the ranks of society', Trollope's novels accordingly looked artificial and trivial; but to those who have immersed themselves in the private correspondence and public statements of Victorian statesmen, his picture carries a remarkable verisimilitude.

To those who have not, his view continues to seem specious. Bradford Booth complained that Trollope's political novels were spurious because there was no political philosophy in them; Morris Speare repeated the impeachment, with similar distaste.[41] Trollope would not have been surprised at their reaction. 'Men and not measures are, no doubt, the very life of politics. But then it is not the fashion to say so in public places.'[42] Barrington Erle's horror at politicians who profess principles, which seemed an appalling piece of cheap cynicism to critics like Speare, was presented by Trollope satirically but feelingly.

According to [Erle's] theory of parliamentary government, the House of Commons should be divided by a marked line, and every member . . . required to stand on one side of it or on the other . . . He thought that debates were good, because of the people outside, – because they served to create that public opinion which was hereafter to be used in creating some future House of Commons; but he did not think it possible that any vote should be given on a great question, either this way or that, as the result of a debate; and he was certainly assured . . . that any such changing of votes would be dangerous, revolutionary, and almost unparliamentary. A member's vote . . . was due to the leader of that member's party. Such was Mr Erle's idea of the English system of Parliament.[43]

Ideas, by and large, get short shrift in the novels, partly because of the nature and background of the sort of people who participate in politics, where personal relationships outweigh all other factors (as hilariously shown in Silverbridge's election speech for Frank Tregear[44]). Lady Glencora begins by producing theories in *Phineas Finn* ('the tendency of all law-making and all governing should be to reduce inequalities'), but she rapidly retreats into social manipulation, the visceral pleasures of 'real' politics, and the capricious adoption of dubious people rather than definite causes; while her husband, who is a theoretician (and in *The Prime Minister* produces the longest discourse on political theory in Trollope), is mercilessly disillusioned. The artifices and collusions of the mid-Victorian political world, as well as the unspoken assumptions of the age, are preserved in Trollope's political novels: what the young Winston Churchill called 'that line of half-chaffing, half-candid intercourse which prevails between people who know each other though on opposite sides, in this country almost alone of modern countries'.[45] Even in Trollope's own age, it was frequently remarked that in the future historians would use his books as a quarry for the temper of the times; later writers like Asa Briggs, W.L. Burn and J.L. Hammond followed the injunction.[46] But it is only recently that we have come to see that he recorded the way high politics happened just as accurately as social and intellectual attitudes.[47]

III

A fuller understanding of the significance of Trollope's political novels is only possible after a backward look at those of Disraeli. The relationship between the two, in literature and politics, is a curious one. Trollope hated Disraeli as a mountebank and 'conjuror', and the sharpest passage in his elaborately even-tempered autobiography is reserved for Disraeli's novels:

> The glory has been the glory of pasteboard, and the wealth has been a wealth of tinsel. The wit has been the wit of hairdressers, and the enterprise has been the enterprise of mountebanks. An audacious conjuror has generally been his hero, – some youth who, by wonderful cleverness, can obtain success by every intrigue that comes to his hand. Through it all there is a feeling of stage properties, a smell of hair-oil, an aspect of buhl, a remembrance of tailors, and that pricking of the conscience which must be the general accompaniment of paste diamonds.[48]

Moreover, these conjuror qualities were also perceived by Trollope in Disraeli's political behaviour. And yet Trollope's picture of politics in his novels is overwhelmingly as Disraeli practised them. (Whether or not either would have admitted it is beside the point.)

There are other connections too. Trollope attacked Peel by name in *The Three Clerks* and *The Bertrams* for having lowered the tone of public life by his deliberate expediency; Disraeli made the same charges more famously in *Coningsby* (1844). Disraeli, like Trollope, could barely 'conceive a masculine character who did not want to enter Parliament'.[49] The resemblance does not carry much further, however. Disraeli's political novels are overrated by some critics for the very reason that they underrate those of Trollope: simply because they are written to demonstrate theories. As the preface to *Coningsby* admits, the tract is the thing: 'The main purpose of the writer was to vindicate the just claims of the Tory party to be the popular political confederation.' In being written to score a didactic point they are not necessarily unusual, or ineffective. (*Alton Locke* was written, like so much of Kingsley's work, as a tract too, and set out deliberately to refute many of the panaceas mooted in *Coningsby*: notably Eustace Lyle's weekly dispensing of alms, which is rejected by Eleanor in *Alton Locke* as counterproductive.) But Disraeli's novels are most effective where they depart furthest from retailing 'ideas': the surprisingly rich and convincing milieu of Dandy Mick and Devilsdust in *Sybil* (1845), or the manoeuvrings of Rigby and the confabulations of Tadpole and Taper in *Coningsby*.

These emphases were not, however, a priority of Disraeli's political novels. They were written to demonstrate, first, the historical descent of rapacious Whiggery (which was read back to the dissolution of the monasteries, or even the Norman Conquest, when the context suited); and, second, to articulate and disseminate an imaginative (and imaginary) tradition of Toryism, which would unite nobleman, manufacturer and worker through the inspirational acts of the New Generation. Chapters like the third in *Sybil* use the springboard of explaining the hero's family history in order to declaim a far larger historical epic, where real actors (inevitably Wellington and Peel) are introduced with bewildering rapidity; *Coningsby* opens with Lord Grey's defeat, and for several chapters alternates between real and fictional politics. Where Trollope used fiction to translate politics into a shorthand, Disraeli manipulated his novels in order to explain what had happened (or, regarding the 1830s, what had gone wrong), and moved from this to theorizing.

The general election of 1832 abrogated the Parliamentary Opposition of England, which had practically existed for more than a century and a half. And what a series of equivocal transactions and mortifying adventures did the withdrawal of this salutary restraint entail on the party which then so loudly congratulated themselves and the country that they were at length relieved from its odious repression! In the hurry of existence one is apt too generally to pass over the political history of the times in which we ourselves live. The two years that followed the Reform of the House of Commons are full of instruction, on which a young man would do well to ponder. It is hardly possible that he could rise from a study of these annals without a confirmed disgust for political intrigue; a dazzling practice, apt at first to fascinate youth, for it appeals at once to our invention and our courage, but one which really should only be the resource of the second-rate. Great minds must trust to great truths and great talents for their rise, and nothing else.[50]

The sententious tone could not be further from Trollope; nor could the 'alternative history' of the 1830s that follows this passage, in which names are named and fingers pointed. Here and elsewhere, Disraeli's tendency in his political novels to oscillate between ponderous journalism and jejune theory obscures the intended effect. This is all the more transparent because the issues pinpointed by Disraeli (writing in, and of, the 1840s) had to do with exactly the kind of social upheaval and class warfare which the denizens of Trollope's political salons twenty years later felt they could safely ignore. And the accusation of 'conjuror' is all the more apposite, since the driving idea behind Disraeli's trilogy was to conjure a change of spirit without an alteration in political practice.

'Do you think, then, there is a wild desire for extensive political change in the country?'

'Hardly that: England is perplexed at the present moment, not inventive. That will be the next phasis in her moral state, and to that I wish to draw your thoughts. For myself, while I ascribe little influence to physical causes for the production of this perplexity, I am still less of the opinion that it can be removed by any new disposition of political power. It would only aggravate the evil. That would be recurring to the old error of supposing you can necessarily find national content in political institutions. A political institution is a machine; the motive power is the national character. With that it rests whether the machine will benefit society, or destroy it. Society in this country is perplexed, almost paralysed; in time it will move, and it will devise. How are the elements of the nation to be again blended together? In what spirit is that reorganization to take place?'[51]

Thus Sidonia to Coningsby. By the time of *Sybil*, a year later, the 'physical causes' of England's 'perplexity' were given more weight, though 'the condition of the people' was held to be 'the consequence . . . of the derivation and character of political parties' as explored in *Coningsby*. Both novels end rather weakly on an open question (as does *Contarini Fleming*): the aristocratic hero is delivered by a fortuitous inheritance to wealth, title and a symbolic marriage (to a daughter of Manufacture in one, and of Chartism in the other). He stands on the edge of public life; what will he do next?

In terms of formal structure, the answer is contained in the commercially unsuccessful *Tancred* (1847), which sets forth 'the duties of the Church as a main remedial agency, the most effectual means of the renovation of the national spirit'. This lays Disraeli open to the same accusation that can be levelled at Arnold Toynbee: faced with the impossible intellectual conundrum of how to end an open-ended story, he produced religion like a rabbit out of a hat (the conjuror again). But this is to forget the pedigree that lies behind the novels. Disraeli wrote them to Henry Hope's order, after being urged during a Young England weekend at Deepdene to 'treat in a literary form those views and subjects which were the matter of our frequent correspondence'. The development can be traced through occasional earlier writings like 'The Gospel of Youth', 'The Poor Law and the Tower of St Geneviève', 'The Principle of Reason and Utilitarianism versus Imagination', 'The Jew in History', 'The Doge Theory of Venetian Government in English History' and the 'Theory and Position of the Anglican Church'. The personnel of Young England appear in *Coningsby* as well as their ideas (Lord John Manners as Lord Henry Sydney, Baillie-Cochrane as Buckhurst, Ambrose Philips as Eustace Lyle, George Smythe as Coningsby himself). Harvie makes the point that Disraeli's 'real hero was the author as character, taking his dolls out of their box and setting them up on the stage';[52] and, lurid as the high-society detail is, the actors and their ideas are firmly grounded in what Disraeli and his friends were trying to do at the time. The free introduction of living personages added to the effect (and the caricature of J.W. Croker as Rigby added to the fun).

This element of actuality forms a vein of resilient matter among the tinsel: the world of political gossip, the back rooms of hangers-on and journalistic hacks, the undercover life of party organization have been epitomized in the many catch-phrases that descended from Disraeli's novels into political commentary at large. The definition of 'sound Conservative government' as 'Tory men and Whig measures'; Lord Liverpool as 'the Arch-Mediocrity'; Methodists as safe Tory voters; the Tamworth Manifesto as 'an attempt to construct a party without principles'; the very names of Tadpole and Taper – all these images and clichés descended into political discourse and history textbooks, and many of them lodged there.[53] If its *roman à clef* aspect helped

Coningsby sell three editions in three months,[54] its political generalizations ensured it another kind of longevity. Similarly, *Sybil* gave currency to phrases like 'the two nations' (whether or not it originated them[55]), and a number of baroque set-pieces ranging from Victoria's coronation to Dandy Mick's initiation into a trade union.[56] More importantly, the language of Disraeli's political novels, and to a lesser extent their ideas, recurred in the New Social Movement of 1871, and more directly provided the Tory Democracy of the 1880s with its rhetoric. J.E. Gorst, Sir Henry Drummond Wolff and Lord Randolph Churchill, as the rebellious Fourth Party within the Conservative ranks, eulogized Disraeli after his death with a fervour they had been very far from feeling when he was alive. Much of Young England's fancy-dress was unpacked for their onslaught on the provincial constituencies in 1883–4, and rediscovered by Churchill during his wilderness years after 1886. (By then, however, he had inimitably vulgarized it by references to the English aristocrat and workman being united against the middle classes by their 'common bond of sport and immorality'.)

In more serious mode, the word 'Venetian' used to designate 'Whig' was a staple Fourth Party catchword; and when Churchill, in the article entitled 'Elijah's Mantle' written against his leaders, referred to 'the old men who croon over the fires at the Carlton', he was lifting a phrase and an image from *Coningsby*.[57] He was also quoting *Endymion* (1880) when on another occasion he declared that there was 'no gambling like politics'. In 1883 the rubric of the Primrose League declared its intention to represent 'the alliance between the noble and the worker foreshadowed forty years ago in *Coningsby* and *Sybil*'. It was perhaps fortunate for Disraeli that he was no longer alive to be appealed to; such ideas had faded with accession to office, and from the mid-sixties he (like most other politicians) had been preoccupied instead with an attempt to become Palmerston *redivivus*,[58] while the reality of the Conservative Party's suburbanization put paid to Tory Democracy's rhetoric of class reconciliation. But the notions expounded in Disraeli's political novels, as well as the novels themselves, have been exhumed whenever the Conservative Party has enjoyed one of its periodic fits of reassessment, or when a moderate backlash within the party has been occasioned by the articulation of survival-of-the-fittest doctrines from the far right. This has happened in the early 1900s, the 1920s, and the 1980s.

In further ways also Disraeli's political novels set up resonances for the future: just as the creator of brilliant youths storming their way to the summit himself became Prime Minister of England, the events and images of the novels were oddly predictive. The great Jewish banking family helping the rulers of nations with swiftly arranged loans (the Neuchatels in *Endymion*) followed the reality of the Rothschilds and Suez; but the suggestion in *Tancred* of making the ruler of England Emperor of India long antedated the fact. (In the novel Disraeli wanted the entire court transferred there as well.) Finally, he withdrew to the House of Lords bearing the title which he had invented for a character in *Vivian Grey* over fifty years before. Trollope's novels mirrored political life through his own oblique prism; but elements of Disraeli's life oddly imitated his fictions, which is why, for all their tractarian intentions, their chief interest is for students of the author rather than of his times.

IV

If an imagined politics, mixed with an idiosyncratic political history, makes up the world of Disraeli's political novels, and that of the insider coterie is accurately reflected in Trollope's, at least two 'sports' should be considered in contrast: novels which dealt with the politics of Trollope's age from the vantage of outsider. Being written by two of the major Victorians, they are inevitably discussed in any commentary on the political novel; but they are rarely placed with the care they deserve. Both George Eliot's *Felix Holt* and George Meredith's *Beauchamp's Career* are concerned with the English political world at local level; both show a hero whose beliefs and instincts are 'Radical', who finds the formulae of 'Radicalism' somehow lacking, who stands on the edge of formal political involvement, and who eventually opts for the less easy answer of raising the level of popular political consciousness by other means. Much of the interest of both novels lies in their provenance: they are political testaments by authors who were committed to Liberalism while believing that utilitarian creeds and visionary solutions were ill adapted to the organic processes of English society. The fact that both novels have been critically underrated in literary terms is an added reason for studying them (though not, for present purposes, a primary one).

Felix Holt confronts the question of 'engineered' political change from the vantage of 1866, and projects its ideas back to the years immediately following the first Reform Bill: Disraeli's period, from a very different angle. From the beginning (indeed, from the subtitle, *The Radical*), two kinds of radical politician are juxtaposed: the opportunist, Harold Transome, who sees that identification as the coming vogue, and the idealist, Felix Holt, for whom a 'Radical' critique and commitment mean the necessity to avoid seduction by upward social mobility, and to use his brains and education to tell unpleasant truths to his own class. Transome may be a deliberate parody of a Disraelian hero: in his *A Year at Hartlebury* (1824) Aubrey Bohun, like Transome, returns from the Levant to contest a borough as a Radical. But George Eliot reverses the structure of the Disraelian political novels, where a legacy elevates a hero towards conquering new worlds, from an accepted and lofty position in society; for Felix's determination to cling to his roots is echoed by Esther Lyon's decision to renounce her inheritance of sterile, deadlocked Transome Court.

Much of the counterpointing between the two worlds is undeniably clumsy; critical hypothesis sees the political theme as a later imposition upon the more coherent Transome plot. But themes of corruption, decay and stasis unite the aristocratic world and that of electoral manipulation of the new franchise, which is the novel's political preoccupation. The emphasis is on a world of deferential and social politics at local level, and the continuation of this syndrome despite legislative change: a subject which waited until a hundred years after *Felix Holt* before finding full exposition in the works of historians.[59] This state of affairs could not be ended by abstract revolutionary theory (what Eliot elsewhere called 'the miserable fallacy . . . that the working classes are in a condition to enter at once into a millennial state of *altruism*, wherein everyone is caring for everyone else and no one for himself'[60]); nor by aristocratic poseurs (Aubrey Bohun or Disraeli himself no less than Harold Transome). Her peculiar definition of 'Radical', as well as her apprehension of the ambivalences of intention whereby many landlords 'of old family and large estate voted for the [Reform] Bill',[61] led to critical misunderstanding of the book by contemporaries and later commentators; Felix may justly be called as much a Tory as a Radical in his implicit attitudes, but the novel is no less 'political' for that, and no less realistic. The comment in the author's introduction that in 1831 'there were pocket boroughs, a Birmingham unrepresented in Parliament . . . and other departed evils' is obviously ironic; much that follows clearly demonstrates Eliot's knowledge that effective pocket boroughs lasted on, and that Birmingham's exiguous representation since 1832 had meant very little change.

The point has been made that Eliot, while no less distrustful of political programmes than Trollope, yet confronts the problems of collective social identities and change in a way which Trollope evaded.[62] This is both to ignore the pervasiveness of political forms in Trollope's novels and to mistake his pessimism for superficiality; but it is important to establish Eliot's ambivalent positivism and her belief in the elevation of 'public opinion' as the necessary basis of any desirable political change. That her novels were written to make ideas 'incarnate' need not, here or elsewhere, imply a duty to 'suggest practical solutions to North Loamshire's political problems'.[63] For the historian, what matters in *Felix Holt* is the extraordinarily well-defined social and historical context within which political activity is both realized and constrained: from the celebrated author's introduction (a super-realist journey through changing rural England), through the slow build-up of forces behind the North Loamshire election, to the ultimate denouement in the riot on polling day. The arguments by which Harold Transome convinces his uncle, a Tory parson, that Peel and Wellington have made it incumbent upon gentlemen of spirit to become Radicals, provide more resonant demonstration of the political traumas attendant upon 1832 than anything in *Coningsby*.[64] The interaction of politics, religion and industrialization in Treby Magna, whereby the Catholic Emancipation crisis reverberates in a particularly idiosyncratic way, traces out the background to the conflicts which provide the theme of the novel.

> Thus Treby Magna, which had lived quietly through the great earthquakes of the French Revolution and the Napoleonic wars, which had remained unmoved by the *Rights of Man*, and saw little in Mr Cobbett's *Weekly Register* except that he held eccentric views about potatoes, began at last to know the higher pains of a dim political consciousness; and the development had been greatly helped by the recent agitation about the Reform Bill. Tory, Whig, and Radical did not perhaps become clearer in their definition of each other; but the names seemed to acquire so strong a stamp of honour or infamy, that definitions would only have weakened the impression. As to

the short and easy method of judging opinions by the personal character of those who held them, it was liable to be much frustrated in Treby. It so happened in that particular town that the Reformers were not all of them large-hearted patriots or ardent lovers of justice; indeed, one of them, in the very midst of the agitation, was detected in using unequal scales – a fact to which many Tories pointed with disgust as showing plainly enough, without further argument, that the cry for a change in the representative system was hollow trickery. Again, the Tories were far from being all oppressors, disposed to grind down the working classes into serfdom; and it was undeniable that the inspector at the tape manufactory, who spoke with much eloquence on the extension of the suffrage, was a more tyrannical personage than open-handed Mr Wace, whose chief political tenet was, that it was all nonsense giving men votes when they had no stake in the country.[65]

Beneath the ironies, Eliot provides, as did Disraeli, an alternative political history of her times, as a background to the desire of her hero to proselytize on behalf of a new sense of politics. Felix early on determines that 'till they [the colliers] can show there's something they love better than swilling themselves with ale, extension of the suffrage can never mean anything for them but extension of boozing. One must begin somewhere; I'll begin at what is under my nose.'[66] Alcohol remains the motif of political consciousness-raising, however; and the tension between Felix's abrasive message to the miners and the emollience with which the established Radical election agent offers treating at the polls is repeated in the exchange when Harold Transome comes canvassing for Rufus Lyon's influence:

'It is rather too much for any man to keep the consciences of all his party,' said Harold. 'If you had lived in the East, as I have, you would be more tolerant. More tolerant, for example, of an active, industrious selfishness, such as we have here, though it may not always be quite scrupulous: you would see how much better it is than an idle selfishness. I have heard it said, a bridge is a good thing – worth helping to make, though half the men who worked at it were rogues.'

'O yes!' said Felix, scornfully, 'give me a handful of generalities and analogies, and I'll undertake to justify Burke and Hare, and prove them benefactors of their species.'[67]

Such an exchange about means and ends in politics prefigures much in *Daniel Deronda*, as well as the recurrent refrain in Trollope. Its resolution in *Felix Holt*, however, amounts to a repudiation of the collusive parliamentary game, especially as played by those whose opportunism ignores the determining power of wider social realities (expressed, as so often with Eliot, in the logic of historical continuity[68]). Elsewhere, Felix states that 'making one's way' in politics and society, and ambition itself, cannot but be corrupting.[69] Eliot gave him two great 'addresses' (one within the action of the novel, when he contradicts the Chartist on nomination day, and another published as an addendum in *Blackwood's Magazine* of January 1868[70]): both present her own ideas about the importance of 'knowledge' before mechanistic political amelioration, and the danger of 'justifiable resistance', if unchecked, becoming 'damaging convulsion'. In this, and in a searching exploration of the multiple and anomalous identifications which make up a 'class interest', the view of English political life portrayed through the action of the novel is given theoretical exposition.

A similar ambivalence and an equal ability to integrate action and theory distinguish Meredith's *Beauchamp's Career* (1874). It is an oddly neglected novel, perhaps because Meredith remains (like Swinburne) one of the few great Victorians still treated as a period piece. This early novel epitomizes the bravura qualities which later burst out in the sustained brilliance of *The Egoist*; but the problems addressed in *Beauchamp's Career* were those observed by Meredith during his friend Frederick Maxse's Radical candidature for Southampton, and it illuminates the politics of a whole locality, not the balletic manoeuvres within a single country house. Beauchamp is, on the surface of things, no Felix. In Meredith's novel of feminist politics, *Diana of the Crossways* (1885), he created a heroine doubly an outsider: changing Lady Caroline Norton, by a Trollopian quirk, into the Irish Diana Merion. But Beauchamp comes from the inside: a brilliant youth, born to an aristocratic tradition, full of wild ambitions and half-baked notions. However, he shares Felix's thorny idealism and dislike of expediency, as well as his Radicalism – in Beauchamp's case thrown as a gauntlet against his feudal family and county neighbours. Aversion to political cant is also a theme which recurs throughout: Beauchamp's early inspiration is Carlyle, and his political mentor, Dr Shrapnel, speaks in Carlylese. This is applied, however, to what is defined as 'the politics of impatience', which become the politics of egoism.

> [Dr Shrapnel] is the earnest man, and flies at politics as uneasy young brains fly to literature, fancying they can write because they can write with a pen. He perceives a bad adjustment of things; which is correct. He is honest, and takes his honesty for a virtue: and that entitles him to believe in himself: and that belief causes him to see in all opposition to him the wrong he has perceived in existing circumstances: and so in a dream of power he invokes the people: and as they do not stir, he takes to prophecy. This is the round of the politics of impatience. The study of politics should be guided by some light of statesmanship, otherwise it comes to this wild preaching. These men are theory-tailors, not politicians.[71]

What Beauchamp, thus inspired, throws himself against is 'his indifferent England' as well as his peers: the theme of the novel concerns the percussion of conflicts, both hilarious and pathetic, set off by his impetuous commitment. Romfrey, Beauchamp's uncle, epitomizes a feudalist English history as Disraeli might have conceived it; but the mockery of Meredith's treatment is more reminiscent of Trollope's Anglo-Saxonist Miss Thorne of Ullathorne. Here, as in the other novels under consideration, a view of English history itself plays the part of actor, and the political novelist uses conceptions of past history to highlight present conflicts. Towards the end Beauchamp suddenly marries the Radical doctor's niece, in a union as symbolic as that of Coningsby or Egremont. But the best that he can do in the practical world is to enforce upon his medievalist uncle a humiliating apology to the unspeakable Dr Shrapnel – which is, ironically, seen as Beauchamp's great achievement. And his only one: he meets a quixotic death by water at the end, while saving a floundering urchin. In an extraordinarily resonant finale, Beauchamp's uncle and Dr Shrapnel are left blankly staring at each other, thinking, '"This is what we have in exchange for Beauchamp!" . . . after they had examined the insignificant bit of mudbank life remaining in this world in the place of him.'

This chillingly offhand conclusion may imply a certain elitist valuation of brilliant individual qualities over and above the common ruck: the people, to whom Beauchamp literally as well as metaphorically gives his life, seem curiously unworthy of it, even though his legacy is the fortuitous reconciliation of enemies. The events of his public life have been equally unpromising throughout. A corrupt borough is ringingly contested from an ultra-Radical platform, and rejects him – a contest reflected and described through hilariously convoluted conversations, alternately baroque and slangy, on the circuit of county dinner-tables. Journalism is embraced, with the intention of founding a Radical newspaper called the *Dawn*, which ignominiously splutters out. What is left on the credit side is Beauchamp's manic charm, his utter unconcern about making a fool of himself, his unabashed energy, and his small success in liberalizing the opinions of the aristocratic girl he was to have married, if not those of his uncle.[72] Towards the end, a more limited and practical vision is beginning to suggest itself to him, through his sceptical and intelligently conventional wife (the novel's feminist bias is subtle but pervasive).[73]

It is a strangely oblique story, full of fudged encounters and missed opportunities. Through the novel, political discourse is conducted in Meredith's inimitably idiomatic conversations, often cast in the form of paradoxical transmission of information to the prejudiced or uninitiated. Politics come filtered through levels of preconception.[74] Meredith probably began work on the book shortly after Maxse's defeat in 1868, though it did not commence publication until 1874; and, like *Felix Holt*, the ambivalences and uncertainties in the novel reflect the adaptation of ancient political formalities to comparatively sudden change.

Mr Tuckham was at that moment prophesying the Torification of mankind; not as the trembling venturesome idea which we cast in doubtful winds, but as a ship is launched to ride the waters, with huzzas for a thing accomplished. Mr Austin raised his shoulders imperceptibly, saying to Miss Halkett: 'The turn will come to us as to others – and go. Nothing earthly can escape *that* revolution. We have to meet it with a policy, and let it pass with measures carried and our hands washed of some of our party sins. I am, I hope, true to my party, but the enthusiasm of party I do not share. He is right, however, when he accuses the nation of cowardice for the last ten years. One third of the Liberals have been with us at heart, and dared not speak, and we dared not say what we wished. We accepted a compact that satisfied us both – satisfied *us* better than when we were opposed by Whigs – that is, the Liberal reigned, and we governed: and, I should add, a very clever juggler was our common chief. Now we have the consequences of hollow peacemaking, in a suffrage that bids fair to extend to the wearing of hats and boots for a qualification. The moral of it seems to be that cowardice is even worse for nations than for individual men, though the consequences come on us more slowly.'[75]

Austin's is the voice of liberal Toryism, presented respectfully, if not always sympathetically, by the author: the Trollopian tone of regret for the days of Lord Brock should be noted. Beauchamp's contradictions are indicated as mockingly by Meredith as by his insufferable cousin Cecil. But at the same time his conception of moral politics is vital: '"Socially and politically mean one thing in the end," said Beauchamp. "If you have a nation politically corrupt you won't have a good state of morals in it, and the laws that keep society together bear upon the politics of the country."' Felix Holt would have put it no differently. Meredith himself described the novel as 'an attempt to show the forces round a young man of the present day in England, who would move them and finds them unutterably solid, though it is seen at the end that he does not altogether fail, he has not quite lived in vain . . . A certain drama of self-conquest is gone through, for the hero is not perfect.'[76] The point is that the effort has been made, and that it should be seen to have been made.

V

Thus *Felix Holt* and *Beauchamp's Career* indicate an awkwardness arising in political questions by 1880: the contradictions which to an inquiring mind could no longer be dealt with either by Disraelian glosses or by Trollope's existentialist scepticism. By the early 1880s it was being robustly observed by Conservative authorities that 'no man professes Conservatism who has not got something to lose' and that 'the great political struggle of our century is the struggle between property, be its amount small or great, and more numbers'.[77] This was an open admission which would disrupt Trollope's world of easy collusion, as well as making the nostrums of Disraeli's trilogy even more fanciful than when he had written them. The silver forks continued to rattle in the fringe political novels like those of Justin McCarthy and W.F. Rae, which reproduced or caricatured many of the publicity politicians of the 1880s:[78] but more central to the genre were those works, equally third-rate in literary terms but more analytical on a political level, which attempted to confront the questions of democracy and class politics. (It is no coincidence that these are the very issues which were continually debated in the heavyweight journals at this time.) If the most notable political event of 1886 seemed to posterity (and historians) the defeat of Gladstone's first Home Rule Bill, to contemporaries it was the West End riots.

The response in fictional terms was notable; and propaganda for Tory Democracy could be delivered in novels by W.H. Mallock as well as in speeches by Randolph Churchill.[79] The novels of the eighties and just after tended to concentrate on politics outside the charmed circle at Westminster; to the heroes the dream of a seat in the House was no longer sufficient guarantee of influence to change the world. Mark Rutherford's *The Revolution in Tanner's Lane* (1887) confronted the question of a radical (even republican) tradition in British politics – and what had happened to it. But his curiously displaced characters do not look to Parliament for articulation of their problems, any more than the revolutionary Hyacinth does in James's *The Princess Casamassima* of the previous year.

Despite the new wave of political novels in unparliamentary language, the old formula was still adhered to by some politically minded novelists. One was Mrs Humphry Ward, which is predictable, considering her own obsessive interest in parliamentary debates and her immersion in high political society.[80] Her *Sir George Tressady* (1896) is often mawkish and stilted, but the theme is significant: the fortunes of a bill for the regulation of labour, drawn up by Lord Maxwell, a noble politician, and his socially conscious wife (as plaster a saint as any of Disraeli's heroines, having lost the ambiguity which made her a memorable heroine in *Marcella*).[81] The fortunes of the Maxwell Bill turn upon the decision of Sir George Tressady, a rising politician attached to a Fourth Party (Lord Randolph Churchill appears in the novel as the group's leader, Lord Fontenoy[82]). Tressady's devotion to Lady Maxwell, and growing doubts about the Social Darwinist values preached by Fontenoy, lead him to go against his party and support the bill; in fact, he adopts the line of behaviour seen by Trollope's Barrington Erle thirty years before as 'dangerous, revolutionary and almost unparliamentary'.[83] (Gladstone, interestingly, agreed, thus demonstrating his adherence to the values of an earlier age; he told Mrs Ward that Tressady's conduct was 'inconceivable in a man of honour'.[84]) Admittedly, there is much in the novel which repeats the traditional political novels: the 'humbug' of elections, the social manipulation of country-house politics, set-piece debates at Westminster, the conflict between 'emotion' and 'argument'. But conversations in the novel refer to Marx and Ibsen, and many of the political themes herald a new age. The ex-Tory mavericks under Fontenoy appear as a 'party of freedom', articulating Spencerian ideas against labour regulation: 'a new cleavage of parties was being everywhere brought about by the new Collectivism'.[85] The conditions of labour are researched by politicians with the help of sociologists. (Mrs Ward was herself aided by Beatrice Webb, who had served an apprenticeship under Booth.[86]) Lady Maxwell, like James's Princess Casamassima, takes a house away from the fashionable quarter to be among 'the people' – though her pilgrimage is to the East End, not Paddington, and her motives are genuinely lofty.

The bill which the Maxwells draw up is designed to restrict working hours and outlaw 'sweating'; the Sweated Trades and Labour Commission of 1890–92, and a diet of Blue Books, gave Mrs Ward her theme. But the fictional measure is noticeably moderate, and the gesture essentially Disraelian (the Maxwells are Tories). A Bismarckian system of state aid and national insurance has no part in the vision, much less any tincture of socialism. Parliament is still seen as the only appropriate forum for the introduction of this kind of reform: one great speech affects the lives of 'dim, toiling thousands' (though Tressady's relation with the miners on his own estate continue grim). The Maxwell Bill indeed prefigured some of the legislation of Asquith's government thirteen years later, but the anxious attempt to import the issues of class politics into the structure of traditional formalities remains unconvincing. The new politics could not be accommodated within the traditional framework. The morality of Parliament, Dickens's question of a generation before, was back on the agenda.

This is in a sense the message of a political novel which appeared fifteen years later, much disliked by Mrs Ward. 'Who, after a few years more, will ever want to turn to the restless, ill-written, undigested pages of *The New Machiavelli* again?'[87] Her dislike of H.G. Wells was tinged with an authentically Victorian distaste for the demotic ('Mr Wells seems to me a journalist of very great powers, of unequal education, and much crudity of mind, who has inadvertently strayed into the literature of imagination'[88]). And this is as it should be, for *The New Machiavelli*, intentionally vulgarian and often brilliantly funny, could never have been produced by the nineteenth century and in many ways deliberately set itself to negate Victorianism. For that reason, it cannot occupy much space here. But it should be pointed out that, besides the feminist windowdressing and the attack on the Fabian Society (particularly the Webbs) for which it is most often remembered, Wells's novel is a satirical portrait of those who try to import nineteenth-century shibboleths into a twentieth-century world: significantly, one of the figures most bitingly lampooned is the nostalgic historian G.M. Trevelyan, who appears as Edward Crampton, 'at work then upon the seventh volume of his monumental Life of Kosciusko'. Complacency about European liberalism 'on the English model' will no longer answer.

The opportunism of Remington, the narrator, is of a different order to that of Trollope's or Disraeli's young men; his repudiation of parties, 'decency' and eventually ideology is a sort of meteoric rake's progress in politics. At the end, he is undone by coming up against sexual hypocrisy, which comes to stand for Victorian political values as well.[89] This may seem rather a tired conjunction now, but was a really modern idea seven years before *Eminent Victorians*.

At the same time, the novel is a biography of its time. 'In my life,' begins Remington, 'I have paralleled very closely the slow realizations that are going on in the world about me.'[90] Wells provided a mocking monument to 'New Liberalism' and progressivist utopianism; by its very targets, the novel demonstrates the newness of the times. The politics are those of flux and experiment, in party lines as well as over women's suffrage and the 1909 Budget: 'a splendid disorder of forces' is everywhere evident. With Remington, humanitarianism, socialism, Liberalism and rejuvenated Toryism succeed each other and give way to his great platform of State Endowment for Motherhood, a bizarre blend of feminism and eugenics. However, it is an unprogrammed and untheoretical impulse that wrecks him in the end: his reflections are issued from exile in Italy after a politically disastrous elopement.

Contemporary readers of the novel took Remington's panacea too much at face value; what is striking about *The New Machiavelli*, in the context of the tradition of political novels, is its contemptuous dismissal of the formal political world. Remington's reaction to Westminster and its rituals is frustrated impatience; his picture of the House after the 1906 election, full of fuddled Liberals discussing 'what we shall do' and withal 'enormously taken up with moribund issues and old quarrels', is a judgement not upon the Liberal Party alone but on the system at large. The result of his determined exploration of other political groupings was a sensation that my political life didn't in some way comprehend more than itself, that rather perplexingly I was missing the thing I was seeking . . . my general conception in politics [now became] the conception of the constructive imagination working upon the vast complex of powerful people, clever people, enterprising people, influential people, amidst whom power is diffused today, to produce that self-conscious, highly selective, open-minded, devoted aristocratic culture which seems to me the necessary next phase in the development of human affairs.[91]

There are elements in this formula of the guiding preoccupations of Disraeli, Trollope, George Eliot, Meredith and even Mrs Humphry Ward; but Remington has to abandon the articulated world of the formal English political structure. Though he begins political life as a Liberal MP, and re-enters Parliament after starting his neo-Tory *Blue Weekly*, it is the world of manipulated publicity and intellectual elitism which provides his real milieu, and his anticipated achievement of office will utilize backing from both parties. He fulminates against the trivia and lack of ideas attendant upon parliamentary discourse; where Trollope's politicians reminisced affectionately about the days of Lord Brock, Remington jeers at pious acolytes, wanting to erect a plaque where Disraeli sat, and liable to murmur in pained tones, 'Mr Gladstone would not have done that.' Finally Remington destroys his career for love; but love has already been responsible for his breaking out of the old political forms. 'Instead of abstractions and blue-books and bills and devices, I had realized the world of mankind as a crowd needing before all things fine women and men. We'd spoilt ourselves in learning that, but anyhow we had our lesson. Before her I was in a nineteenth-century darkness . . .'[92] The reconciliation of public statecraft and private weakness is the Machiavellian theme that runs through the book; and the British way of life and politics – manipulation, compromise and mutually accepted limitations – is contemptuously rejected as no longer providing any of the answers. 'I feel so much that the best people in every party converge,' says Evesham (Balfour). 'We don't differ in Westminster as they do in the county towns. There's a sort of extending common policy that goes on under every government, because on the whole it's the right thing to do, and people know it. Things that used to be matters of opinion become matters of science – and cease to be party questions.'[93] But this Trollopian message is held up to ridicule, as a philosophy appropriate only to days gone by.

Wells's novel forecast (and looked forward to) a war with Germany; within four years of its publication this very eventuality, along with economic decline and the advent of class politics, changed the ground-rules of the British political world. How these changes have been reflected in twentieth-century fiction is another subject; but it is worth observing that political novels since then are a disparate collection, which will record for future historians the amorphous sense of twentieth-century politics. 'In the beginning of the twentieth century you could not see the ground for clever men,' wrote G.K. Chesterton in a futurist novel that is also a political allegory. 'They were so common that a stupid man was quite exceptional, and when they found him, they followed him in crowds down the street and treasured him up and gave him some high post in the state.'[94] The formal world of twentieth-century politics is represented with equal acidity in the novels of C.P. Snow, dominated by squabbling mandarins, or in Angus Wilson's metaphorical *The Old Men at the Zoo* (1961); it is recorded as a repository of rewards for the pompous and the unworthy in the work of Anthony Powell and Evelyn Waugh; more recently, it has been reflected as a kind of oblique and symbolic looking-glass world in the fiction of Nicholas Mosley.[95]

The classical development of the nineteenth-century political novel as *Bildungsroman* is long gone. In those romances young heroes – usually outsiders, sometimes Irish – took on the world through the massive, carefully articulated structure of Parliament and public activity, and learned the lessons of life in the process of improving society as well as extending their own prospects. By a surprising irony (or possibly a Hegelian illustration of Minerva's owl on belated flight), real-life politicians in the 1980s began complacently declaring their affection for Trollope's novels. Partly, this may have been inspired by an intention to show that they were really civilized consensus-people, unlike the simplistic right-wing Radicals in power: they, the Trollopians, had a realistic and humanistic comprehension of the political world as it 'really' operated, and they might be trusted to become Harold Macmillan *redivivus* – the Palmerston of his day. A similar intention may lie behind Michael Foot's vociferous but rather plaintive adoption of Disraeli as hero-figure. But the Victorian world and the system Trollope's novels reflected are still imperfectly understood by historians; and the exploration of nineteenth-century fiction must be conducted by them with a rigour and a commitment which is not simply content with embellishing discussions about elections by ritual references to Percycross and Eatanswill, or agonizing about minor inaccuracies in parliamentary *romans-à-clef*. A careful reading of nineteenth-century novels should be buttressed by analysis of their implicit internal assumptions, as well as the reasons why they were read. The examination of a political culture is in question, which involves an understanding of culture as well as an apprehension of politics. And this is, after all, exactly the combination of qualities represented by the work of the best nineteenth-century political novelists, but not often demonstrated since.

9

Paddy and Mr Punch

These days, representation of 'The Other' in art, fiction and journalism has become a fashionable preoccupation; as mentality becomes an accepted part of historical analysis, expressions of attitudes (subconscious as well as conscious) are seen not only as legitimate but as essential subjects for deconstruction. In the case of the representation of the Irish in Victorian Britain, this subject actually came into focus before the widespread influence of Foucault and his followers, at least in the English-speaking world. Partly, this had to do with the sensitivity of a marginalized element in British society towards being stereotyped as stupid, feckless and idle – a stereotyping that had been very prominent, and often noted, since the first colonial interactions between Britain and Ireland.

In the early 1960s it came under new analysis, particularly in America; this was probably related to the Kennedy ascendancy, and the revaluation of Irish stereotypes which that phenomenon necessitated. Principally, two books by Perry Curtis, *Anglo-Saxons and Celts* (1968) and *Apes and Angels: The Irishman in Victorian Caricature* (1971), began a long-running discussion. In Curtis's vigorous scheme, the image of the Irishman was 'simianized' by Victorian caricaturists, with a deliberate intent to portray him as subhuman, and therefore a candidate for oppression in the debased pseudo-Darwinian science of racial superiority. The argument fitted in well with new approaches to the psychology of colonialism, like those of Franz Fanon and, later, Ashis Nandy.[1] This conjunction happened just when the British army was moving into Northern Ireland; many wanted to learn more about what appeared to be a long-established historical habit of rationalizing British treatment of the Irish as an inferior race given to animal-like bursts of violence and amenable only to coercion.

There is much that is convincing and original in Curtis's argument, though, as I shall later indicate, it has a problematic side too. For our purposes, what is interesting is his indictment of one of the chief carriers of this racialist virus: *Punch*.

Punch began in 1841. Peel was coming into his great reforming ministry, Daniel O'Connell was apparently at his apotheosis in demotic Irish politics, and the Irish Famine was nearly five years in the future. None the less, Ireland had been a dominant issue in the politics of the last decade – from Catholic Emancipation to Church reform, from O'Connell's campaign for Repeal of the Union to the controversial endowment of the Catholic seminary at Maynooth. It was inevitable that the new satirical magazine would take up Irish subjects. And there were other reasons too. One of *Punch*'s founders, Joseph Sterling Coyne, was Irish; he did not last long, being considered unreliable and finally convicted of plagiarism; he lifted some material from a Dublin paper and was relentlessly hounded out by Mark Lemon. Half a century later, someone who had been an office-boy at *Punch* in those days reminisced to Marion Spielmann: 'With regard to the Stirling [*sic*] Coyne incident I was compelled to hear the conversation between Messrs Mark Lemon and Henry Mayhew . . . I cannot forget the contemptuous way in which Mr Lemon spoke of Mr *Paddy* Coyne and the emphasis he laid on the Paddy.'[2] Thus from the very beginning we may sense a tempestuous relationship between Paddy and Mr Punch.

But a far more influential *Punch* figure always retained a close interest in Ireland: Thackeray. Tragically married to an Irish wife, having many friends in Ireland, incessantly introducing Irish figures into his novels, Thackeray's commentary on Ireland is of profound interest. Analysis of it is usually restricted to his *Irish Sketch-Book* of 1843, a fascinating and ambiguous commentary on Irishness and English attitudes to it – especially to middle-class, lace-curtain Irishness. But there are also the Irish journalists of *Pendennis*, Mr Hoolan and Mr Doolan, and the Bohemian Irish milieu frequented by Captain Costigan and his friends. Thackeray reproduced here the kind of world that *Punch* sprang from. And, in a symbiotic way, he used the pages of *Punch* to follow through his ideas about Irishness. In his 'Book of Snobs', serialized in *Punch*, the Irish Snob has a section to himself;[3] it is horribly accurate, but ends affectionately with an injunction to the Irish to be realistic. In this, he strategically ignores the necessary psychological and historical pressures upon the Irish to be *unrealistic*; rather like that well-meaning traveller in Ireland, Mrs S.C. Hall. Touring Ireland around the same time as Thackeray, she sympathetically asked an inmate of Longford Workhouse why she had gone on poor relief. The courteous answer was: 'Sure I'd do anything within reason, ma'am, to please the gentry; *and so I came in here*.'

That could be a *Punch* cartoon, in its savage early days. Thackeray would have understood the irony of it; the *Irish Sketch-Book* records many such shafts. But his Irish commentary in the first years of the magazine tended to be more predictable. Here, for instance, we can find his parody of Charles Lever, which appeared as one of the *Punch* Prize Novels, '*Phil Fogarty, A Tale of the Fighting Onety-oneth*, by Harry Rollicker',[4] where jokes about Lady Morgan are mixed in with hilarious name-dropping about the Napoleonic court, and every Wild Geese cliché going. Here too there are countless stage-Irish stories, usually signed 'Fusbos';[5] Irish jokes based on misspellings and baroque misapprehensions; recurring characters (a favourite *Punch* mode in its early days), like 'Deaf Burke'.[6] All these are par for the contemporary course, along with stereotypes of the Scots and the French. And some of the stereotypes had a firm basis in fact; such as the violent 'Election of Ballinafad', which merely bears out the picture of Irish elections in the mid-nineteenth century given by Theo Hoppen, the great historical authority of the subject.[7] Other stereotypes harp on drink, over-ingenuity and bigotry. Much of this is fair comment, and a send-up of O'Connell's Irish Utopia, where all the stereotypes are piously reversed, is genuinely funny.[8] Moreover, for all its robust anti-Catholicism, *Punch* supported the Maynooth grant and made pointed fun of those who did not; it also satirized Orange demonstrations in Ulster with a free hand.[9] Nor were the Irish mentioned in early *Punch* only as stereotypical head-breaking peasant micks: a great butt was Lord Waterford, often ridiculed for arrogant and drunken behaviour,[10] and Lady Morgan's conversaziones were also fair game.[11] Another favourite Irish target was the Chartist leader Feargus O'Connor, but he was attacked for his politics and his delusions of grandeur, not for his Irishness.[12] The Irish presence in mid-nineteenth-century British life was an infinitely more complex, stratified and influential sector than is often realized; *Punch* gives a more varied representation of it than might be expected. In its early years, it could be anti-Irish; but no more obsessively than it was anti-medical students, or anti-politicians, or anti-income tax. Nor were its representations of the Irish very pronouncedly different in physiognomy from the representations of English plebeians.[13]

As Spielmann points out, the magazine could, in fact, be resolutely pro-Irish in its early years.[14] A famous cartoon shows Britannia indicating to Russia that her own treatment of Ireland gives her little moral ascendancy over the Czar in the matter of Poland: 'Brother, we are both in the wrong'.[15] When O'Connell's movement to repeal the Union between Ireland and Britain was attacked, it was often on the reasonable grounds that it was never fully defined, and changed its nature on demand[16] – a criticism recently repeated by O'Connellite historians.[17] O'Connell himself was something of a favourite character with *Punch* in its first years. His theatrical, self-parodying, larger-than-life elements were much appreciated; foxy, sometimes brusquely ironic, and nobody's fool, but with a heart of gold, O'Connell appears in the early volumes as a sort of Irish Mr Punch. His unmistakable appearance and his Old Testament name lent themselves to brilliant cartoons like 'A Daniel Come to Judgement'.[18] So did his notorious money difficulties,[19] though his sex life was left alone. There was enough else about O'Connell's reputation that was made for *Punch*'s satire: such as going off to prison in the Lord Mayor's coach, and living like a lord when he was there.[20] And even if Mr Punch could not countenance the O'Connellite programme in politics, he admitted that it could be bought off only by 'justice to Ireland'.[21]

This, however, was not to last. Partly, the change in *Punch*'s attitude from the mid-forties must be looked for in changes within the newspaper itself: what R.G.G. Price has called 'the shift from radicalism'.[22] Not that Douglas Jerrold's Radicalism was ever necessarily pro-Irish: but it certainly was anti-stereotypes. (This was sometimes so unexpected that it was misapprehended. An ironic attack on the *Morning Post*'s anti-Semitism, for instance, was too clever to be understood, and had to be laboriously explained in a subsequent issue.[23]) However, events in Ireland from this time conspired to change the Irish image, and *Punch*'s attitude. One was the polarization of Irish politics, with the rise of an extreme-nationalist wing which challenged O'Connell's supremacy: the so-called Young Ireland

A DANIEL—A DANIEL COME TO JUDGMENT!

movement. *Punch* first of all responded with some interest, addressing a serious and intelligent 'Appeal' to Thomas Davis, the leader of the movement;[24] the challenge to O'Connell was attractive material for cartoons like 'Family Jars at Conciliation Hall'. But as Young Ireland became more Anglophobic and irreconcilable (with good cause), *Punch* lost all patience. The open endorsement of violent tactics by the Young Ireland leaders was the final straw, leading to one of *Punch*'s first and most famous anti-Irish cartoons: 'Young Ireland in Business for Himself'.[25]

It is interesting to compare the depiction of the anonymous arms-dealers in this cartoon to the representation of O'Connell and Smith O'Brien in the earlier work. Here is the 'dangerous Irishman' later so familiar in *Punch*, more than a decade before *Origin of Species* and the debasement of Darwinian typology. The resort to force in pursuit of Irish rights was anathema to Jerrold; his brand of radicalism could excuse the English agricultural labourers as poor devils driven to rick-burning by Peel's harshness, but had little patience with an Irish populace force-fed reform policies by successive British administrations, and still unreasonably demanding more. The other circumstance impelling this attitude was, of course, large-scale Irish immigration – always a cause for worry. If the Irish were so resolutely anti-Union, asked *Punch* complacently, why did they come here in droves?[26] (Economic realities were never the magazine's strong suit.) From the early forties there had been squibs about 'Irish tranquillity' in urban slum areas like St Giles, and police apathy about it. From 1845, with an avalanche of starving Irish emigrants landing up in British cities, the attitude hardened.

For the reason behind this was the same as the cause of Young Ireland's desperate espousal of extreme tactics: the Great Famine. *Punch* was conscious of this from an early stage. The preface to vol. 9 (July–December 1845) struck a sombre note: 'The New Year has a dejected look: for he hears the voices of millions bewailing the potato blight.' Two years later, the 'Political Summary' for 1847 grimly recounted Irish Famine conditions. Early on, there is radical criticism of the government's do-nothing line; a first-rate satire of a Privy Council meeting has the Councillors defining hunger as 'a vulgar habit – a wretched prejudice of the common people. Nothing more.'[27] However, the attitude towards Irish expectations of relief on a special and unprecedented scale were seen as essentially unrealistic; the epithet

YOUNG IRELAND IN BUSINESS FOR HIMSELF.

of 'spongers' is often disturbingly implicit in squibs about the fortunate Irish, being let off the income tax.[28] And the Famine changed *Punch*'s line on O'Connell. If British money was needed to bale out stricken Ireland, argued *Punch*, surely this exploded the delusion of repealing the Union?[29] Thus the fact that O'Connell continued to collect Repeal rent for his political campaigns was mercilessly emphasized: his idea of 'relieving his country', Mr Punch remarked, was relieving it of £22,000 per annum. In a moment of seriousness, Mr Punch addressed O'Connell and begged him to desist: 'My brazen old brother buffoon'.[30] The final disenchantment of *Punch* with O'Connell is preserved in one terrible cartoon: 'The Real Potato Blight'.[31]

Through 1846, this dual approach to the Irish crisis continued: attacking O'Connell through the administration of his own estate at Derrynane[32] on the one hand, offering serious recipes for 'how to cure Ireland' on the other. Steel, lead, forcible restraint and hemp were not prescribed; a liberal diet, three meals a day, and the application of a tough Poor Rate to absentee landlords were advocated instead.[33] 'The sufferings of Irish landlords' was taken as a matter for parody,[34] and a bitter ballad contrasted deaths from starvation at Clonmel and the record weights of prize cattle at the Dublin Show. The title was a classically mordant *Punch* pun: 'The Land of Bulls'.[35]

At the same time, political extremism in Ireland was waiting to make its play, and as the rhetoric of Young Ireland became more frenetic, *Punch* portrayed the movement as congenitally impossible to please, biting the hand that fed it, and vitriolically parodied Smith O'Brien's variety of patriotic rhetoric.[36] Ingratitude rather than starvation became the leading characteristic of the Irish represented in the magazine: 'slander cast back in requital for food'.[37] The Irish emblem should be the hyena, Mark Lemon decided, whom 'kindness cannot conciliate, nor hunger tame'.[38] It may or may not be surprising that the cartoonist whose work drove this message home, John Leech, was Irish on his father's side; at a later date R.J. Hamerton, one of the most brutal traducers of Irish apishness, was Irish too. Many of the most influential *Punch* commentators were marginalized from the mainstream of Englishness, in one way or another, which may have made them define the concept all the more emphatically; it seems that some of the transplanted Irish entered into this process of psychological compensation with an almost unholy gusto.

Thus *Punch*'s sympathy for the starving diminished in proportion as

THE REAL POTATO BLIGHT OF IRELAND.

(FROM A SKETCH TAKEN IN CONCILIATION HALL.)

Irish public opinion demonstrated support for the extreme line taken by Young Ireland. The climax of this came in another scorching lead cartoon: 'The Height of Impudence'. Here, a beggar approaches John Bull: 'Spare a thrifle, yer Honour, for a poor Irish lad to buy a bit of . . . a Blunderbuss with.' 'Grateful Paddy' apparently preferred to buy guns rather than bread, and therefore forfeited any sympathy that Mr Punch might have left.[39] By early 1848 open scepticism about Irish suffering was expressed in *Punch*. Soyer's soup kitchens were considered a legitimate subject for mirth; and the grand discovery was announced, of Ireland's real disorder: the Irish were all mad, and the obvious cure for their distress was wholesale incarceration in the new lunatic asylums.[40] Other remedies suggested included enforced emigration on a national scale, unconsciously raising echoes of ideas which had actually been played with in all seriousness by Elizabethan colonizers.[41] Meanwhile, *Punch* rather forlornly regretted the simplicities of a decade before, and called for more Irish Bulls and a return to jolly, joking Paddy. 'The only humour which Ireland has evinced of late has been dreadfully sour.'[42]

The climax of these tasteless jokes, in *Punch*'s eyes, was the so-called 'cabbage patch rebellion' of 1848, which gave cartoonists and satirists another heaven-sent opportunity for Irish ridicule. From now on, Ireland was presented in the classic colonial paradigm: an idealized family.

> Ireland strikes us as being the Prodigal Son of England, always going astray, then coming back, repenting and being forgiven. JOHN BULL may occasionally have been a harsh parent, but we are sure the old fellow means well. It is too bad to see father and son at daggers drawn in this way. When will Ireland be a good boy, and learn to remain quiet at home?[43]

All the clichés are summoned up for a cartoon of 1848, showing Lord John Russell, 'Alfred the Small', visiting the Irish camp.[44] Liberal policies like a £50,000 grant-in-aid for relieving Famine distress were attacked as subsidizing lazy Irish peasants rather than deserving English agricultural labourers.[45] Even Father Mathew's Temperance Crusade was contemptuously mocked, for all *Punch*'s own exhortations to the Irish to sober up. Educative injunctions were still made; the Queen's visit in 1849 was covered in great detail, and provoked a serious plea: 'Let Erin Forget' (a play on Thomas Moore's popular drawing-room ballad, 'Let Erin Remember'). What was

THE ENGLISH LABOURER'S BURDEN;

OR, THE IRISH OLD MAN OF THE MOUNTAIN.

needed, according to *Punch*, was a non-historical, problem-solving, modern-minded approach; suggestions included industrialization, urbanization, alternative energy sources like windmills, all encapsulated in a rather Heath Robinsonish cartoon about the possibilities of peat-derived power.[46] How seriously this was really embraced is another matter. When an Irish sugar-beet industry was mooted in 1852, *Punch*'s reaction was a revealing sketch about race and commerce:

The lazy West Indian Negro – the contented pumpkin-consumer, hateful to gods and Thomas Carlyle – will, in his sluggard slumbers, be tortured with the nightmare. Paddy, twenty times increased with beetroot, magnified to the mast of 'some tall amminal', dancing upon the blackamoor's sooty breast, and calling upon him to get up, and bring out his cane, and meet him with it in open market, like a man. Why, beetroot shall be to Ireland the root of all goodness. Sweets found in Ireland! Think of that, contemplative men, who tread the wharf of Liverpool – the quay of Bristol – and see vomited from hundreds of ships, to crawl like wingless vermin over the country, tens of thousands of Irish: the sons and daughters of beggary; the blight of their own land, and the curse of the Saxon.[47]

All in all, by 1850, when the preface to vol. 18 recorded a visit to Mr Punch from 'Respectability', the magazine's views on Ireland were 'respectable' beyond reproach.

In the ensuing decade, the so-called papal aggression brought on a bilious attack of anti-Catholicism among the respectable. Triumphant papal apes and dishonest Irish bishops conspire in *Punch*'s lead cartoons, and 'the last Irish grievance' is represented as the need to overcome bigotry and bring in non-denominational educational reform.[48] 'Remedies for Ireland' still abound; and Ireland is yet again portrayed as an irrational child, 'peevish, fractious, squalling, shrieking, teething'. The remedy, according to *Punch*, is the measles – as England had three hundred years before. Decoded, the message is Froudian (James Anthony, not Sigmund). Give Ireland the bacteria of Repeal, Rome Rule and wholesale Protestant emigration. A few years of fevered Romish tyranny would bring about the desired reaction: a Protestant Reformation, and a subsequent age of civilization.[49]

Not that the Irish abroad showed many signs of successful inoculation, in *Punch*'s terms. By the second half of the nineteenth century, the Irish in Britain were an established butt: a sarcastic note in 1852 wondered if they were losing their nationality, as they were evidently

THE NEW IRISH STILL.

SHOWING HOW ALL SORTS OF GOOD THINGS MAY BE OBTAINED (BY INDUSTRY) OUT OF PEAT.

becoming as frugal and provident as the Scots. But on examination, this was because the men were saving their wages by dint of sending their wives out to beg.[50] A significant satire, 'The Vision of St Patrick', inveighed against Irish idleness and superstition, and their refusal to move from dirt and degradation.[51] Those British people who became pro-Irish fared no better; a favourite target for withering satire was Frederick Lucas, founder of the *Tablet*, Catholic convert, and devotee of all things Irish. Lucas's claims that the Irish were discriminated against or unfairly stereotyped were savagely lampooned in *Punch*.[52] And though the 'loyal Irish' – invariably portrayed as firm-jawed and sturdy – could still be appealed to as special constables in the fight against Fenianism from the 1860s,[53] by that stage the image of the disloyal Irish had been fixed. Given *Punch*'s eye for a current debate, and its brilliance at conflating two news stories into a memorable image, it was perhaps inevitable that the Irish Other should quickly appear in a chilling neo-Darwinian mode:

> A creature manifestly between the Gorilla and the Negro is to be met with in some of the lowest districts of London and Liverpool by adventurous explorers. It comes from Ireland, whence it has contrived to migrate; it belongs in fact to a tribe of Irish savages; the lowest species of the Irish Yahoo. When conversing with its kind it talks a sort of gibberish. It is, moreover, a climbing animal, and may sometimes be seen ascending a ladder with a hod of bricks. The Irish Yahoo generally confines itself within the limits of its own colony, except when it goes out of them to get its living. Sometimes, however, it sallies forth in states of excitement, and attacks civilized human beings that have provoked its fury.
>
> The somewhat superior ability of the Irish Yahoo to utter articulate sounds, may suffice to prove that it is a development, and not, as some imagine, a degeneration of the Gorilla.[54]

In the ensuing years, the magazine's contempt for Irish extremism remained evident whenever the revolutionary secret society of Fenianism was in the news, though Gladstone's efforts at Irish legislation in his mid-career were sometimes sympathetically noted. However, the next period of particular interest is another era of high drama where Ireland is concerned: the polarization of politics and society that began with the Irish land crisis of 1879–81, and subsequently saw the establishment of Charles Stewart Parnell, the icy, aristocratic leader of the Irish nationalists at Westminster, as the arbiter of party politics in the House of Commons.

Fenianism had given full rein to the image of the bestial and violent Irishman; Parnell in a sense was the obverse of this, being classically handsome and dignified, and impeccably descended from Anglo-Irish gentlefolk and a celebrated American family. Even when represented in traditional Paddy attire of billycock hat, breeches and pistol, *Punch* cartoonists still gave him noble (if rather wild-eyed) good looks; they were also capable of presenting him as a Jekyll-and-Hyde figure, or as a Frankenstein who created, but could not control, the ape-like monster of Fenianism and the Land League. However, there was another tradition of representing Parnell and his followers, also found in *Punch*; it did not rely on visual effects, but was no less influential for that. This was the political diary kept by Henry Lucy under the sobriquet of 'Toby, MP'.

Lucy was a star political columnist, who had taken over and transformed the old 'Essence of Politics' series. Present-day commentators like Alan Watkins and Edward Pearce owe much to him; he originated the faintly weary, intimate, offhand tone which they have perpetuated, and like them, he often presented Westminster as a schoolroom of unruly boys, with a schoolroom's feuds, alliances and strategies for fighting off boredom. Lucy's columns often idiosyncratically devoted more space to a completely incidental exchange in the smoking-room, or a fully elaborated fantasy about how a certain MP spent his leisure hours, than to a debate on an actual political issue. Like all school stories, his object was to make readers believe they understood the arcana of an elite world. In the process, he made reputations and created stereotypes, which their owners later obligingly tried to resemble. One notable example was Lord Hartington, another Lord Randolph Churchill; Lucy's impressionistic pen-portraits, illustrated by Harry Furniss and leading into the great mock-heroic compositions of Linley Sambourne and Tenniel, created their images indelibly for their contemporaries, and for posterity.[55] And the same was true for the generation of Irish politicians who made up Parnell's legendary party: tightly disciplined footsoldiers, led by a dictator, whose oratorical abilities and unbreakable nerve could enable them to filibuster out an entire session and reduce the proprieties of the House to a nullity. Lucy helped construct the reputations of politicians like Joe Biggar, the hunchbacked Belfast pork-butcher, who developed the obstruction technique; his account of a holiday Biggar spent in France, gravely iterated as told through Biggar's Belfast accent, is farce of a very high order.[56] He also immortalized one Philip Callan, a shifty and bellicose drunkard forgotten by contemporaries, but seen by Gladstone (probably through Lucy's eyes) as the only Parnellite of talent.[57] In 1893 Furniss's ruthless caricature of another forgotten Irishman, J.G. Swift MacNeill, provoked his subject to mount a 'technical assault' on the person of the artist as he was sketching in the lobby of the House.

Most of all, Lucy polished up the portrait of Parnell: the brooding, inscrutable, magnetic dictator, whose habitual composure was a mask for raging neurosis, and who conjured up demons only to icily disassociate himself from the results.[58] Accompanying cartoons pressed the message home. *Punch* did more in the 1880s to establish the accepted picture of the Parnellite ascendancy than contemporaries realized at the time, or historians realize now.

The conditions of the 1880s also gave free rein to traditional *Punch* themes for Irish behaviour: all the old clichés about the Kilkenny Cats or the Donnybrook Fair.[59] The very idea of the parliamentary device of 'Obstruction' was ready-made for cartoons of Irish life, especially when represented by actual figures like the duelling octogenarian Major O'Gorman Mahon, who might have been invented by Thackeray. (The O'Gorman Mahon, as he liked to style himself, probably inspired another recurrent *Punch* invention, 'The O'Bugaboo'.[60]) From late 1879, nearly every lead cartoon had an Irish reference.

Jokes that were not about Ireland tended to be about the unprecedentedly wet weather; and that too would have its Irish implications, as yet unknown to *Punch*. For the conditions of that winter produced an agrarian subsistence crisis in the west of Ireland. As reports came in, *Punch* remained as jauntily sceptical as ever. A cartoon of 8 November 1879 showed rapacious and dishonest tenants saving their capital to buy into new holdings, while claiming rent reductions on the grounds of destitution.[61] The favourite cliché of the Irish pig as 'The Gintleman that Pays the Rent' was converted into a murderous wild boar, armed with a blunderbuss: 'the gentleman that *won't* pay the rent'.[62] By now, radical journals like the *Pall Mall Gazette* took it upon themselves to condemn *Punch* for its anti-Irish cartoons.[63]

As in the 1840s, however, a parallel interpretation was projected as well. Some of the evidence from Ireland was incontrovertible, and by midwinter of 1880 a starving Hibernia was portrayed, solaced by her elder sister Britannia: '*That* I can, and *will*, help.' As before, a real problem supposedly brought them together and displayed the integrity of the Union.[64] Nevertheless, it was impossible to resist the picture of devious Paddies exploiting the relief funds organized respectively by the Lord Mayor of Dublin and the Duchess of Marlborough: 'We're feedin' three pigs on the Mansion House and atin' the Duchess ourselves.'[65] And as the tactics of resistance became increasingly violent, and the spectre of Fenianism arose once more, Mr Punch enlisted an old comrade to admonish the murderous Land Leaguers. Daniel O'Connell, the 'brazen brother buffoon', reappeared like Hamlet's father, a ghost lecturing on the lost ways of morality. The 1842 title, 'A Daniel Come to Judgment', was used again here. But this time the judgement was solemn: 'No political reform is worth the shedding of one drop of blood.'[66] Once again the Irish had to await reform until they had abjured violence.[67] This approach was thoroughly vindicated in *Punch*'s eyes, at least, by the horrifying Phoenix Park Murders of May 1882, which inspired Tenniel's classic treatment of 'The Irish Frankenstein', though this was an image much used for Irish matters already.[68] Serious and rather portentous poems addressed the Irish propensity for violence, and the need to combat it wherever it raised its malevolent fist.[69] And Toby's Diary inimitably addressed the subject in his oblique way, recording the effect on the House of Commons of a Fenian bomb at the Local Government Offices near by. Toby remarked to a policeman in the lobby, '"They will be trying this place next." "No sir," says Al [the policeman], lowering his voice confidentially and pointing with thumb over shoulder to the House. "There's too many of them there, and they're regler sitters." Don't know what he means. Dursn't ask.'[70]

When the turn of the Law did come, Punch was predictably cynical. And yet there was far less open abuse of the reformers than one might have expected. Gladstone was repeatedly represented as a white knight, bearing the scroll of the 1881 Land Act to Hibernia in distress;[71] *Punch* also endorsed his idea of a royal residence in Ireland,[72] angrily scouted by the Queen. The editorial influence of Francis Burnand, a Catholic as well as a Liberal, was entering the ascendant. Even when Gladstone went for Home Rule, *Punch*'s attitude was less

JUSTICE TO IRELAND!

BRITANNIA (*to* HIBERNIA). "YOU'VE TROUBLES ENOUGH, MY POOR SISTER, WITHOUT *STARVATION*. *THAT* I CAN, AND *WILL*, HELP."

"A DANIEL COME TO JUDGMENT!"

SHADE OF O'CONNELL. "EVERY MAN WHO IS GUILTY OF THE SLIGHTEST BREACH OF THE LAW IS AN ENEMY TO IRELAND. *NO POLITICAL REFORM IS WORTH THE SHEDDING OF ONE DROP OF BLOOD.*" (*See* JUSTIN M'CARTHY'S *History.*)

contemptuous than might have been expected. Lucy, with remarkable prescience, forecast exactly the way the political cards would fall, at the very beginning of January 1886, when the game was still apparently in the air. In a spoof letter from Hatfield, he outlined Salisbury's tactics: cut out Randolph Churchill's neo-Home-Rule posturings, woo moderate Liberals, force Gladstone to the front under a Home Rule flag, 'and then we go to the country with the cry "the Empire in danger"'. This, in a nutshell, was what happened; and *Punch* was not displeased.[73] But Gladstone's *démarche* was portrayed quite sympathetically in cartoons and squibs: at worst, he was the ageing Merlin, led astray by the Irish witch Vivien, in rather a good Tennysonian parody,[74] or a devious dressmaker trying to persuade Mrs Britannia into a divided skirt – one culotte embroidered with the harp, the other with lion and unicorn.[75] And when the great play failed, and Home Rule was rejected by the House of Commons, a lead cartoon showed 'Hibernia Consolatrix': a beautiful colleen gave Gladstone, her fallen knight, a cup of water as he sat disconsolately in the ditch.[76]

By the later 1880s, Irish matters were far less prominent, though the revelations of the *Times* Special Commission gave them ammunition – even if the main evidence against Parnell turned out to be a forgery, at least the forger was himself Irish. However, when the once-great Parnellite party foundered in acrimony over the O'Shea divorce case in 1890–91 and Parnell's refusal to stand down, *Punch*'s treatment was curiously oblique. Not for them the jokes about fire-escapes and Parnell's adulterous sobriquet of 'Mr Fox', which were so joyfully seized upon by other comic papers after the divorce-court evidence. (Lucy made many plays in his column about eviction and tenure, and the Fox joke did creep, subtly, into an Uncle Remus parody; but by the standards of the opposition this was extremely tasteful.[77]) The disgraced leader was represented, at worst, as a refractory carriage-horse which Hibernia could not control: 'If your tandem leader turns vicious, and kicks over the traces, where are you?'[78] Most miraculous of all, there is no reference to those tired Kilkenny Cats in all the unedifying weeks of the Parnell split; though Farmer Smith is blocked on his road by two quarrelling Irish pigs. 'Bad enough when there was only one.'[79] Through that terrible year, *Punch* pursued its target of Ibsen (and what it called 'Ibsenity') with far more ruthless commitment than its campaign against the unfortunate Irish. And when Parnell died suddenly at Brighton on 6 October 1891, his back to the wall and his great cause in ruins around him, *Punch* responded with a dignified ode, which saw him (not for the first time) as Marmion. 'He fell by his own action, as he rose.' His bravery deserved a laurel wreath:

> . . . but the task
> Of coldly keeping up the Stoic mask
> O'er-taxed him at the last; it fell and lo!
> Another face was bared to friend and foe.[80]

History, in *Punch*'s view, would be kinder to Parnell than to those foes – mean, merciless, venomous, petty, ignoble. (It is, in fact, an early statement of the Yeats myth about Parnell.) As with O'Connell, *Punch* could handsomely apostrophize a great Irish leader as long as he was dead.

By this point, as even Curtis admits, the penchant for bestializing and simianizing the Irish had passed. There are a number of *Punch* cartoons from the 1880s and 1890s which show other kinds of Irish: the impecunious 'Irish gent' or the family of an Irish local politician anticipating the Prince of Wales's visit;[81] and their features, while caricatures, are caricatures in no way different from the caricatures of English subjects. *Punch* had, certainly, helped establish the image of the bestial Irish extremist; but the magazine's record is more ambivalent than it might seem from some recent commentary.

Punch itself was rather sensitive on the subject. In 1886 the Irish MP Timothy Healy (a favourite subject of Toby, MP) bitterly denounced the record of the journal. 'Whenever [O'Donovan] Rossa [the Fenian polemicist] wanted a quotation or a couplet against Ireland,' said Healy, 'he could always find one to his purpose in *The Times* or *Punch*.' The editor replied specifically to the charge:

> *Mr Punch* is the true friend of Ireland; not of Orangemen or Ribandmen, or of Invincibles or Incorrigibles. He is the true and sincere friend of Distressful HIBERNIA, the Cinderella sister of BRITANNIA and CALEDONIA, and, as such, he has ere now pictorially, and with the deepest sympathy, represented her.
>
> *Mr Punch* (is not PUNCH an Irish name? And is there not Punch's Town? Go to!) has no steel pen hard enough, and no pencil black enough, to

represent the agrarian crimes, the Moonlighters, and the assassins, who are at once the terror and disgrace of the country, nor can he from time to time exempt from his righteous indignation those in authority who palliate such crimes, or who, by their silence, appear to favour them, any more than he can too strongly reprobate those on the other side who are willing to accept, without careful examination, as true, and thereupon to promulgate, any story which may keep at fever-heat the bad blood between the two great factions into which the Irish people are divided . . .

So go on and prosper; get the best you can out of the two Bills [Land and Home Rule, currently under debate]; recollect '*Codlin*'s your friend, not *Short*', and to quote the real original Tiny Tim, 'Bless us all!' says the true and just friend of everybody, PUNCH.[82]

How far can this genial defence be sustained? As we have seen, *Punch*'s classic characterization of the Irish remained much the same from the 1850s on; and it was by and large bestial. By contrast the *Graphic* and the *London Illustrated News*, though they were far from endorsing Irish nationalist politics, showed Irish crowds as handsome, well formed and physically varied; and the *Illustrated News* employed many ex-*Punch* cartoonists. But the point is that the *News* was not in the business of caricature; and *Punch* was. As mentioned already, their representation of all working-class types was dark and brutish; all enemies, especially class enemies, tended to the monster. (French apes were a commonplace.) This went with the territory. It might be pointed out that Irish comic papers of a nationalist bent represented the English as grasping, prognathous, subhuman bogeymen; J.F. O'Hea created a memorable and horrifying stereotype for *Zozimus* in 1870, who was christened 'Bill Stiggins of Uxbridge'.[83] It should also be noted that many of Curtis's most bestial examples of simian Irishmen, including his cover illustration, come not from *Punch* but from American journals; the implication is that genteel journalism, on both sides of the Atlantic, saw the Irish as a threatening underclass rather than a colonized subrace.

This said, one cannot get away from the intellectual and scientific (or pseudo-scientific) context of such stereotypes. Why were the Irish presented as apes? As Curtis himself points out,[84] the relationship of jaw and mouth to the upper part of the skull was a generally accepted nineteenth-century criterion for measuring the development from primitivism to civilization. It had been developed by Lavater and

Camper in the eighteenth century, and was broadly applied, in *Punch* as elsewhere, to out-groups defined in terms of race and class. Similarly John Beddoe's ideas on skin colour – 'nigrescence' – were influential in finding dark-skinned 'melanous' characteristics in the Irish and Welsh. Up to mid-century, these characteristics were developed fairly freely by cartoonists; from then, they become applied nationally, specifically to the peasant Irish, in *Punch* as elsewhere.[85]

Yet Hibernia is pure and lovely, with classical limbs, and a pure line from forehead to chin which approximates to Camper's ideal ninety degrees. And Irish types were by no means restricted to the murderous savage. As Sheridan Gilley points out in a brilliant critique of the Curtis thesis,[86] Celticism and Saxonism were extremely ambiguous concepts in the nineteenth century; and many who, by a selective reading, appear intransigently anti-Celt can be demonstrated from other evidence to have valued the Celtic input into what was conceived of as the British identity.

But that Celtic element had to remain acceptably subordinate. As *Punch* progressed, Thackerayan sympathy for a wide range of Irish types and Irish issues, and the recognition of specific Irish qualities and legitimate Irish causes, was moderated from the 1850s into a reflexive Victorian clubman's view of the Irish as hopeless cases. Mr Punch followed the same trajectory as Anthony Trollope, described elsewhere in this book.

It remains doubtful whether the generalizations of simple racial prejudice against the Irish really apply (intermarriage, for instance, was not counted miscegenation but rather a valuable conversion process). Class and religion were more central preoccupations in constructing an alien identity for the Irish than Curtis will admit; the whole process may relate more to resentment of the Irish attack on property and the Union, and also resentment against Irish resentment of the Union. How *could* they not know what was good for them? Certainly, the attitude was colonial; the Irish were weaker brethren. As the answer to Tim Healy demonstrates, by the 1880s *Punch* none the less endorsed Home Rule. But this could not negate decades of representing one Irish element, the propensity to violence, as Caliban (or O'Caliban, in a famous Tenniel cartoon[87]). The other Irish image, a sort of platonic ideal which must be protected from Caliban, was Hibernia – 'Britannia's Cinderella sister', according to Mr Punch's reply to Healy. But neither Mr Punch nor his cartoonists ever followed through the implication of the metaphor: that Britannia was therefore Hibernia's Ugly Sister, exploiting her at home and keeping her from the ball.

10

Good Behaviour: Yeats, Synge and Anglo-Irish Etiquette

William Butler Yeats and John Millington Synge were thrown together by circumstance, and remain welded by literary history; their relationship, as self and anti-self, has been the subject of intensive analysis.[1] Synge appears to have accepted philosophically Yeats's tendency to turn him into part of the Yeatsian myth, even while he was still alive; after Synge's premature death Yeats's hands (and his imagination) were comparatively untied. Thus, receiving the Nobel Prize in 1923 and talking about the Irish Dramatic Movement, he announced that a 'young man's ghost' should have stood on one side of him, and on the other 'an old woman sinking into the infirmity of age'. At a stroke, he cut out the Fay brothers from the foundation of the Abbey; he prematurely aged Lady Gregory, who still had a good few years ahead; and he claimed Synge. 'I no more foresaw her [Lady Gregory's] genius than I foresaw that of John Synge,' he remarks in *The Trembling of the Veil*; but, in fact, Synge was cast early on for a great role in Yeats's drama of his own life.

The great text of this remaking is, of course, Yeats's essay 'J.M. Synge and the Ireland of his Time'. It was dated September 1910 and appeared, elegiacally, in *The Cutting of an Agate* (1912) but had been begun as a kind of general introduction to Synge's work, and a reflection on the significance of the *Playboy* riots, probably in August 1908.[2] It could not appear as the introduction to Synge's posthumously collected works, because of Yeats's disagreement with the family's decision to include work rejected by Synge himself. But publishing it in this form gave Yeats the opportunity to concentrate on the riots that had greeted the first run of *The Playboy of the Western World* in

1907. Thus his preoccupation was the reaction to Synge's work, rather than the work itself – as a vital emblem of the significance not only of Synge but of the Abbey and of Yeats. 'I stood there watching,' he wrote, 'knowing well that I saw the dissolution of a school of patriotism that held sway over my youth.' Significantly it was in this essay too that he published in prose a sort of early draft of 'Easter 1916', in the passage about hearts enchanted to stone by a fixed idea. Thus Synge focused for Yeats all the ambiguity he felt about conventional Irish nationalism.

Yeats's response to the riots provides a key not only to his political and intellectual odyssey, but also to his relationship with Synge. Synge enabled Yeats, in certain ways, to adopt a stance which he had been nervous about beforehand. (Lady Gregory had something of the same effect, but with less bravura.) Both Synge and Yeats mixed hatred and love in their reactions to Ireland, and interrogated themselves about the relative proportions of the two emotions.[3] But there are other keys as well in unlocking the significance of what Synge meant to Yeats. Principally, one might consider what Synge's life, background and demeanour – and what he made of them – meant to Yeats's imaging of his own life. For Yeats's social and psychological insecurities were unconsciously thrown into relief by Synge, in a way that has great significance for Yeats's personal myth.

Certainly, after knowing Synge, Yeats's attitudes to class, family, background and (in a sense) race took a new turn. This can be monitored in the journal he kept in 1909, and later partially published in the long essay mentioned above; and, a few years before, while Synge was still alive, in his preface to *The Well of the Saints*. It is significant that Synge's effect on Yeats goes back to the early 1900s, because it must be read in terms of what Yeats was making of Nietzsche; clear clues lie in phrases Yeats uses of Synge like 'astringent joy and hardness'.[4] Later on, Yeats's constantly refined image of Synge was similarly put through yet another filter of philosophizing, when he was writing *A Vision*: here we find him trying to create a system of archetypes of human personality, through a sort of do-it-yourself transactional analysis. And here, too, Synge (or Yeats's idea of him) plays a vital part, in characterizing people of the twenty-third phase. So through his career Yeats memorialized Synge for his own purposes, building him into his philosophies, invoking him in his speeches, and finally, in the late 1930s, depicting him in the heroic frieze of 'The Municipal Gallery Revisited'. Perhaps the first thing to do is to scrape some of the varnish off that frieze and go back to how they were when they met, in Paris, probably on the 21st of December 1896.

II

Yeats recorded it in a famous passage – often recycled, but worth quoting in the version he published while Synge was still alive.

Six years ago I was staying in a students' hotel in the Latin Quarter, and somebody, whose name I cannot recollect, introduced me to an Irishman, who, even poorer than myself, had taken a room at the top of the house. It was J.M. Synge, and I, who thought I knew the name of every Irishman who was working at literature, had never heard of him. He was a graduate of Trinity College, Dublin, and Trinity College does not, as a rule, produce artistic minds. He told me that he had been living in France and Germany, reading French and German literature, and that he wished to become a writer. He had, however, nothing to show but one or two poems and impressionistic essays, full of that kind of morbidity that has its root in too much brooding over methods of expression, and ways of looking upon life, which come, not out of life, but out of literature, images reflected from mirror to mirror. He had wandered among people whose life is as picturesque as the Middle Ages, playing his fiddle to Italian sailors, and listening to stories in Bavarian woods, but life had cast no light upon his writings. He had learned Irish years ago, but had begun to forget it, for the only literature that interested him was that conventional language of modern poetry which had begun to make us all weary . . . I said 'Give up Paris. You will never create anything by reading Racine, and Arthur Symons will always be a better critic of French literature. Go to the Aran Islands. Live there as if you were one of the people themselves; express a life that has never found expression.'[5]

The inaccuracies in this superb sketch have been relentlessly explored.[6] Yeats did not tell Synge to turn away from French things; in fact, he continued to advise him to go in for reviewing French literature. If he did give such advice to Synge when they first met, it was in 1896, not 1899, as this preface claims; though they *were* in Paris together in 1899, Synge by then had been to Aran. On the other hand, Yeats had just discovered Aran in 1896, so would probably (in his characteristic way) have been posing as an authority on it. On 21 June 1898 he wrote to Synge that at Coole they could 'talk about Aran and your work there . . . Try if the people remember the names of Aengus & Mannanan & the like; & if they know anything of the Dundonians as I have heard the De danaans called.'[7] (He was also much more under Arthur Symons's sway in 1896 than in 1899.) In any case, it has been amply demonstrated that family connections with the island meant that Synge did not need Yeats to tell him about Aran. What should be noted is Yeats's determination to present himself as Synge's tutor; and also the significance of Paris as a meeting-place.

To Yeats, Paris meant a number of things. It signified cosmopolitanism; decadence; occultism as a general practice; and the intoxicating world of Maud Gonne, whose base it was. It also meant the theatre. Here his artistic life had been illuminated by seeing a performance of *Axël*; here too he was present at the first night of *Ubu Roi*. And in 1899 (in *Beltaine*) he had declared that the Irish theatre movement must 'do in Dublin something of what has been done in London and Paris'. France, in his mind, his fiction and his autobiographies, always symbolized various forms of liberation; but, unable to speak French, and deeply conscious of his own limitations, he experienced it through magus-figures like MacGregor Mathers and Maud Gonne. It was no accident that he dropped Symons's name when putting Synge in his place: Symons was his guide to the French Symbolists. For Synge, Paris would also remain important – especially in artistic terms.[8] But he was far more at home there than Yeats. This was only one of the differences between them – and it was a difference of the sort which Yeats was not keen to emphasize, preferring to stress the quite untrue fact that Synge was 'even poorer' than he was. Let us look at them when they met in 1896.

They were both young, Yeats thirty-one to Synge's twenty-five. Both, obviously, were Irish; both middle-class Protestants, from clerical families. But Yeats's background was an important notch or two down that carefully defined ladder. Synge's ancestors were bishops, while Yeats's were rectors; Synge's had established huge estates and mock castles, while Yeats's drew the rent from small farms and lived in the Dublin suburbs. Yeats had no money, while Synge had a small private income. Yeats had no university education, whereas Synge had been to Trinity, as Yeats noted (in a feline way). Both retained powerful and emotive links to ancestral parts of Ireland; but Yeats's roots were with bourgeois business people in Sligo, whereas the Synges remained closely connected to Wicklow country houses, and the memory of Glanmore Castle. Synge, in fact, was located in Wicklow and Dublin Protestant society in a way that Yeats, always marginalized by his Bohemian background, was not. That Synge reacted against all this is irrelevant. Both shared the sense of growing up in a minority, against a background of lost social influence; but Yeats experienced this at a much more elemental level than Synge did.[9]

Another important difference between them, which reflects upon background and education, is that Synge, for all his unpretentiousness, was really cosmopolitan; whereas Yeats, when they met, was desperately trying to be. Synge was practically bilingual, wrote notebooks in French, translated Villon; Yeats rather bitterly later recalled, 'I have never heard him praise any writer, living or dead, but some old French farce-writer.'[10] That might have been one way in which Synge got a quiet revenge for Yeats's condescension: by invoking a writer whom Yeats could not read. Because for all his readiness to hand down advice, his lordly name-dropping of Symbolist critics, his relationship with Maud Gonne, his links in the romantic world of patriots in exile, his commitments to murky occult and drug-taking circles, Yeats was not quite at ease in Paris. It was the world he tried, clumsily, to evoke in his early unfinished novel, *The Speckled Bird*, which he was working on at this time. 'You wonder why I am in Paris,' he wrote to Robert Bridges on 10 January 1897, '& I can allege no better reason than a novel which I have undertaken to write and which brings its central personage from the Arran [*sic*] Islands to Paris.'[11] The novel delineates the same axis between cosmopolitanism and Gaelicism which he prescribed to Synge. The unsureness of that fragmentary fiction reflects his own unsureness in the world where Maud Gonne and Arthur Symons had swept him. The action swings from fishing-boats tossing off the Galway coast, to half-ruined castles in the west, to occult investigations in the British Museum and the Bibliothèque Nationale, to mysterious encounters with sages and gurus in Paris streets; while half-told loves change shape, renounce and flit by each other in a vague penumbra of signs and symbols. Most of all, it is full of people whom the author tries to make dignified and mysterious, but who rarely quite succeed in bringing it off. Embarrassing as it may be, it is an illuminating approach to Yeats when he was still remaking himself.

Synge, as presented in the famous Yeats quotation, fits into this world – a wandering music student with mystic interests.[12] And Yeats writes of him as if he were a draft character from *The Speckled Bird*, for whom Yeats himself was an all-knowing magus-figure. In fact, their connections in Paris were not so very close. Synge rejected Maud Gonne's extreme circle round *Irlande Libre*; and his interest in mysticism and the supernatural was very different from the occult incantations of MacGregor Mathers. There were many ways in which mutual suspicion between the two young Irishmen was as likely as mutual sympathy. For one thing, at Trinity, Synge had been a student of Edward Dowden, to whom Yeats was at this time fiercely antipathetic. Again, the Trinity reference in that much quoted description is relevant here. When they met in the 1890s, Yeats was still deeply sensitive on the subject of Trinity, rarely losing an opportunity to make a gibe at the institution as a repository of the undead, maintaining a suffocating influence on Dublin life through its resolute philistinism. He was determinedly repudiating the assured world of the Dublin *haute bourgeoisie*, where Synge was objectively located (whether he wanted to be or not).[13]

The two apprentice Irish Protestant Bohemians, then, had cause for mutual distrust. And when Yeats used Synge's life as subject for his art (because Yeats's prefaces and autobiographies are nothing if not art), he deliberately abstracted Synge from that background, making him an icon for artistic loneliness, integrity, authenticity and rejection. Some of this is relevant, but it does not fit the Synge known by his family or by Molly Allgood. He was also someone whose art sprang from his life, if not as automatically and directly as his family biographer Ned Stephens thought. But Yeats was determined to show not only that Synge liberated himself from surrounding influences in order to create great art, but also that he, Yeats, had a part in this transformation.

'Placing' his friends in different sections of *A Vision*, he wrote of AE: 'I no more accept his visionary painting, and his visions of "nature spirits", as true to phase, than I accept the gloomy and self-conscious verse and prose of Synge before he learned to write in dialect.'[14] He put Synge in Phase Twenty-three (with Rembrandt, Michelangelo, Balzac and, oddly, Daniel O'Connell), where the creative genius ('CG') was greatest. But 'of all phases, it most misuses its faculties'.[15] And, in an interrogation conducted through his wife's automatic writing, he clarified that for Synge 'Personal life can enter the art but the art is from without'.[16] Synge, it was decided, had to undergo 'an aesthetic transformation, analogous to religious conversion, before he became the audacious joyous ironical man we know'. It was important to Yeats that he himself should have been an agent of that transformation. Synge's qualities and his progress were much in his mind as he tried to pin down the process of creative genius in *A Vision*; he visited the Wicklow valley of Glenmalure in March 1918, probably because it was where *The Shadow of the Glen* was set, at the very time when he and his wife George were conducting the most intensive automatic-writing sessions. By then Synge was nearly a decade dead, and the process of his assumption into the Yeatsian heroic frieze was well advanced.

III

What had fixed him there was the great theatrical collaboration with Yeats and Gregory. It was symbolic – though possibly no more – that Synge had visited Coole Park in 1899, when he returned to Ireland from Paris, at the very time when the Irish Literary Theatre was coming into being; this enabled Gregory to claim he was there from the beginning.[17] Though he was an observer, he does not really become a presence until *The Shadow of the Glen* was produced in 1903; it is the third volume of Hogan's and Kilroy's indispensable history of Irish drama, covering the period from 1905, that is called *The Years of Synge*.[18] In these years, he was at the centre; 'we three always', as Gregory reminisced to Yeats after his death. In 1905 he was part of the rather draconian takeover by that triumvirate – though his strategy had differed from Yeats's, and there were resentments below the surface.[19] In crises like Marie Walker's alienation from the Fays, Yeats was all for vehement offensive tactics, while Synge more wisely wanted 'TO LET THE HARE SIT'.[20] Yeats, unheeding, sent Synge dictatorial letters about the need for someone to take a decisive and 'dangerous' line, and in the process alienated Walker for good.

Synge said, quite correctly, that Yeats was too impetuous to deal with the actors; he 'had everything by the wrong end and was quite hostile, but when I explained everything to him he quite came over . . .'[21] He takes the same judicious line when writing to Yeats himself ('It would probably be best for you to come the day before meeting so that Russell may not have time to fight with you'[22]). He sounds both older and wiser than Yeats; he also appears more at ease in dealing with people.

This was especially true when they had become – as the actors now were – employees.[23] It may have been true, as W.G. Fay declared, that democracy was unworkable in a theatre; and Yeats may have been the Machiavelli who arranged the change of organizational structure.[24] But it still was noticeable, and perhaps rather unfortunate, that the three directors were all Ascendancy Protestants. Given the fact that those who seceded from it tended to argue along nationalist lines, and went on to present deliberately nationalist works, the original, reorganized company was inevitably seen as non-'national'.[25] This was probably unfair to Gregory – whatever about Yeats. But thus they were identified. And Synge's close artistic and theatrical connections with Yeats and Gregory rather misrepresented him; as Declan Kiberd has pointed out, up to the time of the Playboy riots many of his inclinations were closer to those of the Drama League.[26] But he did dislike professional *Gaeilgóirí* and pious chauvinists; and the fact that Yeats had used *The Shadow of the Glen* (among other strategies) to dish James Cousins's play *Sold* set the middle classes against Synge for good.

It is also significant, if hardly surprising, that in their private communications, the Abbey triumvirate allowed themselves a certain note of asperity about Catholic pieties – especially evident in Gregory's letters (now in the Berg collection) and Yeats's 1909 journal, by which time he had decided that the 'sense of form . . . the power of self-conquest, of elevation' were all Protestant characteristics in Irish life. In this, Synge's self-transformation and his artistic discipline were important influences. As for Synge himself, he might allow Christy Mahon mock Catholic celibacy; but whether he would have subscribed to Yeats's more sweeping theories may be doubted.

And there were other differences between the directors. Gregory never liked *The Playboy*, though she stoutly defended it; she lost few opportunities, in interviews with journalists, of claiming that she had originated the kind of language used by Synge in his plays, and she was not always very supportive. (Witness her comment to Synge the day after the opening of *The Well of the Saints*. 'What happened to you last night? We thought you had committed suicide.'[27]) When it came to Yeats and Synge, she was completely sure whose side she was on: as when she counselled Yeats to refuse to let *The Pot of Broth* be put on with *The Playboy* in 1907. It was, she told Yeats, 'Synge setting fire to your house to roast his own pig'.[28] Nor did she keep these feelings to herself, telling Synge in December 1906 that Yeats's dramatic work 'was more important than any other (you must not be offended at this) as I think it our chief distinction'.[29]

From the other side, Synge admitted Yeats's practical ability, as Stephen MacKenna recalled. 'He had . . . a curious admiration for Yeats on the practical side of things; he said once Yeats is a genius in bossing carpenters and judging the good qualities of nails and the price of a wooden platform; Synge pined for this power.'[30] But in terms of day-to-day running of the theatre, Yeats was less admirable as a colleague. Synge recorded sardonically in 1908, 'The Fays left us early in January and since then Yeats and I have been running the show i.e. Yeats looks after the stars and I do the rest.'[31] More seriously, Synge increasingly resented Gregory's and Yeats's determination to impose a high proportion of their own plays on to the programme. In 1907, he tells Molly, they show an American producer 'ONE play of mine "Riders", five or six of LG's and several of Yeats. I am raging about it.'[32] It should be said that Gregory's undemanding plays were the bread and butter of the repertoire. But Synge saw their prominence as a recurrent annoyance, and it made him consider withdrawing his work from the Abbey tours. He resented Yeats's lack of tact, as when he sweepingly dismissed *Riders to the Sea* as 'quite useless for the provincial tours'.[33] He had distinct reservations about Yeats's plays, and his poetic satire on AE's Celtic art contains some sharp digs at Yeats too.

> Adieu, sweet Angus, Maeve and Fand,
> Ye plumed yet skinny shee
> That poets played with hand-in-hand
> To learn their ecstasy.
>
> We'll stretch in Red Dan Sally's ditch
> And drink in Tubber fair,
> Or poach with Red Dan Filly's bitch
> The badger and the hare.[34]

His target here is the sexlessness of Celtic Twilight views of Irish reality, and a certain strain was put on his relationship with his fellow Ascendancy directors towards the end of his life because of his love affair with the bewitchingly different Molly Allgood: who was, as someone who knew her once remarked, 'the image of Pegeen Mike'. This not only spelt trouble for Gregory's vigorous notion of noblesse oblige;[35] it was also in marked (and earthy) contrast to Yeats's relationships with women.

Annie Horniman, who paid the piper, was, in a sense, one of Yeats's women, and she deeply disapproved of Synge; when she tried to detach Yeats from the Abbey and bring him to Manchester and pastures new, it was in her mind to get him away from Synge as well as from Gregory.[36] In December 1906, when Yeats was trying to keep Horniman well disposed by manoeuvring William Fay into a different (and subordinate) position, Synge took a very contrary line.[37] Horniman told Yeats on 31 December: 'Over and over again the road has forked before you; at this moment Fay, in the form of Mr Synge, points one way, and I and your interests point in the other.'[38] To her credit, she supported *The Playboy* when the storm over it broke a couple of weeks later; though she continued to bombard Synge with abusive letters on yellow paper. (He said mournfully that he could never look on daffodils with any pleasure again. When he died, in the cold spring of 1909, Yeats remembered this as he walked to the graveside, and noticed Annie Horniman's floral tribute: a large wreath of daffodils.)

Despite these pressures and resentments, the triumvirate of directors stuck to each other; and even after Synge's shattering death, his theatrical presence remained. In 1915 Yeats said: 'Synge has left us a glorious heritage, and I have worked to make the theatre a Synge theatre.'[39] This did both of them justice. He had even, evidently, decided that *Riders to the Sea* was possible for provincial tours after all.

IV

To be fair, Yeats had long hailed Synge as a dramatic genius; and he was right. But there were several reasons why Synge's work spoke so powerfully to Yeats, and some of the most interesting of them concern qualities other than literary merit. For one thing it provided, like folklore, a way into Irishness: a purchase upon native tradition. Part of the appeal of folklore, for Gregory, Hyde and O'Grady as well, was that through its study you could demonstrate and claim 'Irishness' at the very time when this was being defined more and more restrictively.[40] Synge revealingly put his discovery of Ireland as a substitute for a lost Protestant religion. 'Soon after I had relinquished the Kingdom of God I began to take a real interest in the Kingdom of Ireland. My patriotism went round from a vigorous and unreasoning loyalty to a temperate nationalism and everything Irish became sacred.'[41] The elision he makes from 'Protestantism' to 'loyalty' (meaning 'loyalism') is important: it indicates an automatic identification between political culture and religious belief, always a close identification for conventional Irish Protestants. (Lily Yeats was told by the Dean of St Patrick's that a mutual acquaintance 'has no religion but is an out-and-out Protestant in everything else'.[42]) But even a Protestant who had lost his religion was still a Protestant in other, Irish ways; at least in the beady perceptions of the Arthur Griffiths and D.P. Morans of the world. Yeats also had found this, to his cost. For him, and possibly also for Synge, the discovery of the 'folk' and explorations of 'the people' in their 'unspoiled' mode went with a contempt for the new middle classes: expressed early on by Yeats in his antipathy to the plays of Boyle and Cousins, and articulated by Synge in his much quoted letter to Stephen MacKenna after his western tour with Jack Yeats.[43] Such attitudes crystallized hard for both men after the *Playboy* riots; but, in a way, they were always implicitly there.

For Yeats, Synge was from the time of his first Abbey play sanctified as an Irish hero. For one thing, he had become 'baptized of the gutter', and set himself against his class, as Yeats had decreed must be done in the first issue of *Samhain*. (This went with the fellowship of bohemianism.) But what really accomplished his canonization was the *Playboy* riots. For this demonstrated that Synge, having given himself to 'the people', was turned on by the pack, and died prematurely. Yeats had already noted Goethe's remark that Irish Catholics always seemed to him like a pack of hounds, dragging down some noble stag – though he tended to drop the word 'Catholics' and read it as 'Irish' (as well as strategically forgetting that the reflection was inspired by O'Connell). And this interpretation of Synge linked him very powerfully with the figure already coming to prominence in the iconography of Yeats's imagination, as the emblem of Irish nobility: Parnell. Another rebel from the Wicklow Protestant Ascendancy, torn down by the common people, in the name of Catholic morality, after a career spent trying to elevate their cause. For Yeats, the death of Synge (like the death of Parnell) became central to his energy and his vision, and part of his politics. When he describes Synge in the nursing-home turning around and saying 'it is no use fighting death any longer',[44] the adversary is, for Yeats, not so much Hodgkin's Disease as the forces of outraged middle-class Irish philistinism. The circumstances of Synge's death were reinterpreted by Yeats to put him in the category of Parnell, Wilde and Casement.[45]

This was because Yeats had, in a sense, fitted out Synge for the part since the first controversies aroused by his work. The attack on *The Shadow of the Glen* was a vital part of this process, since it was led by William Martin Murphy, the traducer of Parnell. Yeats's great polemic on the subject, entitled 'The National Theatre and Three Sorts of Ignorance', made the connection practically specific. It was also an important stage in the development of Yeats's idea that Irish nationalist politics might be corrupted through anti-intellectualism. 'Extreme politics in Ireland were once the politics of intellectual freedom also, but now, under the influence of a violent contemporary paper, and other influences more difficult to follow, even extreme politics seem about to unite themselves to hatred of ideas.' The figure of Cuchulain in *On Baile's Strand* was specifically linked by Yeats to Parnell;[46] and Synge is in there too. His work and the reaction to it had crystallized Yeats's idea of Parnell as 'that lonely and haughty person below whose tragic shadow we of modern Ireland began to write';[47] these qualities were applied to Synge as well, along with the images of passion, and of an aristocratic will to serve the people – cruelly repaid. It is significant that Yeats's epigram, 'On those that hated *The Playboy of the Western World*', written at the same time as his preface to Synge's poems, used the image of Don Juan in Hell – again, a Parnellite image. And it is from the time of the Playboy riots that Yeats began frequently invoking Parnell in interviews and reflections.[48]

An important aspect of this Parnellite archetype was that 'the people', implicitly, had proved themselves unworthy of the hero; thus Synge, in Yeats's view, knew better than his audience, and was in a sense too good for them. This is hinted in an interview Yeats gave to a newspaper in 1909, at the time of the crisis over Shaw's controversial play *The Shewing-Up of Blanco Posnet*. Yeats compared Shaw's work to that of Synge. The satire of Blanco Posnet, he said, was directly comprehensible and therefore not offensive (Yeats always enjoyed putting down Shaw); but

> Synge's work, on the other hand, is precisely the work that is dangerous with an Irish audience. It is very hard to understand, and, therefore, the very desire to do so makes them impatient with it. They have gradually come to know what he means, and to accept his work without resentment. But it has been a long fight. To him everything was capricious and temperamental, and he could not tell his secret quickly.[49]

For Yeats, then, Synge became (like Parnell) the figure of a great gentleman. In other ways too his Ascendancy aura was subtly stressed. The asperity in his character was Swiftian; and he was a solitary, like Swift and Berkeley, seeking solitude 'as befits scattered men in an ignorant country'.[50] Thus Synge played a part in Yeats's evolving theory of aristocracy. It is significant that Yeats's Italian journey with the Gregorys in 1907 was taken in the aftermath of the *Playboy* riots – in fact, as a sort of convalescence from that excitement. For it was on this journey that he discovered Castiglione, Urbino, and the idea of noble discourse in culture and aristocratic patronage of the arts which he later applied, ludicrously but effectively, to eighteenth-century Ireland.

What Synge was coming to represent to him was the uncompromising attitude that went with elite authority tempered by good manners: always an Anglo-Irish preoccupation.[51] Oddly, Synge also preached the importance of manners in his letters to Molly, and 'wearing a sort of masque after a while, which is rather a needful trick';[52] though Yeats was not to know that Synge also told her 'people like Yeats who sneer at oldfashioned goodness and steadiness in women seem to want to rob the world of what is most sacred in it'.[53] And in manners, too, Yeats knew Synge had an enviable edge over him. He was not only able to speak French, but he could relate easily to the lower classes (including actors) in a way Yeats could not: he could keep his temper, and hold his counsel, which Yeats never managed. This stemmed from insecurity – much as Synge could unaffectedly fall in love with Molly Allgood, whereas one of Yeats's arguments to Maud Gonne against marrying John MacBride was that she would lower herself socially by doing so.[54] As Max Beerbohm remarked when reviewing *The Shadow of the Glen*, Synge possessed an incapacity to be vulgar. The way he struck a visiting Australian in 1904 was exactly as Yeats himself longed to appear. 'He was full of race and good breeding, courteous, sensitive, sincere . . . a simple man; but there was something strange and alluring about him, an indescribable charm expressed in his voice and manner, and, above all, in his curious smile that was at the same time ironic and sympathetic'.[55] Again, this recalls an idealized figure from *The Speckled Bird*; or, indeed, John Morley's description of Parnell. 'Uniformly considerate, unaffectedly courteous, not ungenial, compliant rather than offensive. In ordinary conversation he was pleasant, without much play of mind; temperament made him the least discursive of the human race.'[56]

Yeats read and marked this description; like the Australian portrait of Synge, it evoked a great gentleman. And Yeats knew it described qualities he did not have. He was not unaffected, not considerate, not compliant, not controlled; his temperament made him the *most* discursive of the human race. He feared in himself his own tendencies to vulgarity – his hysterical over-reactions, his agonized self-examination, his obsessive insecurities. All these qualities he tried to school out of himself.[57] Much later, in 'Coole Park, 1929' he remembered how he 'ruffled in a manly pose/For all his timid heart', and put this in immediate apposition to Synge's 'slow and meditative' qualities. Ironically, this undemonstrative, detached quality of Synge's was something which Yeats 'in real life' often resented, as did Augusta Gregory. After his death they privately commiserated with each other over the way he never complimented them or their work. 'I have often envied him his absorption,' Yeats wrote, adding mysteriously, 'as I have envied Verlaine his vice.' Maybe he meant that both were mechanisms for blocking out the distracting world, which was always too much with him.

Synge, however, could remove himself through a certain aristocratic discipline, like Parnell; and this became Yeats's ideal, and influenced his half-envious, half-affectionate view of the younger playwright. Synge's influence, like Parnell's, matured in Yeats's mind and his work. A Synge-like voice emerged in the Crazy Jane poems – their rhythm as well as their content. It is echoed in *Purgatory* (where the references to the old man's son being born from a tumble with a tinker girl in a ditch recalls a controversial exchange in the first version of *The Well of the Saints*). The conflation of myth and bawdy realism in Yeats's late work recalls poems of Synge's like 'Queens'; and what Yeats called Synge's 'hunger for harsh facts, for ugly surprising things'[58] has direct relevance to his own work throughout the 1930s. It went back to what W.J. Lawrence in 1907 had interpreted as 'the Swift-like horror of humanity that renders so much of the work of the Irish National Theatre Society repulsive'.[59] (This was in contrast to the wholesomeness of the Ulster Literary Theatre.) By 1930, when Swift had joined Parnell, Synge, Wilde, Casement and Berkeley in Yeats's Ascendancy gallery, this endorsement was exactly what he wanted. Synge had contributed this element early on – which we nowadays see as a celebration rather than a horror of 'humanity'. It continued to represent for Yeats something admirable, with which his own dramatic work never quite connected. So, on a wider level, personally and psychologically, did Synge himself.

As a coda, some reflections about fishing. This was one of the things that Synge did most, and did best. It is beautifully caught in Ned Stephens's evocative description of fishing with his uncle:

> We usually went to Annamoe bridge and each fished alternate pools as we went down the river past the rectory. John carried his old brown rod, which used to lie against the chimney-piece in the back drawing-room, as he did not trouble to take it down unless we were going to fish at a distance. He had an old leather fly book in his pocket, a spare cast round his hat, and a fish basket on his back, but he used no other equipment. The trout in the Annamoe river were not so large as to make a landing net necessary and John never thought of waders. He wore his usual knickerbockers, home-knit stockings, and strong shoes and was quite indifferent as to whether he walked on the bank or in the water. I often watched him excited and intent, standing with his feet firmly set apart among slippery stones and crouching slightly while he watched cast after cast on the end of a rapid as it slid in decreasing waves to calm in a deep pool.
>
> When it was too dark to see our tackle we walked home, often in silence except for the measured squelch of water from John's shoes. It was pleasant to slide fish out of his basket when we reached home and lay them evenly on a plate under the lamp. I caught very few, but John said that the gift for

catching fish would come to me with practice and would seem to come quite suddenly . . .[60]

Fishing is a matter of sensitivity – especially trout-fishing. It needs leisure and skill; it sets the countryman apart. This means that it is often taken as an index of gentlemanly status, although this can be over-interpreted. There is a striking passage in the Irish critic Denis Donoghue's memoir, *Warrenpoint*, where he describes being, as he thought, condescended to in Cambridge by the Anglo-Irish scholar Tom Henn. Henn told Donoghue, then a gauche young lecturer, that he was off to the ancestral home in Clare to fish. Donoghue inquired whether he would catch salmon. Henn said yes, he expected to 'kill' some salmon. Donoghue, decades afterwards, agonized at the correction, the condescension, the pulling of rank which he read into this exchange.[61] In fact, it is simply a country usage, derived directly from the Gaelic: the condescension is that of the countryman to the townsman, not, as Donoghue thought, the Anglo-Irish Protestant to the working-class Catholic. But it demonstrates the sensitivity of the question.

Yeats would have loved to be able to fish. He posed as a fisherman at Coole, writing with elaborate casualness about going out to fish, and was described by fellow guests as arraying himself in full and magnificent costume (including a sky-blue mackintosh). He wrote of trout-fishing as an image of solitude and disdain ('And maybe I shall take a trout/If but I do not seem to care'[62]); it was also, quintessentially, a gentleman's pursuit and a gentleman's skill. Unfortunately, in the marshy lakes of Coole, all he could pursue were plebeian pike. But staying there with his new wife in 1918, he was still trying. He attempted to impress her by suggesting they go mayfly-fishing for trout. They struggled to a stream with their equipment, where it slowly became clear that he had no idea what to do next. Finally he gestured vaguely at the cloud of summer insects darting above the water and asked her helplessly which, she supposed, might be the mayfly? This ignorance revealed, they abandoned fishing, sat on the bank, and he told her about Florence Farr's love-life instead. They probably both preferred this.

But he still wished he could fish. A few years before, he had thought of Synge, already abstracted into a pure Ascendancy icon, when he was writing 'The Fisherman'.[63] Both Henn and Nicholas Grene have drawn attention to Synge's presence in that poem as 'The dead man that I loved'; he is compared implicitly to the hangers-on of Dublin pub culture who now pass for literary figures. But he is also suggested by the central image of the confident, skilled, solitary fisherman, in his

> . . . grey Connemara cloth,
> Climbing up to a place
> Where stone is dark under froth,
> And the down-turn of his wrist
> When the flies drop in the stream;
> A man who does not exist,
> A man who is but a dream . . .

Synge was still in Yeats's mind when in 1930 he called on the Swift/Berkeley/Burke tradition whose task was to 'preserve that which is living and help the two Irelands, Gaelic Ireland and Anglo-Ireland, so to unite that neither shall shed its pride'.[64] Synge also came from an eighteenth-century tradition of intellectual toleration and Protestant elitism; and he had his part to play in the celebration of Gaelic Ireland. This, in a way, is what 'The Fisherman' was about: and it was also about Yeats's despairing aspiration to play such a part himself. It shows us, too, how in the forty years since their Paris meeting Yeats (who had then posed as Synge's mentor) reversed their positions. He had made Synge a mentor and an inspiration for himself – utterly different from the seedy magus-figures of his Paris period but, in some ways, just as unreal an idealization. And, like those figures, his image of Synge was necessitated by the insecurity which accompanied Yeats's own genius; and which, for all his efforts, stayed with him throughout his life.

11

Protestant Magic: W.B. Yeats and the Spell of Irish History

I

Irish historians have always had to confront Yeats, just as Yeats periodically confronted Irish historians. Both as a nationalist propagandist and as a totemic national figure, he is an enormously important presence in the establishment of Irish independence: he presided over the process, in a sense (if not the sense he later claimed). But if the historical view is taken to mean a simple chronological approach to his life, that will not answer (though it might help solve some knotty problems of dates of composition and strategies of publication), because the life was lived on so many levels, in bursts of parallel intensity. Then there is the disingenuousness of Yeats's own approach to his life: the complications arising from examining the life of someone who ruthlessly imposed patterns on his life in retrospect, and consciously constructed a reputation for himself from – it sometimes seems – about the age of fifteen.

And with the personal history is the larger question of national history, past, present and future. T.S. Eliot said, famously, that Yeats was 'one of those few poets whose history is the history of their own time, who are part of the consciousness of an age which cannot be understood without them'.[1] You can, however, stand this on its head. Yeats certainly shaped history for posterity. But also – and particularly for the historian – the curious and powerful resonance of Yeats's personality and his work is inseparable from the historical tradition and social subculture which produced him. Literary criticism has demonstrated how Yeats made history; historians might modestly indicate ways in which history made him. There are many facets to this process, but here I simply want to look at one: the theme of his Irish Protestant background.

An Irish Protestant identity is not necessarily to be expected of a nation-building Irish nationalist. And traditionally, the self-consciously Protestant Yeats emerges only in the 1920s: when, sixty years old and after a lifetime of ostentatious Celticist and nationalist sympathy, he turned on the Catholic guardians of morality in the new Irish Free State and assailed their outlawing of divorce. Suddenly Yeats invoked the tradition which bore him: Protestant liberalism. Conor Cruise O'Brien puts it with characteristic punchy insouciance: 'The Protestant now re-emerged with an audible sigh of relief. It had been stuffy in there, and getting stuffier.'[2] However, the Protestant had been battering at the walls for some time. That strain in Yeats and its inheritance had always been powerful factors. And this aspect of Yeats, besides clarifying certain political commitments and social attitudes, can help a biographer around one of the great stumbling blocks left by the poet for those tracing his path: what Auden called the Southern Californian side of Yeats, his lifelong commitment to occultism and magic.

It should be grasped early on that Irish Protestantism, even in its non-Ulster, non-demotic mode, is as much a social and cultural identity as a religious one, and that it is a more complex formation than is often realized. In his triumphalist and stately post-1920s Ascendancy style, Yeats celebrated his literary and theatrical partnership with Lady Gregory and John Millington Synge, where artistic commitment was shaped by the social identity of an elite.

> John Synge, I and Augusta Gregory, thought
> All that we did, all that we said or sang
> Must come from contact with the soil, from that
> Contact everything Antaeus-like grew strong.
> We three alone in modern times had brought
> Everything down to that sole test again,
> Dream of the noble and the beggarman.

This picture disguises the variety of backgrounds, and the social fissures, represented by that formidable triumvirate of Abbey Theatre directors who formed the national theatre. Lady Gregory came from the world of country houses, vast western estates, family retainers and imperial service. Synge was the descendant of Church of Ireland bishops and secure county gentry. Yeats's forebears were merchants, rectors, professional men and lawyers. By the time of 'The Municipal Gallery Revisited', written in August 1937, social spaces between the various levels of Irish Ascendancy mattered less (there were so few of them left). And Yeats had elevated himself to their upper reaches by a sort of moral effort and historical sleight of hand. Much earlier in his career, however, he had been mercilessly mocked by the novelist George Moore (son of a Catholic Big House far grander than Lady Gregory's). There is one famous account of Yeats crooning over the fire about his ducal Butler ancestors; Yeatsians tend to see it mostly in terms of the poetry and memoir which this attack provoked from Yeats (and, oddly, from Ezra Pound). But to a historian the comments are worth noting for what they say, representing the analysis of a shrewd social observer who knew the Yeats background well. Moore put it even more specifically and more offensively earlier in the same recollection, when he described Yeats at a public meeting to raise money for Hugh Lane's collection of Impressionist paintings in 1904.

[Yeats] began to thunder like Ben Tillett against the middle classes, stamping his feet, working himself into a great temper, and all because the middle classes did not dip their hands into their pockets and give Lane the money he wanted for his exhibition. When he spoke the words 'the middle classes', one would have thought that he was speaking against a personal foe, and we looked around asking each other with our eyes where on earth our Willie Yeats had picked up the strange idea that none but titled and carriage-folk can appreciate pictures. And we asked ourselves why Willie Yeats should feel himself called upon to denounce his own class, millers and shipowners on one side, and on the other a portrait-painter of distinction.[3]

As Moore pinpoints, the Yeats family, especially in the impoverishment spectacularly embraced by Yeats's artistic father, existed historically at a different level from the Gregorys and even from the Synges – though by the twentieth century an overwhelming solidarity had had to assert itself, faced with the rise of Catholic democracy. This is one of the aspects not often remarked upon in analysis of the great correspondence between Gregory, Synge and Yeats. The shared dream of the noble and the beggarman also meant a shared exasperation with Catholic demos, and a refusal to allow that element the monopoly on being 'Irish'. And this only clarified the lessons of Yeats's childhood and background.

II

His father, John Butler Yeats, uninterested barrister turned failed portrait-painter and world-class talker, constantly stressed the value and values inherent in 'genuine Irish Protestants'. This was all the more necessary by the time of his eldest son's youth, for the condition of the caste was already drastically changed from the palmy days of eighteenth-century Ascendancy (which W.B. Yeats would later rediscover and celebrate). By the 1860s, when Yeats was born, a survey showed that Catholics now possessed five out of the twelve judgeships in the Irish Supreme Court, half the administrative power in the banks, the control of three great Irish railway lines, and were by far the largest beneficiaries of sales of landed estates in the Encumbered Estates Court.[4] Political upheavals and land agitation from the 1870s would destroy Ascendancy power completely. But even before then, the establishment was no longer exclusively Protestant. And the isolation, or marginalization, of the Southern Irish Protestant had been mercilessly highlighted since the 1830s – by the geographical breakdown demonstrated by religious censuses, as well as by less concrete demonstrations and threats. The once-ascendant Protestant minority (about twelve per cent of the population at this time) were potentially in eclipse by the year 1865, when W.B. Yeats was born in a suburban Dublin villa at Sandymount, called No. 1, George's Ville. Symbolically, the older Yeats generation still lived in a nearby dwelling called 'Sandymount Castle' – a rambling, crenellated but not particularly grand old house. Thus was neatly captured not only the distance between insecure middle-class present and receding aristocratic past, but also the physical uncertainty of present Protestant life. George's Ville was such an inconsequential house that (though it still stands) its correct address has been squabbled over for generations and appears wrongly on Yeats's birth certificate. And Sandymount Castle, like so many Irish castles, was not a castle at all: a comfortable but bogus accumulation of architectural styles, deliberately reminiscent of past grandeur.

One way of understanding the ethos of the Protestant Ascendancy is through their architecture. It is epitomized in the creation of a deliberately grand imperial city, as well as in the stylish, plain, small Georgian houses scattered through rural Ireland, like Lady Gregory's

Coole Park. Literary critics have on occasion referred to them as 'granite boxes' 'affronting' the Irish landscape, which seems exactly wrong. Elizabeth Bowen, more poetically, described them as 'ships out at sea'.[5] But they do stand for an evident need on the Ascendancy's part not only to lay claim to land recently won, but also to convince themselves that they would remain. The little battlements and Strawberry Hill windows of a Sandymount Castle may represent a declaration by its inhabitants of the antiquity of their claim to an Irish house – in an age when their right to be 'Irish' was beginning to be questioned by the new wave of Irish nationalism.

It has been mentioned earlier in this book that Anglo-Irish writers obsessively use houses as symbols and personifications. From the inside of the demesne wall, a sense of threat was inevitable. And as the nineteenth century wore on, Ascendancy marginalization was reflected in their relation to architecture as well as to landowning. Dublin was reduced to echoing, cavernous, half-abandoned public buildings and streetscapes. Its atmosphere is preserved in a subculture of absorbing fourth-rate fiction. In these novels, another image recurs: that of the country house barricaded against mysterious night marauders, often taking the form of an exotically named secret society, out to reclaim the land. (In *The Kellys and the O'Kellys*, Trollope mocks this superbly in a conversation between two Irish Protestants, one of them convinced, against all rational evidence, that he has been the subject of such an attack.[6]) Later, the erosion of Ascendancy landownership under the dual onslaught of Parnellite land agitation and Gladstonian land purchase legislation is reflected in better fiction, like George Moore's *Muslin* or Somerville's and Ross's *The Real Charlotte*. In that novel of 1894, what the grasping central character really wants is one particular little 'gentleman's house': a Georgian farmhouse, fallen on evil days, with a *déclassé* owner and a grass-grown avenue.

Yeats and his family were alive to the issue that preoccupied Somerville and Ross, and has continued to interest economic and social historians of Ireland: that is, the emergence of a successor class to the Ascendancy in the seismic upheavals of the late nineteenth century. Collaborationist strategies for the survival of the Protestant Ascendancy had been sketched out by political leaders like Isaac Butt and, more daringly, Parnell, in their movements for federalism or Home Rule. (The Yeats and Butt families were, interestingly, very closely associated.) However, in terms of economics, the writing was on the wall. The Land War of the 1880s and the legislation which it precipitated may have preserved some of the landlords' property. But, together with agricultural rent and price movements which advantaged the tenants and disadvantaged the landlords, plus franchise extension and local government reform, the Ascendancy's social *raison d'être* was removed long before Irish independence – even if they were bought out at a good price. (Unlike the landless cottiers and agricultural labourers, who were the real losers of the Land War.)

It is important not to misapprehend the nature of this conservative revolution; for the next step, politically speaking, was that the successor class would provide not only leadership of establishment politics (John Redmond), but also, with the upheavals of 1912–14, an extremist political leadership that for the first time was not commandeered by Protestants reacting against their background, like Tone or Mitchel. The revolution of 1913–21 was led instead by the children of Catholic teaching orders like the Christian Brothers (metaphorically speaking, of course). Yeats's poems 'Easter 1916' and 'Parnell's Funeral' are only two of the contemporary texts which express a certain bemusement at this turn of events. Late in his life he summed it up more brutally, recalling his fellow Senators in the Irish Free State parliament:

> hot and vague, always disturbed, always hating something or other ... [they] had destroyed a system of election and established another, made terrible decisions ... signed the death-warrant[s] of [their] dearest friend[s] ... Yet their descendants, if they grow rich enough for the travel and leisure that make a finished man, will constitute our ruling class, and date their origin from the Post Office as American families date theirs from the *Mayflower*.[7]

He does not write as if the process greatly appeals to him.

For the Irish Protestant Ascendancy, their eventual marginalization manifested itself economically, politically and spiritually. Religiously, what is an Irish Protestant's country? The episcopalian Church of Ireland, tempered in the zealous fires of the Irish seventeenth century, retained certain brutally reductionist Low Church characteristics, well expressed in the tone adopted by some Trinity College Dublin academics. But this ethos tended to dogged stasis rather than upbeat evangelicalism: and to a certain philistinism, attacked from outside the charmed circle by both Yeats and Shaw, the latter putting his own faults of 'vulgarity and savagery' down to having 'sat once upon a time every Sunday morning in an Irish Protestant church'. Apart from briefly picking up evangelical fervour in the 1850s, the Church of Ireland remained locked into the guardianship of its privileges. None the less, it saw its parishes and revenues rationalized and its tithes commuted by one reforming British government in the 1830s, and its established status removed by another in the 1860s. By the time of the First World War, the social reality of the Ascendancy, its Church and its houses, was as usual best reflected by Somerville and Ross. Here is a private letter from one of that duo, Violet Martin, written after a visit to County Galway (Lady Gregory's territory) in 1912:

I was driven off to a little desolate awful church, to which the Ardrahan clergyman drives out. I have *never* been at anything so wretched – the little church quite well built, but coated with mildew and damp, the decaying old prayer books stuck to the seats with fungus. The clergyman came out and dusted a pew for me before he allowed me to sit in it – I, a young man, and a policeman were the congregation. The parson gave out a hymn, started it very well; I struck in, and he and I then sang a duet. When he found that I was well set, he sang an *excellent* bass in a low baritone. The youth and the policeman listened reverently to this unique performance.

In the afternoon Tilly Redington and I drove over to Tyrone House. A bigger and much grander edition of Ross – a great square cut-stone house of three stories, with an area – perfectly empty – and such ceilings, architraves, teak doors and chimney-pieces as one sees in old houses in Dublin. It is on a long promontory by the sea – and there *rioted* three or four generations of St Georges – living with country-women, occasionally marrying them, all illegitimate four times over. Not so long ago *eight* of these awful half-peasant families roosted together in that lovely house, and fought, and barricaded and drank, till the police had to intervene – about 150 years ago a very grand Lady Harriet St Lawrence married a St George, and lived there, and was so corroded with pride that she would not allow her daughters to associate with the Galway people. She lived to see them marry two men in the yard. Yesterday as we left an old Miss St George, daughter of the last owner, was at the door in a donkey trap – she lives near, in a bit of the castle, and since her people died she will not go into Tyrone House, or into the enormous yard, or the beautiful old garden. She was a strange mixture of distinction and commonness, like her breeding, and it was very sad to see her at the door of that great house – If we dare to write up that subject![8]

Much later, her collaborator did, in *The Big House at Inver* (1925). But so, interestingly, did Yeats, who took an equally garbled version of this Galway story for his last play, *Purgatory*, which, like the Somerville novel, is preoccupied with decline, miscegenation, the death of a house and the hauntings of history. Its inspiration is closely associated with the ethos delineated in Violet Martin's letter, where she locates these same elements against a background symbolized by a rotting Protestant church with a congregation of three – one of them, significantly, a policeman.

This was the point to which the once-triumphant Ascendancy was declining through Yeats's youth. But in terms of intellectual history, a process of marginalization and psychological insecurity is traceable from the early nineteenth century. As the Ascendancy took to castellating their houses, they gothicized their fiction, possibly for similar reasons. The condition of the embattled Irish Protestant from the early nineteenth century was epitomized by figures like Charles Maturin, an eccentric but acute Dublin cleric and author, or another Huguenot-descended Irish intellectual, Sheridan Le Fanu. Le Fanu was a non-practising lawyer, conservative journalist and congenital depressive, who lived a reclusive life in Merrion Square, absorbed in Swedenborg and fears for Protestant Ascendancy. And what he and Maturin had in common is striking: both, in their successive generations, pioneered the nineteenth-century tradition of Irish supernatural fiction.

Maturin created *Melmoth the Wanderer*, published in 1820, a figure who echoes Faust and prefigures Count Dracula: the undead, wandering the world to claim the issue of a corrupt bargain. Le Fanu wrote numerous classic ghost stories and one authentic masterpiece, *Uncle Silas* (1864); though ostensibly set in Derbyshire, it was long ago spotted by Elizabeth Bowen as an Irish story in disguise, dealing with exploitation, imprisonment, fractured identity and hauntings.[9] He was a devoted reader of Swedenborg, as was Yeats. Le Fanu is also responsible for a prototype lesbian vampire story, *Carmilla*. And this topic would later be carried on by yet another respectable Dublin Protestant, Abraham – Bram – Stoker.

Over forty years ago V.S. Pritchett acutely characterized Le Fanu's ghosts as frightening because 'they can be justified: blobs of the unconscious that have floated up to the surface of the mind . . . not irresponsible and perambulatory figments of family history, moaning and clanking about in fancy dress'.[10] This is true of more Irish ghost stories than Le Fanu's; and, particularizing further, the line of Irish Protestant supernatural fiction is an obvious one, though it has not been analysed as such. It leads from Maturin and Le Fanu to Bram Stoker and Elizabeth Bowen and Yeats – marginalized Irish Protestants all, often living in England but regretting Ireland, stemming from families with strong clerical and professional colorations, whose occult preoccupations surely mirror a sense of displacement, a loss of social and psychological integration, and an escapism motivated by the threat of a takeover by the Catholic middle classes – a threat all the more inexorable because it is being accomplished by peaceful means and with the free legal aid of British governments. The supernatural theme of a corrupt bargain recurs again.

Indeed, a strong theme in Protestant gothic is a mingled repulsion and envy where Catholic magic is concerned. The Jesuit order in *Melmoth* manipulates darker forces than the eponymous hero. In *Dracula*, Van Helsing is a Dutch Catholic who brings the Host, with a papal dispensation, to combat the undead at Whitby. Yeats, who read about vampires in Joseph Ennemoser's *The History of Magic* (1854), wrote in *The Land of Heart's Desire* about demon children who flinch from the crucifix; the undead in *The Shadowy Waters* cast no shadows; his fairies cannot be watched eating and are invisible in mirrors. For those who have accompanied Jonathan Harker through Dracula's castle, none of this is new. Yeats knew Stoker; he inscribed a copy of *The Countess Cathleen* to him in 1892,[11] read *Dracula* with Ezra Pound, and was only put off a proposed visit to Dracula's original castle (though Yeats thought it was in Austria, not Transylvania) by the outbreak of a world war in 1914.[12]

Equally Stokerish is Yeats's interest in Catholic versus Protestant magic. He wrote to Lionel Johnson in 1893: 'My own position is that an idealism or spiritualism which denies magic, and evil spirits even, and sneers at magicians and even mediums, (the few honest ones) is an academical imposture. Your Church has in this matter been far more thorough than the Protestant. It has never denied *Ars Magica*, though it has denounced it.'[13] By 1909, however, he had decided that the Protestant mind was readier to accept magic. The pedantry of Irish Catholic education, he wrote in his journal, 'comes from intellectual timidity, from the dread of leaving the mind alone among impressions where all seems heretical, and from the habit of political and religious apologetics. This pedantry destroys religion as it destroys poetry, for it destroys all direct knowledge. We taste and feel and see the truth.

We do not reason ourselves into it.'[14] This theme appears in the stories he published as *The Secret Rose*, where magical insight is defined against unthinking Catholicism. Here too there are echoes of *Melmoth*: the invented text, the esoteric book, the idea of esotericism as aristocratic domination, perhaps – for an Irish Protestant – the reclamation of an elite authority. 'The dead,' he once wrote, 'remain a portion of the living.'[15] A critic as imaginative as Terry Eagleton might see the crowds of dead people whom Yeats or Elizabeth Bowen discern walking the roads of Ireland as the souls of dispossessed tenants. I do not; but, while accepting the Neo-Platonic and Swedenborgian pedigree of ideas about the dead partaking in the life of the living, the particular appeal of the supernatural for Irish Protestants deserves decoding.

Yeats was a man of his late nineteenth-century time in being influenced by the general occult revival of the late 1880s, unequalled until the 1960s. Éliphas Lévi's *Mysteries of Magic* had been translated in 1886, Cornelius Agrippa's *Natural Magic* a few years later. An explosion of public interest in Rosicrucianism had affected Europe. MacGregor Mathers's *Kabbalah Unveiled* and A.P. Sinnett's *Esoteric Buddhism* were sacred books for a certain element of the avant-garde. (Sinnett's book was presented to Yeats by a Sligo Protestant aunt.) There was a belief in a coming dawn of wisdom which would rout eighteenth-century rationalism and nineteenth-century materialism. But Yeats already had his reasons for repudiating these beliefs: they had helped bring about the decline of the Protestant Ascendancy. And he had access to his own occult tradition too.

Irish occultism was often identified by Yeats, for public purposes, as part of the Celtic mind-set; but the superstitiousness of Irish Protestants was legendary. A fear of three candles burning together, or the unlucky colour green, or a hotel bedroom numbered 13, governed the private life of Charles Stewart Parnell.[16] Roger Casement's father dabbled in spiritualism at Ballymena.[17] Elizabeth Yeats would never allow her publishing company to begin printing a book on a Friday.[18] In the house of Yeats's Pollexfen relations at Sligo, a long-dead great-grandfather and his four-year-old daughter, victims of the cholera, walked in the garden of an evening, and the dogs ran to greet them. The Dublin Protestant middle class had frequent recourse to fortune-tellers and wise women, long before AE and Yeats tried to bring them Theosophy, seances and astral travel in the

1880s. And Yeats's early fellow occultist and schoolfriend, Charles Johnston, came from the last redoubt of Protestant extremism, a Northern Irish Orange stronghold called Ballykilbeg: where, Yeats noted, 'everything was a matter of belief' in Protestant salvation and Catholic damnation.[19]

It does not seem frivolous or irrelevant to locate Yeats in this context – Protestant marginalization – as much as in the world of international occultism, Byzantine studies, Indian mysticism and London bohemianism: for it antedated these influences on him, as did his interest in supernaturalism. 'Without the arbitrary,' he wrote, 'there cannot be religion . . . because there cannot be the last sacrifice, that of the spirit.'[20] For a Catholic, religious authority provided the arbitrary; an Irish Protestant had to look elsewhere. Yeats found it in magic. As he himself wrote of Blake, 'He was a man crying out for a mythology, and trying to make one because he could not find one to his hand. Had he been a Catholic of Dante's time he would have been well content with Mary and the angels.'[21] But the supernatural dimension of the Irish Protestant subculture provided a further impulse – less personally, more historically derived – and one which he shared with several similarly marginalized members of his increasingly marginalized class and caste.

III

It is worth looking in some detail at the specific case of Yeatsian marginalization, a concept always present in Yeats's own work. (His own favourite among the stories in *The Secret Rose* is called 'The Crucifixion of the Outcast'.[22]) What was the family's background? The Yeats side were classic clerical-bourgeois Irish Protestants, land-agents rather than landlords, fallen on poorer times. Yeats's own grandfather, after whom he was named, resigned his living under a cloud. On his mother's side the Pollexfens were Protestant business-men, millers and shippers of fairly recent Irish vintage. The Yeatses were sociable, easy, graceful, unsuccessful; the Pollexfens were money-minded, puritanical, introverted, with great reserves of feeling. Or so John Butler Yeats read them. He was obsessed with the distinctions, contrasts and dissonances between the two families, and so, in his way, was W.B. Yeats.

To a certain extent, Yeats's father's obsessive commentary has created and preserved the idea of two clashing family cultures which produced, by some sort of Hegelian dialectic, the poet. More to our purposes is the way that the Yeatses and Pollexfens, taken together, represent the varieties of social identification across the Protestant middle class. The Yeatses were very conscious of their Protestant tradition, in the sense of social caste rather than religious commitment; they treasured the aristocratic Butler component. John Butler Yeats also noted, again and again, Pollexfen shortcomings which he attributed to their business background. Nor was he the only one. Another element of social marginalization stemmed from the social distance between the Pollexfen world and the great houses of the neighbourhood like Hazelwood, Markree and Lissadell. Yeats's autobiographical writings preserve the litany of names, the grey ancestral roofs glimpsed through trees and across high walls. His youth has usually been seen refracted through a Celtic mist. Reading his memories, it recalls something very different: the Combray childhood of the good bourgeois Marcel in *A la recherche du temps perdu*, wandering along the hawthorn paths by unattainable demesnes. And Yeats, like Marcel, would later conquer their inhabitants through charm and the social power of art. The county lady Violet Martin, hearing about Yeats on a visit to Lord Morris in 1901, picked up the impression that: 'He has a sense of humour, and is a gentleman – hardly by birth, I fancy – but by genius.'[23] That had been the option open to him, and he had taken it.

The Pollexfen house, Merville, looks large enough to us now; it was certainly a step up from the old Pollexfen residence on Union Street, Sligo, and Yeats emphasized the length of its avenue,[24] a rigorous test of gentility since the days of Jane Austen. But as Jack Yeats remarked, 'we had no gate lodges and no carriage drives'.[25] John Butler Yeats wrote to Rosa Butt (herself from the marginalized and financially insecure Protestant middle class): 'One reason why I am so incensed against class distinctions is because these very small gentry round Sligo always excluded the Pollexfens from their friendship. Because they were engaged in business they were not fit company.'[26] And when W.B. Yeats finally visited Lissadell socially in 1894, he remembered it as a cause of great pleasure to the Pollexfens.

He can be seen, then, as a figure at odds with his various contexts; and in this he expresses the wider dislocation of his caste. The Yeatses, unlike the Gore-Booths, did not have a demesne to cultivate when the Land Acts turned their tenants into proprietors. The heavily mortgaged farm at Thomastown which provided John Butler Yeats with his meagre private income disappeared before the turn of the century. The Yeatses, in fact, did not even have a house, especially in the Irish sense. John Butler Yeats rented a series of seedy Dublin houses, remembered with horror by his son. 'We lived in a villa where the red bricks were made pretentious and vulgar with streaks of slate colour, and there seemed to be enemies everywhere.' Elsewhere: 'That Rathgar villa where we all lived when I went to school, a time of crowding and indignity.'[27] There is the authentic Ascendancy shudder, and the authentic Ascendancy fear of the enemies outside the walls.

Blenheim Road in suburban London's artistic Bohemia was the family's only real home, rented though it was; and it went in 1901. Yeats's only base for over twenty years after leaving home was a couple of rooms near Euston Station: and, for every summer from 1897, his collaborator Lady Gregory's house, Coole Park.

Coole was the epitome of the small Irish Georgian house which Yeats had once dismissed as 'ugly and box-like' before he learned to celebrate the eighteenth century as 'that one Irish century that escaped from darkness and confusion'[28] – and a time when Yeatses were Yeatses. At Coole he discovered 'a life of order and of labour', of ceremony, of libraries (the people who opposed Synge's *Playboy of the Western World*, said Yeats, 'had no books in their houses'[29]). Coole was an imperial house, memorializing generations of service to the Empire. Here Yeats rediscovered the Protestant virtues. It is less often remarked that he also rediscovered a robust contempt of Catholic values, reflected in many off-the-cuff remarks in Lady Gregory's letters, and culminating in Yeats's Senate speeches in the 1920s. There was also his admiration of Lady Gregory's autocratic way with Lord-Lieutenants. ('What many old Abbey Theatre actors remember most about being in the presence of Yeats and Lady Gregory,' one researcher has found, 'is simple fear.'[30])

Vitally, Lady Gregory provided Yeats with a house where he could be, for the summers, a resident; where he could attempt to go fishing, like any country gentleman; where he could belong. Houses, and an insecurity about whether they will last, pervade Yeats's writings, as they do Elizabeth Bowen's. In 1894 the idea of burning down landlords' houses horrified him; by the time of *Purgatory* he could write

to kill a house
Where great men grew up, married, died,
I here declare a capital offence

– a view which I think the play's author, as well as its central character, endorses. With marriage and a certain amount of worldly success, he could get his own house; so, of course, he moved to a castle (even if it were only 'a tower/Half dead at the top'). And as Lady Gregory tartly remarked to her American friend John Quinn, 'He already feels such a real Irish landlord that he has begun by putting a mortgage on it.'[31]

This, as much else, was a deliberate reassertion of an Irish Protestant identity denied him by historical and family circumstances. In youth, his reaction had been to over-compensate: he attacked Unionist Dublin as resembling 'that fabled stony city of Arabia'[32] and preserved a special animus against the quintessentially Protestant institution of Trinity College Dublin. In his angry youth Yeats said that the only instinct for religious veneration experienced by Irish Protestants was directed towards Trinity College. In a public letter of 1900 he referred to 'that Death whose most manifest expression in this country is Trinity College . . . and which has already turned our once intelligent gentry into readers of the *Irish Times*'.[33] That journal was the quintessential Unionist newspaper; and perhaps it is relevant to cite a short story in *The Celtic Twilight*, where a country woman is vouchsafed a vision of the devil, disguised as a newspaper blowing along the road: 'she knew by the size of it that it was the *Irish Times*'.[34] A supernatural view of Irish Protestant institutions looms into view once more.

Yeats's relationship to Trinity continued highly charged. He did not attend the college (where his father and grandfather had won prizes) for a number of rather disingenuously expressed reasons. He continued to rail against the Trinity establishment, sometimes referring to it as 'the middle class'. In a carefully recorded dream, he visualized 'a certain portentous professor of Trinity' as a lap-dog set to guard the gates of hell.[35] Most of all, he assailed one emblematic figure with Oedipal passion: the Professor of English Literature, his father's friend Edward Dowden. Dowden, whom Yeats took as the personification of Protestant Dublin, had been an early supporter of his poetry. In later life Yeats felt somewhat guilty about all this, and wrote nervously to his father that he had treated Dowden rather unfairly as 'a little unreal, a specious moral image . . . [a symbol] for the whole structure of Dublin, Lord Chancellors and all the rest'.[36] In the same mode, at the same time, he would reject Swift and Berkeley as not really Irish, while claiming Blake and Emily Brontë as countrymen. In the act of classifying a canon, anything that smacked of Trinity was illegitimate. But, just as later he discovered Swift and Berkeley as intellectual ancestors, and exponents of Ascendancy virtu, so too he came near capturing the castle that was Trinity. In 1910 and again in 1913 he was canvassed (not very enthusiastically) for the succession to Dowden's chair, and found himself very interested. So was his father, who fantasized happily about Yeats walking in the front gate of Trinity in such august circumstances. Yeats never became a Trinity professor. But here too, by about 1913, a wheel had come full circle and a reconciliation with a tribal tradition had been made.

There was, moreover, another aspect to the Dowden connection, which raises yet again the Irish Protestant predilection for the occult. Dowden's pioneer scholarship was devoted to the Shelley circle; in the mid-1880s he read to Yeats and his father parts of his unpublished life of Shelley. And the works of Shelley's circle included not only Mary Shelley's *Frankenstein* but also Polidori's Byronic tale, *The Vampire*. It was Dowden's account of Shelley's experiments with demonic invocation at Eton that inspired Yeats and AE to attempt spirit-raising in the mid-1880s.[37] And Dowden's star student was the brilliant son of a professional Dublin Protestant family, Trinity Gold Medallist, Auditor of the College Philosophical Society, Double First and civil servant – Bram Stoker. Stoker's first book, long in use, was called *Duties of Clerks of the Petty Sessions*. Only an Irish Protestant could have graduated so easily from that to *Dracula*. The genesis of the latter masterpiece has recently been demonstrated, with the discovery of Stoker's working notes, now deposited in Philadelphia. They represent seven years of Yeats-style research into folklore, myth, armchair anthropology, medieval history and magic, particularly diabolism.[38] Stoker had even found a treatise on the peasants of Transylvania which remarked on their 'many points of resemblance to our friend Paddy. He is grossly superstitious, as the number of crosses by the roadside and on every eminence testify; and, like his prototype, he lives in abject terror of his priest, of whose powers he has the most exalted ideas.'[39] The Irishness of Dracula must be left aside here. But Dowden's influence had a part in Stoker's imagination, as it did in Yeats's. From adolescence, Yeats set out on his lifelong path to constructing occult alter egos, to membership in the Hermetic Order of the Golden Dawn, to the long parade of mediums and seances and occult evocations. And this path may lead back not to studios in Fitzrovia in the 1890s, but earlier: to Dowden's large villa on Temple Road, Rathmines, Dublin, where in the early 1880s the mutinous young Yeats and his irrepressible father used to visit Dowden for breakfast and then walk argumentatively into the city together: the young Yeats dropping off at the High School, Harcourt Street, the elder continuing on to his studio at Stephen's Green, while Dowden alone – symbolically – terminated his journey at the Grand Mosque of Irish Protestantism, Trinity College Front Square.

IV

As his career developed from this marginalized base, Yeats remade an Irish identity in his work and in his life. In the process he reclaimed Ireland for himself, his family and his tradition. He began by asserting a claim on the land, particularly the Sligo land, through its people: the discovery of folklore and fairy belief. Difficulties arose: he could, for instance, be attacked as incapable of interpreting Ireland religiously, as he was a *Protestant* mystic. But folklore and anthropological interests, besides being often connected in the 1890s with theosophical or occult investigations, opened a way into nationalism via 'national tradition' (as Scott and others had shown long before). It could also demonstrate the links between Yeatses, Pollexfens and the 'real' Irish people around them. Landed Irish Protestants had always had a special relationship (for better or worse) with Ireland – denied to the landless bourgeoisie whence Yeats was sprung. So he claimed the land in his own way. And the process could assert, yet again, intuitive, organic, traditional forms of wisdom – even 'secret' wisdom – against scientific, 'rational' modes of thought, and against an increasingly Establishment Catholicism. Defending his views against an antagonist in the *Outlook* as early as 1898, he wrote: 'If your paragraphist, who is, perhaps a Catholic, will wait until I have completed the series of essays . . . he will find that the Irish peasant has invented, or that somebody has invented for him, a vague, though not altogether unphilosophical, reconciliation between his Paganism and his Christianity.'[40] Perhaps that was the function of the Irish Ascendancy occultist? In the same year he prophesied that Art in Ireland would usurp the role of religion: artists must 'take upon [themselves] the method, and the fervour of a priesthood . . . We must baptize as well as preach.'[41] In early works like his collection of *Fairy and Folk Tales of the Irish Peasantry* there is a highly charged mixture of calculation, belief and proselytism.

Even before Lady Gregory's more expert tutelage, Yeats was a committed gatherer of folklore, and an equally committed enemy of rationalizing folklore scholarship. Folktales embodied a secret truth, of the sort denied by the priests but asserted by the hero and the country people in Yeats's unfinished novel *The Speckled Bird*:

One of the young priests [from Maynooth] asked if the fishermen were attentive to their religious duties, and Michael began to praise them for their sense of an overhanging spiritual life and went on, without weighing his words, to speak of apparitions they had seen.

One of the priests said, 'People used to imagine they could see things of that kind, but they are too well educated now,' and the other priest added, 'These superstitions are all dead, I am glad to say.'

Michael, thinking that some chance had kept them ignorant of what was his greatest interest in life, said: 'You are entirely mistaken. I have spoken to many who have seen such things.'

The priest who had first spoken was silent for a minute and then said in the heavy voice of one who is repeating a lesson, 'They may tell such things as stories, but they no longer believe in them.'[42]

It was necessary for Yeats passionately to adhere to the idea that Sligo people did believe in fairies and talked about them all the time. So they did, of course – to *children*, as Lily Yeats remembered.[43] The difference was that her brother expected to go on being talked to about them. This tendency is powerfully connected with laying claim to the lost domain of childhood, symbolized for all the displaced Yeats children by Sligo, their one rooted place. Still obsessively discussing this lost Eden in 1936, Yeats said to his sister Lily: 'No one will ever see Sligo as we saw it.'[44] The lost world of childhood also stood for a long-lost world of social dominance.

Folklore also asserted another identity: the gentry's liking for the disappearing type of 'pure' Irish peasant memorialized by the plays of Synge. Strong farmers, cattle dealers, gombeen men and enforced emigration do not characterize Yeats's landscape; mysterious, self-confident, independent (but polite) people living in close communion with dhouls and fairies do. Like Douglas Hyde, who was from a similar background, Yeats recurs to the class distinctions among the Irish faery: tall, well-made, aristocratic *Sidhe*, attended by pygmy plebeian smiths, cattledrovers and shoemakers. 'Folk art is, indeed, the oldest of the aristocracies of thought . . .'

Yeats's autobiographies asserted this view of the countryside of his youth, much as he rewrote the history of Ireland during his adulthood. He had learned from one of his obscure occult mentors, MacGregor Mathers, that 'images well up before the mind's eye from a deeper source than conscious or subconscious memory':[45] a trained spiritual visionary had access to a sort of universal random memory bank, and thus the visionary poet was the ideal historian.

In Yeats's influential version, the quarter-century from 1891 to 1916 was 'the stirring of the bones', and the 1916 rising the inevitable apocalypse – gestated almost supernaturally in the transference of energy from politics into culture after the death of Parnell, a process midwived by Yeats and his friends. This may be unconvincing and ahistorical;[46] but it had the advantage of putting Yeats at the centre of Irish history. 'Did that play of mine send out/Certain men the English shot?' he asked in a famous couplet; his *Autobiographies* provide an extended, affirmative answer. (This contrasts with the answer implied in a recent version by the Ulster poet Paul Muldoon: 'If Yeats had saved his pencil lead/Would certain men have stayed in bed?'[47])

The Yeats version distorts the continuing power of the constitutional political movement, ignores the context of the First World War and the contingent nature of the 1916 rising, and wrongly identifies cultural and political revolution as fundamentally the same thing. But the process welds the marginalized Yeats into the mainstream of Irish history and presents him not only as the cultural founding-father which he came to be, but as the political patriarch which he certainly was not. The reality of Yeats's public position (and the attitude of mainstream Ireland towards its marginalized Protestant intellectuals) is probably more accurately preserved in a coded newspaper attack on Yeats and AE in 1901:

The type of Non-Catholic Nationalist to whom we refer has been pampered in vanity. He could not be a mere Home Ruler, so he found it necessary to differentiate and be a Protestant Home Ruler; he thinks that Ireland practically never had a leader who was not a Protestant – that is one of the fruits of commencing Irish history at the year 1782; he sometimes writes poetry which no Irishman understands or rather which no Irishman troubles his head to read; he thinks Catholics are superstitious and believes in spooks himself; he thinks they are priest-ridden and he would like to go back to Paganism; he is a bigot who thinks that he is broad-minded; a prig who thinks he is cultured; he does not understand Ireland – a fact which would not be of much import if he did not firmly believe that he is a philosopher. However, he means well.[48]

By this stage, condescension was exercised by the Catholic middle class towards the Ascendancy, instead of the other way round. Notwithstanding, Yeats's continuing preoccupation with the occult did enable him to lay a claim upon Irishness, while retaining a hold upon his own marginalized tradition. His own occult short stories, like 'Rosa Alchemica', are not often enough seen as contributions to the Protestant Gothic tradition, continuing the Maturin–Le Fanu–Stoker theme of occultism as a strategy to compete with Catholicism and to deal with the hauntings of Irish history (including spectres from the seventeenth and eighteenth centuries).

Yeats's discovery of the eighteenth century restored to his personal pantheon the one figure who could enable him to square the circle of reconciling Augustan values with scepticism about 'rationalist' apprehensions of reality: Bishop Berkeley. Occultism also enabled him to make common cause with the Protestant Freemason tradition, epitomized by his uncle George Pollexfen in Sligo – friend of his father's youth, seer of visions, caster of horoscopes, initiate of the Order of the Golden Dawn and pillar of the Masonic order. Freemasonry, a vital presence in Irish Protestantism, hovers in the background of *fin de siècle* occultism; Yeats's own hermetic order, the Golden Dawn, was begun by three Freemasons, and Maud Gonne left it because of these associations. For an Irish Protestant, of course, the Masonic order continued to offer one of the few convenient avenues to the irrational, the arbitrary and the sense of a secret society (except in Ulster, where they had their own routes to these destinations). Yeats cannot have been unsympathetic. Perhaps this predisposition lay behind the otherwise surprising fact that one of the few enthusiastic reviews of Yeats's occultist handbook, *A Vision*, appeared in the *Church of Ireland Gazette*.

By 1913, not yet fifty, Yeats had begun to write his memoirs and rewrite his past. He was well embarked on his development into a new and uncompromising tradition, in poetry as in stagecraft – encouraged by his secretary and companion, Ezra Pound. He would look to the East, to Europe and eventually back to Ireland. And like Pound, he found his way to a literary culture which could embrace a politics of conscious, unashamed and authoritarian elitism. This again had its Irish Protestant echoes. His 1909 journal is preoccupied by aristocracy, anti-egalitarianism and occasionally anti-Catholicism, tutored by Lady Gregory and by what Yeats conceived as the lesson of Synge's life and death: 'Friendship is all the house I have.' The baseness and intellectual corruption of Catholic education is stressed; the adherence of Protestantism to form, and Catholicism to formlessness;[49] he is even on his way to a sneaking sympathy with Protestant fears about Home Rule becoming Rome Rule.

That same 1909 journal repeated his belief that 'national feeling' was dying out, and his disillusionment with the Irish ethos.[50] Later he would have to rewrite this, as part of his interpretation of modern Irish history inevitably setting hard towards the rising of 1916. The poet, after all, *was* the ideal historian. He had, much earlier, wondered whether Ireland's 'whole history' might 'be fiction . . . sung out of the void by the harps of the great bardic orders'.[51] (Many analysts of medieval sources would be in general agreement.) In any case, by the first publication of his great collection entitled *Responsibilities* in 1914, Yeats's approach to history, Irishness and Protestantism was more or less set – well before *A Vision*, or the 1916 rising, or his political experience as a Senator of the Irish Free State.

This *tour d'horizon* of some general as well as specific circumstances surrounding Yeats's life may beg some questions, but it answers others. It may, for one thing, present some excuses for a historian taking on the biography of a poet. It may make some sense of Yeats's 'finished' image or persona as the reconstructed Protestant gentleman from his fifties on. A home first in Merrion Square (like Sheridan Le Fanu),[52] then a suburban estate at Rathfarnham (which he leased just after Coole was broken up); summers in the west; the Kildare Street Club; Horse Show Week; Punchestown races, even; worries that if his son goes on to the new-look Trinity after his public school (St Columba's), he may meet and marry a Catholic. If this is a marginalized existence, it had become, at last, marginalized in much the same way as others of his tribe who lived on under the Free State.

And at the same time, the other Protestant tradition was sustained: the Yeatsian variety of occultism. A ceiling in the Merrion Square house was painted with mystical gold stars (and afterwards the decorator was often seen stopping outside the house with a friend, pointing at it, and laughing loudly). Mrs Yeats, miraculously adept at automatic writing, summoned up voices and messages from the spiritual void. Mystic familiars made their presences known, to Yeats at least, through magic auras and unexplained perfumes. He proudly wrote to Ezra Pound that he was 'making a sensation' by publicly debating spiritism with a Catholic priest: 'I am confident that I finished him off.'[53]

This essay began with a quotation from Eliot on Yeats, and in conclusion another remark of his comes to mind. Speaking in Dublin in 1936, he expressed regret that Yeats 'came to poetry from a Protestant background', since that might account for his 'wanderings among oriental philosophies and dubious mysticisms, journeys unsafe for any but the Christian, and which the Christian informed about the historic wealth of his faith has least need to make'.[54] This may be Eliot at his most insufferable. But certainly to understand Yeats it seems necessary to recapture and combine aspects of the curious subculture from which he came: an insecure middle class, with a race memory of elitism and a predisposition towards seeking refuge in the occult. He is too often seen as someone who becomes an 'advanced nationalist' in the 1880s and later retreats into being a 'reactionary'. The process of retirement into a cultural Big House of his own building is far more deeply rooted than that. *Pace* recent commentators like Edward Said, the Irish traditions which Yeats was conditioned by and reclaimed were not automatically those supposed 'nationalist' (at least in the sense of Anglophobic, Gaelic Revivalist and puritanically Catholic–Republican). But they constituted no less an Irish subculture for that.

12

To the Northern Counties Station: Lord Randolph Churchill and the Orange Card

I

On 22 February 1886 Lord Randolph Churchill stepped out of Belfast's Northern Counties Station and into the demonology of Irish nationalist history. He proceeded to the Ulster Hall and, in a speech which was taken to threaten unconstitutional action, promised Ulster Unionists the help of the Tory Party in their resistance to Home Rule. He had only visited Belfast once before, and never went there again; he did not say 'Ulster will fight and Ulster will be right';[1] but he created an identification which lasted almost exactly a century, until a Conservative government outraged Ulster Unionist opinion by signing the Anglo-Irish Accord with the Irish Republic at Hillsborough in 1985.

To contemporaries, however, the identification of Churchill and die-hard Unionism came as an abrupt surprise. Interpretations of this sudden *démarche* tended to rely on opportunism or original sin. In a famous and flippant remark to his great Irish friend Gerald FitzGibbon, he mentioned his decision that 'the Orange card would be the one to play. Please God it may turn out the ace of trumps and not the two.'[2] Looked at in context, there is a pattern behind that fateful trip to Belfast; but it must be traced down unexpected paths. For to consider the development towards the triumphal progress from the Northern Counties Station to the Ulster Hall in 1886, it is necessary to go back nine years, to the arrival of Churchill's father, the seventh Duke of Marlborough, in Ireland as Viceroy, following the involvement of both his sons in a celebrated Victorian scandal.

The strangeness of the Castle world, an admixture of Gilbert and Sullivan with Mr Pooter, must have struck the Marlboroughs forcibly: on the one hand public jeers at their financial embarrassments, on the other an extraordinary avalanche of private letters bitterly contesting questions of personal politics and social precedence, still incongruously preserved in Blenheim Palace.[3] But for the majority of their tenure, the Marlboroughs made a remarkable public success of the viceroyalty. Duly warned, the duke kept social life up to expectations; and he adroitly followed an 'Irish' line in policy most untypical of Disraeli's last administration. He travelled widely in the country, opposed coercion, called for religious toleration in the North, supported land purchase for small farmers, and cultivated a public image far removed from the hauteur of predecessors like the Duke of Abercorn.[4] Most of all, he strongly identified himself with the Catholic side in schemes for intermediate and higher education, working closely with Hicks Beach, his Chief Secretary, and enthusiastically corresponding with the hierarchy from the beginning.[5] The outcome, a cautious intermediate scheme introduced by James Lowther in 1878, was disappointing, as was the eventual abandonment by the government of the university scheme worked out by Isaac Butt and the O'Conor Don, and warmly supported by Marlborough; the substituted plan for the Royal University only indirectly subsidized the Catholic University. There was talk of the Viceroy resigning over this. He and Beach had been assured by their clerical contacts that 'in Irish politics the education question has practically displaced even the home-rule question and the land question',[6] an analysis in which they devoutly believed. They were bombarded by Butt with letters telling them that Catholic opinion was more favourable to a Conservative than a Liberal government,[7] and they took this seriously, though under no illusions about Butt's own increasingly eroded position. In education, above all, the Viceroy and other Conservatives in Ireland backed an approach which was essentially alien to the government's approach in England.

The liberal-minded duke, decent and often slightly bemused, bears some resemblance to Trollope's Plantagenet Palliser; and his wife quickly showed certain similarities to Lady Glencora. She swiftly emerged as an energetic politician obsessed with the need for good publicity and famous for her dedication to 'feeding the press' at Castle receptions.[8] Besides the routine involvements of a Viceroy's wife, she cultivated a network of Irish contacts, to which the correspondence at

Blenheim bears loquacious witness. They ranged from liberal landlords like Sir William Gregory to a phalanx of clerics from Cardinal Cullen down. Her late sister, the Countess of Portarlington, had been converted to Catholicism and entertained a stream of clerical admirers at Emo Park; here the duchess met men like Dr William Delany, the Rector of St Stanislaus College, Bishop Nulty of Meath and Dr Molloy of the Catholic University, who were duly invited to Blenheim. Such people were firm Conservatives, but they put her in touch with coming men like the future Archbishop Walsh. These contacts were invaluable in projects like her famine distress fund. And when she left Ireland the duchess was showered with addresses and poems from all over Ireland, many in Irish, and some no less fulsome in her praise for declaring parenthetically a pious wish to repeal 'the curse of union'.

The initiatives and attitudes of the Marlboroughs gave their reign a characteristic identity, which was added to by the presence of their *déclassé* and socially disgraced son Lord Randolph, the hitherto undistinguished MP for Woodstock. His position at the Castle was anomalous; it was decided he could not occupy a paid private secretaryship, but the official private secretary had to give up his house to Lord Randolph, and pledge that he would defer to him behind the scenes. And he figured largely in Castle life, accompanying his father on political tours (including a sole prophetic visit to Belfast in 1877), meeting his future friends at viceregal parties and in the Dublin Castle offices, and imbibing the political atmosphere at a time when the *Freeman* was still able to hold out hopes of the 'Irish catholic conservative' as a desirable political phenomenon;[9] Churchill worked at the Castle on the education schemes which had this very end in view. Given this, the fact that Butt dined regularly with him need not seem surprising.

Certainly, Churchill eschewed the great houses of the Ascendancy in favour of cultivating Irish friends; but, despite biographers' comments about his 'close contact with intellectual home rulers',[10] his contacts were not nationalists. They may not have been quite as exotic as claimed in a recent study devoted to proving that Churchill was Jack the Ripper; this traces his involvement back to being sworn as a Freemason into the First Lodge of Ireland in 1878, under the alias 'Rudolph H. Spencer'.[11] Murderous Masons or not, Churchill cultivated an overwhelmingly 'Trinity' clique of professional men, educated Tories, the products of an immensely distinguished university generation – David Plunket, Michael Morris, Edward Gibson, John Pentland Mahaffy, Gerald FitzGibbon.[12] They took him up, launched him on the College Historical Society in TCD as his first Irish public appearance, and in many ways formed his thinking on Ireland.

FitzGibbon was the most important of these. Law adviser and then Solicitor-General in the Irish administration, he came from a robustly Tory and Protestant legal family.[13] Fourteen years older than Churchill, he was already well known for his success in nearly every 'heavy case' that came on in Dublin. His advancement to Lord Justice of Appeal in 1878 need not have been due to viceregal favour, for he was conspicuously able; even the unenthusiastic Beach lamented his 'waste' in Dublin legal life.[14] FitzGibbon himself would probably have preferred politics, in which he was immersed behind the scenes, but the promised seat for Dublin University went instead to Gibson in 1875. FitzGibbon was a realistic, decisive, superficially flexible but basically intractable Unionist and Protestant: an influential Freemason, whose mother came from Belfast.[15] The fact that he had a wide circle of Catholic friends and contacts was in no way incompatible with this, contemporary English ideas of Ireland notwithstanding.

FitzGibbon formally promised to keep Churchill informed on Irish politics; which he did, in a flow of marvellous letters, until the end of Churchill's life. Despite his complaint that advising his mercurial friend was 'crying in the wilderness through the privacy of the penny post',[16] time and time again a public Irish initiative of Churchill's followed, in both senses, private advice from FitzGibbon. His reiterated lesson to Churchill was that there were *other* Irish Unionists than landowners to be considered; himself of the professional middle class, he deeply resented 'the identification of the union and of constitutional rule with the collection of rent'.[17]

He pressed the claims of the denizens of Dublin's professional squares, and also of the Northern brethren; time and again this theme recurs. His circle included no landowners. Plunket and Gibson were careerist lawyer-politicians, later sundered by politics; Gibson's success alienated most of his Irish associates, and Churchill, after briefly considering him Fourth Party material, came to dislike him intensely for his affiliation to his *bête noire* among the Conservative leaders, Sir Stafford Northcote. Gibson could appear all things to all men, being suspected in 1886 of secret Home Rule sympathies by authorities as varied as Lord Carnarvon, Wilfrid Scawen Blunt, and the Kildare Street Club.[18] Morris (later Lord Morris and Killanin and first Catholic Lord Chief Justice of Common Pleas in Ireland) was a Spartan pessimist from a Galway background, though educated at an Erasmus Smith school, and a Trinity Gold Medallist. He combined intransigent Unionism with a dislike of most Englishmen, believing that the Irish question arose from a quick-witted race being governed by a slow-witted one. Like Plunket and Gibson, he had been a protégé of Disraeli (an even more untypical Englishman than Churchill); like FitzGibbon, he left direct politics through lack of money. He advised Churchill closely, and became more relentlessly Unionist as the years went by;[19] but he always disagreed with coercive legislation, seeing a typically English lack of imagination in the government's inability to use the ordinary legal processes.

Churchill's single contact among the Irish landlords was made outside the FitzGibbon circle – his uncle, Lord Portarlington, who has been presented as a disapproving high Tory but was in reality an extraordinarily liberal landlord who praised Archbishop Croke's pronouncements, believed in a peasant proprietary, and eulogized Gladstone's Land Bill of 1881 in the House of Lords.[20] But generally, Churchill's friends were in the FitzGibbon set: Lord Chief Justice Ball, Ben Williamson of Trinity, the celebrated wit Dr Nedley, and the indefatigably socialite parish priest of Little Bray, Father Healy. Healy, though no snob, was noted for his dining out in grand houses (which he called 'my outdoor relief'). In no way a typical Irish priest, he regularly visited Trinity high table and the viceregal lodge, involved himself in Conservative politics, and was close to Tory politicians like Balfour and Orange families like the Leslies, opposing Archbishop Walsh on national questions.[21] In England he was welcome at Blenheim and Hatfield, as well as at Gladstone's breakfasts; and both Churchill and his father dined often at his little house in Bray, where the fare was invariably boiled mutton, but the company could include, at one sitting, Monsignor Persico, Lord Powerscourt, Archbishop Walsh, Lord Morris, Chief Baron Palles, Prince Edward of Saxe-Weimar and the ubiquitous Gibson.

Against the background of his parents' initiatives and his friends' opinions, Churchill's celebrated speech at Woodstock in September 1877, attacking the government's neglectful Irish policy as causing the antics of the obstructionists at Westminster, need not be seen as unduly surprising; it was no more than what educated Irish Conservatives were saying in private, probably at viceregal dinners. The duke mollified Beach by the supposition that his unofficial private secretary had been drunk, but there are other aspects to be considered. The speech can be seen as an attempt by Churchill to put himself between parties, or to steal the thunder from Gladstone's coming visit to Ireland.[22] However, press opinion made much of it; traduced by the *Morning Post* and treated with some embarrassment by the *Irish Times*, he was welcomed by the *Freeman's Journal* as demonstrating *noblesse oblige* (a quality dear to the heart of the editor, Edmund Dwyer Gray). Though Churchill rapidly mended his fences in England, the speech had a spectacular and lasting effect in Ireland.[23] A friendly relationship began between the *Freeman* and Churchill, who carefully referred to it in public as 'the best-written paper in Ireland'; Gray rewarded him by greeting even his defection over the Irish borough franchise in 1879 'more in sorrow than in anger'.[24]

Churchill was, moreover, determined to become a Tory 'Irish expert'. From 1876 he had energetically followed the family interest in intermediate education; this culminated in his publication in early 1878 of a pamphlet which argued firmly in favour of denominational education, and condemned the organization of Protestant educational trusts. It pressed strongly for a restructured system, with the aid of the surplus fund of the disestablished Church, to provide state intermediate schools catering for the Catholic middle class; this fairly represented enlightened Castle thinking.[25] The scheme devised by Beach and passed in June 1878 resembled it in many points, though not actually endowing Catholic education and not reorganizing the endowments monopolized by Protestant schools. When Beach's measure was introduced, Churchill (who had been actively involved in the preceding negotiations) called for a commission of inquiry into endowed schools in Ireland, attracting the support of Chamberlain and William Forster, annoying Lowther, and earning grateful mention in the nationalist press. A commission was appointed, though with only limited advisory powers, and was commandeered by Churchill, FitzGibbon and Mahaffy, under the chairmanship of the Earl of Rosse. Such membership did not encourage Catholic opinion, and it was looked on in some quarters as an attempt to preserve a Protestant initiative in education; but it compiled an interesting and effective report,[26] obediently following the lines set out in Churchill's pamphlet. His own attendance at sittings of the commission was regular, and his questioning highly pertinent, as well as markedly hostile to administrators who had contrived to make their endowments exclusive.[27] Unique among the commissioners, his questioning was forensic and tendentious, trying to draw out suggested remedies and alternatives, despite the commission's limited scope. Churchill's questioning also concentrated upon the management of landed estates; and his overall reactions indicated an impatience with rickety Ascendancy institutions which had outlived their function. His prime consideration may have been to make a figure, but at the same time he learned a lot.

The same is true of his involvement in the duchess's famine relief fund, which she set up in December 1879 after taking lengthy soundings from her landlord and clerical friends, and against the advice of Castle officials.[28] By mid-December her formidable publicity machine was in action, English politicians canvassed, and the Mayor of London set to producing a steady flow of £2,000 cheques from a parallel fund in Britain. And almost at once the Dublin Lord Mayor, Dwyer Gray, began the Mansion House fund for a similar purpose; after initial amity, the two organizations were soon in violent opposition, the duchess having been warned early on that any co-operation with Gray would dry up the English contributions which accounted for the majority of her takings. William Gregory consoled her with the assurance that such vendettas were part of Dublin life,[29] but the war was soon prosecuted on a wider front; Disraeli's indolent attitude towards Ireland hardened into intransigence with the land crisis, and on 8 March 1880 he sent a famous open letter to Marlborough about the 'pestilential' nature of the Home Rule movement. The duke had already boycotted the Mansion House, for the ironic reasons of Dwyer Gray's supposed support of extremists; after agonized tacking and veering Gray had to abandon attendance at the Castle, and neither he nor the *Freeman* ever forgave Marlborough.[30]

The duchess's fund carried on, a prodigy of organization and financial productivity, attacked by English Protestants for 'favouring Catholics' and by Irish nationalists for deliberately concealing the government's responsibility for the distress; and racked by internal crisis when an embezzling secretary threw himself into the canal in a drunken fit of remorse (a story which at all costs had to be kept from the Mansion House fund).[31] After the election defeat the duchess left Ireland with a *grande dame* circular letter in Irish and English addressed to the distressed districts, and her harassed trustees finally wound things up at the end of the year, receiving abusive epitaphs in the Dublin press.

Throughout, Churchill was a moving spirit. He drew up for the duchess a cautious and considered memorandum on the extent of agricultural distress, advising against hasty commitment and looking at the question almost entirely from the angle of political priorities.[32] When the fund was started, however, Churchill as Honorary Secretary worked incessantly: corresponding with bishops, organizing liaison in London, arranging local distribution of seed and potatoes, advising about the feud with the Mansion House, and showing a tactless degree of impatience at the objections to 'favouring Catholics'. At the end of it all he arranged for the dispersal of surplus funds in an emigration scheme. It was, taken with his work on the endowed-schools commission, a baptism into Irish politics.

Meanwhile, the duke was increasingly alienated from public opinion in the transforming country under his nominal command. Long before the election, he announced his intention not to return; he had even lost favour with the episcopacy; and after leaving office he continually called for coercion in the House of Lords. The duchess, too, had hardened; she believed that in the winter of 1881 the Irish gentry would be living 'as in the dark days of the French revolution'.[33] When Marlborough died suddenly in 1883, the *Freeman* used the occasion to resurrect all the contentious issues it could: a thankless end to all the duchess's unsparing efforts to feed the press.

Though their son cannot have been unaffected by this, he had also absorbed and retained a variety of progressive and activist attitudes towards Ireland. He had made a figure. Educated Unionism was interested in him. Though someone of William Gregory's orientation could rate him very highly indeed,[34] the normal Irish landlord interest thought him an enemy and told him so, in private letters as well as in slightly ridiculous incidents like barring him from their meetings. This, however, should not be identified with a 'Green' coloration. Butt may have been a friend, but he was desperately courting the Conservatives; Father Healy may have been an intimate, but his political opinions were 'unpalatable to the majority of his own cloth in the country'.[35] And antipathy to the landlords was a characteristic of the staunchly Unionist FitzGibbon circle, which kept Churchill in touch with Ireland, bringing him back nearly every year to FitzGibbon's famous Christmas house party at Howth. Here the faithful, arriving at the seaside house by train like Madame Verdurin's 'little clan', convened to talk, drink, play whist and cook their own suppers. Besides Plunket, Morris, Mahaffy, Gibson and Father Healy, the party could include stray English politicians, John Butler Yeats, Archbishop Walsh or the Viceroy. In later years John Morley became an incongruous regular. But the parties originated 'to enable Lord Randolph to meet many of his Irish friends'.[36] Winston Churchill, Edward Ashbourne and others claimed that these gatherings were 'unpolitical'; given the personnel, this could hardly be so. FitzGibbon sometimes called his annual gathering 'the feast of the holy innocents', but he also referred to it as 'the *haute école* of intelligent toryism',[37] and this was nearer the mark. Sometimes the company was eclectic enough to frighten off even Churchill; but then he generally came for the New Year instead. And, to anticipate, the Christmas of 1885 was just one of his returns to FitzGibbon's '*haute école*', when the intelligent Tories introduced him to the unintelligent but potent Toryism of Colonel Saunderson and the Ulster Unionists.

II

Churchill's behaviour in relation to Irish issues after he left the country in 1880 is often explicable in terms of Fourth Party politics: the running skirmish carried on against both front-benches by back-bench Tory *enfants terribles* composed of Churchill, J.E. Gorst, Henry Drummond Wolff and – at a slight distance – Balfour. The fact that the Fourth Party's policy (a loose term) was more often than not to place themselves between parties meant that they automatically seemed aligned with the Irish; the recurrent rumours of their break-up were generally seen as meaning a set-back to the Irish cause.[38] The Fourth Party consolidated this impression by presenting arguments which used the Irish case, on issues like the parliamentary *clôture*. However, many of the issues chosen by Churchill to differentiate himself from his leaders' low-key approach had to do with attacking the government for not proceeding firmly against the Irish malcontents.[39] Escalation of confrontation attitudes was in the Fourth

Party's interests; Gorst proudly told Churchill that Charles Russell believed they were responsible for most of the threatening letters in Ireland.[40] Their priority was to use language so extreme that, for instance, Northcote wondered in November 1881 if the government might arrest Churchill on his next visit to Ireland.[41] The Irish appreciated the raising of the political temperature, but they often ignored the actual implications of what Churchill was saying.

At the same time, he continued to represent himself as an Irish expert, referring to his first-hand knowledge of the country on every possible occasion (his recurrent desire to become Chief Secretary may have been manifesting itself early on). To an extent, he was successful; even the despised Northcote referred to him on Irish affairs. But his line on Ireland was not as sympathetic to the nationalists as it sometimes seemed. In the Fourth Party, both Gorst and Wolff were far more radical on the issue of Home Rule. Gorst had his own Irish connections; he visited the country on fact-finding tours; he disliked Ulster Tories and Southern landlords; and he dreamt of working Home Rule into an expansive imperial framework.[42] He wrote to Churchill about this, wondering if the Fourth Party should 'shadow out' such a scheme in Parliament. Wolff was nearly as adaptable. He too had Irish connections; and, like Gorst, he could cheerfully accept the inevitability of Irish separation. He believed that whatever measure of Home Rule might arrive would make little enough difference in the end. Like Gorst, he was ready to anticipate the trend, in the Conservative interest.[43]

But Churchill never committed himself thus far, at least on paper; maybe because such was not his practice (when he wrote at length and discursively there tended to be a motive of publicity in the background), or maybe because he did not believe in the idea. Nor did Balfour commit himself: possibly indicating the difference between Wolff and Gorst, 'scholarship boys' in politics, and their allies, who were born to inherit the political earth and expected, with good reason, to do so. The others never felt they could rely on Balfour, who in his turn suspected Churchill of too much Irish trafficking. But he may have been absorbing from Churchill the decisive ideas on Irish policy which he, and not Churchill, would eventually have the opportunity to put into practice as Chief Secretary – though only at a stage when they no longer provided a sufficient answer.

Even if Churchill avoided theoretical commitment in these years, his actions gave rise to widespread suppositions of a covert relationship with the Irish. He was capable of light references to the inevitability of Home Rule in private; and there was a considerable sympathy on the personal level, as well as identity of political interest, between the Parnellites and Churchill.[44] There was also a frivolous public camaraderie between them, which involved Churchill having long discussions with Justin McCarthy about recent novels during dull debates, and making Mrs Jeune sing 'The Wearing of the Green' at dinner parties attended by Northcote. Churchill also got on remarkably well with Joe Biggar and communicated closely with Tim Healy; he met Parnell at Mrs Jeune's, one of the few social waterholes frequented by the Irish leader, and was often noticed sitting with him, Thomas Sexton, and Henry Labouchère round the stove in the lower smoke-room of the House of Commons.[45] McCarthy emphasized how Churchill liked to create the *impression* of an alliance. Numerous Conservative authorities have concluded with relief that no actual compact existed. There certainly, however, seemed to be an 'understanding'. When Churchill brought an anti-Irish line into debate, it was as often as not simply in order to raise a contentious point at a juncture in the session which precluded any real discussion. When he came round to supporting coercion for Ireland in early 1881, it was in such an ambivalent way that he was thought to be abandoning the Fourth Party; he continued to taunt Forster's policy as being at once draconian and inept,[46] and to be referred to by Gladstone as the Irish Parliamentary Party's 'single English ally'. As the Prime Minister kept pointing out, Churchill's position in regard to the Irish was shared by no one else in the House.

But in many ways his idiosyncratic approach could be attributed to his particular Irish *Unionist* bias. He disapproved of the Liberal policy of coercion unaccompanied by remedial measures, as did FitzGibbon and Morris; and he railed against the government's inability to use the existing jury law more intelligently for the maintenance of order, again like any Conservative Dublin lawyer. To attack the Errington mission, to call for grants to Irish fisheries, was also in this tradition. The exigencies of parliamentary tactics could lead onlookers to infer an alliance: Churchill could, for instance, begin a speech on the Land Bill of 1881 by congratulating Parnell on it, then denounce it as an expropriating measure, and finally mount a campaign of amendments related to it, despite anguished requests from W.H. Smith to cease.[47]

Over land purchase, too, Churchill combined extravagant public denunciation with sober private investigations. On the issue of franchise extension in Ireland he changed front not once but twice; at a juncture when one can certainly see the pressures of British party politics far outweighing any actual analysis of the Irish situation.[48]

Whether or not this was always the case is difficult to say; but Irish nationalist opinion held out great hopes for him, and usually gave him the benefit of the doubt. In England, his stand over the Irish franchise in 1884 was seen purely in terms of opportunism or power politics; in Ireland, the *Freeman* hailed him as '*the* man of his party'.[49] He was also seen as 'recognizing the influence upon the Irish youth of education and the study of the past history and present political position of their country', a reference to the fact that he was pursuing his continuing involvement in Irish educational schemes – principally through FitzGibbon and the duchess's old friend Dr Molloy (described by FitzGibbon as 'a colourless philomath who attends evening parties at Dublin Castle but is a gentleman').[50] Molloy and others believed that Churchill alone was reliable regarding Catholic educational claims, and nurtured dreams – which they shyly shared with him – of seeing him as Chief Secretary. When the Tories briefly entered power in 1885, they did do something for Irish education, in the Educational Endowments Act, which went some way towards the kind of financial restructuring outlined by Churchill in his pamphlet and on the Rosse Commission. This took place via a concerted effort by FitzGibbon, Hugh Holmes (Conservative Attorney-General for Ireland and a protégé of FitzGibbon), and Churchill himself.[51] Sexton was also involved and, at a later stage, Dwyer Gray – dealing directly with Churchill. The measure was passed on 14 August, the last day of the session.

When the constitution of the commission set up by this act ran into trouble with the Irish hierarchy, Churchill involved himself; at FitzGibbon's request, he sent a letter full of 'vigour and vertebra' to bring the bishops to heel.[52] But when FitzGibbon went on to drive a rift between the moderates, such as Delany and Molloy, and the increasingly intransigent figure of Archbishop Walsh, Churchill baulked. The story of education commission politics in 1885–6 has a symbolic interest: the clerics who had been so pleased to work with the Marlboroughs in the 1870s can be seen as crushed between the immovable Presbyterian interest on one side, and the equally intractable Walsh on the other. There was a new dispensation at work. Churchill failed to see it; he pressed FitzGibbon not to play episcopal politics, telling him the bishops were the only bulwark between them and Home Rule, which 'they don't care a damn for'.[53] This may have held good in the 1870s, but by 1885 it was no longer true. Walsh was determined on an intransigent stance, and in December 1885 he formally boycotted the commission after all. Churchill did not give up; he asked Salisbury's permission to 'intrigue with Walsh' on his Irish trip in that month, believing that FitzGibbon had not understood him.

But FitzGibbon had decided that Churchill's policy of winning over the bishops was no longer viable, an assessment also reached by the Viceroy, Carnarvon. Carnarvon decided that therefore Home Rule must be accepted; FitzGibbon drew the opposite conclusion. Churchill continued to back FitzGibbon in his parleys about Catholic university education (and had drawn up plans for this in a sweeping remedial outline of Irish policy which he presented to Salisbury in November 1885). However, on university education, too, Walsh stuck fast, after lengthy negotiations; taking his ground on the point most impossible for Irish Unionist opinion to accept, a demand for changes in the status of Trinity College, 'the citadel of ascendancy'.[54] This led to a series of letters from FitzGibbon to Churchill, remarkable for their uncharacteristically desperate tone. The existence of non-landed Irish Protestants, he wrote, depended upon Trinity; already an exodus of professional men had begun from Dublin, for the sake of their children's education.[55] Walsh's obstinacy and FitzGibbon's alarmism came at just the point when Churchill was switching to a confrontation policy. And he had visited Dublin twice that autumn and winter; he saw much of the Howth symposium; he ended by falling back on a violent Unionist initiative. If there were objective Irish reasons as well as obviously expedient English ones, it seems logical to look at the suddenly embattled attitude of his Dublin contacts, and the breakdown of negotiations with the traditionally friendly Irish episcopacy.

There were also, of course, party manoeuvres, which can provide reasons for this as for everything else. Intense negotiations between Churchill and the Irish during the summer were alleged by everyone from John Dillon to Herbert Gladstone, and a Home Rule undertaking was widely inferred; but others had heard that Churchill anticipated, early on, a policy which involved ditching the Irish by occupying a strong anti-Home Rule platform.[56] A shadowy dimension is added to Churchill's dealings with the Irish by his links with less savoury members of the party like Philip Callan and William O'Shea. Callan, the contentious MP for Louth who was the first to raise in public the spectre of the O'Shea liaison against Parnell, wrote to Churchill in 1885, making ominous allegations about the Home Rule leader, asking for money to continue in politics, and later soliciting a job in India.[57] Cardinal Manning urgently asked Churchill to oblige; perhaps he knew Callan's secrets, and his proverbially loose tongue.[58] O'Shea, too, was on close terms with Churchill (he turns up in 1881 in the bizarre role of Churchill's second in a threatened duel with Lord Hartington). They themselves later crossed swords metaphorically on several occasions, Churchill at one point mischievously referring to O'Shea in public as 'a person who from every point of view is absolutely repugnant and loathsome politically and from every point of view' to the Irish party. O'Shea took violent exception to this, and it is likely that Churchill was throwing out a hint; Parnell's private life was stale gossip in Churchill's circle by 1886.[59] O'Shea later worked with Churchill over Catholic education. Possibly Churchill retained links with Callan and O'Shea because of the potential advantage to be derived from Parnell's personal position, though it could as well be put down to a Bohemian love of slumming, or a congenital addiction to intrigue.

Not everyone, however, saw him in this light. The Fourth Party wrote derisively to each other about Wilfrid Scawen Blunt, who expected Churchill to be redeemed through Ireland and to assume the 'mantle of conscience' from Gladstone's shoulders, as well as that of Elijah from Salisbury's;[60] he took a long time to disembarrass himself from the conception. Blunt was not alone; W.H. Duignan, a Radical interested in Ireland, also tried to enrol Churchill publicly on the side of the angels. And from the opposite bias, chauvinist Tory Democrats worried desperately about Churchill's seduction by Irish issues,[61] which seemed to contradict their hopes of him. Similarly, the gimcrack iconography of the Primrose League had nothing to do with remedial ideas about Ireland.

It is a moot point how far all these expectations and fears would have been upheld if Churchill had ever become Chief Secretary. A rumour of this reached Portarlington in June 1885, and delighted him.[62] Even though Churchill went to the India Office instead, he still presented Salisbury with an enormous memorandum on Irish policy in November; this took an impeccably anti-Repeal line, which may or may not have been principally dictated by a wish to tell Salisbury what it was politic for him to hear. In January 1886 Churchill suggested himself as an alternative to Smith for the chief secretaryship, an idea that recurred in June, when Beach shuddered at it as 'an ideally bad appointment'.[63] Through 1885–6 Churchill was constantly receiving advice about Ireland, with several Tory contacts there advocating a constitutional alliance with Parnell and remedial legislation 'only short of a separate legislature'; even Morris suggested an above-party solution, incorporating Parnell. Churchill sent a *non possumus* reply, in terms of strict ministerial piety: 'radical work must be done by radical artists', he chided Morris, who must have gulped.[64] But copies of such letters were simultaneously sent by him to an approving Salisbury, self-presentation being as ever an urgent priority.

There was also a constant thread of advice from FitzGibbon, who more and more emphatically urged Churchill 'not to touch the national question'; rumours had reached Dublin of a halting Tory Home Rule scheme in December 1885.[65] There is an implication in this and other letters that FitzGibbon was not sure of Churchill's reliability on the issue. This urgency heightened as rumours of Gladstone's impending conversion to Home Rule entered circulation in mid-December; but Churchill was due at Howth for Christmas (he had already been there in September, as well as encountering FitzGibbon at Ashbourne's French holiday house in August). Pressure would be applied then. Nationalist opinion in Dublin continued to have hopes of a Tory conversion under Churchill; in early 1886 reference was still being made to the chance of a settlement represented by the Catholic–Conservative ethos.[66] Much attention had been paid earlier to Churchill's criticism of the Dublin Castle system just published in the *Pall Mall Gazette*. When he first entered office, the *Freeman* referred to him approvingly as 'a friend to Ireland'; a Unionist correspondent informed him 'you are popular to a surprising degree in Ireland'.[67]

Historians have obsessively monitored the political shifts of 1885–6, with careful attention to Churchill's part in them. Afterwards, he himself chose to see these bewildering months in terms of the realization by the Conservatives that they could not govern without coercion – despite the fact that he for one had made it clear he could not enter a government committed to such a policy. For this basic contradiction Churchill violently, and conveniently, blamed Gibson's erroneous and self-interested advice on the Irish situation to Salisbury. Others did not see Churchill's progress towards advocacy of coercion in mid-January 1886 as a moral dilemma, but simply as trimming. He was in an impossible position; his genius for giving easy impressions out of office was called to account once power was gained. July 1885 had seen his celebrated challenge to his leaders in the Maamtrasna debate, when he went against prearranged Conservative tactics by denouncing the Spencer regime and promising the Parnellites an inquiry into the Maamtrasna Murders: this was supposed by many to formalize a Conservative–Parnellite alliance.[68] Salisbury was not particularly bothered, but the Ulster Unionists were infuriated. Churchill attempted to mollify them with a speech at Sheffield, geared, not very convincingly, to ridiculing the very idea of a Parnellite alliance. But the Ulstermen were not appeased; to Churchill's chagrin, Lord Claud Hamilton (a moving spirit in defence organizations in the province as well as a creator of the Ulster Unionist base in Parliament) refused to share a platform with him in Liverpool the next month. Conservative candidates in November inundated him with requests to make it publicly clear that he had not sold his political soul to the Parnellites, though they also begged him for help with the Irish vote in their constituencies. His Irish Unionist contacts reinforced the message. Visiting Dublin in September and October, Churchill attempted to reassure them, informing Holmes that 'we must have nothing to do with home rule in any shape or form'.[69] Holmes, a flinty Unionist lawyer with an Ulster background, hardly needed telling; the intention was primarily to clarify Churchill's own position and provide reassurance. Christmas saw him once more at Howth.

On this visit, Blunt believed Churchill was still talking Home Rule to select acquaintances, though he had already made his position after Gladstone's embrace of Home Rule clear to McCarthy and to Blunt himself. Back in London in January, he began his withdrawal from formal opposition to coercion, constantly bombarded by FitzGibbon, as he did so, with calls for firm measures.[70] Carnarvon, who had been led along by Churchill through a halcyon Irish summer of Home Rule half-promises, where many of his contacts and ideas echoed

Churchill's, was scandalized to see his supposed ally a convert to draconian measures by mid-January. At this point Churchill floated the idea of proclaiming the National League and arresting prominent politicians and National League leaders. There is a key in the fact that, as outlined initially to Holmes, this scheme was part of a plan which involved – yet again – Churchill going to Ireland as Chief Secretary.[71] But Carnarvon could only take refuge in the comforting assumption that Churchill was mad.

This was not (yet) the case. But Churchill had heard, via Henry James and Labouchère, that Parnell would not be fobbed off with remedial measures;[72] he wanted a powerful initiative, probably led by himself, in Ireland; he had been apprised by FitzGibbon of the significance of the hierarchy's new hard line; and he had to allay suspicions of his own reliability on the Home Rule question. As for Carnarvonism and Carnarvon, Churchill had never been committed to the Viceroy, who had been brutally categorized by the FitzGibbon circle as a 'gusher'; Holmes thought him 'weak, vain, and emotional', and Churchill followed this line too. Later, he magnanimously described Carnarvon to McCarthy as 'a Don Quixote', adding unnecessarily, 'I am not that kind of man at all.'[73] Nevertheless, by this point, he was engaging himself to go adventuring in Ulster, where windmills tilted at rhetorically could turn out to be giants after all.

III

Immediately following these shifts in emphasis, Churchill publicly identified himself with hardline Ulster Unionism in February 1886. This *rapprochement* was begun before the Tories left office, though he would have seemed the most unlikely of candidates a year before. But besides the events of the moment, there were some inner strands of logic in the development. One might go back as far as his mother's Ulster background, and both the Marlboroughs' disenchantment with Ireland after 1880, as well as his own observation of the Irish political situation in the late 1870s and early 1880s, when activity in the North was beginning to escalate. In 1880 he had vague thoughts of making an 'inflammatory' tour in Ulster, but confided to Gibson that he 'feared Kane'.[74] Dr R.R. Kane was a Grand Master of the Belfast Orangemen, who suspected Churchill of secret commitment to nationalism; Churchill did not enlarge on why he feared him in 1880, and one might wonder in what direction the inflammation was intended. Certainly his references to Ulster Members at this time tended to be hostile. FitzGibbon thought Churchill cared too little for Ulster, warning him in October 1883 (apropos of Northcote's visit) that he ignored the real and deserving Unionism of the Ulstermen: 'no doubt the orange flag is given to frightening otherwise steady horses, but it is the only one which gathers any rank and file together in Ireland who would not cut all your Britishers adrift tomorrow if they could, and cut all *our* throats the day after'.[75]

This points up the fact that FitzGibbon's advice, despite his network of Catholic contacts and his support of denominational education, all tended towards unflinching, Ulster-oriented Unionism. And shortly after this letter came the celebrated Rosslea incident, giving Churchill the opportunity to play a small Orange card in late 1883, which he did with gusto. Lord Rossmore, dismissed from the magistracy in Fermanagh for Orange bias in a public affray, provided a new-minted Protestant hero. Just after this, a speech at Edinburgh in December 1883 also shows Churchill bringing out the theme of the indivisible Union, in an extreme formulation. However, his line on Irish franchise the following year was seen as a direct threat by the Ulster Unionists; and it is only when Churchill had to mend his fences after the Maamtrasna debate that we find him again referring, in a speech at Sheffield, to the wisdom and probity of the Ulster MPs.

In the same month, September 1885, Carnarvon had visited the North of Ireland; Beach, who gloomily expected little good from his journey, hoped that Churchill would soon do likewise.[76] Such ventures were a stock in trade for Conservative politicians: Northcote, for instance, had sent Gibson off there in 1880 and made his own tentative visit in 1883. The heightened political activity in the province over this period made Tories like Northcote worry whether the party really ought to be identified with Orangeism;[77] but Irish Conservatives paid more attention to Orange cries from 1884 on, including Churchill's friends Plunket and Gibson. At the same time, nationalist opinion adhered to the comfortable belief that Orange intransigents in the North were a small minority.[78] In November 1885, when pressing his remedial Irish plans on Salisbury, Churchill denounced 'those foul Ulster tories who have always been the ruin of our party'.[79] This was in the wake of the Maamtrasna debate, but it was not an uncommon reaction; Beach held similar views. Yet at the same time the growing importance, as well as the potential usefulness, of Ulster Unionism can never have been far from Churchill's mind, for all his dislike of the crudity and aggressiveness of its proponents at Westminster. And essentially his attitude towards this lobby moderated from the time of the Rosslea incident in late 1883, and was stiffened by FitzGibbon's messages of increasingly embattled Unionism in 1885–6. The course thus adopted was a departure from the 'Catholic Conservative' ideal which, given a calm social background of prosperity and a defused land problem, seemed once to have been capable of producing the kind of Home Rule that meant the opposite of Repeal.

From 1884, however, Churchill was liable to use Parnellism, Home Rule and Repeal interchangeably, despite the efforts of correspondents to point out semantic differences. And the events of 1885–6 pushed him inexorably northwards. In early December 1885 an apprehensive Blunt noticed 'an odd mischievous look come over his face' at the mention of Ireland, and expected a change of direction.[80] In mid-December he warned Labouchère of his readiness in certain circumstances 'to agitate Ulster to resistance even beyond constitutional limits'; the hung election result and Gladstone's initiative supplied the necessary conditions. Labouchère at once passed the message on to Healy, as Churchill had probably intended.

In Dublin at Christmas, FitzGibbon and Holmes put Churchill in touch with Colonel Saunderson.[81] He then returned to London and contacted Lord George Hamilton, who enthusiastically assented to an Ulster venture. Churchill followed this by carefully paying warm tributes to Saunderson in the House of Commons, and urging Salisbury to sweeten the Ulster Members in private meetings. At the end of January the first press rumours of a Belfast visit appeared. Nationalist papers took an injured tone; even Tory ministers were rumoured to fear bloodshed. Minds cannot have been set at rest by Churchill's first speech to his new constituents at South Paddington, a week before he went to Ulster. This was a violent Orange tirade, during which he unleashed a volley of backs-to-the-wall Protestant clichés, to the surprise and delight of die-hard Ulster opinion, called up images of civil war brought about by Gladstone's 'monstrous and unparalleled combination of verbosity and senility', and repeatedly offered the assistance of English hearts and hands to their beleaguered co-religionists. This speech (which referred to Protestants rather than loyalists, and contained a direct attack on the Catholic hierarchy) was far more extreme than anything he was to say in Belfast. There were at once some scandalized calls for his arrest; more reasoned opinion saw it as evidence of the government's adoption of hard-line orthodoxy, with the *Telegraph* describing it as 'restoring morality to politics'. Churchill followed it up with a public letter of markedly die-hard Protestantism, denouncing his mother's old friend Archbishop Walsh especially as a 'separatist';[82] he had learned that the bishops could no longer be used against Home Rule. The nationalist press, in tones of lugubrious disappointment, finally abandoned their hopes of Churchill; the editorial in the *Freeman* read like the most regretful of obituary notices.[83] Which, in a sense, it was.

But looked at from the North this new champion, despite his equivocal record, had been visible in the distance for some time. Ever since the Charles Bradlaugh affair in 1880, when he had opposed an atheist's right to affirm, he had been approached by belligerent Anglican bishops with a view to becoming the spokesman of militant Protestantism in Parliament. And after the Rosslea incident of October 1883, Churchill took up the Protestant martyr's case with ostentatious enthusiasm, sending a letter to Lord Arthur Hill in which he expressed violent approbation of Rossmore's action.[84] One reason for his speedy adoption of this cause may have been its popularity with Tory Democracy on his home ground; among the letters of sympathy and support received by Rossmore there was a noticeably large proportion from Conservative working men's organizations,[85] and Churchill was at the time absorbed in his epic struggle for control of their National Union. He remained identified with the affair, which was raised in the House of Lords by Churchill's friend and parliamentary ally, Lord Dunraven. The Rosslea incident and its aftermath became a *cause célèbre*, monopolizing the editorials in Irish papers for two months and raising at an early stage the issue of Conservative support for Ulster Unionism even in situations of doubtful constitutionalism. At one point Churchill engaged in a heated exchange with Parnell over it, daring him to put himself in the position of an Ulster Orangeman and then be in favour of Home Rule (called, of course, 'repeal' by Churchill).[86]

None of this was necessarily incompatible with his dislike of 'foul Ulster tories', much less his initiative in Catholic education. And he had contacts in Ulster which went back further than the hectic switches of 1885–6. Sir John Leslie, who had convened the Rosslea meeting, was connected to him by marriage; Leslie, an unreconstructed die-hard, had proposed at Rosslea a resolution to exclude Catholics from Parliament.[87] His son, Lady Randolph's brother-in-law, was to accompany Churchill to Belfast in February 1886. Lord George Hamilton pressed his political friendship on Churchill after Rosslea, urging him to visit his father, the Duke of Abercorn, at Baronscourt and view 'the northern farming class, who are the best conditioned people in the United Kingdom'.[88] Churchill's reluctance to do so need not be taken as an aspersion on the Northern farming class; he would also have had to meet Abercorn's daughter, the injured Lady Blandford – who as his brother's wife had been an innocent party in the scandal which sent the Marlboroughs to Ireland nine eventful years before.

But the most recent of Churchill's Ulster contacts was the most important. This was the leader of the Ulster Unionists in Parliament, Colonel Saunderson (a glowing exception to the rule that anyone educated by the Jesuits at an early age is theirs for life).[89] An unlikely associate for Churchill, he mixed a taste for violent practical jokes with a matter-of-fact approach to revivalist religion, and was politically of a Liberal background. He came to Orangeism in the 1880s, returning to politics by starring at a demonstration organized by William Johnston of Ballykilbeg in 1882. In 1884 he formally renounced the Liberals, appearing with Plunket and Gibson at a Rotunda demonstration in Dublin. Besides emphasizing the need for a rearmed Orangeism, he was dedicated to 'giving it hot to Northcote', which must have appealed to Churchill; he also seems to have been one of the MPs approached by Callan in his one-man campaign against Parnell in 1885.[90]

Churchill was impressed by Saunderson's public claims about exerting a balancing influence at Westminster in 1885. In the Christmas of that year, their meeting was arranged by the Howth circle of 'intelligent tories'. According to Saunderson, Churchill said little, and Saunderson told him roundly that Ulster did not trust him. In any case, Churchill must have been slightly nonplussed by Saunderson, who chose to present himself as an uncompromising political innocent. (For one thing, Saunderson all his life denounced the idea of an official Catholic university as a trick of Satan; whereas Churchill would have scattered such foundations all over Ireland, including

Armagh.) Their liaison was, however, made. Churchill returned to London and contacted Hamilton. He then started negotiations (along with Gibson) for Ulster Unionist support at Westminster. On 26 January 1886, Saunderson recorded, Churchill 'came to me and pledged himself at my disposal for a meeting in Ulster whenever I thought it necessary to hold one'.[91] 'It seems queer to me,' he added, 'to become suddenly a political personage, hobnobbing with cabinet ministers . . .'

The way was open to further contacts, like the celebrated William Johnston of Ballykilbeg. As soon as Johnston heard of Churchill's projected visit, he determined to identify it with Orangeism rather than simple Unionism, and began a publicity campaign to this effect.[92] From the beginning of February until his speech on Churchill's platform in Belfast, it was obvious that he was trying to do what Northcote had so feared regarding himself in 1883: 'giving an Orange character to the visit'.[93] Churchill's political friends in England reacted less energetically. Beach was surprised the visit was going ahead; he had thought of accompanying his colleague, but had decided activity in London would be more productive, and commiserated with Churchill on not being able to get out of it. Press leaks and the Paddington speech made Churchill's intention public; FitzGibbon wrote in excited approval; the schedule for the visit took shape. At the principal meeting Churchill was to be proposed by Dr Kane – somewhat ironically, as Kane had once declared that if Churchill ever set foot in Ulster 'things would be made very hot for him'.[94] Lord Arthur Hill, Lord Deramore, Reverend Crawford and other stalwarts were also busily involved in preparations; the strangeness of these bedfellows for Churchill did not go unremarked.

Churchill left London on 21 February with Lord Rossmore, W.E. McCartney, Robert O'Neill, Saunderson, and Jack Leslie.[95] He arrived the next morning to a muted welcome in Larne, suffering from his habitual seasickness. After lunch there, he made a brief speech and proceeded to Belfast via Carrickfergus on a special train. He arrived at the Northern Counties Station in York Street to a tumultuous welcome. Addresses were presented, several harking back to the golden age of the Marlborough viceroyalty, a theme repeated by Churchill himself. Reporters noted his own gravity and thoughtfulness (or perhaps seasickness). He travelled to the Ulster Hall and received more addresses, those from Orange lodges taking marked precedence (though some lodges had allegedly stayed away because of Churchill's suspected Home Rule affiliations). Despite the Duke of Abercorn's habitual prominence at such gatherings, all the Hamiltons also stayed away; possibly for the same reason, or possibly out of solidarity with Lady Blandford. Churchill replied to the addresses with a low-key speech, mostly about his Ulster ancestors.

That evening he returned to the Ulster Hall for the main meeting. At Larne he had told his audience that their privileges were worth fighting for, but that it might not come to that; here, however, he approached more nearly the appropriate tone, accusing Gladstone of an ambition to convert Trinity College into 'a Roman Catholic seminary' and calling up the horrors of 1641. Given his own record, his strictures on the franchise and on Parnell's position represented many piquant self-contradictions.[96] On the religious issue, he assailed the Catholic Church for encouraging sedition in the guise of an appeal to loyal Catholics and a commiseration with their trials. Archbishop Walsh was – as had become usual for Churchill – singled out for special attack. And if the Protestant faith was threatened they must remember 'No surrender' and give practical meaning to 'the forms and ceremonies of Orangeism'. He instructed them to make their demonstrations orderly and, for the moment, to wait and prepare. The storm might blow over; but 'if my calculations should turn out to be wrong, then I am not of the opinion, and I have never been of the opinion, that this struggle is likely to remain within the lines of what we are accustomed to look upon as constitutional action'. He rounded off with a reference to the American Civil War, and a promise of physical support from England in the dark hour.

One academic interpretation of this speech is that he was attempting to defuse the situation and counsel calm;[97] if so, it only goes to show how little he understood Ulster. And exhortations to moderation in Churchill's speech were probably directed towards preventing riots following the meeting. His fellow speakers followed the more belligerent emphasis. Saunderson promised another Boyne and added a Nietzschean epigraph: 'my experience of the present age is this – that the age values one thing only, and that is force'. Johnston followed and, like Saunderson, emphasized that Churchill's presence in Belfast represented a triumph for Ulster Unionism, and Orangeism in particular. As the guest of honour drove back to the house of his host, Sir Edward Harland, Lord Mayor of the city (and a friend of

FitzGibbon), rioting broke out in the streets. Churchill stayed the night, lunched next day at the Ulster Club, and left the province, never to return.

'Churchill's crusade' had a striking immediate effect. Salisbury swiftly congratulated him. The nationalist press contrived to see it as a failure.[98] English Conservative papers applauded it, though piously regretting the inevitably sectarian overtones. From the other side, motions were drafted to accuse him of incitement to civil war; individual Irish nationalists were less upset (at least in private) than disillusioned political innocents like Blunt.[99] Saunderson saw it all as 'a splendid success'; foreign arms firms began to send him catalogues for rifles.

Immediate reasons of political advantage have been powerfully adduced as the only causes of Churchill's appearance in Belfast, and whether it actually made a categoric difference to how affairs in Ulster immediately developed has been queried.[100] But it can be seen as representing a long-term development in Churchill's career, as well as a process which has a wider importance in the sphere of Anglo-Irish relations. It is worth noting that after February 1886 his range of Irish contacts diminished; militant Unionists and cranks predominate among his correspondents. At least one old acquaintance, however, had witnessed the Belfast epic, and applauded it. FitzGibbon's brother Henry, another Dublin Tory, and professional man, had travelled to Belfast, drawn by solidarity with Ulster and 'I trust not a morbid desire to see and hear you as a public man'. From his hotel on Royal Avenue he watched Churchill's entry:

> You can have no idea of the imposing sight it was . . . For a whole mile as far as the eye could reach there was a dense and orderly mass of respectable men marching after your carriage. I did not see a single drunken or disorderly person in the vast crowd. The contrast in this respect with the other demonstrations which it has been my misfortune to be a witness of was *most* striking. I congratulate you on your enterprise in coming here, and it cannot fail to open the eyes of the Saxon 'just a wee bit'.[101]

Harland had got FitzGibbon into the Ulster Hall to hear Churchill's speech, 'which I would not have missed for anything; you have made a big score, and I hope you will accept my sincere congratulations as they are meant'.[102] Belfast had the blessing of the Howth symposium.

It is doubtful if Churchill saw the venture as presaging a departure any further into the Orange spectrum. Alvin Jackson has demonstrated that many Conservatives took Ulster Unionism very seriously from then on; but Churchill was not one of them. He detached himself from the Ulstermen as swiftly as was decent, fulminating against their lack of parliamentary manners and vainly trying to keep Saunderson quiet. Statements like his admission a month after Belfast that he had 'for a considerable time hoped to be able to work in alliance with the Irish party' appalled Ulster. But Saunderson implacably ignored his pleas for moderation, and Churchill's new allies continued to behave proprietorially towards him, asking for his support in local power struggles, and reiterating to him that they were unfairly vilified in the English press ('the tarring of the man Johnson at the Island has been tremendously exaggerated').[103] It was an alien subculture to Churchill, and he complained about its demands on him.[104] But his position was an awkward one; for instance, he had now to have police protection against assassination attempts, and several Conservative MPs upbraided him for identifying Protestantism with loyalism.

Some Ulster Tories, of course, never trusted him – as Abercorn wrote triumphantly to Salisbury after Churchill's stunning resignation as Chancellor of the Exchequer and Leader of the House at Christmas 1886.[105] Out of office, he was a less and less likely champion for Ulster Unionism. In the wilderness he reverted to southern Irish initiatives (Beach had feared that he was after the chief secretaryship again in July 1886). However, an Orange penumbra remained, and made him less approachable; those trying to negotiate him into the Liberal camp concentrated upon Ulster as a probable stumbling-block.[106] FitzGibbon still advised him as closely as ever; and on issues like land purchase and the *Times* Commission, Churchill followed the FitzGibbon line exactly. Educational intrigues had never ceased. Even before his resignation, Salisbury had rejected an Irish local government plan backed by Churchill as 'too much like real home rule'; in 1889 Churchill recurred to such a scheme, collaborating with Carnarvon, FitzGibbon and Hartington. By that year, Irish die-hard opinion had begun once more to fear him as too progressive.[107]

But little ever happened – for reasons partly to do with Churchill's health, partly with Balfour's policy, partly with changes in Ireland itself. In 1890 Churchill drafted three long articles on Irish land purchase, denouncing the idea of bailing out landlords ('rent-chargers and encumbrancers') and advocating a scheme reliant upon wide measures of local government. Irish initiative was the only valid dynamic for legislation, and retreat from a policy that had been proved unwise was the only politic approach.[108] This could have stood as an epigraph for his own position *vis-à-vis* Irish affairs; but since February 1886 the verities had changed. The hardening of attitudes through the events of the eighties had caused even the heroically decisive FitzGibbon to have doubts. In February 1888 he watched from his drawing-room in Merrion Square as a Union of Hearts demonstration surged past en route from Ballsbridge to Rutland Square. Afterwards he wrote to Churchill:

The scene from our windows here was your Belfast entry by mud and rebellion out of torchlight, with T.D. Sullivan fresh from Tullamore jail as first gentleman, and Ripon K.G. and ex-governor-general of India and then Morley, freethinker from the privy council, both playing second. In ten minutes after the last band had played 'God Save Ireland' and the last star-spangled banner had gone by, my wife, daughters and I drove off to Dublin Castle: never got there or back so quickly or so easily, and never saw there a larger or more 'brilliant' assembly. Which Rome is burning, and who is hero?[109]

This uncertainty prevailed; he could think of 'no new views on Ireland', being unsure about 'the reality of anything on either side'.[110] Like other intelligent Unionists, he favoured moderate devolution by 1889; but, as he wrote to Churchill, what now loomed in the background was 'the impregnable Ulster unionist province'.

It cannot be made a subdivision of united Ireland, without depriving all the congenial inhabitants of the rest of the island of their only hope and support, and at the same time exposing the 'masses' living in Ulster to the most unbending and to them repugnant rule of the extreme Ulster party, and sacrificing all the 'loyalists' everywhere else. On the other hand it can't be kept as an England in Ireland without raising a frontier question of the most utterly insoluble character, and it can't be forced under the hateful yoke of home rule without destruction of its prosperity, if not without actual force.[111]

In 1886 FitzGibbon's emotional Unionism had been amplified by his resentment at the terms of land purchase, and by what he saw as a general sell-out to the anti-British elements in the south at the expense of the Trinity-educated professional classes, traditionally faithful to the British connection. He had introduced Churchill to Saunderson, encouraged his Belfast initiative, and backed him with all the accustomed weight of Howth Toryism. By 1890 he had reverted to the idea of Churchill's completing the Union by a positive, conciliatory Irish policy, probably in alliance with Rosebery: a notion shared by Churchill himself. But the constructive Unionist initiative was no longer sufficient answer; the spirit of the 1870s was as dead as the seventh Duke of Marlborough. And the kind of atavistic political emotions and literal apprehensions of rhetoric, which Churchill played with in the North, were essentially foreign to a flexible pragmatist like himself. Images of Faust as well as Pandora, over-simplifying though they are, remain inescapable.

The story of Churchill's Orange card, seen in context, can be an enlightening one, both in terms of what was afterwards made of such a tactic, and how Churchill's behaviour was interpreted at the time. It is illustrative of Churchill's imaginative but imperfect apprehension of the Irish problem – noted by contemporaries, but only recently re-emphasized by historians. If he had nationalist contacts, they were not among those so assiduously maintained in Dublin; and wondering whether he was a covert Home Ruler seems less relevant than considering the extent to which politicians used Home Rule as it suited them, and what Home Rule actually meant, as opposed to what it stood for. Churchill may have been exceptional in his adaptability, and was often exceptional in the specific nature of his policy statements. He was also exceptional in having a quasi-Irish background in the 1870s, and a permanent conditioning influence exerted upon him from Howth.

From education in 1877 to the *Times* Commission in 1889 and land purchase in 1890, Churchill's public ideas were preceded by private advice from FitzGibbon; and Ulster came in between, at a juncture when the influence from Howth, the impressions left by his Irish stay, and the bewildering prism of high politics combined to lead him out on a political limb. Even without his self-destructive resignation, it is doubtful if he could ever have regained the creative initiative in Irish policy which – had he ever had his ambition of the chief secretaryship – he would once very likely have carried out.

IV

On a foggy afternoon in November 1947, sixty-one years after Lord Randolph's Ulster visit and more than fifty after his premature death, his son Winston decided to use some of his enforced idleness to copy a portrait of his father – 'painted for one of the Belfast Conservative Clubs about the time of his visit to Ulster in the Home Rule crisis of 1886'.[112] Deeply absorbed in studying the painting and his own canvas, turning from his subject to the large mirror which he had set up to reflect it, he

> suddenly felt an odd sensation. I turned round with my palette in my hand, and there, sitting in my red leather upright armchair, was my father. He looked just as I had seen him in his prime, and as I had read about him in his brief year of triumph. He was small and slim, with the big moustache I was just painting, and all his bright, captivating, jaunty air. His eyes twinkled and shone. He was evidently in the best of tempers. He was engaged in filling his amber cigarette-holder with a little pad of cotton-wool before putting in the cigarette. This was in order to stop the nicotine, which used to be thought deleterious. He was so exactly like my memories of him in his most charming moods that I could hardly believe my eyes. I felt no alarm, but I thought I would stand where I was and go no nearer.[113]

A conversation developed, of the kind which his son must often have dreamed about. The ghost addressed gently mocking queries about the state of the world, and the ex-world leader returned modest answers which concealed his own part in history. Lord Randolph's shade expressed scepticism about the survival of the monarchy, pleasure that horse-racing 'still goes on', and approval that the socialists sometimes wore sweaters to Buckingham Palace. Eventually, after declaring his astonishment at the negligible results of female suffrage, he asked about Ireland.

> 'Did they get Home Rule?'
>
> 'The South got it, but Ulster stayed with us.'
>
> 'Are the South a republic?'
>
> 'No one knows what they are. They are neither in nor out of the Empire. But they are much more friendly to us than they used to be. They have built up a cultured Roman Catholic system in the South. There has been no

anarchy or confusion. They are getting more happy and prosperous. The bitter past is fading.'

'Ah,' he said, 'how vexed the Tories were with me when I observed that there was no English statesman who had not had his hour of Home Rule.' Then, after a pause, 'What about the Home Rule meaning "Rome Rule?"'

'It certainly does, but they like it. And the Catholic Church has now become a great champion of individual liberty.'

'You must be living in a very happy age. A Golden Age, it seems.'[114]

This illusion was dispatched by a subsequent exchange about the world wars and the new Tsar in Russia ('It's another family. He is much more powerful, and much more despotic'): before fading, the apparition expressed profound relief that he had not lived to see the events of the twentieth century. Both ghost and interlocutor, however, seemed quite happy about the state of Ireland, north and south. Alive or dead, Lord Randolph's insouciance indicated not only cynicism but tunnel vision: and an inability to sense the results of actions outside his own arena.

He also believed in the dual nature of politics, public and private, his public reactions often being decided upon either flippantly or with a ruthless priority of manoeuvre. In Belfast, however, he was nearly led into a Midlothian-style crusade, conferring authority on an area of Irish policy which he probably never intended. Irish politics in many essentials operated outside the charmed circle of the English high political world – which can provide such an entertaining reflection of how things were done at Westminster. Churchill failed to grasp this; and the educated Dublin Tories from whom he took so much of his policy also misjudged reality in 1886. The result had a decisive effect on Churchill's career; it also made its mark on Irish history.

13

Thinking from Hand to Mouth: Anglo-Irish Literature, Gaelic Nationalism and Irish Politics in the 1890s

I

Macaulay, in his *History of England*, postulated an appropriately mechanical 'explanation' for the scientific revolution of the late seventeenth century: 'The torrent which had been dammed up in one channel rushed violently into another. The revolutionary spirit, ceasing to operate in politics, began to exert itself with unprecedented vigour and hardihood in every department of physics.'[1] It is the sort of analysis whose ingenuousness raises an indulgent smile now. But an analogous process of reasoning has dominated commentaries on Ireland after the fall of Parnell. The torrent of 'politics' was seen suddenly to run into the channel of 'culture', in a curiously unquestioned way, creating a ferment which is automatically assumed to have been the necessary precondition of the 1916 rising.

Thus Nicholas Mansergh sees post-1891 as

> a shift of interest from Westminster to Ireland, from the source of constitutional reform to the breeding-ground of rebellion . . . Encouraged in their romanticism by the poetry of Yeats and his circle, dreaming of the regeneration of Ireland with Douglas Hyde, the young men marked out as their goal, not the pedestrian Home Rule haven of the Nationalist party, but the independent Ireland of the Fenians.[2]

This led Mansergh on to a suggestive treatment of 'The Influence of the Romantic Ideal in Irish Politics', which fundamentally presented the contemporary argument of Yeats's friend John Eglinton. 'Yeats, and the literary movement in which he was a commanding figure, may be said to have conjured up the armed bands of 1916.'[3] F.S.L. Lyons endorsed this, though with characteristic (and increasing) caution,[4] and so did Conor Cruise O'Brien, Richard Ellmann and George Dangerfield.[5] The 1890s were presented as the seedbed of cultural revolution, absorbing energy that had somehow diverted itself from political to intellectual agitation, as with Macaulay's physicists. The question of what – or whose – energy was thus diverted tended to be left aside; so was the question of whether the energies that produced the cultural efflorescence of the 1890s would ever have found their way into political channels. The idea was too potent, and too inspirational, for questions as mundane as that.

This was largely because the thesis was so well expressed by the generations who lived through the upheavals of the early twentieth century. In fact, even as the 1890s drew to a close, in a celebrated lecture to the Gaelic League in September 1899, Father Peter Yorke of San Francisco denounced the passing decade. It had been a time of disastrous apathy, a 'lull' in politics while the Gaelic League alone kept the faith. In relating his lecture directly to the progress of proselytizing on behalf of the Irish language, and mounting an onslaught on supposed organs of Anglicization, he advanced the idea that anything productive in Irish life since Parnell's fall had been cultural.

Yorke would not have looked to the revolution in local government of 1898, or to the mass movement of land agitation which was at that very time galvanizing the west. Nor, as an extremely bigoted Irish American, would he have been an admirer of the already celebrated W.B. Yeats. But Yeats was already outlining a similar analysis in public letters at this time, and later (in 1923) gave classic form to the Yorke thesis during a lecture delivered to the Royal Academy of Sweden:

> The modern literature of Ireland, and indeed all that stir of thought which prepared for the Anglo-Irish War, began when Parnell fell from power in 1891. A disillusioned and embittered Ireland turned from parliamentary politics; an event was conceived; and the race began, as I think, to be troubled by that event's long gestation.[6]

The 'event' mentioned was, of course, the 1916 rising. Thus, just like the luckless Chief Secretary Augustine Birrell, Yeats saw the rising as inevitably looming up from the debris of post-Parnellite politics, and inevitably brought about by the cultural events which started twenty-five years before.

Birrell, whose political career was destroyed by 1916, had his reasons for laying this emphasis. But it is essentially a very Whiggish version of history, telescoping a quarter-century and viewing it retrospectively through the prism of 1916. Whig history might be forgiven in a Liberal littérateur; it is less expected from that firm irrationalist and devotee of catastrophe theory, W.B. Yeats. And the analysis must provoke some questions.

What happened, first, to Irish politics after 1891? The supposed 'lull' in politics should not be taken as read. An assumption that literary activity took over politics leaves out not only the Irish Parliamentary Party (both wings) which continued to hegemonize the world of Irish politics, but also the agrarian mobilizing of the United Irish League, William O'Brien's new mass movement of the tenantry, which towards the end of the 1890s set the terms for a major political initiative. Both the Irish Parliamentary Party and the United Irish League had little to do with literature, but they were no less politically energetic and productive for that. 'Productivity' need not necessarily take in the second Home Rule Bill of 1893, which showed Gladstone sustaining a classic fudge by stating that he was 'requesting full equality' for Ireland and in the same breath accurately defining the bill as a 'wide extension of the privileges of local self-government'.[7] But real local government reform five years later was another matter; as, indeed, was the record of reforming Unionism in the 1890s. Recent work has stressed this, not so much as an effort to kill Home Rule by kindness, but as a series of measures contingent upon immediate political pressures, which sometimes led their devisers further than expected.[8] Local government in 1898, for instance, was a vital step in entrenching nationalist influence on county councils; and the extension of land purchase provided similarly concrete gains, as, potentially, did the plethora of schemes for agrarian investment and experimentation.

All this provided a solid substratum for nationalist advance. The ideas and atmosphere of the 1890s are well profiled in the pages of the *New Ireland Review*, an important forum, which first printed D.P. Moran's celebrated onslaught on 'shoneenism' and cultural Anglicization, later published as *The Philosophy of Irish Ireland*. There too can be found regular bilingual pieces by Douglas Hyde on the religious poetry of Connacht, or more unequivocal pieces dealing with 'The Race Type in Celtic Literature'.[9] Hungary also occurs early on as a model for Irish aspirations.[10] But the periodical is equally notable for articles with titles like 'Where Does Ireland Stand?', which analyse current politics in the tones of hard-headed constitutionalism and advocate tactical alliances with the Conservatives; and for floating influential ideas on land tenure, the forestry question, the work of the Recess Committee, the Financial Relations issue, and the perennial education question.[11] Mixed in with all this are pieces eulogizing any radical separatists just so long as they are dead. The whole thing is an odd compound of Gaelicism and constitutional reformism, linked by unstinting criticism of Britain if not the British connection.

This brings us rather nearer to the ethos of the Irish Parliamentary Party, a curious blend of Trollopian fixers, political journalists, respectable ex-Fenians and closet imperialists. They excelled in the politics of sleight of hand, and rested on the powerful local machinery inherited from the 1880s. Their backing from the Catholic clergy dated from the same era, ever since Parnell's concordat over education in 1885. The Catholic ethos also influenced them in their critical stance regarding welfarist fads. Despite the split over Parnell, the party retained vitality; despite the lack of detailed sources (and of a modern biography of John Redmond), they should not be consigned to the dust-heap of history before their time. And several of them were conscious of the need for a high political profile, especially given the revived land agitation in the west.[12]

For the land question had not been taken out of Irish politics after Gladstone's 1881 Land Act, or even the 1886 Plan of Campaign. And the late 1890s sees the last stage of the uncompleted Land War, beginning with the concerted agitation mounted by western farmers against the large-scale stock-grazing interests. This mobilized political energy in the shape of the United Irish League, which spread at such a rate and posed such a political threat that by 1900 it provided the means of reunifying the Irish Parliamentary Party (which then subsumed it). It is a movement curiously written out of Irish history, despite a growing academic interest. (The same is true of its successor, the All-for-Ireland League.[13]) This was partly because it failed (the UIL, starting out as a movement against the graziers, ended by co-opting them into the leadership of the movement), and partly because later developments in Irish history followed a different tack.

Vampirized by the Irish Parliamentary Party, it dropped from sight; its leaders, however, had a firmer idea than Redmond and Dillon about the possibilities of land purchase, and the unsatisfied interests it represented would crop up again in the War of Independence, greatly alarming the conservative leaders of the Irish revolution.

What should be emphasized is the power of what began as (so to speak) a grass-roots movement against graziers in the west, but spread across the country, claiming 33,000 members by 1899 and mustering 60,000 to 80,000 by 1900.[14] The politics of boycott and trade war had taken over in certain areas: there was a National Directory, with offices in Dublin; a newspaper, the *Irish People*, was founded in September 1899, calling for a public movement 'wide enough to give free play to every school of honest Nationalist conviction from the believer in a Gladstonian parliament to the believer in an Irish Republic'. The movement mobilized anti-Parnellites and Parnellites alike; it entered urban politics, to considerable effect; it fought the new local elections with conspicuous success (more success than it showed in altering traditional rural power structures).[15] The issue was politically galvanic, all the more so as the UIL agitators were preaching Home Rule as part of their message. If the Irish Parliamentary Party had not taken steps to subsume the UIL, the UIL might very well have subsumed the Irish Parliamentary Party. And even after the reunion in 1900, and the ostensible defusing of the land issue by the 'Wyndham' Land Act of 1903, a core of radicalism remained, articulated by the volatile William O'Brien.

For those involved in cultural revivalism, all this was irrelevant. Yeats gives the accepted, withering view of the politicians from the Land War era on:

> And so was founded an agitation where some men pretended to national passion for the land's sake; some men to agrarian passion for the nation's sake; some men to both for their own advancement . . . they had grown up amid make-believe, and now because their practical grievance was too near settlement to blind and to excite, their make-believe was visible to all . . .[16]

Faced with the necessary venality of contemporary politics, both Yeatsian and Fenian iconography preferred the image of the dead Parnell as an icy, aristocratic Anglophobe. Thus Yeats again:

> I had seen Ireland in my own time turn from the bragging rhetoric and

gregarious humour of O'Connell's generation and school, and offer herself to the solitary and proud Parnell as to her anti-self, buskin followed hard on sock, and I had begun to hope, or to half-hope, that we might be the first in Europe to seek unity as deliberately as it had been sought by theologian, poet, sculptor, architect, from the eleventh to the thirteenth century.[17]

A more visceral tone enters his memory of Sir Charles Gavan Duffy, Young Irelander turned imperial constitutionalist:

One imagined his youth in some little gaunt Irish town, where no building or custom is revered for its antiquity; and there speaking a language where no word, even in solitude, is ever spoken slowly and carefully, because of emotional implication; and of his manhood of practical politics, of the dirty piece of orange-peel in the corner of the stairs as one climbs up to some newspaper office; of public meetings where it would be treacherous amid so much geniality to speak or even to think of anything that might cause a moment's misunderstanding in one's own party. No argument of mine was intelligible to him . . .[18]

Elsewhere, too, he appears to indict the parliamentary politicians more on the grounds of excessive clubbability than anything else. It is probably relevant to remember Yeats's own social insecurity and marginalization at this stage of his life; and, for all his contempt of the bourgeois, his mentors in nationalism, John O'Leary and Standish O'Grady, were anything but radical, despite Yeats's claims to the contrary.

Parnell's image, even a decade after his death, was more important than his record. It is characteristic that R.M. Henry, writing *The Evolution of Sinn Féin* from first-hand knowledge in 1920, presents Parnell as the usual 'strong, romantic and mysterious personality' who held the future of Irish politics in his hand. This is contrasted with 'the story of small intrigues, base personalities, divided counsels and despairing expedients' after his death, presided over by the flunkey Redmond. However, Henry adds, apropos Redmond's call for Home Rule within the Empire: 'It is true that Parnell would have obtained little more than this, if he had lived; but he would have obtained it in a different way, and would have accepted the concession with a gesture of independence.'[19] In other words, the difference was simply one of rhetoric and style. Yeats himself unguardedly implied as much elsewhere, admitting that in the 1890s few wanted separation from

Britain, and that he himself viewed the actuality with some misgivings.[20] Talking about it, in the right tone, was apparently something else.

In the light of this, Redmond's strategy of accepting what reforming Unionism had to offer does not appear quite so pusillanimous. Land tenure reform, the Congested Districts Board, a Department of Agriculture, the achievement of Sir Horace Plunkett's influential Recess Committee (which lay behind this step) and revolutionized local government were decent payments on account – not to mention the Childers Financial Relations Committee reassessing Ireland's dues to imperial revenue, in which Redmond had been extremely influential. In retrospect, this may look like settling for half a loaf; contemporarily, it had a different resonance. Unduly optimistic though he was, Horace Plunkett had some reason for remarking that 'the decade of dissension which followed the fall of Parnell will, perhaps some day, be recognized as a most fruitful epoch in modern Ireland's history'.[21]

From certain points of view, then, by the time Redmond succeeded to the leadership of a united party in 1900 constitutional politics could be seen to be working. Conventional rhetoric might not have allowed the case to be stated. But, as has been well remarked of an earlier period, 'popular Irish nationalism was a matter of self-assertiveness of the Catholic community and of a search for material benefits rather than a question of yearning for constitutional reforms'.[22] And much of the rhetorical criticism even at the time came not from the cultural nationalists (who held themselves above the detail of material benefits), but from Young Turks within the constitutional movement like the Young Ireland branch of the UIL. Vacuum theories notwithstanding, politics went on happening.

By 1907 Redmond was even receiving letters from the veteran Irish American physical-force man, Patrick Ford, couched in glowing terms:

> You are of course aware that the bitterest enemies of the Irish cause are those of our own household. They iterate and reiterate that Ireland will never get Home Rule except by fighting for it. These men can take care to make no allusion to the victories won by the Irish Parliamentary Party.[23]

Such indulgence is surprising, coming from someone always suspicious even of Parnell's nationalist probity, who had only supported the UIL in the hopes that they would 'invite the constabulary to shoot the people down in an eviction campaign inaugurated for the purpose'.[24] Perhaps equally significant, for the present purposes, is the fact that when Standish James O'Grady wrote excitedly in 1897 of a 'new Irish movement which has risen with the suddenness and power of a tidal wave', letting loose 'forces whose play no man can predict', he did not mean the Gaelic League; he was referring to the Financial Relations Committee and the co-operative constitutional agitation that lay behind it.[25] The cultural movement of these years only replaces 'politics' when viewed strictly in retrospect.

II

When considering to whom cultural revivalism appealed, and how it related to political agitation, it is interesting to revert to the archetypal organ of Gaelic Revivalism in a Catholic, Irish-speaking sense: the *Celt*, a weekly periodical of 1857–8 edited by a committee of the Celtic Union. It produced the usual exhortation to the youth of the country to read up on dead heroes, and the usual vague calls to action ('not only, in our judgement, does the history of this country remain to be written – it requires to be acted'). But it also invariably looked back rather than forward; and, despite coinciding with the founding of Fenianism, it emphasized that the evils caused by the British connection 'may be remedied in a manner within what is called the constitution, and not outside the law'.[26] It even threw up, in July 1858, a leader under the title 'Home Rule', pointing out Australian and Canadian parallels and adding, 'we do not view this question at all as a physical force question . . . we look for Ireland's rights by moral and constitutional means and will dream of and listen to none other, until these have failed. And if properly used, they cannot fail, and must win.' All this, twelve years before the foundation of Butt's Home Government Association, went with calls to revive the language as a 'vehicle for national thought', and fulminations against degrading English influence. 'To be Anglicized is to lose our national and characteristic identity, to merge everything Irish and Celtic in, not a British union, but a British supremacy.' The point here is that a violent predisposition against Anglicization was not incompatible with a realistic commitment to constitutional reform. And the amateur poets and antiquarians who shortly began recycling the most bloodthirsty pieces of ancient mythology in order to draw apparent parallels for contemporary separatist heroics do not themselves appear to have adhered to anything like revolutionary beliefs: a mild collection of vegetarians, Theosophists, India Office civil servants, and so on, whose glorification of fighting was literary trope rather than political exhortation to anything more radical than Home Rule.[27]

Similarly, in the 1890s Gaelic zealotry happened, and mattered, at a different level from that of politics; nor were the cultural ideologues those who would ever have taken part in politics under the previous dispensation, as the Yeats thesis seems to imply. The Gaelic Revival is, reasonably enough, approached through key texts like Douglas Hyde's 'On the Necessity for De-Anglicizing the Irish People', a presidential address delivered to the National Literary Society on 25 November 1892 and subsequently published. It is too often forgotten, though, that Hyde's lecture began by presenting de-Anglicization as a strategy that should appeal to Unionists as much as to nationalists, while emphasizing – rather innocently – Anglophobia as the motive power of a movement that still need not be separatist.

It is the curious certainty that come what may Irishmen will continue to resist English rule, even though it should be for their good, which prevents many of our nation from becoming Unionists upon the spot. It is a fact, and we must face it as a fact, that although they adopt English habits and copy England in every way, the great bulk of Irishmen and Irishwomen over the whole world are known to be filled with a dull, ever-abiding animosity against her, and – right or wrong – to grieve when she prospers, and joy when she is hurt. Such movements as Young Irelanders, Fenianism, Land Leaguism, and Parliamentary obstruction seem always to gain their sympathy and support. It is just because there appears no earthly chance of their becoming good members of the Empire that I urge that they should not remain in the anomalous position they are in, but since they absolutely refuse to become the one thing, that they become the other; cultivate what they have rejected, and build up an Irish nation on Irish lines.[28]

In the end, however, Hyde presents the priority of poetry over politics, and casts his argument entirely in a Home Ruler context. 'We can, however, insist, and we *shall* insist, if Home Rule be carried, that the Irish language, which so many foreign scholars of the first calibre find so worthy of study, shall be placed on par with – or even above – Greek, Latin and modern languages in all examinations held under the Irish government.'

That was to be the real revolution (and that is what worried the English-speaking Yeats).[29] Like all Gaelicists, Hyde was anti-O'Connell because of his Anglophone policy; but that was one of his few political stances. Costume and place-names remained his chief preoccupations, outside his own beautiful translations. Nor was he alone; Eoin MacNeill, for one, thought the early Gaelic League exhibited a strong streak of cautious Home Rulerism.[30]

What then of the strong subsequent tradition of Fenianism within the League – and the traditional identification of John O'Leary, veteran Fenian leader, as cicerone to the Yeats generation in cultural and separatist politics alike? It should be remembered that by now O'Leary was seen by his Irish Republican Brotherhood colleagues as (according to police reports) a 'fossil'[31] or 'an old crank full of whine and honesty'. He had become the classic armchair Fenian, incensed by the revival of land agitation which decimated his *rentier* income, and endlessly writing the history of the movement for publication in the *Weekly Independent*. (When Yeats reviewed it as a book, it was a severe blow to their intimate association.) Fenianism overlapped with cultural associations; four out of the original seven founders of the Gaelic Athletic Association were Fenians; the IRB organization was behind the famous guard of honour carrying draped hurley sticks after Parnell's coffin. But at the same time, by the early 1890s the number of members in good standing was falling.[32] Assistant police commissioner Mallon believed in October 1892 that there were only fifty active IRB men, and he could put his hand on every one of them; he may well have been right.

What, however, was an 'active' Fenian? The image of a pledge-bound, conspiratorial, Malatesta-influenced group, dedicated to revolutionary separatist action by means of violence, was technically true of the leadership cadres in Paris and America. But recent work has given us a picture of Fenianism in Ireland which was casual, public and recreational in a way that suggests the voluntary associations of *petit bourgeois* England, such as the Oddfellows or the Foresters. In late nineteenth-century Ireland the same large crowds reported at nationalist demonstrations apparently turned up cheerfully again for royal visits: the play was the thing. Fenianism was as much a verbal (and social) commitment as an ideological one.

If this was the case, it is easier to see how even Redmond could be fingered as a Fenian;[33] it could be as political a gesture as joining the Ancient Order of Hibernians. The word was being widely used to mean *any* kind of nationalist as early as the 1860s. To see it as the ideological counter-pole of the Irish Parliamentary Party is an oversimplification (even leaving aside the fact that the movement had itself splintered into the Invincibles, the Irish National Brotherhood, and so on; the latter being joined by Yeats, who remained rather vague about their antecedents).

Fenianism had its own tradition of cultural nationalism from the late 1850s, when many Fenians were involved in the Society for Promotion and Cultivation of the Irish Language, dominated by A.M. Sullivan (who could not himself speak Irish, but was no less anti-English for that). The rhetoric of Fenian-influenced literary journals like the *Shan Van Vocht* tended to portray Home Rulers as cringing royalists; but rhetoric it was. And the great Anglophobic outburst of the 1798 centenary celebrations should be seen as therapeutic Anglophobia as much as an endorsement of separatism. Going back to the 1860s, a strident Catholic nationalism had not meant the same thing as a commitment to Republican values; Fenian cadres throughout the country had worked readily for Home Rule candidates in by-elections. Fenianism reflected the variousness and sophistication of Irish nationalism: 'the concept of a pure Fenianism incapable of compromise with a corrupt political world is largely an invention of the 1870s; it had as a corollary a cult of physical force and that alone, which for many was, unconsciously, a cult of inaction'.[34] More generally, it attracted the 'joiners' of Irish society at certain quite well-defined levels, many of whom joined other associations as well (Yeats had a Fenian acquaintance who was also a member of the Primrose League). To quote Vincent Comerford again, 'From the 1860s being a Fenian was a mode of life in Ireland in the same way as being anti-clerical or republican was in provincial France.'[35] One might add that being a Parnellite after 1891 was to subscribe to a cult of safely romantic leader-worship which was rather analogous to Bonapartism.

This idea of Fenianism should be borne in mind when considering how far the cultural revivalists thought of themselves as Fenians. When Eoin MacNeill's biographer finds it 'surprising' that the unpolitical and pacific Hyde used a Fenian analogy for the Gaelic League in its work of revivification, he misses the point: it was not as dangerous as it retrospectively sounded.[36] The Catholic identification of the League should be noted, which took over so quickly that by 1900 people like T.W. Rolleston were proposing a parallel Gaelic League for Protestants. In both the League and Fenianism, Anglophobia and confessionalism were provided for; but revolutionary separatism need not necessarily be inferred.

And though Hyde stressed the non-sectarian and unpolitical nature of the League, he himself passionately declaimed against 'the creeping Saxon'; the message was quickly read in a climate where organizations like the Celtic Literary Society demanded that members be of Irish descent. But though Pearse would in 1913 claim the League as a nursery of practical revolution, it did not look like it in 1900.[37]

Another 'classic' example of Fenian infiltration is provided by Arthur Griffith, the influential Gaelicist ideologue who later founded Sinn Féin. His Fenian connection supposedly led to his becoming Chief Organizer of the INB. But this was part of an ideological 'package', not an all-consuming involvement. Griffith was pro-Boer, anti-British, the moving spirit behind the Transvaal Committee; the flavour of the organizations which he inspired is epitomized by Cumann na nGaedheal, an anti-British (but not a separatist) organization founded in 1900, which met in premises owned by the Celtic Literary Society. A hilarious police report on the first meeting profiles the committee: two habitual drunkards, two 'corporation scavengers', two schoolboys and a car-driver who was also bandmaster of the Milltown Band. Yet one of their number produced a very impressive account of the meeting for newspaper publication, giving a long list of distinguished but imaginary attenders; if this stood alone as source material, it would lead historians to much more portentous conclusions. (The police spy later watched impassively as the author, after a long evening's drinking, set off to deliver the article and 'spent a quarter of an hour trying to find the letter-box in the door of the publishing office of the *United Irishman*'.[38])

According to police reports, the most active associations in Dublin in 1901 were the Celtic Literary Society, the Gaelic League and the Gaelic Athletic Association. The 1798 Centenary Committee had fizzled out, and embezzlement had put paid to the funds of the Wolfe Tone Memorial Bazaar. The tiny clubs of extremists were seen as negligible, and probably were. The whole scene is strongly reminiscent of the atmosphere delineated in James Joyce's *Dubliners*, rather than the ferment of cultural revivalism and revolutionary politics recalled in the disillusioned tranquillity of the Free State. It is worth remembering Joyce's vitriolic picture of the genteel Gaelic Revivalists in 'A Mother', and the appalled Ascendancy reactions of Synge, Yeats and Moore to the *petit bourgeois* bigotries of Gaelic League society; Moore saw Hyde as having crossed over to become 'the archetype of the Catholic Protestant, cunning, subtle, cajoling, superficial and affable'.[39]

The relationship of any of these attitudes to practical planning towards revolutionary separatism is hard to assess. Clerical influence militated against it (as well as against romantic Parnellism: Eoin MacNeill, visiting the Aran Islands to commune with the pure Gaelic spirit, found the islanders firmly anti-Parnellite on strict moral grounds). The ill-starred Sir Antony MacDonnell probably got it about right when he wrote in a memorandum: 'The information I receive . . . does not invest the Gaelic movement at all events with malign and disloyal objects, though the objects are certainly "national".'[40] Cultural nationalism was, of course, Anglophobic, as Yeats nostalgically remembered:

> New from the influence, mainly the personal influence, of William Morris, I had dreamed of enlarging Irish hate, till we had come to hate with a passion of patriotism what Morris and Ruskin hated. Mitchel had already poured some of that hate drawn from Carlyle, who had it of an earlier and, as I think, cruder sort, into the blood of Ireland, and were we not a poorer nation with an ancient courage, unblackened fields and a barbarous gift of self-sacrifice?[41]

The de Valera vision of Ireland was also anticipated, defined against English materialism:

> We Irish do not desire, like the English, to build up a nation where there shall be a very rich class, and a very poor class . . . I think the best ideal for our people, an ideal very generally accepted among us, is that Ireland is going to become a country where, if there are a few rich, there shall be nobody very poor. Wherever men have tried to imagine a perfect life, they have imagined a place where men plough and sow and reap, not a place where there are great wheels turning and great chimneys vomiting smoke. Ireland will always be a place where men plough and sow and reap.[42]

Yeats, unlike many extreme nationalists, maintained a warm support for Horace Plunkett and the Irish Agricultural Organization Society, whose strategy was to make the Union work in economic terms. At the same time, he could declare (at the Pan-Celtic Congress in 1901) that the Gaelic movement 'would soon be shaking governments'. But this was like Hyde remarking that 'every speech we make throughout the country makes bullets to fire at the enemy'. Violent metaphors were employed without any necessary thought of revolution.

There is a strong case for saying that Yeats's approach to politics had become more serious, more realistic and more committed by the time he was writing his memoirs in the 1930s: whereas in youth, he remarked grandly, 'one can grow impassioned and fanatical about opinions which one has chosen as one might choose a side upon the football field'.[43] In the 1890s and 1900s he was demonstrably disingenuous about thorny issues like speaking Irish;[44] and even at his most committed there was always the congenital ambivalence of the Protestant bourgeois. For all his identification with the Gaelic ethos, a wistful hope remained for leadership from a regenerated landlord class. Thus, writing to Katharine Tynan in 1895 from Sligo about the fashion for things Celtic among the local gentry:

> These people are much better educated than our people & have a better instinct for excellence. It is very curious how the dying out of party fealing [*sic*] has nationalized the more thoughtful Unionists. Parnellism has greatly help[ed] also, & the expectation of Balfours threatened emmense [*sic*] local Government scheme. However this is to[o] big a subject to get into at the end of my second sheet.

This is of a piece with his remarks to Alice Milligan the previous September: 'My experience of Ireland, during the last three years, has changed my views very greatly, & I now feel that the work of an Irish man of letters must be not so much to awaken or quicken or preserve the national idea among the mass of the people but to convert the educated classes to it on the one hand to the best of his ability, & on the other – & this is the most important – to fight for moderation, dignity, & the rights of the intellect among his fellow nationalists.'[45]

Occultism predisposed him to expect a revolution, but that was something else. Stuart Merrill, talking to him a year later, recorded their conversation:

> Yeats, who has a very clear idea of social questions, and who sees them from

a lofty level, favours a union of superior forces for revolutionary action. He envisages revolution after an impending European war, like us all. He has even collected the prophecies of various countries on this subject, and all are agreed that the war will be unleashed during these next years.[46]

Playing with prophecy and rejecting British materialism, however, did not lead to any very specific pronouncement on separation from Britain. Malcolm Brown noted some time ago what John Kelly's definitive edition of Yeats's letters has recently made very clear: that his references to Parnellite or nationalist politics in correspondence during the 1880s and early 1890s are extremely scarce and vague.[47] Even his nationalist poetry for the *Gael* was expressed in conveniently backward-looking balladry about the Cromwellian period, rather reminiscent of Fanny Parnell:[48] far less bloodthirsty and more tentative than even the gentle Hyde. With all three, one senses the tensions and over-compensations of cultural deracination, as much as a specifically political commitment.

Even before Parnell's death, Yeats had been prophesying 'an intellectual movement at the first lull of politics'; his desire to fulfil the prophecy encouraged him to define the post-1891 period as the expected lull, when 'Ireland was to be like soft wax for years to come'.[49] But it is not surprising that his efforts to mould the wax were brutally abused as fey and half-hearted posturing in the 1898–9 *New Ireland Review* articles by D.P. Moran.

Moran's brilliant and vitriolic journalism has been taken as the text for exclusivist Irish nationalism from that day to this; certainly, his hatred and contempt for Anglicization and for Anglo-Ireland still burn off the page. But what comes across nearly as strongly, on a careful reading, is his ambivalence about separatism. There is an attractively robust line on the 'nonsense' of complaints about 'England stealing our woollen industries some hundreds of years ago', and he is very hard indeed on 'prating mock-rebels'.

A great many people in Ireland, unfortunately, live from hand to mouth; most of them, apparently, think after that fashion also. They not only think in that unsatisfactory way, but they impose arbitrary limits on their thinking. There are certain things which the average Irish mind will never allow as debatable. The spirit of nationality is eternal – that is a fine-flowing Irish maxim. No one ever thinks of asking himself – Is it? We nearly won in '98; we may win another time. Another undisputed view. No one ever dares to ask himself – Can we?[50]

Moran remained realistic about the necessity for economic initiative rather than 'rebel clap-trap'. Economic opportunities and language revival were at least as important as Home Rule (though he also expressed a distaste for gombeen commercialism – 'the greasy draper rubs his hands and dilates on "the circulation of money"' – which curiously anticipates the Yeats of 'September 1913'). Irish nationality should recognize its limitations: 'We can never beat England, can't even remain long in a fight with her, on her own terms. All we can do, and it should be enough for us, is remain Irish in spite of her, and work out our own destiny in the very many fields in which we are free to do so.'[51] Even his famous and chilling dictum that 'the Gael must be the element that absorbs' is prefaced by a much less often quoted passage:

No one wants to fall out with Davis's comprehensive idea of the Irish people as a composite race drawn from various sources, and professing any creed they like, nor would an attempt to rake up racial prejudices be tolerated by anyone. We are proud of Grattan, Flood, Tone, Emmet and all the rest who dreamt and worked for an independent country, even though they had no conception of an Irish nation; but it is necessary that they should be put in their place, and that place is not on top as the only beacon lights to succeeding generations. The foundation of Ireland is the Gael, and the Gael must be the element that absorbs.[52]

Moran objects to 'racial hatred' of England as a bogus stratagem: 'Privately, some of the hillside men will tell you that all the wild rebellion talk is nonsense, but that it is necessary to keep up the national spirit.' And a surprising degree of his contempt is reserved for, of all things, Fenianism. He draws a brilliant picture of the career of an Irish snob, in which his hero begins by joining the Fenians as a necessary but harmless involvement.

He joined a revolutionary society, where they talked wisely of foreign complications and held a picturesque midnight drill occasionally. He tried to persuade himself as long as he could that a few of the members were not drunkards, and he exhausted his ingenuity in attempting to square his youthful idea of a revolutionary hero with the characters of several of his comrades. He held on to the society for a few years, but it did nothing. There was one informer; two suspected of informing; one who bolted with the funds; and the great body of members – mostly honest, enthusiastic youths like himself – were getting sick of all the boasting and lip-rebellion that went on. He dropped out of it after a while and attended to his business, but still held extreme opinions.[53]

He ends up 'fat and comfortable in a mansion in Rathmines, the butt of every young Nationalist politician who little suspects that, unless conditions alter, a similar ending awaits him should he prosper in life'.

What Moran preaches, like Hyde, is language revival and a plague on politics. 'The fact of being a sound political nationalist of any stamp, from a constitutional Home Ruler to a fire-eating revolutionist, does not necessarily mean that one is Irish at all'; he is more scathing about separatism and revolutionary 'desperadoes' than anything else.[54]

III

In some ways this general picture holds good for the period after the 1890s. There is a case for saying that by 1900, when Moran's last article appeared, there was little ground for expecting political separatism to be practically encouraged by cultural revivalism; and, moreover, to see the Irish Parliamentary Party as morally bankrupted by a decade of sterile bickering is equally to miss the point. Looking briefly ahead, the Sinn Féin movement founded by Griffith seems similarly unimpressive if judged at this stage as an avatar of independence. It began by calling for a restoration of the 1782 constitution, and how far it proceeded from this before its effective reconstruction during the First World War is a moot point. It tried to square circles from Parnellism to Fenianism, following the rhetorical tradition of Irish nationalism, and was always careful to emphasize that it would not reject Home Rule.[55] From 1910 to 1913 it had sunk to a low ebb, before its traumatic reformation by the Young Republicans and the Independent Labour Party of Ireland. Though allegedly permeated by the IRB, this should be modified by a realization of what Fenianism actually meant, and by remembering that the historian of the IRB sees it as practically moribund in 1905, though it was entering upon its revitalization. By about 1910 the name 'Sinn Féin' had come to stand for a combination of various policies rather than a movement. (In this sense, the much derided contemporary British view of 1916 as a Sinn Féin rebellion may have something to be said for it after all.)

What flourished after the 1890s, as before, was Anglophobia and confessional identification, both well established for good historical reasons, and epitomized by Joseph Devlin's Ancient Order of Hibernians – one of the chief elements that dissipated O'Brienism, the All-for-Ireland League and the initial impetus of the United Irish League. Looking ahead even as far as 1910, one should still be cautious about assuming that cultural revivalism had produced an implicit revolution in politics. Not many Dubliners were reading the new literature.[56] In some ways, their energies had flagged; even Pearse, virulent in 1899 about Yeats ('a mere English poet of the third or fourth rank') and the Irish Literary Theatre ('more dangerous, because less glaringly anti-national, than Trinity College'), was by 1905 praising Yeats's opinions on nationalism and literature and sending honeyed letters to Lady Gregory.[57]

It is possible that the real seeds of the separatist crisis were sown only in the Volunteer movements of 1913, with the formation of the Ulster Volunteer Force and the National Volunteers: a reaction sparked off by the Home Rule impasse. MacNeill's odd idea that Edward Carson could march his Volunteers to Cork and receive a tumultuous welcome from their nationalist counterparts in joint defiance of Britain may have marked a new level of self-delusion.[58] But the events of the next few years moved with bewildering speed; and Pearse's graveside speeches of 1913 to 1915 mattered more, in the end, than Yeats's *Cathleen Ni Houlihan*.

Moreover, the vital conditions of germination were provided by the First World War. The greatest military cataclysm of the modern era affected Ireland too, though in post-1921 historiography it was somehow hived off as a British involvement.[59] 1916 depended on the European War scenario. Reactions to the subsequent government repression, and the anti-conscription movement, may have mobilized more Irish people politically than the Gaelic League or the Irish Parliamentary Party or Sinn Féin or the IRB ever dreamt of. The support of the Catholic Church was equally important: Anglophobia and confessionalism again.

Both these reactions seemed amply justified by British policies in Ireland over the next six years. Still, when it was all apparently over in 1922, a significant remark was made in the Free State Senate. Proposing the unlikely figure of Lord Glenavy as Chairman of the assembly, John McLoughlin superbly quoted Léon Gambetta: 'I refuse to ask the date on which any man became a republican.'[60] Given the realities of Irish history over the previous thirty years, this was just as well.

In all this, the Yeatsian view of the 1890s as the stirring of the bones, and the race being troubled by the long gestation of the 1916 rising, seems rather at odds. So does the idea that political energy was 'diverted' into culture. Yeats astutely saw the confusion at the time; in a public letter of December 1893 he attacked the 'stupefying' effect of oratory which led the Irish 'headlong into unreality'.[61] But this did not stop him from drawing out his own artful patterns. When Richard Ellmann was discussing Yeats with the poet's shrewd widow, she pointed out to him that 'one quality of her husband never ceased to astonish her . . . This was his extraordinary sense of the way things would look to people later on.'[62] To which must be added his extraordinary ability to impose his view of how things *should* look to people later on. 'Man can embody truth but he cannot know it.' In Yeats's terms, this gave the poet of revelations, the interpreter of unconscious manifestations, a dual identity as the ideal historian.[63] This is nearly as risky as making him an unacknowledged legislator. Perhaps our tendency to accept the poetic version of that quarter-century from 1891 to 1916 arises not so much from ideological inflexibility, as from simple suggestibility: 'thinking from hand to mouth' again.

14

Marginal Men and Micks on the Make: The Uses of Irish Exile, *c.* 1840–1922

I

On 4 July 1842 William Makepeace Thackeray, inquisitive travel-writer newly arrived in Dublin, sat down to breakfast and devoured the local papers (like any Paul Theroux or Jonathan Raban of his day). His eye lit on one announcement, perfect for his purposes: 'Miss Hayes will give her first and farewell concert at the Rotunda, previous to leaving her native country.' 'Only one instance of Irish talent do we read of,' adds Thackeray triumphantly, 'and that, in a desponding tone, announces its intention of quitting its native country.'[1]

The cultural context of this vivid observation could bear intensive deconstruction: characteristically condescending and astute at the same time, it fits neatly in with the Victorian fictionalization of Irishness which Thackeray did so much to promote, and which nowadays so preoccupies Irish cultural commentators. Some, indeed, have taken verbal cleansing to the agonized extent of banning the very word – 'Irishness' being seen as a corrupt concept predicated upon some notion of 'Britishness'.[2] But that interaction and duality is of particular interest, however uncomfortable a subject. It is intimately connected with the ragged edges and loose ends of the fiction of Union since 1800, discussed elsewhere in these pages.[3] And in terms of nineteenth-century cultural influence and exchange, the issue which comprehends and conditions it is the great social fact of emigration.

The 'originary colonial moment' of Britain's cultural influence on Ireland has been expansively interpreted in terms of Edmund Spenser, or the Statutes of Kilkenny;[4] but the cultural implications of the export and interchange of people in the modern period have been curiously ignored, or approached on a very narrow canvas indeed. These extend not just to displaced ballad-singing in Birmingham (or the Bronx), but to the way that emigration at once defined, reinforced and diluted Irishness in the modern period. The strategies and conduits which characterize this process have been looked at in terms of oral culture and the social history of 'immigrant communities'. But it is less often considered how the process affects commentators like Yeats and Shaw, whose cultural influence is inseparable from their emigrant status. Another process which deserves attention is, in a sense, the reverse image: while a certain type of emigrant creates or discovers an Ireland abroad, this process is mirrored by the migration towards Ireland of cultural or political brokers from the colonial centre, working out their own displacement or identifying with Ireland as an appropriate arena for moral endeavour.

From an early period, disaffected British people used Ireland for dreams or ideas or insecurities too uncomfortable for home; the young Shelley is a classic example. Such people were usually misfits, as often Tories or Radicals or socialists as liberals. It is a minority strain but an engrossing one, uniting odd combinations like Friedrich Engels, Anthony Trollope, Lord Randolph Churchill and Maud Gonne: as a sort of shorthand, they may be called (for the purposes of this essay, and temporarily sacrificing gender-consciousness to alliteration) 'marginal men'. The other strain of cultural exchange which I wish to examine are some of those nineteenth-century Irish emigrants who went to England and made a good thing out of it: especially those aspiring careerists and *arrivistes* who may be referred to as 'micks on the make'. The encounter of Thackeray and Miss Hayes (through the medium of the morning paper) on that summer morning in 1842 is a meeting of these two archetypes. And for both categories, the crisis of the early twentieth century coincided with a traumatic transition in their views of themselves, and their ideas of what Ireland was for.

II

The conditions of life under the Union imposed a divided identity. We find it easier to visualize this for denizens of Northern Ireland today, or disorientated Anglo-Irishry after 1922, than to reconstruct the consciousness of nineteenth-century Irish people who saw much of their focus and most of their career opportunity as lying across St George's Channel. But for many of the Victorian Irish middle class, life was spent travelling back and forth across the Irish Sea, observing and participating in British forms of government, reading English books, attending British educational institutions, looking for employment within the structures of the British Empire[5] and speaking English. It was never an identity comfortably accepted. A scathing reference in the *Dublin University Magazine* for 1842 describes the atmosphere of Dublin – 'shrewd lawyers, suave doctors, raw subalterns and fat country gentlemen – waiting in town for remittances to carry them to Cheltenham – that Paradise of Paddies and Elysium of Galway Belles'.[6] But the writer was Charles Lever, who sought his own fortune out of Ireland rather than in it. So did Gerald Griffin, another neglected novelist, who was equally sarcastic about the Holyhead boat in 1827, where he itemized 'members of the exiled Parliament, made up for the winter campaign; and adventurers of every description who devoutly believed gold and fame grew like blackberries upon hedges everywhere except in poor Ireland'.[7] In the same mode, the romantic poet Tom Moore made a national reputation in England out of lyrically regretting Ireland – crashing the highest of high society while he was at it, and having his memoirs edited by an English Prime Minister. Emigration as a concept must also include the kind of people observed on the packet-boat by Gerald Griffin: the middle-class or *petit bourgeois* careerists, Civil Service exams or journalistic apprenticeship behind them, and the office desks of the metropolis ahead. It should take in the political and social *arrivistes* making their way in Victorian London, their Irishness no impediment but even a ticket of passage. In contemporary fiction Meredith's Diana Merion reflects this no less than Trollope's Phineas Finn.

From the 1890s, careers and reputations like these came under heavy attack, though both literary and historical revisionists have now got their hands on Moore. But throughout the nineteenth century an enduringly interesting question concerns the English aspect of Irishness and the Irish aspect of certain Englishnesses, inseparable from the fact of the Union. Historical hindsight, or theoretical predisposition, may tempt us to discount these themes as craven collaborationism on one side, and hypocritical exploitation on the other. Still, they raise questions worth rescuing from the condescension of posterity.

The micks on the make were not the average Irish emigrant; but who was? Emigration dominates nineteenth-century Irish history; it is bound up with the history of the Union, beginning on a large scale well before the Famine exodus, and reflecting the discouraging history of the Irish agrarian economy under the Union. By 1861 the Irish-born population of England, Scotland and Wales had reached 805,000, or 3.5 per cent of the population. It had declined to 655,000 in 1891; but these figures do not include those born of Irish parents in Great Britain, which raises the debated question of the extent of an Irish community within the larger island. The 1872 survey carried out by the *Nation* newspaper indicated that these figures should be doubled to arrive at a real idea of the *soi-disant* Irish community; and the whole area is haunted by statistical anomaly.[8]

General patterns are more readily accepted. The combination of changing agrarian patterns, de-industrialization from the 1820s, and the magnetic effect of apparently limitless employment in Britain and America created the fundamental economic conditions. The endogenous social conditions which presented emigration as the overwhelming option are just as significant. The congestion of Irish people on Irish land had something to do with the exploitative and self-perpetuating nature of the Irish landholding system; something to do with farming methods which allowed subsistence-level existence for large numbers living on small plots of land; and something to do with a family economy and social order that encouraged early marriage and steady procreation.[9] All these processes were facilitated by the pre-Famine potato economy up to the mid-1840s, with a plentiful supply of highly nutritious home-grown food. But even so, another expansion-valve was necessary: large-scale and self-sustaining chain-patterns of emigration. These structures were in place, and large-scale emigration under way, by the 1830s, when subsistence crises in agriculture can be closely related to subsequent boosts in emigrant figures. With the failure of the potato crop in the mid-1840s, this was drastically exacerbated. And the effect of the Famine, which varied from region to region, affected most seriously those areas where the structures of chain emigration were already in place: leaving behind in Ireland, according to Sir William Wilde (father of the well-known emigrant Oscar), a population disproportionately 'poor, weak, old, lame, sick, blind, dumb, imbecile and insane'.[10]

The haemorrhage of emigration settled by the end of the 1840s to a steady flow, sustained by complex mechanisms. Attitudes towards it among economists and social planners were generally favourable, though the principle of subsidy was bitterly debated. Despite individual subsidies and government aid towards settling the colonies, emigration to Britain tended to be autonomous rather than planned. Nationalist rhetoric disapproved of the principle, though several individual nationalists privately supported colonization schemes. Self-starting emigration was cheap; it could be embarked upon at short notice and before second thoughts. The step was also facilitated by a sort of unofficial 'twinning' process between specific Irish regions and foreign destinations. Where families and young children emigrated, they tended to come from the more prosperous eastern counties; but the classic Irish emigrants came from the poorer west and south-west and were young, unmarried, unskilled and slightly more often male than female. They were also more unlikely to return, though the figure of the seasonal labourer, working in Britain for the winters and Ireland for the summers, remained to bedevil statistics.

All Irish emigrants tended to be lumped together for generalization by the host country. But there was also an outflow at other levels of Irish society, up to the artisanate and aspiring middle class. Many of these would help create and re-create images of Irishness in exile. And even at the conventional level of Irish emigration, many of the expected images turn out, on historical re-examination, to be wrong; a recent wave of research on the Irish in Britain has questioned many of the stereotypes.[11] Was the Irish influx responsible for swelling the size of English cities to unbearable limits? Evidently not; this was the result of rural migration from the hinterlands.[12] Did the Irish presence incite locals to violent demonstrations of antipathy? Outside Lancashire, which has its own baroque religious history, this did not happen: the attitude of natives towards the incursors has been analysed as 'for the most part passive and unconcerned'.[13] Were the Irish imported to break strikes? Very rarely.[14] Were they highly represented in the Chartist movement? No, or at least not in terms of total numbers.[15] In fact, they were rather politically apathetic. Did they depress other workers' living standards? No.[16] Did they import disease? No, they were probably healthier than the English natives.[17] Did they invariably live in ghettos? No, according to several local surveys; they were distributed across working-class areas, and by no means as endogamous or ethnically exclusive as usually assumed. And finally: did they inevitably stay lower class? This question elicits an increasingly audible negative, as proliferating local studies show the Irish emerging into the middle class in London, Liverpool, Manchester and Glasgow – and Irish communities in towns like Stafford and Winchester come into focus.[18] And this is connected with the final revision: regarding English attitudes towards the Irish.

III

That the Irish were discriminated against is a 'given': nineteenth-century fiction is full of anecdotal evidence. The labour *agents provocateurs* in Elizabeth Gaskell's *North and South*, Charles Kingsley's *Alton Locke*, and who knows how many other condition-of-England novels are all Irish, and represent the perceived weaknesses of the race – put into a classic dialectic in *Alton Locke*, where two Chartists debate whose fault it is that the Irish are 'a nation of liars' and savages.[19] Friedrich Engels (honorary Marginal Man) put it in equally classic form, at an early point in the trajectory of his opinions on Ireland, in the *Condition of the Working Class in England*. 'The southern facile character of the Irishman, his crudity, which places him but little above the savage, in contempt for all humane enjoyments . . .' But, tutored by Mary and Lizzie Burns, mick mill-girls on the make, he soon adopted the Marxian romantic view of the Irish as nature's revolutionaries, instinct with the moral superiority of the oppressed, possessing the secret of capitalism's overthrow. Later again, however, both Marx and Engels rather lost faith and reverted to a racial typology of 'national character' as explaining the inexplicable about Ireland.[20] As this parabola indicates, the nature of anti-Irish prejudice requires careful tracking.

Nineteenth-century English attitudes towards the Irish are clearly prejudiced, relying on a well-worked grid of assumptions and stereotypes. This is hardly surprising; so are nineteenth-century Irish attitudes towards the English. The question is what it signifies. For a start, it is worth noting that the stereotypes are riven with contradictions. The Irish are quick-witted and verbally ingenious but also stupid. They are lazy but laborious; bellicose but shifty; roistering but melancholic. No wonder that the Irish so ruthlessly used their own stereotype against literal-minded observers. (The Victorian traveller Mrs S.C. Hall was cheated and accused her guide of 'cunning', getting the reply: 'Sure why wouldn't we be cunning? Isn't it our strength?') The anti-Irish stereotype certainly helped confirm the outcast status of many immigrants: in the first generation they often stayed marginal in a literal sense, residing near their ports of entry, and remaining outside the metropolitan economy. But this had changed by the end of the century, as even Engels admitted in 1892. And there were internal, Catholic routes to educational and social mobility as well (though the revisionists have sceptically reassessed the religious devotion of Irish immigrants too). What needs to be examined is how far anti-Irishness was based on a covertly or overtly racialist assumption of superiority.

This is often claimed, and throw-away remarks by Kingsley, Froude and even Trollope might seem to confirm it – not to mention the often-canvassed cartoons in *Punch*.[21] At the same time, however, *Punch* often portrayed Hibernia as a classic Greek beauty; the Irish occupied administrative and legislative roles in the imperial hierarchy which would never be allowed to Africans or Indians; intermarriage was never tabooed. Not only Matthew Arnold and J.R. Green, but also Charles Kingsley, advocated intermarriage with the quicksilver Celt in order to alleviate Saxon cloddishness. Still, how could Trollope, for instance, state on one occasion that the Irish were a lesser breed, and on another that the Irish working classes were far cleverer than the English working classes, and that Irish gentlemen were gentlemen in a real sense almost unknown in England? How could he make his favourite hero an Irish Catholic *arriviste* in high-political circles? How could Disraeli remark that 'this wild, reckless, indolent, uncertain and superstitious race have no sympathy with the English character',[22] and yet advance in politics clever but impecunious young Irishmen like Edward Gibson (later first Baron Ashbourne and Lord Chancellor), David Plunket (first Lord Rathmore and Solicitor-General) and Michael Morris (first Lord Killanin and Lord Chief Justice)?

The answer is that just as there were English and English in a class society, there were Irish and Irish. Phineas Finn, Edward Gibson, David Plunket and Michael Morris were acceptable Irishmen. They might claim Gaelic stock and Catholic religion, like the fictional Finn and the real Morris; they might be middle-class doctors' and lawyers' sons; but they fitted into the known bourgeois world, and the world of the Union. There, Irishness did not count against them; in many ways, Trollope makes it favour Phineas Finn. The prejudice against Irish iniquity was not always so very different from the prejudice against English iniquity, where the iniquitous were the terrifying underclass of St Giles or Jacob's Island. Then, as now, anti-Irish prejudice owed more to class than to race.

The generalizations about Irish emigration remain based on the notion that it was invariably both proletarian and involuntary; and that it was inseparable from a sense of exile. This is taken to mean banishment from a territory – mental and spiritual as well as physical – which still imposes the psychological norms of reality, and exerts a compulsion to return which will never be fulfilled. Kerby Miller has devoted a vast book to analysing this theme for Irish Americans;[23] the fact that this does not seem to have been their invariable experience makes its imagery no less potent. It is certainly an inseparable component of expatriate Irish rhetoric; alienation persisted as a literary trope, even among the prosperous emigrants who had no intention of ever returning home. It was sustained by a long native tradition: religious poetry derived from the cult of St Columkille, the folk memory of Cromwellian transplantations, the romance of the Wild Geese. All these associations stressed the inseparability of Irishness and exile, and the links between Anglicization and displacement. And this could be ingeniously utilized, as in a baroque petition to the Colonial Office on behalf of the Irish emigrants. 'Our feet, wearied night and day by exorbitant labour for impoverished masters, now tremble with feebleness whilst treading the paths of uncompensated toil. Our heads, long bent beneath a Slavish yoke, require support and encouragement towards their being raised to a natural consistency . . .'[24]

It is tempting to ask – certainly in terms of Irish American experience – a more robust question: if the emigrant Irish were so trapped in a state of permanent yearning nostalgia, why did they do so well? Is there a case for seeing the emigrant laments as a kind of therapy, and the extremely low numbers of those who returned as representing a deliberate option, not evidence of imprisonment abroad? Certainly the literary tropes of exile expression became increasingly a reflex action, not only bearing less and less similarity to emigrant experience as actually lived in the second and third generations, but also diverging more and more markedly from the reality of life in the old country.

In some ways, emigration to Britain is generically different, if only because the emigrants were flocking to the country of the ancient oppressor. (Poles did not emigrate to Russia, nor Italians to Austria.) In both Britain and America, the Irish emigrant was often emigrating from a Gaelic-speaking to an Anglophone culture, which imposed another kind of distance; though this was less and less the case as the century wore on and use of the language declined. But it is relevant to point out that demotic exile literature is an expression, by professional intermediaries, on behalf of the inarticulate – very much in the tradition of Irish ballad poetry. And, as with Irish ballads, the texts over time assume a rigid form and represent an experience held in suspension, governed by a set of accepted and expected norms, providing psychological reinforcement in an alien terrain, conjuring up consoling and familiar images. They also helped provide an alternative hierarchy to that of received English pronunciation, or 'No Irish Need Apply' notices, and sustained a valuably buoyant self-image. (This, ironically, entered the stereotype too.) Moreover, Irish consciousness abroad, vitalized by ethnic defensiveness and a network of social and political organizations, fed back into the construction of nationalist consciousness at home – as the history of the Fenian movement demonstrates.

But did this typify the majority emigrant experience? One of the dangers of using 'exile' expressions is that we may be generalizing from the aggressively articulate voice of a minority – those who did not emigrate successfully. Listening hard, other voices come through, which strike a new note.[25] And this leads to the question of the middle-class Irish emigrants to Britain; statistically invisible and ideologically unattractive though they may be to many commentators, they existed. It is often commented upon how many Fenian organizers in London were Irish doctors; it is less often noted that they *were* Irish doctors. And the Irish middle classes in England would not generally have been visible Fenians; in immigrant societies, the further up the class scale, the more pronounced the phenomenon known beguilingly as 'ethnic fade'. The Irish middle classes make their presence felt more obliquely than their compatriots in the slums: they must be traced by clues like the fact that by 1897 they had bought up many of the plots in the smartest Dumbarton cemetery.

But the history of the middle-class Irish on the make can be traced through one profession in particular: the press. Immigrant society created its own needs, and fortunes were made in catering for a Catholic readership by entrepreneurs like Charles Diamond, who emigrated from Maghera to Newcastle and built up an empire of thiry-seven journals. But in the larger world of secular journalism, too, Irishmen were remarkably prominent. Thackeray lovingly satirizes this in *Pendennis*, where he compares Irish journalists to the seventeenth-century Wild Geese fighting in foreign armies. Mr Hoolan and Mr Doolan, producing the *Dawn* and the *Day*, and Jack Finucane on the *Pall Mall Gazette*, are at the heart of the London hack world into which the hero unintentionally drifts. Thackeray knew similar types like Daniel Owen Madden;[26] his own first editor was a Corkman, the redoubtable William Maginn of *Blackwood's*.[27] Later real-life figures included people like T.P. O'Connor and Justin McCarthy: ambitious young men from the aspiring Catholic middle classes of provincial Victorian Ireland, educated in the Queen's Colleges, nationalist by inclination but opportunist by nature, looking to London as a cultural focus. 'Who but an Irishman,' O'Connor once lamented, 'can know the full hopelessness of a youth born into the lower middle classes of an Irish country town?'[28] His own book, *The Parnell Movement*, and his own life offer a fascinating commentary on those determined to get out. He served his apprenticeship in Fleet Street and Bohemia (Irish political opponents later accused him of living off the immoral earnings of *two* ladies in St John's Wood – a charge, he urbanely remarked, 'more flattering to my charm than my morality'.[29]) After working on the *Daily Telegraph* and the *Pall Mall Gazette*, his own papers the *Star* (founded in 1887) and *T.P.'s Weekly* (1902) were legendary successes. He wrote sharp biographies of Disraeli, Parnell and others, was himself a nationalist MP for forty-four years, and became Father of the House of Commons (as well as first President of the Board of Film Censors, a prophetically 'Irish' touch). His political identity owed as much to English Radicalism as to Irish Parnellism.

His friend and colleague Justin McCarthy migrated from Cork journalism into the world of Fleet Street, literary salons and Westminster with equal ease. He too became a Parnellite MP, and was briefly leader of the party after Parnell's fall. He called his autobiography, slightly defensively, *The Story of an Irishman*, but took

England as his oyster and always claimed that neither his religion nor his politics 'ever interfered in the slightest degree with my way in journalism or in literature, here in England'.[30] Men like McCarthy followed the kind of ascent traced by Trollope in *Phineas Finn*, where an Irish hero, not well off (Finn's father is a Catholic doctor), but with brains, charm and natural good manners, gets to the top while adhering firmly to Irish identity – and to unpopular Irish politics. Trollope used earlier models like William Gregory, Chichester Fortescue and John Pope-Hennessy, who came from a level of Irish society above the O'Connors and McCarthys: but by the later nineteenth century, this element had made its way.

At this stage, however, fundamental change was set in motion. First the shift in Irish political expectations, and British political parties, attendant upon the age of Parnell; then the political polarization of the early twentieth century, which would brand the O'Connors and McCarthys and Finns as shoneens or West Britons, and the Gregorys and Fortescues as not Irish at all. Perhaps the transitional figure was George Bernard Shaw, a middle-class Irishman on the make who felt no guilt at all about emigration. 'Every Irishman who felt that his business in life was on the higher planes of the cultural professions,' he wrote in an autobiographical fragment, 'felt that he must have a metropolitan domicile and an international culture: that is, he felt that his first business was to get out of Ireland.'[31] Shaw came from what he described as the 'downstart' element of *déclassé* middle-class Irish Protestants; emigrating to England in 1876, he never tired of, on the one hand, railing against Irish obduracy and, on the other, deriding English stupidity. The key texts are the 'Preface for Politicians' to *John Bull's Other Island*, and his splenetic pieces in the *Irish Statesman* during the 1920s. But by the time of the latter, the Union was over. It had been helped to its end by a new generation of micks on the make, working with a new strategy.

IV

But before considering this it is worth looking at the other side of the coin, and the other half of my title: those nineteenth-century marginal men and women who seized on Ireland as an appropriate area for activity, and fiercely identified with it. The literature of mid-nineteenth-century travellers in Ireland provides intriguing clues. Many were simply determined to point a moral, produce a panacea, and help their career as a pundit: a process explosively derided by Carlyle at the end of his own Irish journey. 'Remedy for Ireland? To cease generally from following the devil: no other remedy that I know of.'[32] But Thackeray, tragically married to a demented Irish wife, and closely linked to London-Irish journalists and littérateurs, was obsessively interested in all that made up Irishness. He produced in his *Irish Sketch-Book* a passionate commentary on what Ireland meant to a self-proclaimed Cockney who was also a radical critic. As a text, it is obscured by the resentment and criticism it occasioned at the time – notably from Charles Lever, yet another *émigré* Irish journalist, who must surely lurk behind the indebted Irish editor Shannon in *Pendennis*, tactfully remaining resident in Boulogne. The *Sketch-Book* is preoccupied by Irish–English traffic and borrowings. For Thackeray, as for Trollope, Ireland represented a highly literate populace – ragged boys leaning on a bridge in Cork discussing 'one of the Ptolemies' – and good manners, of the kind lost to modern England. 'More *gentlemen* than in one place I ever saw – gentlemen of high and low rank . . . shrewd and delicate of perception, observant of society, entering into the feelings of others, and anxious to set them at ease or to gratify them.'[33] The point of this *beau idéal* is that it reflects the novelist-observer, as Thackeray and Trollope knew themselves to be, unappreciated as they were for it in England. Their experience of Ireland in the 1840s (Thackeray as traveller, Trollope as resident Post Office surveyor) led them to brood on manners, representation, social relations, self-deception and the nature of truth. 'And where is [the truth] to be had in the country?' cries Thackeray on the last page of the *Sketch-Book*. 'There are two truths, the Catholic truth and the Protestant truth.'[34] In *Pendennis*, the raw and self-deluding hero on his erratic progress towards truth is surrounded by unreliable Irish ciceroni like Captain Costigan of Costiganstown, and the journalistic mafia already mentioned. They are hardly the best moral tutors, but they lead him along a certain path towards reality.

Trollope, even more than Thackeray, came to Ireland afflicted by personal troubles, and found far more answers than Thackeray there. 'From the day on which I set foot in Ireland all . . . evils went away from me. Since that time who has had a happier life than mine?' 'When I meet an Irishman abroad I always recognize in him more of a kinsman than I do in an Englishman.'[35] Previous inertia, depression and failure fell away. He learned to measure himself by his own standards, not those imposed by his formidable mother. He met his wife there; he wrote his first novels there, taking Ireland as his theme; he put his impressive mark on the organization of the Irish Post Office, still commemorated by the first Victorian pillar-box, an elegant octagon on a street-corner in Galway. His early Irish novel, *The Kellys and the O'Kellys* (1848), is an unwinking, accurate and thoughtful observation of Irish conditions just before the Famine; but it is also a celebration of the complexities of Irish social relations, at once offhand and sophisticated. The stereotypes are never stereotypical; his latest and best biographer has pointed out that he actually acquired his typical 'English' mode of address and behaviour in Ireland.[36] His appetite for Ireland remained omnivorous.

And yet there is another side to it. Trollope wrote a series of public letters defending the organization of Famine relief which are determinedly rosy and insouciantly muddle-headed.[37] His opposition to Home Rule was violent, and his unfinished last novel, *The Landleaguers* (1883), is a crude treatise against Irish rural savagery, worthy of Froude or Kingsley. In his late autobiography he tried, unconvincingly, to disown the necessary Irishness of Phineas Finn. The qualities of perception which make him the best 'Irish' novelist of mid-century had by old age been thrown into reverse. Is this simply a case of Lord Denning syndrome, or something more significant?

Before trying to define what Ireland really provided for the marginal men, it is worth instancing a few more of them at random. One figure who might have been invented by Trollope has been already considered in this book: Lord Randolph Churchill. Exiled to Ireland in disgrace in 1876, he became a politician there, made his best friends there, continued to take much of his political advice from clever Irishmen, always spent his Christmases in slightly *louche* Dublin company, and remained more interested in Ireland than anything else. (He is unique among British politicians in that he actually requested the Irish chief secretaryship: perhaps this was seen by his colleagues as an early symptom of the dementia which killed him in the end.[38]) Then there is Frederick Lucas, an ex-Quaker connected to John Bright by marriage, who converted to Catholicism, founded and edited the *Tablet*, and moved it to Dublin in 1849. He subsequently became MP for Meath, threw himself into nationalism and tenant right, and challenged the Irish bishops to take a more prominent part in nationalist politics (to their well-bred horror).[39] There is the evangelical Sophia Sturge, removing herself to Letterfrack in Connemara in 1888, to the astonishment of her relations, and starting a basket-works with the help of local priests.[40] And there is that most marginal of men, the historian James Anthony Froude: constantly returning to Ireland, writing beautifully of the therapeutic qualities of life in County Kerry – but whose Irish obsession also produced his extraordinary study of *The English in Ireland in the Eighteenth Century* (1881). This is a sustained invective against Irish self-government, argued on impeccably prejudiced Carlylean grounds of Irish unreliability. But the language of his preface suggests that the book really represents an insecure Victorian over-reaction against something insidiously attractive. The Irish are 'passionate in everything – passionate in their patriotism, passionate in their religion, passionately courageous, passionately loyal and affectionate, they are without the manliness which will give strength and solidity to the sentimental part of their dispositions, while the surface and show is so seductive and so winning that only experience of its instability can resist the charm'. The key words tell their own tale: passion, manliness, seduction, resistance.

Froude's attack reminds us of Trollope's reaction and Randolph Churchill's eventual (and utterly unexpected) political embrace of 'foul Ulster Tories' in the interests of embattled Unionism. What purposes had Ireland really served for these marginal men, to make them react so violently? In some ways, like Thackeray, they had been searching for a non-existent 'truth'. Put another way, Ireland provided an alternative kind of reality. Categories changed and were jumbled after landing at Kingstown; the angle of the universe suddenly tilted. For awkward young people at odds with the received truths of the mother country, this could be welcome. There was also a different social integument, and an arrangement of social relations, which appealed to those impatient of restrictive English modes – rather as other displaced English people discovered Arabia for their own purposes. In this way the exploitation of Ireland by the marginal men was a kind of colonialism: on other cultural levels, 'Celticism' might be approximated (rather crudely) to 'Orientalism' or 'negritude'. But it is an extremely complex phenomenon. While colonially derived, it was the obverse of the original Spenserian colonial attitude, which had argued that Irish cultural values were inevitably corrupting and therefore must be extirpated. Nor was it an assimilationist approach. The marginal men usually expressed the kind of idealization that Shaw satirized in *John Bull's Other Island*. He raged against Englishmen 'always gaping admiringly at the Irishman as at some clever child prodigy. He overrates him with a generosity born of a traditional consciousness of his own superiority.'[41] Personally, Shaw said elsewhere, he liked Englishmen better than Irishmen because they made more of him. (Perhaps this is why Yeats only had affairs with Englishwomen.) Shaw followed through his theme in the Wildean 'Preface for Politicians':

> I am English enough to be an inveterate Republican and Home Ruler ... When I look round me on the hybrid cosmopolitans, slum poisoned or square pampered, who call themselves Englishmen today, and see them bullied by the Irish Protestant garrison as no Bengalee now lets himself be bullied by an Englishman; when I see the Irishman everywhere standing clearheaded, sane, hardily callous to the boyish sentimentalities, susceptibilities, and credulities that make the Englishman the dupe of every charlatan and the idolater of every numskull, I perceive that Ireland is the only spot on earth which still produces the ideal Englishman of history.[42]

(Elsewhere he posits Nelson, the typically sentimental, theatrical Englishman, against Wellington, the typically laconic and unemotional Irishman.)

You could, of course, experience Ireland as an English intellectual and cordially loathe it: for example, Carlyle, Newman and Gerard Manley Hopkins. But those who took Ireland for their own purposes identified with it more passionately and interrogated Irishness more enthusiastically than, for instance, native Anglo-Irish intellectuals like Sheridan Le Fanu or Edward Dowden, who, while disliking the thought of life in England, retired into a sort of gloomy internal exile in Ireland, awaiting the barbarians.[43] Lord Randolph Churchill, working round the clock to manoeuvre Catholic bishops and Presbyterian dominies into accepting an Intermediate Education Bill, or Frederick Lucas, excitedly setting up the *Tablet* in Dublin, present a very different kind of engagement. And it is no coincidence that so many of the marginal Victorians who had chosen Ireland as the appropriate area in which to exercise their moral authority, or who had in one sense or another found themselves there, reacted powerfully against the idea of losing it. When Home Rule advanced on to the real agenda of politics in the 1880s, Froude, Churchill and Trollope were all to be found frantically opposing it – with an irrational intensity which cannot simply be put down to anti-Popery or imperial dementia. Something they valued personally was being taken from them – a part of their achieved personality – and they clung to it. This brings us to the significance of the end of the Union, both for the marginal men and the micks on the make.

V

From the 1880s, and escalating from the turn of the century, the picture changed. By this decade, a certain kind of Irish literary emigrant was advancing to prominence: notably Wilde, Shaw and Yeats. Yeats's background and ethos partake both of marginal man and mick on the make. His family and background, Protestant clerical-bourgeois, were completely Irish – as his sister Lily sharply pointed out in a private letter. 'We are far more Irish than all the saints and martyrs – Parnell – Pearse – Madame Markievicz – Maud Gonne – de Valera – and no one ever thinks of speaking of them as Anglo-Irish.' Yeats's youth was spent between England and Ireland, the background of one defining the image of the other. His early fascination with Wilde was for a fellow countryman who had remade himself in London – both his natural focus and a stronghold of the enemy, to be conquered. Wilde was, of course, destroyed in cross-examination by another Irish *arriviste*, Edward Carson. Shaw, Yeats, Wilde and Carson were all from the reaches of the Protestant Dublin middle class – the first three from its Bohemian fringe. Marginalization and duality at home made translation to England both easy and necessary. Yeats could not have remade his Irishness in the way he did if he had been permanently based in Dublin; nor could he have achieved his vision of an Irish community, worldwide, united by 'imaginative possessions'. His rooms in Bloomsbury were for decades his only fixed home: symbolically, across the road from Euston Station, where the Irish Mail departed every evening and arrived every morning. Sometimes it brought a visitor from Ireland whose first port of call was breakfast with Yeats in Woburn Buildings. Often it was Lady Gregory or Maud Gonne; on one awkward occasion it was the definitive voice of exile-as-opportunity, James Joyce.

Joyce's use of exile is well known; Yeats's careful manipulation of his permanent status as temporary emigrant has been less considered. One of his earliest works, the novel *John Sherman* (1891), deals with a divided man, caught between provincial, rooted Ireland and the metropolitan temptations of England; his first great popular success was a poem about exile, 'The Lake Isle of Innisfree' (1890), which he later came heartily to dislike. His own early conditioning owed much to the London artistic milieu of Bedford Park, before his explorations in the Celtic Twilight; time and again, at crisis points in his life, he determined to live in England rather than in Ireland (though such resolves had to be elided in his autobiographies). He could use Irishness with artistic ruthlessness, but his nationalism, while *sui generis*, remained intense. He was a cultural founding father of the new state, returned to live there at the height of civil war, became a senator and a formidable committee man. But in the last decade of his life he was again living between England and Ireland.

The interactions discussed here depended, in a sense, upon the Union: certainly upon the various forms of collusion, implicit and explicit, which it created and evoked. From the early 1900s, with the return of the Liberals to power and the resumption of a balance-holding role by the Irish Parliamentary Party at Westminster, the Union was under strain. At the same time, the phenomenon known, loosely, as the 'new nationalism' was coming into focus. This meant that distinctively Irish modes of cultural expression were emphasized by an elite avant-garde, and a deliberate process of reclamation embarked upon. This came, not after a period of immiseration and confrontation, but as a response to modernization, Anglicization and deracination. In the last fifty years of the nineteenth century, there had been a dramatic shift of language, landownership, communications, commercialization and population – all phenomena which involved Anglicization. The gradual revolution in economics and society would be followed, in the decade 1912–22, by a political revolution: private armies, constitutional confrontation, armed rebellion, a guerrilla war of 'liberation'.

The actual pattern of cause and effect is more complex than it might seem. But a particular aspect of it which has not been much looked at concerns the making of the revolutionary generation. Apart from the pioneering work of Tom Garvin, their social and economic background has not been comprehensively analysed; and their cultural background tends to be taken as read.[44] Looking at them anew, they tended to come from *petit bourgeois* 'middling' occupational groups, frustrated in many areas of life. They were often educated to a certain level of expectation, and then unemployed. Their parents tended to be artisans, journalists, minor civil servants, clerks, shopkeepers. Rather than an insurrectionary peasantry or proletariat, they are nearer to Marx's idea of the *déclassé*, or Putnam's 'overeducated and underregarded outgroups'.[45] Their education, and the influence on them of the new class of National Teachers (after the 1885 Intermediate Education Act), needs analysis. (So does the interesting fact that the Irish populace was, in a sense, educationally experimented upon from the 1830s to the 1930s.) Their political impotence enabled them to adopt the rhetoric of political extravagance, at the expense of the comfortably establishment Irish Parliamentary Party; it also encouraged a warm glow of Anglophobia. An ex-peasant class, many of them resented the limitations of life for those without land in *fin de siècle* Ireland; but they were educated to higher expectations than their rural ancestors, and reached the UK job market at a higher level. They often became junior civil servants or teachers.

Significantly, Yeats's poem 'Easter 1916' opens by memorializing the revolutionary generation before the apocalypse:

> I have met them at close of day
> Coming with vivid faces
> From counter or desk among grey
> Eighteenth-century houses . . .

Georgian Dublin has become tenanted by solicitors' and government offices; and the vivid faces trapped there despised the generation of nationalists such as the Irish Parliamentary Party who lived, in a sense, in mid-Irish Sea, paying lip-service to an idea of separation which most of them never wanted to happen. Thus the *Leader* on T.P. O'Connor in 1900:

> The Ireland in which he rose to fame is gone. It must be strange to him when he finds that sentimentality and treacle are drugs on the market, but no doubt he has made the discovery already. If he has nothing else to offer, he had better go home to England, where life is so hard-working and practical

that treacle and sentimentality may be eagerly taken as a condiment. We who, alas, have taken them so long as our staple food have had our fill of them.[46]

It is striking how emphatically the voices of Irish-Irelandism – newspapers like the *Leader* or Arthur Griffith's *United Irishman*, the Catholic establishment of the National University, and so on – identified English cultural norms with corruption (just as Spenser had once identified Irish cultural norms). It is also striking that the new, Anglophobic, culturally separatist organizations did not, unlike the old Home Rule structures, appeal to the Irish in Britain. (The Catholic Church in Ireland supported Sinn Féin; the Church in Britain did not.) Further to the Green Left, the old Fenian movement in nineteenth-century Britain had been by and large a moderate, leisure-oriented, rather open identification, mostly in the hands of a few ubiquitous committee men (like the doctors already mentioned); but even so, it did not appeal to the great majority of the Irish in Britain. By the 1890s, individuals of Irish descent were politically prominent in the new politics of radical trades unionism, providing much of the leadership for the gas and dock strikes. In Scotland, many defected to the new Independent Labour Party, but the response of the Irish in Britain to the new-wave separatist political organizations was more or less apathetic. New-wave cultural groups rooted themselves more readily – like the Irish Literary Society, originating in Southwark, which is still active. Local Gaelic League branches meant much to the transplanted Irish; a survey of 32 early Gaelic Leaguers shows that 17 had been emigrants, and 12 had joined the League while living out of Ireland.[47] But the transference to political extremism is unproven.

Thus many of the old ambivalences and dependencies continued; and beneath the rhetoric of *völkisch* nostalgia, the revolutionary generation sustained a correspondingly ambiguous relationship with Englishness. Where, then, to locate the micks on the make? The interesting thing is how many of the revolutionary generation had experienced a spell of temporary emigration. One of the few relevant pieces of statistical research shows a correlation between foreign residence and extremism.[48] Between forty and fifty per cent of the future revolutionary leaders had lived in Britain, or were of returned emigrant stock (like James Larkin and James Connolly, the two great socialist leaders).

Several came from the traditional location of *émigré* London journalism, like W.P. Ryan, editor of the *Irish Peasant*, and D.P. Moran of the *Leader*. Ryan's son Desmond, who was one of Patrick Pearse's aides in the 1916 rising, provided a poignant record of the revolution in his autobiography, *Remembering Sion*. It is written from the focus of someone brought up in Dulwich, perennially crossing the Irish Sea: the book begins and ends with an evocation of Ireland seen from England. It takes its place with the works of Joyce, O'Casey, Ernie O'Malley and others who preserved received epic images of Ireland, conjured up in emigration. Another literary nationalist of the new generation who discovered his nationalism and Gaelicism while living in London was the writer Robert Lynd. He had received one piece of careers advice from his Belfast schoolmaster: 'Escape. Fly while there is time!'[49]

Many of the Sinn Féin leaders had taken this advice when young, and later returned; P.S. O'Hegarty and Arthur Griffith come to mind and so, most of all, does the future guerrilla supremo, Michael Collins. Collins's career was classic (the supermick on the make?). A respectable Cork farming background, apprentice journalist, successful in his Post Office clerkship exams, the emigrant boat, nine years in London; joining his sister, his cousin, and his friend P.S. O'Hegarty in the Post Office Savings Bank, later moving to running the messengers' department at a City solicitor's, then to the Guaranty Trust Company. Throughout, he remained an omnivorous reader of the English classics as well as a cynical commentator on the prejudices and practices of the sister island. His future would make him, in his twenties, Minister of Finance to the underground Sinn Féin parliament, President of the Irish Republican Brotherhood, and negotiator of the Anglo-Irish Treaty in London. He might be seen as the classic successful returned emigrant.

In fact, Collins's emigrant experience remained central to him. His nine years in London enshrined a view of Ireland left behind which provided a powerful emotional impetus. He once said he stood for

> an Irish civilization based on the people and embodying the things – their habits, ways of thought, customs – that make them different – the sort of life I was brought up in . . . Once, years ago, a crowd of us were going along the Shepherd's Bush road when out of a lane came a chap with a donkey – just the sort of donkey and just the sort of cart that they have at home. He

came out quite suddenly and we all cheered him. Nobody who had not been an exile will understand me, but I stand for that.[50]

At the same time, like O'Hegarty, residence in London had modified his Anglophobia (and probably strengthened his anti-clericalism). And 'exile', for all its romantic and mournful connotations, could be a liberation and an education too, as it had been for generations. (This is how it is represented in George Moore's seminal Irish short stories published as *The Untilled Field* in 1902.[51]) Desmond Ryan, that 1916 revolutionary bred in Dulwich, wrote:

> To leave Ireland often means to know Ireland better, and too few of those who should leave their country for their country's good have the sense to do so. The 'expatriates' . . . do for Ireland what Ireland too seldom does for herself. This is no great virtue on their part: looking back over their shoulders they see the thing half seen before.[52]

And in the revolutionary era, what of the marginal men – those who relied on Ireland to provide something they lacked or missed in England or in themselves? The syndrome continued, but in a different generation. Ireland now, apparently, provided a haven for displaced revolutionary identities – first in the realm of culture, then of politics. A good transitional example is Annie Horniman: heiress to the Pure Tea fortune, from a Manchester Quaker background, preoccupied by mysticism, the artistic avant-garde, and the idea of a new theatre. She was also, to her misfortune, half-consciously in love with W.B. Yeats. In a sense he 'was Ireland to her' (as Yeats himself would say of Maud Gonne). She came to Ireland in 1904, having bought a theatre for Yeats and the nascent Abbey Theatre Company. And Ireland, which was to provide her with a fulfilled alternative identity, let her down. 'She paid and paid, but what she paid for was never delivered. She tried to buy the love of Yeats; lacking that, an Irish theatre society; lacking that, the Abbey Theatre building. In the end she was relieved of the title of the building, with £1,500 remaining of a £13,000 investment, and of her relationship to Yeats.'[53] She was initially dazzled by Dublin Bohemia, and by being allowed to design costumes as well as pay the bills. 'Do you realize that you have now given me the right to call myself "artist"? How I thank you!'[54] But Yeats rewarded her by telling her, in front of the entire cast, that her medieval costumes for *On Baile's Strand* made them look like a row of

'Father Christmases and fire extinguishers'. Failing artistic initiatives, Horniman fell back on economic power: she tried to keep the sixpenny classes out of the pit, she attempted (like a nineteenth-century landlord) to control the lives and marriages of her tenants. She told the stage manager that she had spotted his unsuitable fiancée 'going into a shop with a common-looking girl',[55] but this merely started a canard that Miss Horniman was in love with him herself. Again like a landlord, she tried to enforce a 'no politics' rule for the Abbey. Her own political and emotional agenda was never far below the surface. 'We will conquer your country,' she told Yeats, 'with the help of mine.' And Lady Gregory compared her influence to inviting the Normans into Ireland, or 'giving up Parnell to please an English howl'.[56] By 1907, according to one observer, Miss Horniman's 'hatred of everything Irish amounted to lunacy'.[57] She returned to England with what she could salvage and started an avant-garde theatre in Manchester instead. It is all very like a Shaw plot – the other side of *John Bull's Other Island*, that comedy of Irish–English interactions which Shaw actually wrote for Yeats's theatre company but which they never performed.

The cautionary tale of Annie Horniman shows a last marginal figure, trying to write on the supposedly blank Irish slate a message that would make sense of her own difficulties. It is significant that one of the rocks which split her venture was politics, for the new marginal men and women of the early twentieth century were figures who found in Ireland the revolutionary identity, and revolutionary potential, so regrettably lacking in England. In some ways, they are like the 'superfluous men' of late nineteenth-century Russia described by Isaiah Berlin in his famous essay on Alexander Herzen:

> They belonged to the class of those who are by birth aristocratic, but who themselves go over to some freer and more radical mode of thought and of action . . . [They] exercise a peculiar kind of personal freedom which combines spontaneity with distinction. Their minds see large and generous horizons and, above all, reveal a unique intellectual gaiety of a kind that aristocratic education tends to produce. At the same time, they are intellectually on the side of everything that is new, progressive, rebellious, young, untried, of that which is about to come into being, of the open sea whether or not there is land that lies beyond . . . intermediate figures who live near the frontier that divides old from new, between the *douceur de la vie* which is

about to pass and the tantalizing future, the dangerous new age that they themselves do much to bring into being.[58]

The revolutionary era in Ireland magnetized many such people. In a sense much of the revolutionary language, the articulation of the separatist rationale, came not from the micks on the make but from the marginal men. The nascent revolutionary generation in Ireland produced no particular keeper of the revolutionary conscience – staying with the Russian parallel, there is no figure analogous to Vissarion Belinsky. But the cohort who made Ireland the cause which centralized their marginal existences produced several such figures, often harking back to the Shelley tradition: English romantics identifying Ireland's cause as their own, or possibly their own as Ireland's. Maud Gonne, English débutante, French anti-Dreyfusard, Irish revolutionary and consummate stylist, was one ('the Colonel's daughter still', as Seán O'Casey, disenchanted mick on the make, witheringly described her). Another was Erskine Childers: quintessential English adventure-hero, Haileybury and Trinity College, Cambridge, Boer War, DSC for his achievements in the Royal Navy Air Service, inspirational figure for John Buchan, imperial propagandist – then a Pauline conversion in 1919, Director of Publicity for Sinn Féin, eventually executed by his ex-comrades in the Irish Civil War. Aodh de Blácam, born Hugh Black in England, was another convert to high-souled Sinn Féin values and eventual guardian of purist Irish nationalist culture. Charlotte Despard, Maud Gonne's companion in arms (and sister to the Lord-Lieutenant of Ireland), is another: Dubliners knew them as 'Maud Gone Mad and Mrs Desparate'. And there is O'Casey's other *bête noire*, Constance Markievicz, daughter of the Sligo Ascendancy turned 'Irish rebel' (a description she insisted upon).

Markievicz's contribution to the debates over the Anglo-Irish Treaty is significant for this argument. When the time came in 1922 to debate the Treaty that ended the Union, and rearrange the terms of the Irish–British relationship, where did the micks on the make stand in relation to the marginal men? It is interesting to look at the background of those who went to London, negotiated the Treaty, and brought it back to a bitterly contested debate. Most prominent and glamorous was Michael Collins, last in London as the junior clerk on the Shepherd's Bush Road, now pursued by society hostesses and driving a hard bargain with Lord Birkenhead and Winston Churchill. The other members of the Irish delegation included Arthur Griffith, South African agitator and journalist turned state-builder; Robert Barton, English-educated son of an Ascendancy house in Wicklow, ex-British army; George Gavan Duffy, son of the Irish Prime Minister of Victoria, educated at Stonyhurst, and a successful London barrister before taking up the Sinn Féin cause in 1918; and Erskine Childers, whose background has been described. As the terms of the Treaty were beaten out, most particularly the Oath of Allegiance, the micks on the make were most ready to come to an agreement; the marginal man Childers opposed it, and eventually persuaded his cousin Barton to do likewise. In the debates back in Dublin, the same division is discernible – epitomized by Constance Markievicz's attack on Collins. She should have been sent to negotiate, she claimed, because as a renegade, with an English mother, she understood the English mind. 'By that bad black drop of English blood in me I know the English – that's the truth. I say it is because of that black drop in me that I know the English personally better perhaps than the people who went over on the delegation.'[59] Collins, she insinuated, had been seduced by his own opportunism and his vulnerability to English corruptions. The Treaty debates are full of such exchanges, redolent with ironies, and expressing a tangled history of Irish–English interactions and borrowings of identity. And just like their Victorian precursors, the marginal men and women wanted Ireland to go on being Ireland as they knew it – and as it answered to their needs.

In a sense the same was true of Irish nationalists conscious of an English cultural conditioning: like Yeats. The new nationalism was, however, determined to deny him the right to sustain this dual identification. All through his life, and for months after his death, newspapers like the *Leader*, the *Catholic Bulletin* and the *Irish Monthly* engaged in a bizarre exercise they called '"placing" W.B. Yeats' (or 'Pensioner' Yeats, or 'Pollexfen' Yeats), inevitably deciding with pleasure that *The Times* and the *Spectator* and other English organs that claimed him as an English poet were absolutely correct.[60] Yeats would not have been surprised. In the 'General Introduction to My Work', unpublished in his lifetime, he attempted his own analysis, writing that

no people hate as we do in whom [the] past is always alive. There are moments when hatred poisons my life and I accuse myself of effeminacy because I have not given it adequate expression ... Then I remind myself that though mine is the first English marriage I know of in the direct line, all my family names are English; that I owe my soul to Shakespeare, to Spenser, to Blake, perhaps to William Morris, and to the English language in which I think, speak and write; that everything I love has come to me through English. My hatred tortures me with love, my love with hate.[61]

Nor was he the only one: Desmond Ryan was obsessed by Shakespeare; Michael Collins's favourite novel was *The Mill on the Floss*;[62] one 1916 martyr, Joseph Plunkett, had a devoted cult of G.K. Chesterton; another, Thomas MacDonagh, revered Jane Austen. Ryan remembers MacDonagh's last English class at University College before he left for the fateful Easter; the aspiring revolutionaries read *Pride and Prejudice*. '"There's no one like Jane, lads!" he said with deep affection.'[63]

This may demonstrate cultural hegemony with a vengeance. But there are also fruitful ambiguities and tensions in this mixed inheritance, which require careful understanding. Nor do they stop neatly in 1922; emigration certainly did not cease, a fact which created some embarrassment for the theoreticians of de Valera's Ireland.[64] The death of nationalism has been over-anticipated by historians; the 'national idea', in Eric Hobsbawm's words, 'as formulated by its official champions does not necessarily coincide with the actual self-definition of the people concerned'.[65] And the marginal men and women continue to find Ireland an appropriate arena to exercise the conscience of their race:[66] latter-day examples might include Mícheál Mac Liammóir, Bridget Rose Dugdale and Enoch Powell. Dutifully based theories of culture usually break down when posited against the variety and ambivalence of historical experience, but the disciplines of history and literature can throw light on figures caught in the interstices of the Irish–English relationship, and illuminate crooked corners and eccentric alleyways – even if the shadows around them loom more questioningly than ever.

Notes

Introduction

1. See below, p. 122.
2. Donall Mac Amhlaigh, *An Irish Navvy: The Diary of an Exile*, translated from the Irish by Valentin Iremonger (London, 1964), p. 124.
3. Brendan Bradshaw, 'Nationalism and Historical Scholarship in Modern Ireland', *Irish Historical Studies*, vol. 26, no. 104 (1989), p. 349.
4. Ibid., p. 350.
5. Tom Dunne, 'New Histories: Beyond "Revisionism"', *Irish Review*, no. 12 (Spring/Summer 1992).
6. See Brendan Bradshaw, 'Nationalism and Historical Scholarship in Modern Ireland', p. 350.
7. Desmond Fennell, *Irish Review*, no. 4 (Spring 1988), p. 21.
8. Brendan Bradshaw, 'Nationalism and Historical Scholarship in Modern Ireland'; and also the revealingly autobiographical 'The Emperor's New Clothes' in *Free Thought in Ireland*, a supplement to *Fortnight*, no. 297 (July–August 1991, Belfast). For a combative and closely argued response, see Michael Laffan, 'Insular Attitudes: The Revisionists and Their Critics' in M. Ni Dhonnchadha and Theo Dorgan (eds.), *Revising the Rising* (Derry, 1991).
9. Peter Quinn, reported in *Irish Times*, 6 April 1992.
10. See Seamus Deane, 'Wherever Green is Read', in M. Ni Dhonnchadha and Theo Dorgan (eds.), *Revising the Rising* and his 'General Introduction', *The Field Day Anthology of Irish Writing* (Derry, 1991).
11. See Luke Gibbons, 'Challenging the Canon: Revisionism and Cultural Criticism' in ibid., vol. 3, p. 567.
12. Brendan Bradshaw, 'Nationalism and Historical Scholarship in Modern Ireland', p. 349.
13. Peter Quinn to the GAA Congress, reported in *Irish Times*, 6 April 1992.

14. Desmond Fennell in *Irish Times*, 10 November 1989.
15. Brendan Bradshaw, 'Nationalism and Historical Scholarship in Modern Ireland', pp. 347–8.

1 History and the Irish Question

1. Alice Stopford Green, *The Old Irish World* (Dublin and London, 1912), p. 9.
2. John Mitchel, *Jail Journal* (Dublin, 1918 edition), p. xlvi. All the Young Irelanders adopted this approach; see also Sir Charles Gavan Duffy's 'A Bird's-eye View of Irish History', interposed as chapter 4 of *Young Ireland: A Fragment of Irish History* (London, 1880).
3. Parnell with Grattan, for instance, and Pearse with Emmet; see D. Ryan, *Remembering Sion* (London, 1934), p. 119.
4. Sean Cronin, *Irish Nationalism: A History of Its Roots and Ideology* (Dublin, 1980); Tom Garvin, *The Evolution of Irish Nationalist Politics* (Dublin, 1981); D.G. Boyce, *Nationalism in Ireland* (London, 1982).
5. Giraldus Cambrensis (Gerald de Barry), *The Irish Historie Composed and Written by Geraldus Cambrensis* (completed in 1185) in Raphael Holinshed, *The First Volume of the Chronicles of England, Scotlande and Irelande* (1577); Edmund Spenser, *A View of the State of Ireland* (completed 1596); Edmund Campion, *A Historie of Ireland: Written in the Yeare 1571*; Richard Stanihurst, *The Historie of Ireland* (1577; Stanihurst edited Campion and Cambrensis); Sir John Davies, *A Discovery of the True Causes Why Ireland was Never Entirely Subdued . . .* (1612); Fynes Moryson, *An History of Ireland from the Year 1599 to 1603* (written *c.* 1617).
6. See, for instance, N. Lebow, 'British Historians and Irish History', *Éire-Ireland*, vol. 8, no. 4 (1973), pp. 3–38.
7. See Norman Vance's pioneering article 'Celts, Carthaginians and Constitutions: Anglo-Irish Literary Relations 1780–1820', *Irish Historical Studies*, vol. 22, no. 87 (1981), especially pp. 220ff. Since this essay was first published, an important Ph.D. thesis has been written on the subject: Clare O'Halloran, 'Golden Ages and Barbarous Nations' (Cambridge, 1991).
8. Especially Charles O'Conor, *Dissertations on the Ancient History of Ireland* (1780) and Sylvester O'Halloran, *Introduction to the Study of the History and Antiquities of Ireland* (1772).
9. See Clare O'Halloran, 'Irish Re-creations of the Gaelic Past: The Challenge of Macpherson's Ossian', *Past and Present*, no. 124 (August 1989), pp. 69–95.
10. Charles Vallancey, *An Essay on the Antiquity of the Irish Language, being a Collation of the Irish with the Punic Languages* (1772): see Norman Vance,

'Celts, Carthaginians and Constitutions: Anglo-Irish Literary Relations 1780–1820', pp. 266–7.

11. See Jeanne Sheehy, *The Rediscovery of Ireland's Past: The Celtic Revival 1830–1930* (London, 1980), p. 62. An antiquarian priest, Father Horgan of Blarney, finally in desperation built one himself, 'to puzzle posterity as antiquity has puzzled me'. See W.R. Le Fanu, *Seventy Years of Irish Life* (London, 1893), pp. 175–6.
12. Thomas Comerford, *History of Ireland from the Earliest Accounts of Time to the Invasion of the English under King Henry II* (1751).
13. See F. Grannell, 'Early Irish Ecclesiastical Studies' in Fr. Michael Hurley, S.J. (ed.), *Irish Anglicanism 1869–1969* (Dublin, 1970), pp. 39–50.
14. See Sir Laurence Parsons, Bt, *Observations on the Bequest of Henry Flood* (1795).
15. Thomas Leland, *The History of Ireland from the Invasion of Henry II* (1773); John Curry, *An Historical and Critical Review of the Civil Wars in Ireland* (1775).
16. See my *Charles Stewart Parnell: The Man and His Family* (Brighton, 1976), part 1, chapter 2. Parnell-Hayes used illustrations from early Gaelic customs and history which show familiarity with the historiographical developments of the day.
17. See *Transactions of the Gaelic Society of Ireland*, vol. 1 (1808). Other societies included the Iberno-Celtic Society (1818), the Irish Archaeological Society (1848), the Celtic Society (1848) and the Irish Archaeological and Celtic Society (1853).
18. Revd Edward Ledwich, *The Antiquities of Ireland* (1790). For a full critique, see D. Macartney, 'The Writing of History in Ireland 1800–1830', *Irish Historical Studies*, vol. 10, no. 40 (1957), pp. 347–63.
19. Sir Charles Gavan Duffy, *Young Ireland: A Fragment of Irish History*, p. 280.
20. *The Patriot Parliament of 1689, with Its Statutes, Votes and Proceedings*, edited with an introduction by Sir Charles Gavan Duffy (Dublin, London and New York, 1893).
21. See B. Farrell, 'The Paradox of Irish Politics' in B. Farrell (ed.), *The Irish Parliamentary Tradition* (Dublin, 1973), pp. 19–20.
22. See Revd Denis Taaffe, *An Impartial History of Ireland, from the Time of the English Invasion to the Present Time, from Authentic Sources* (1809–11); cf. Francis Plowden, *An Historical Review of the State of Ireland, from the Invasion of that Country under Henry II, to Its Union with Great Britain on the First of January 1801* (1803).
23. D. Macartney, 'The Writing of History in Ireland', p. 359.
24. *Dublin Evening Mail*, 27 March 1844.
25. Habits of the people. Note the general style of the cottages, as stone, mud, slated, glass windows, one storey or two, number of rooms, comfort and cleanliness.

Food; fuel; dress; longevity; usual number in a family; early marriages; any remarkable instances on either of these heads? What are their amusements and recreations? Patrons and patrons' days; and traditions respecting them? What local customs prevail, as Beal Tinne, or fire on St John's Eve? Driving the cattle through fire, and through water? Peculiar games? Any legendary tales or poems recited around the fireside? Any ancient music, as clan marches or funeral cries? They differ in different districts, collect them if you can. Any peculiarity of costume? Nothing more indicates the state of civilization and intercourse.

(J.H. Andrews, *A Paper Landscape: The Ordnance Survey in Nineteenth-century Ireland*, Oxford, 1975, p. 148.) The Institute of Irish Studies in Belfast has now begun the welcome project of publishing these parish surveys.

26. T.F. Colby, *Ordnance Survey of the County of Londonderry. Volume the First: Memoirs of the City and North-western Liberties of Londonderry, Parish of Templemore*. See J.H. Andrews, *A Paper Landscape: The Ordnance Survey in Nineteenth-century Ireland*, pp. 157ff.
27. Alice Stopford Green, *The Old Irish World*, pp. 56–61. Also see Michael Tierney, 'Eugene O'Curry and the Irish Tradition', *Studies*, vol. 51 (1962), pp. 449–62.
28. J.H. Andrews, *A Paper Landscape: The Ordnance Survey in Nineteenth-century Ireland*, pp. 173–7.
29. Sir Charles Gavan Duffy, *Young Ireland: A Fragment of Irish History*, p. 75fn.
30. Ibid., p. 289. See also John Banim, *The Boyne Water* (1826), reprinted in 1976 by the Université de Lille with an introduction by Bernard Escarbelt. On the Library of Ireland, see also M. Buckley, 'John Mitchel, Ulster, and Irish Nationality 1841–1848', *Studies*, vol. 65 (1976), pp. 30–44, which analyses Mitchel's contribution to the series, and D.G. Boyce, *Nationalism in Ireland*, pp. 161–2. Gavan Duffy remarked that Irish history was 'ransacked' for suitable examples and arguments (*Young Ireland*, p. 104).
31. P.J. Dowling, *The Hedge Schools of Ireland* (Dublin, 1935), pp. 111–12.
32. See Mr and Mrs S.C. Hall, *Ireland: Its Scenery, Character, Etc.* (1841–3); Thomas Carlyle, 'Reminiscences of My Irish Journey', *Century Illustrated Monthly Magazine*, vol. 24 (May–July 1882); William Makepeace Thackeray, *The Irish Sketch-Book* (1843). Also below, pp. 287, 292.
33. Alexis de Tocqueville, *Voyages en Angleterre, Irelande, Suisse et Algérie*, edited by J.P. Mayer (Paris, 1958); Gustave de Beaumont, *L'Irlande sociale, politique et religieuse* (1839).
34. Sir Charles Gavan Duffy, *Young Ireland: A Fragment of Irish History*, p. 167; Augustin Thierry, *Histoire de la conquête de l'Angleterre par les Normands* (1825).

35. Marx notably in his articles in the *New York Tribune*: 'A small *caste* of robber landlords dictate to the Irish people the conditions in which they are allowed to hold the land and live on it' (11 July 1853); 'the Irish landlords are confederated for a fiendish war of extermination against the cottiers' (11 January 1859), etc. Engels's view was that 'Irish history shows one what a misfortune it is for a nation to be subjugated by another nation; all the abominations of the English have their origin in the Irish Pale.'
36. In May 1885 Lytton sent Churchill, as commissioned, 'The Lay of the Primrose', of which the last verse ran:

> When, O say, shall the Celt put his blunderbuss down,
> Cease to bully the Commons, and menace the Crown?
> When shall Erin be loyal, and Britain repose,
> Neither fawning to rebels, nor flying from foes?
> That shall be, saith the Primrose, nor ever till then,
> When the country is honestly governed again,
> When the realm is redeemed from the Radical's hand
> And the Primrose comes blossoming back to the land.

(Lytton to Churchill, 18 May 1885 (RCP 1/v/601).) It does not appear to have found its way into print.
37. Samuel Smiles, *History of Ireland and the Irish People, under the Government of England* (1844), p. iv. Cf. Sir Charles Gavan Duffy, *Young Ireland: A Fragment of Irish History*, p. 81: 'Many men refrain from reading Irish history as sensitive and selfish persons refrain from witnessing human suffering. But it is a branch of knowledge as indispensable to the British statesman or politician as morbid anatomy to the surgeon.'
38. Carlyle, predictably, was the exception; see below, p. 292. Earlier he had, however, been impressed by the Royal Irish Academy museum: 'really an interesting museum, for everything has a certain *authenticity*, as well as national or other significance, too often wanting in such places' ('Reminiscences of My Irish Journey', p. 27).
39. John Stuart Mill to J.E. Cairnes, 29 July 1864, quoted in E.D. Steele, 'J.S. Mill and the Irish Question: *The Principles of Political Economy* 1848–1865', *Historical Journal*, vol. 13, no. 2 (1970), p. 231.
40. As incisively demonstrated in ibid., and in 'J.S. Mill and the Irish Question: Reform and the Integrity of the Empire 1865–1870', *Historical Journal*, vol. 21, no. 3 (1970), pp. 419–50.
41. See J.V. Kelleher, 'Matthew Arnold and the Celtic Revival' in H. Levin (ed.), *Perspectives of Criticism* (Cambridge, Mass., 1950), pp. 197–221.
42. His preface to the separate edition of the *History of Ireland* considers at some length the problems of writing Irish history and the steps he had taken to obviate them.

43. See A. Wyatt, 'Froude, Lecky and the Humblest Irishman', *Irish Historical Studies*, vol. 14, no. 75 (1975), pp. 267–85.
44. J.A. Froude, *The English in Ireland in the Eighteenth Century* (1872–4). There is a large secondary literature of refutation by Thomas Burke, W.H. Flood, John Mitchel, J.D. McGee and others.
45. Until, that is, E.R. Norman's *History of Modern Ireland* (Harmondsworth, 1971).
46. H. Montgomery Hyde (ed.), *A Victorian Historian: Private Letters of W.E.H. Lecky 1859–1878* (London, 1947), p. 41.
47. Letter to *The Times*, 9 June 1886.
48. 'The trouble with Ireland was not only social and racial. It could not be explained by unjust land laws or the sway of an alien established church. These were superadded embroilments. The root cause was English autocracy' (Herbert Gladstone, *After Thirty Years*, London, 1928, pp. 263–4).
49. See Churchill to Harcourt, 29 November 1889, Harcourt MSS 217/63, writing 'in support of a plea of "not guilty" to your charge of "bumptious ignorance"', and enclosing a pamphlet based on a speech at Perth (5 October 1889), which involved a lengthy historical exegesis on the Union. Harcourt, who had earlier stated that not 'one honest man' in Ireland approved of the measure, replied at great length, with much historical reference to back up his case (RCP 1/xiv/3340).
50. *Young Ireland: A Fragment of Irish History*, p. 93.
51. Derby's diary, quoted in J.R. Vincent, 'Gladstone and Ireland', *Proceedings of the British Academy*, vol. 63 (1977), p. 223.
52. See 'Parnell and His People: The Ascendancy and Home Rule', below.
53. For Parnell's knowledge of Irish history, see F.S.L. Lyons, *Charles Stewart Parnell* (London, 1977), pp. 37–8, and 'The Political Ideas of Parnell', *Historical Journal*, vol. 16, no. 4 (1973), pp. 749–75.
54. *The Anglo-Irish Quarrel: A Plea for Peace* (1880).
55. *The Rise and Fall of the Irish Nation* (Paris, 1833).
56. T. Newenham, *A Series of Suggestions and Observations Relative to Ireland Submitted to the Consideration of the Lord President and Council* (1825); for Newenham's ideas and influence, see H.D. Gribbon, 'Thomas Newenham 1762–1831' in J.M. Goldstrom and L.A. Clarkson (eds.), *Irish Population, Economy and Society: Essays in Honour of the Late K.H. Connell* (Oxford, 1982), pp. 231–47. His ideas were repeated in Alice Murray's influential *Commercial and Financial Relations between England and Ireland from the Period of the Restoration* (London, 1903).
57. 'One of the capital acts in Irish history; in a few years it changed the face of the land and made Ireland to a great extent an arable instead of a pastoral country.' The case against this and other misconceptions is

trenchantly summarized by Joseph Lee, 'Grattan's Parliament', in B. Farrell (ed.), *The Irish Parliamentary Tradition*, pp. 149–50. 'Foster's Corn Law did not reverse an existing trend; at the very most it slightly accentuated it.'

58. First published 1867; acutely analysed in D.G. Boyce, *Nationalism in Ireland*, pp. 247ff.
59. J. Pope-Hennessy, 'What Do the Irish Read?', *Nineteenth Century*, vol. 15 (January–June 1884), pp. 920ff.

> Abbé MacGeohegan's *History of Ireland from the Earliest Times to the Treaty of Limerick*, with John Mitchel's continuation; D'Arcy McGee's *History of Ireland to the Emancipation of the Catholics*; Duffy's *Four Years of Irish History*, with the preceding fragment, *Young Ireland*; A.M. Sullivan's *Story of Ireland*; Justin H. McCarthy's *Outline of Irish History*; Lecky's *History of the Eighteenth Century*; Walpole's *History of Ireland to the Union*; O'Callaghan's *History of the Irish Brigade in France*; Justin McCarthy's *History of Our Own Times* –, these are the most read; but the works of Macaulay, Hallam, Froude, with Father Tom Burke's *Refutation of Froude*, are read also. In biography Madden's *Lives of the United Irishmen*, *The Life and Times of Henry Grattan*, Moore's *Life of Lord Edward Fitzgerald*, Wolfe Tone's Memoirs, Mitchel's *Jail Journal*, Maguire's *Father Mathew* seem to be favourites (p. 926).

60. *United Ireland*, 13 August 1881.
61. See David Fitzpatrick, *Politics and Irish Life 1913–1921: Provincial Experience of War and Revolution* (Dublin, 1977).
62. See D. Macartney, 'The Political Use of History in the Work of Arthur Griffith', *Journal of Contemporary History*, vol. 8 (1973), p. 67. It is worth, however, quoting Griffith's utilitarian view of the ends of education:

> The secondary system of education in Ireland . . . was designed to prevent the higher intelligence of the country performing its duty to the Irish State. In other countries secondary education gives to each its leaders in industry and commerce, its great middle class which as society is constructed forms the equalizing and harmonizing element in the population. In Ireland secondary education causes aversion and contempt for industry and 'trade' in the heads of young Irishmen, and fixes their eyes, like the fool's, on the ends of the earth. The secondary system in Ireland draws away from industrial pursuits those who are best fitted to them and sends them to be civil servants in England, or to swell the ranks of struggling clerkdom in Ireland.

(*The Sinn Féin Policy*, Dublin [n.d., but delivered as a speech to the first annual conference of the National Council, 28 November 1905].)

63. George A. Birmingham, *An Irishman Looks at His World* (London, 1919), pp. 12–13; see below, p. 74.

64. In 1868 Gerald FitzGibbon's pamphlet *Ireland in 1868* (noted by Marx as the distillation of the Ascendancy case) emphasized the complete lack of tension between Protestant and Catholic at university, on the Bench and in professional life; but the same author's *Roman Catholic Priests and National Schools* (1871) held that the denominational nature of national schools had bred the idea of the true Irishman as Catholic and Celtic, and driven a wedge between those whose interests were objectively identical. The polarization of politics in the 1880s saw the solidifying of this process.
65. See 'Varieties of Irishness: Cultures and Anarchy in Ireland', below.
66. G.B. Shaw, *Prefaces* (London, 1938 edition), pp. 443–4. Cf. E. Estyn Evans, *The Personality of Ireland: Habitat, Heritage and History* (revised edition, Belfast, 1981), pp. 43–4, where an elegant demonstration is given of the 'mongrel' nature of the Irish 'race'.
67. See Fr. Francis Shaw, 'The Canon of Irish History: A Challenge', *Studies*, vol. 61 (1972), pp. 1133–52; Ruth Dudley Edwards, *Patrick Pearse: The Triumph of Failure* (London, 1977); J.V. Kelleher, 'Early Irish History and Pseudo-history', *Studia Hibernica*, no. 3 (1963), pp. 113–27.
68. On MacNeill, see Michael Tierney, *Eoin MacNeill: Scholar and Man of Action 1876–1945* (Oxford, 1981), especially pp. 90–96.
69. He identifies Davis with a commitment to physical force in *Political Writings and Speeches* (Dublin, 1924), pp. 323–4; but Davis, especially in a celebrated essay 'Moral Force', specifically denied that this was an answer. See B. Farrell, 'The Parodox of Irish Politics', p. 19.
70. See, for instance, *A History of the Irish State to 1014*, pp. ix, 85, etc.
71. *A History of the Irish State to 1014*, chapter 6.
72. See especially *Irish Nationality*, pp. 13, 14, 20–21, 28, 76, 95, 165.
73. Notably the work of Kathleen Hughes; for a summary, see E. Estyn Evans, *The Personality of Ireland: Habitat, Heritage and History*, pp. 58–9.
74. See especially D.A. Binchy, 'The Origins of the So-called High Kingship' (Statutory Lecture, Dublin Institute of Advanced Studies, 1959).
75. J.V. Kelleher, 'Irish History and Pseudo-history', pp. 120–22, for the case against the 'Book of Rights' and other sources as twelfth-century creations. 'So extensive was the revision of historical evidence that we have, I would say, about as much chance of recovering the truth about early Christian Ireland as a historian five hundred years from now would have if he were trying to reconstruct the history of Russia in the twentieth century from broken sets of different editions of the Soviet encyclopaedia.'
76. AE (George William Russell), 'Nationality and Cosmopolitanism in Art' (1899), reprinted in *Some Irish Essays* (Dublin, 1906), p. 18.
77. *Catholic Bulletin*, February and June 1925, quoted in Margaret

O'Callaghan, 'Language and Religion: The Quest for Identity in the Irish Free State' (MA thesis, University College Dublin, 1981).

78. Ruth Dudley Edwards, *Patrick Pearse: The Triumph of Failure*, p. 341.

79. 'We think that the powers of the Ministry to regulate and to supervise the books used in schools should be very strictly exercised in the matter of historical textbooks. No books bearing on the subject of history should, without previous official sanction, be permitted to be used in any schools under the Ministry.' Quoted in John Magee, 'The Teaching of Irish History in Irish Schools', *Northern Teacher*, vol. 10, no. 1 (1970).

80. This is reflected by the adoption among historians of George Russell's *Irish Statesman* as the agreed source for quotations showing the sanity and cosmopolitanism of the Anglo-Irish in the Free State; but as O'Callaghan ('Language and Religion: The Quest for Identity in the Irish Free State', n. 85) reminds us, it spoke for far fewer of them at the time than did the less liberal *Church of Ireland Gazette* or *Irish Times*.

81. For a retrospect and a commentary, see Robin Dudley Edwards, 'Irish History: An Agenda', *Irish Historical Studies*, vol. 21. no. 81 (1978), pp. 3–19.

82. The case for interpreting the Land War of 1879–82 as a revolution of rising expectations was asserted by Barbara Solow, *The Land Question and the Irish Economy 1870–1903* (Cambridge, Mass., 1971); Paul Bew, *Land and the National Question in Ireland 1858–1882* (Dublin, 1978); W.E. Vaughan, 'An Assessment of the Economic Performance of Irish Landlords 1851–1881', in F.S.L. Lyons and R.A.J. Hawkins (eds.), *Ireland under the Union: Varieties of Tension* (Oxford, 1980), pp. 173–200; James S. Donnelly, *The Land and the People of Nineteenth-century Cork* (London, 1974), and others. But it is also to be found in contemporary texts like Anna Parnell's astringent *The Tale of a Great Sham*, edited by Dana Hearne (Dublin, 1986), and in Terence McGrath's *Pictures from Ireland* (1880), which described the Land War in terms of an adroit takeover by the middling tenantry, manipulating a credit squeeze.

83. See report 'The Teaching of History in Irish Schools', 1966, in *Administration*, journal of the Institute of Public Administration, Dublin (Winter 1967), pp. 268–85. This committee included historians who were influential in the new school of history-writing, and emphasized throughout the need for impartiality and an international perspective. Also see John Magee, 'The Teaching of Irish History in Irish Schools'.

84. T.W. Moody and F.X. Martin (eds.), *The Course of Irish History* (Dublin, 1967). Previously the field had been held by M. Hayden and G.A. Moonan, *A Short History of the Irish People from the Earliest Times to 1920* (Dublin, 1921) and J. Carty, *A Junior History of Ireland* (Dublin, 1932).

85. L. Ó Broin, *Dublin Castle and the 1916 Rising* (Dublin, 1966).

86. See Fr. Francis Shaw, 'The Canon of Irish History: A Challenge', and for comments, F.S.L. Lyons, 'The Dilemma of the Irish Contemporary Historian', *Hermathena*, vol. 115 (1973), p. 53; Ruth Dudley Edwards, *Patrick Pearse: The Triumph of Failure*, pp. 341–2; Terence Brown, *Ireland: A Social and Cultural History 1922–1979* (London, 1979), pp. 287–9.
87. E. Estyn Evans, *The Personality of Ireland: Habitat, Heritage and History*, p. 59.
88. A.T. Lucas, 'Plundering of Churches in Ireland' in E. Rynne (ed.), *North Munster Studies* (Limerick, 1967), pp. 172–229.
89. F.X. Martin's 1975 O'Donnell Lecture presented this unexpected picture.
90. See R.V. Comerford, 'Patriotism as Pastime: The Appeal of Fenianism in the Mid-1860s', *Irish Historical Studies*, vol. 21, no. 87 (1981), pp. 239–50.
91. D.H. Akenson, *Occasional Papers on the Irish in South Africa* (Grahamstown, S.A., 1991), p. 30. (The generalization refers to the whole Empire, not just to South Africa.)
92. David Fitzpatrick, *Politics and Irish Life 1913–1921*.
93. Barbara Solow, *The Land Question and the Irish Economy 1870–1903*, p. 204, and R.D. Crotty, *Irish Agricultural Production: Its Volume and Structure* (Cork, 1966).
94. Joseph Lee, 'Continuity and Change in Ireland 1945–1970' in *Ireland 1945–1970* (Dublin, 1979), p. 177.
95. G.B.S. [Shaw], 'On Throwing Out Dirty Water', *Irish Statesman*, 15 September 1923; quoted in F.S.L. Lyons, *Culture and Anarchy in Ireland 1890–1939* (Oxford, 1979), p. 165.
96. Dedicatory preface to *A History of Ireland under the Union* (Dublin, 1952). It might be added that this is a work of wide reading and dense texture, in which original documentation and personal reminiscence is used to powerful effect; but it is none the less pervaded by obsession.
97. See H. Glassie, *Passing the Time: Folklore and History of an Ulster Community* (Dublin, 1982), p. 83, which records the 'education' transmitted in rural Fermanagh. '"It took the boys in Fenian days to carry it on until the Men Behind the Wire came . . . The old fight had to be fought, and it had to be fought from the days of eighteen and sixty-seven, and indeed it went back further. Seventeen and ninety-eight, that was the first Rising. That's what you want to know: the background to everything."' Also see ibid., pp. 639ff., for observations about the keeping of 'alternative history' in local communities. In a similar manner, the memory of dispossession lasted on at atavistic levels, noted by Arthur Young, and often since (see, for instance, Tom Garvin, *The Evolution of Irish Nationalist Politics*, p. 16).
98. The work of M.W. Heslinga, *The Irish Border as a Cultural Divide*

(Assen, Netherlands, 1962) has received less attention than might be expected; and Erhard Rumpf's pioneering *Nationalism and Socialism in Twentieth-century Ireland*, published in German in 1959, had to wait until 1977 for an English translation (under the imprint of Liverpool University Press). When carrying out research, Dr Rumpf was told 'by an authority on Irish politics' that he could not hope to analyse the dynamic of Irish nationalism: 'There was no sociological, sectarian or class problem or angle in the Sinn Féin movement, or any part of it, from beginning to end' (p. xv).

99. I. Adamson's book *Cruthin: The Ancient Kindred* (Newtownards, 1974) is interpreted by Unionist ideologues as arguing for an indigenous 'British' people settled in Ulster before the plantations.
100. Elegantly mocked by E. Curtis in the *Irish Statesman*, 7 November 1925: 'We must beat our harps into harpoons and our wolfdogs into walruses.'
101. Goldwin Smith, *Irish History and Irish Character* – 'an expansion of a lecture delivered before the Oxford Architectural and Historical Society at their Annual Meeting in June 1861' (1861), preface and p. 193.

2 Varieties of Irishness: Cultures and Anarchy in Ireland

1. F.S.L. Lyons, *Culture and Anarchy in Ireland 1890–1939* (Oxford, 1979), p. 177.
2. Ibid., p. 54.
3. W.B. Yeats, *Autobiographies* (London, 1955), p. 559.
4. See 'Thinking from Hand to Mouth: Anglo-Irish Literature, Gaelic Nationalism and Irish Politics in the 1890s', below; also my *Modern Ireland 1600–1972* (London, 1988).
5. Dominic Daly, *The Young Douglas Hyde: The Dawn of the Irish Revolution and Renaissance 1874–1893* (Dublin, 1974).
6. 6 February 1904.
7. Tom Garvin, *Nationalist Revolutionaries in Ireland* (Oxford, 1988), p. xi: my italics.
8. This is one theme in an important Ph.D. thesis by Joseph Spence, 'The Philosophy of Irish Toryism 1833–1852' (University of London, 1991), shortly to be published in book form by Oxford University Press.
9. See F.W. Boal and J.N.H Douglas (eds.), *Integration and Division: Geographical Perspectives on the Northern Ireland Problem* (Belfast, 1982), p. 67.
10. See 'History and the Irish Question', above.
11. W.B. Yeats in New York, 1903; quoted in E. Cullingford, *Yeats, Ireland and Fascism* (London, 1981), p. 25.

12. See Dennis Kennedy, *The Widening Gulf: Northern Attitudes to the Independent Irish State 1919–1949* (Belfast, 1988), chapter 7.
13. *Culture and Anarchy*, p. 105.
14. Brian Friel, *Translations* (London, 1981), p. 49.
15. *Nationalist Revolutionaries in Ireland*, pp. 23, 46.
16. 23 September 1899.
17. *Culture and Anarchy*, pp. 1–2.
18. *An Claidheamh Soluis*, 8 November 1913.
19. See Margaret O'Callaghan, 'Language, Nationality and Cultural Identity in the Irish Free State 1922–1927: The *Irish Statesman* and the *Catholic Bulletin* Reappraised', *Irish Historical Studies*, vol. 24, no. 94 (1984).
20. *Culture and Anarchy*, p. 168.
21. See M. Dent, 'The Feasibility of Shared Sovereignty (and Shared Authority)' in Charles Townshend (ed.), *Consensus in Ireland: Approaches and Recessions* (Oxford, 1988).
22. A beginning has been made: see Fintan O'Toole's columns in the *Irish Times* from the mid-1980s and the fiction of Dermot Bolger and Joseph O'Connor.
23. John Hutchinson, *The Dynamics of Cultural Nationalism: The Gaelic Revival and the Creation of the Irish Nation State* (London, 1987), p. 233.
24. Kevin Boyle and Tom Hadden, *Ireland: A Positive Proposal* (Harmondsworth, 1985).
25. Tom Garvin in Charles Townshend, *Consensus in Ireland: Approaches and Recessions*, p. 103.
26. E. Moxon-Browne, *Nationality, Class and Creed in Northern Ireland* (Aldershot, 1983), p. 17.
27. 'Planter's Gothic: An Essay in Discursive Autobiography' in Tom Clyde (ed.), *Ancestral Voices: The Selected Prose of John Hewitt* (Belfast, 1987), p. 9.

3 Interpretations of Parnell: The Importance of Locale

1. Reprinted in *Essays in Applied Psycho-analysis* (London and Vienna, 1922).
2. See Anna Parnell's letter to the *Gaelic American*, 16 January 1907, casting doubt on her mother's Fenian sympathies, quoted below.
3. Obituary in *Truth*, 15 October 1891.
4. 'The Parnell Literature', an unpublished TS, NLI n4657 p4645.
5. See Conor Cruise O'Brien, *Parnell and His Party 1880–1890* (Oxford, 1957; second edition, 1964), p. 10, for a discussion of Healy's claim and Paul Bew, *C.S. Parnell* (Dublin, 1980), for many references to Tully's

critique of Parnell in the *Roscommon Herald* of which he was editor; also Frank Hugh O'Donnell, *A History of the Irish Parliamentary Party* (London, 1910), vol. 1, p. 256.

6. Now edited by Dana Hearne and published as *The Tale of a Great Sham* (Dublin, 1986).
7. See J.B. Lyons, '"What Did I Die of?" The Last Illness of Charles Stewart Parnell', *Irish Medical Journal*, vol. 78, no. 8 (August 1985).
8. T.P. O'Connor, *The Parnell Movement* (London, 1887), p. 150.
9. J.H. Parnell, *C.S. Parnell: A Memoir* (London, 1916).
10. Preserved in *Irish State Catalogues* (1901) in the NLI.
11. Katharine O'Shea, *Charles Stewart Parnell: His Love Story and Political Life* (London, 1914), vol. 1, pp. 235–6.
12. F.S.L. Lyons, *Charles Stewart Parnell* (London, 1977), p. 85.
13. See Jane McL. Côté, *Fanny and Anna Parnell: Ireland's Patriot Sisters* (London, 1991), chapter 8.
14. See Paul Bew, *C.S. Parnell*, *passim*.
15. John Morley, *Recollections* (London, 1917), vol. 1, p. 241. His repudiation of the Gladstonian Home Rule scheme was declared in his address 'To the People of Ireland', 29 November 1890.
16. R. B. O'Brien, *The Life of Charles Stewart Parnell* (London, 1898), vol. 1, pp. 203–4.
17. Letter to the *Gaelic American*, 16 January 1907.
18. Alan O'Day, *Parnell and the First Home Rule Episode 1884–1888* (Dublin, 1986); James Loughlin, *Gladstone, Home Rule and the Ulster Question 1882–1895* (Dublin, 1986).
19. R.B. O'Brien, *The Life of Charles Stewart Parnell*, vol. 1, p. 365.
20. 9 October 1881; see F.S.L. Lyons, *Charles Stewart Parnell*, p. 168.
21. See ibid., p. 628, n. 29.
22. William O'Brien, *The Parnell of Real Life* (London, 1926), p. 125; Standish O'Grady, *The Story of Ireland* (London, 1904), p. 203; Lord Ribblesdale, *Impressions and Memories* (London, 1927), pp. 190–200.
23. William Michael Murphy, *The Parnell Myth and Irish Politics 1891–1956* (Berne, New York, Frankfurt-am-Maine, 1987). This includes tables such as 'Persons Compared with Parnell 1891–1899, with the Number of Comparisons Made' (Balmaceda 3, Ancient Mariner 1).
24. See F.S.L. Lyons, *Charles Stewart Parnell*, p. 385.
25. J.H. Parnell, *C.S. Parnell: A Memoir*, p. 96.
26. Part of this essay derives from a lecture for the inauguration of the Parnell Summer School that year.
27. See Eoin Neeson, *A History of Irish Forestry* (Dublin, 1991), pp. 122–3, for the most recent commentary.
28. For a commentary on the 'middling gentry' of nineteenth-century Cork,

see Ian d'Alton, *Protestant Society and Politics in Cork 1812–1844* (Cork, 1980), p. 26.

29. See 'Parnell and His People: The Ascendancy and Home Rule', below.
30. See my *Charles Stewart Parnell: The Man and His Family* (Brighton, 1976), pp. 120–21.
31. His sister erected a pulpit to his memory in St Johns Church, Laragh.
32. See my *Charles Stewart Parnell: The Man and His Family*, pp. 82–5.
33. Parliamentary speech reported in *Pall Mall Gazette*, 17 June 1881.
34. See NLI MSS 4955, 4962, 3983, 3984, 4965.
35. NLI MS 3988, p. 41, records a payment to 'Mr Healy, who has now established a classical school in Carnew'.
36. See NLI MS 8816 for details of this lengthy saga.
37. See James Grattan's notebook for 1823, NLI MS 5777.
38. See Anon. [W.J. Fitzpatrick], *Memories of Father Healy of Little Bray* (Dublin, 1896).
39. James Grattan's notebooks (see NLI MS 3853) refer to Lord Wicklow's political dictation to his tenants in the 1830s; Chaloner's letter-books indicate that the practice continued in the following period. Wicklow tenant voters, however, had a name for recalcitrance and independence on other estates; see Tottenham Papers, NLI n4905 p4937. And Grattan saw his return in 1832 as accomplished 'in spite of them all', 'them' being the neighbouring grandees (R.F. Foster, *Parnell: The Man and His Family*, p. xix).
40. Robert Chaloner's letter-book, NLI, Fitzwilliam Papers, MS 3987, pp. 211–18, a draft standard letter of April 1848, asking for local support for Howard's candidature.
41. See Brassington's and Gale's 1853 report on the estate.
42. T. Jones Hughes, 'Society and Settlement in Nineteenth-century Ireland', *Irish Geography*, vol. 5, no. 2 (1965), pp. 79–96.
43. For detailed consideration of this point, see my *Parnell: The Man and His Family*, pp. xiii–xiv.
44. See NLI MS 4814, Mrs Caroline Hamilton's family reminiscences.
45. Pp. 59ff.
46. In a letter to Denys Scully, 3 December 1811.

> Why not . . . call every nerve & sinew of the Catholic body into action by quarterly meetings of all the *Parishes* throughout Ireland . . . I perceive a great many more contingent advantages from this plan but I think that you will perceive these too. I shall only mention one; which is affording you a regular fund of money without being burthensome to anyone . . . I think nothing would give more union to the Catholic body than to raise generally & annually a very small voluntary contribution, if only a penny from each labourer, a shilling from

each farmer & five from each gentleman. Your parish collectors & your Treasury would be the connecting medium between you & the people – so small a donation could scarcely become an object of great obloquy. It might be raised for the ostensible purpose for paying the law expenses where poor Catholics were oppressed; & for the necessary expenses of your petitions; but your Executive in Dublin might be allowed a sum for secret service money accountable to a select committee, for contesting the elections of members inimical to your cause, and for remunerating the newspapers & employing the press . . .

In one word instead of a Parliament, I would propose an executive, & the people.

This long letter of strategic advice, of which the above is only an extract, lays down the tactics and organization adopted by O'Connell and Scully a decade later. See Brian Macdermot (ed.), *The Catholic Question in Ireland and England 1798–1822: The Papers of Denys Scully* (Dublin, 1988), pp. 301–4.

47. William Parnell-Hayes, *An Inquiry into the Causes of the Popular Discontents in Ireland* (1807), p. 36.
48. See NLI MS n6–8 p201–3, for Poor Law Union records. It remained true that his doctrinal disagreements with Catholicism ran deep, at least in his youth; see my *Parnell: The Man and His Family*, pp. 40–41.
49. Roscommon was one place where this phenomenon was noted. See also F.S.L. Lyons, *Charles Stewart Parnell*, p. 584.
50. *Waterford Star*, 27 April 1895; quoted in Paul Bew, *C.S. Parnell*.
51. See my *Parnell: The Man and His Family*, pp. 121–2; also J.H. Parnell, *C.S. Parnell: A Memoir*.
52. See 'Parnell and His People: The Ascendancy and Home Rule', below.
53. *Wicklow Newsletter*, 10 October 1891.
54. R.F. Foster, *Parnell: The Man and His Family*, p. 168.
55. For details, see my *Parnell: The Man and His Family*, pp. 113, 128–30, 151, 191, 193–6, 290.
56. T.P. O'Connor, *C.S. Parnell: A Memory* (London, 1891), p. 22.
57. For Parnell's discovery, see his letter to Katharine O'Shea in her *Charles Stewart Parnell: His Love Story and Political Life*, vol. 2, p. 53; for the Ordnance Survey reference, J.H. Andrews, *A Paper Landscape: The Ordnance Survey in Nineteenth-century Ireland* (Oxford, 1975), pp. 166–7. According to this information, gleaned by OS 'field collectors' just before the objectives of the Survey were summarily limited, the Ballyknockan quarries had then been in operation for fourteen years and were considered the best 'in this part of the kingdom', employing 160 men.
58. See my *Parnell: The Man and His Family*, pp. 200ff.

59. 'Parnell as a Prisoner in Kilmainham', *Irish Weekly Independent*, 7 October 1883.
60. Rather to Carnarvon's bewilderment; see his account in Carnarvon Papers, British Library, MS 60829.
61. See, for instance, Standish O'Grady, *The Story of Ireland* (London, 1904), p. 203.
62. F.S.L. Lyons, *Charles Stewart Parnell*, p. 278, for the circumstances. An interesting illustration of Parnell's preoccupation, not often noted, occurs on pp. 190–200 of Lord Ribblesdale's *Impressions and Memories* and describes 'A Railway Journey with Mr Parnell' in the summer of 1887. Parnell talked vehemently about the possibilities of local industrial development under Home Rule, as well as afforestation, fisheries and tillage improvement.
63. See my *Parnell: The Man and His Family*, p. 138.
64. Ibid., p. 170.
65. *Pall Mall Gazette*, 14 December 1880.
66. For Redmond's remarks, see *Wicklow Newsletter*, 7 December 1881.
67. Evidence to the Land Commission as reported in *Pall Mall Gazette*, 17 June 1881. See, however, Hansard 3, clxii, 1597, for unfavourable remarks from Corbet, who said that Lord Fitzwilliam was 'kind and indulgent' only to 'sycophants and parasites' and claimed that leases and administrative practice on the estate left much to be desired.
68. Published extracts are in M. McGusty and D. Thomson (eds.), *The Irish Journals of Elizabeth Smith* (Oxford, 1980); the diaries are the subject of an important Ph.D. thesis by Andrew Tod, 'The Smiths of Baltiboys: A County Wicklow Family and Their Estates in the 1840s' (Edinburgh, 1978).
69. Dr Martin made this point in the lecture 'Parnell and the Problem of Biography', which was part of the inauguration ceremony for the Parnell Memorial fellowship at Magdalene College, Cambridge, in October 1991.
70. Paul Bew, *C.S. Parnell*, *passim*. See Hansard 3, cccii, 151ff. for a particularly interesting speech of 21 January 1886 by Parnell on Home Rule, the Empire, landlords and his own Protestantism.

4 Parnell and His People: The Ascendancy and Home Rule

1. The mental world of this group has been brilliantly explored in J.A. Spence's Ph.D. thesis, 'The Philosophy of Irish Toryism 1833–1852' (London, 1991).
2. As in the broad promises about land legislation and denominational

education in the 1868 election. David Thornley, *Isaac Butt and Home Rule* (London, 1964), pp. 30–32.

3. The tradition that the HGA was 'Tory nationalism' incarnate is enshrined in A.M. Sullivan's *New Ireland* (see 14th edition, 1881, p. 328). Sullivan himself was something of an admirer of Irish Protestant probity; he told Galbraith he would accept the Church of Ireland Synod as a parliament for Ireland, knowing that it would lead to full and equal Home Rule (J.G. Swift MacNeill, *What I Have Seen and Heard*, London, 1925, p. 126).
4. David Thornley, *Isaac Butt and Home Rule*, pp. 96, 113.
5. Ibid, pp. 125–6. This was not restricted to 'Protestants with horses'; Bishop Delany of Cork, who had cautiously supported the HGA, was one Catholic Conservative who had hoped it would lead to something like a 'national Grand Jury for Irish affairs' (ibid., p. 129).
6. This was a belief that had been reiterated in Gerald FitzGibbon's *Ireland in 1868*, a pamphlet appealing to the 'Roman Catholic gentry' and the common interests of all right-thinking men of property; later itemized by Engels as an archetypical Irish Conservative broadside.
7. David Thornley, *Isaac Butt and Home Rule*, pp. 195–6. The men in question include figures like Sir John Esmonde (Wicklow), Thomas Tighe (Mayo), Sir George Bowyer (Wexford), George Morris (Galway).
8. Esmonde was from the first doubtful about the whip. Morris and White supported him. The O'Conor Don, Bowyer, Montagu and King Harman sat on the conservative side. Sir Colm O'Loghlen provided the classic rationale against tight party discipline (David Thornley, *Isaac Butt and Home Rule*, pp. 218–9). All the same, Esmonde, Morris and the O'Conor Don supported Butt's proposal to give Home Rule another hearing when Parliament opened; and in meetings of the party in 1876–7, only Blennerhasset of the landed element was a regular absentee.
9. See Butt's open letter to Father Murphy of Ferns, *Freeman's Journal*, 7 September 1877. Also Terence McGrath's satirical *Pictures from Ireland* (1880), which profiled a typical Home Ruler thus:

   > When Mr Butt's scheme of Home Rule was proposed Mr O'Carroll accepted it, and kept well within constitutional lines in his advocacy of the measure. He was one of the committee that deliberately chose a Protestant candidate pledged to Mr Butt's principles, in opposition to one of his own faith. Such moderation must, he argued, have its effect in the attempt to induce the British Parliament to grant the measure, or the Protestants of the North of Ireland to combine in seeking for it . . . (p. 81).

   See also Paul Bew, *C.S. Parnell* (Dublin, 1980).
10. See *Sixty Years' Experience as an Irish Landlord: Memoirs of John Hamilton,*

DL, of St Ernan's, Donegal, edited with an introduction by Revd H.C. White (London, 1894). Hamilton still felt that Irish patriotism had left 'a legacy of vain aspirations of national glory as a *little* independent nation, instead of the truly glorious position of being an independent part of the United Kingdom'.

11. James S. Donnelly, *The Land and the People of Nineteenth-century Cork* (London, 1974). The best general summary of this controversy is in K.T. Hoppen, *Ireland since 1800: Conflict and Conformity* (London, 1989), chapter 4.
12. 23 May 1856; see Karl Marx and Friedrich Engels, *On Ireland and the Irish Question*, edited by Richard Dixon (London, 1971).
13. K.T. Hoppen, 'Landlords and Electoral Politics in Ireland', *Past and Present*, no. 75 (May 1977), pp. 62–93.
14. Terence McGrath, *Pictures from Ireland*, pp. 185ff.; Clifford Lloyd, *Ireland under the Land League* (London, 1892), pp. 218–19; Anna Parnell, *The Tale of a Great Sham*, edited by Dana Hearne (Dublin, 1986); Samuel Hussey, *The Reminiscences of an Irish Land Agent* (London, 1904).
15. H.M. D'Arcy Irvine, *Letter to the Rt Hon. W.E. Gladstone on the Irish Land Bill* (1870), p. 8. Another example is Rigby Wason, *A Letter to the Rt Hon. Chichester Fortescue* (1869).
16. Published London, 1870. Also see Henry Dix Hutton, *History, Principle and Fact in Relation to the Irish Land Question* (London, 1870).
17. Samuel Hussey, *The Reminiscences of an Irish Land Agent*, p. 31.
18. W.R. Le Fanu, *Seventy Years of Irish Life* (London, 1893), p. 5. For a more extended treatment of 'golden age' notions, see below, pp. 68, 100.
19. This is the implicit message of K.T. Hoppen's magisterial *Elections, Politics and Society in Ireland 1832–1885* (Oxford, 1984).
20. 'The late Thos. Conolly, the Hamiltons, the Marquis of Coyningham, Mr Brooke of Lough Eske, and some others', quoted in Terence de Vere White, *The Anglo-Irish* (London, 1971), p. 142.
21. Mr and Mrs S.C. Hall, *Ireland: Its Scenery, Character, etc.* (1841–3), vol. 1, pp. iii–iv.
22. Epigrammatically described by W.E. Vaughan as 'rustic statesmen with proconsular functions'; also see Somerville's and Ross's *The Real Charlotte*, where the Desart agency conferred 'brevet rank of gentleman' on Roddy Lambert.
23. Introduction to 1872 edition of *Traits and Stories of the Irish Peasantry*, p. 13.
24. Of the authorities cited, see, *passim*, M. McGusty and D. Thomson (eds.), *The Irish Journals of Elizabethan Smith* (Oxford, 1980) and Mr and Mrs S.C. Hall, *Ireland: Its Scenery, Character, etc.*; Samuel Hussey, *The Reminiscences of an Irish Land Agent*, p. 116; Clifford Lloyd, *Ireland under the Land League*, p. 62; Terence McGrath, *Pictures from Ireland*, pp. 56–7.

25. NLI MSS 3853, 5776.
26. As reported in the *Pall Mall Gazette*, 17 June 1881. On the unpopularity of such ideas, see Barbara Solow, *The Land Question and the Irish Economy 1870–1903* (Cambridge, Mass., 1971), pp. 82–5; on the reasons why they were not more generally adopted, W.E. Vaughan, 'An Assessment of the Economic Performance of Irish Landlords 1851–1881' in F.S.L. Lyons and R.A.J. Hawkins (eds.), *Ireland under the Union: Varieties of Tension* (Oxford, 1980) and Cormac Ó Gráda, *Ireland before and after the Famine: Explorations in Economic History 1800–1925* (Manchester, 1988).
27. NLI MS 5777.
28. Anon. [W.J. Fitzpatrick], *Memories of Father Healy of Little Bray* (London, 1896), p. 131.
29. Like J. O'Connor Power, who attacked Parnell on these grounds in *The Anglo-Irish Quarrel: A Plea for Peace* (1880): see above, pp. 11–12.
30. Hansard 3, ccxxxix, 1160.
31. See 'To the Northern Counties Station: Lord Randolph Churchill and the Orange Card', below.
32. For instance, his letter to the Dundalk electors about Philip Callan: *Pall Mall Gazette*, 30 March 1880.
33. Described by Captain Nolan, one of its progenitors, as 'not directed against a class', but intended to bring the peers into county administration, and presented by Butt as a measure to integrate gentry and people (Hansard 3, ccxxvii, 377, 765; ccxvxii, 87–9). Parnell often used similar language, as when arguing that rents should be fixed in May 1880.
34. 'Home Rulers at Home', *University Magazine: A Literary and Philosophic Review*, vol. 1, no. 2 (1878) p. 216.
35. *An Irishman Looks at His World* (London, 1919), pp. 1, 12, 13.
36. Ibid., p. 208.
37. '"And Mr Parnell's a gentleman too. I wonder how he can ally himself with such blackguards," gently insinuated Mrs Barton, who saw a husband lost in the politician.' (Ebury edition, 1915, p. 44).
38. Ibid., p. 253.
39. Found in Samuel Hussey, *The Reminiscences of an Irish Land Agent*, p. 178, but elsewhere too.
40. T. Maguire, *England's Duty to Ireland, as Plain to a Loyal Irish Roman Catholic* (Dublin, 1886).
41. J.M. Synge, *In Wicklow and West Kerry* (Dublin, 1912), pp. 48–9.

5 Knowing Your Place: Words and Boundaries in Anglo-Irish Relations

1. Hansard 3, xxii, 1092ff.
2. 30 June 1874; Hansard 3, ccxx, 700ff.
3. See the Dáil Éireann Official Report, *Debate on the Treaty between Great Britain and Ireland* (Dublin, 1922), especially pp. 27, 152.
4. Hansard 6, lxxxvii, 780–85 (Hume, 26 November 1985); 912–18 (McCusker, 27 November 1985).
5. *Debate on the Treaty between Great Britain and Ireland*, cols. 234ff.
6. See 'History and the Irish Question', above, n. 53.
7. See 'We are All Revisionists Now', *Irish Review*, no. 1 (1986). A rather involved attempt to pin down 'revisionism' has been made by Brendan Bradshaw in 'Nationalism and Historical Scholarship', *Irish Historical Studies*, vol. 26, no. 104 (1989), pp. 329–51, but much of this is based on the idea that so-called 'revisionists' believe themselves, inaccurately, to be impartial and 'value-free', which is a red herring, easily disproved. More germane are the comments of L.M. Cullen in the *Newsletter* of the Economic and Social History Society of Ireland, no. 2 (Spring 1990).
8. Thus Joel Mokyr, *Why Ireland Starved: A Quantitative and Analytical History of the Irish Economy 1800–1850* (London, 1983) and Cormac Ó Gráda, *Ireland before and after the Famine: Explorations in Economic History 1800–1925* (Manchester, 1988) are querying recent views of the Famine, and to a certain extent re-establishing the old orthodoxies on firmer quantitative foundations; while K.T. Hoppen, *Ireland since 1800: Conflict and Conformity* (London, 1989) and others are questioning the view of the Land War established in the early 1970s by Barbara Solow, *The Land Question and the Irish Economy 1870–1903* (Cambridge, Mass., 1971) and others.
9. For instance the Victorian historian, Robert Dunlop, when reading the depositions taken at the time of the 1641 insurrection, found his view of them inescapably coloured by the politics of 1882.

> I began to experience an uncomfortable feeling that my evidence was not so strong as I would have liked it to be. True, the depositions were very explicit and apparently incontrovertible; but I was living in Dublin at a time when the power of the Land League was at its height, and I could not help asking what value depositions taken by a body of Orange magistrates as to nationalist outrages were likely to possess for an impartial estimate of the state of Ireland during the

government of Earl Spencer. Was the state of affairs in 1642 more favourable for an impartial inquiry than it was in 1882?

(R. Dunlop, *Ireland under the Commonwealth*, Manchester, 1913, pp. i, vii.)

10. See Padraig O'Malley, *Northern Ireland: Questions of Nuance* (The John W. McCormack Institute of Public Affairs, University of Massachusetts at Boston, 1990), pp. 4–5, and Anthony Kenny, *The Road to Hillsborough: The Shaping of the Anglo-Irish Agreement* (Oxford, 1986), pp. 96–7.
11. See E.J. Hobsbawm and T.O. Ranger (eds.), *The Invention of Tradition* (Cambridge, 1983).
12. See especially Linda Colley, *Britons: Forging the Nation 1707–1837* (London, 1992).
13. Edward Maurice, *A Sermon Preached in Christchurch, Dublin, on Thursday the 23rd of October 1755, being the Anniversary of the Irish Rebellion* (1755), p. 7; I owe this reference to Gerard McCoy.
14. *Debate on the Treaty between Great Britain and Ireland*, p. 66.
15. See the *United Irishman* for the early months of 1970, as quoted in Henry Patterson, *The Politics of Illusion: Republicanism and Socialism in Modern Ireland* (London, 1989), p. 129.
16. See, for instance, S.J. Connolly, *Priests and People in Pre-Famine Ireland 1780–1845* (Dublin, 1982) and Peter Brooke, *Ulster Presbyterianism* (Dublin, 1988).
17. See 'Varieties of Irishness: Cultures and Anarchy in Ireland', above.
18. This process is discussed in the conclusion to Marianne Elliott's definitive *Wolfe Tone: Prophet of Irish Independence* (London, 1989), pp. 411–19.
19. Marianne Elliott, *Wolfe Tone: Prophet of Irish Independence*, p. 418, for a discussion of this statement. For the original formulation, see W.T.W. Tone (ed.), *The Life of Theobald Wolfe Tone* (Washington, 1926), pp. ii, 46.
20. C.S. Andrews, *Man of No Property* (Cork, 1982). And Peadar O'Donnell, speaking at Bodenstown in June 1931, took the 'men of no property' formulation as the manifesto of the breakaway socialist Republican movement, Saor Éire: see *An Phoblacht*, 27 June 1931.
21. Written in Paris in August 1796; see Marianne Elliott, *Wolfe Tone: Prophet of Irish Independence*, pp. 309–12, 411.
22. See James Connolly, *The Reconquest of Ireland* (Dublin, 1915).
23. See E.J. Hobsbawm's Wiles Lectures on nationalism, published as *Nations and Nationalism since 1780: Programme, Myth, Reality* (Cambridge, 1990).
24. See *Ireland 1912–1985: Politics and Society* (Cambridge, 1990), *passim*.
25. See 'Marginal Men and Micks on the Make: The Uses of Irish Exile, *c.* 1840–1922', below.

26. Henry Patterson, *The Politics of Illusion: Republicanism and Socialism in Modern Ireland*, p. 120.
27. Paul Bew, *Conflict and Conciliation in Ireland 1890–1910: Parnellites and Radical Agrarians* (Oxford, 1987), p. 239.
28. See Henry Patterson, *The Politics of Illusion: Republicanism and Socialism in Modern Ireland*, pp. 50–51.
29. Ibid., p. 122.
30. See Padraig O'Malley, *Biting at the Grave: The Irish Hunger Strikes and the Politics of Despair* (Boston, 1990).
31. Reported in the *Round Table*, vol. 18 (May 1928).
32. Joseph Lee, *Ireland 1912–1985: Politics and Society*, p. 522.
33. *Saorstat Éireann Official Handbook* (Dublin, 1932): a beautiful and richly illustrated volume, ironically celebrating a 'State' whose days were already numbered.
34. See David Kirby, 'Nationalism and National Identity in the New States of Europe: the Examples of Austria, Finland and Ireland' in Peter M.R. Stirk (ed.), *European Unity in Context: The Inter-war Period* (London, 1989), p. 120.
35. See J.R. Vincent, 'Gladstone and Ireland', *Proceedings of the British Academy*, vol. 63 (1977).
36. Brian Harrison, 'Violence and the Suffragettes' in *Peaceable Kingdom: Stability and Change in Modern Britain* (Oxford, 1982), p. 37.
37. See a speech at Maryborough, October 1901:

    > My guiding principle in public life is perfectly simple. I have no faith, and never had, in any English political party. I have no faith, and never had, in English benevolence towards Ireland. I have no faith, and never had, in the possibility of any class of our population getting justice in the smallest particular for mere reason or argument or persuasion. No! We have never got anything, from the days of O'Connell down to today, without labour or suffering or sacrifice on our part, or without making a movement dangerous and menacing towards England.

    (Quoted in Liam de Paor, *Unfinished Business: Ireland Today and Tomorrow*, London, 1990, p. 21.)
38. See John Lonsdale, 'Mau Maus of the Mind: Making Mau Mau and Remaking Kenya', *Journal of African History*, vol. 3, no. 3 (November 1990).
39. Dan Breen, *My Fight for Irish Freedom* (Dublin, 1924), pp. 32–3.
40. See *Debate on the Treaty between Great Britain and Ireland*, p. 128 (Mary MacSwiney) and pp. 228–9 (Liam Mellows).
41. Paul Bew, *Conflict and Conciliation in Ireland 1890–1910: Parnellites and Radical Agrarians*; also 'Varieties of Irishness: Cultures and Anarchy in Ireland', above; and 'Thinking from Hand to Mouth: Anglo-Irish

Literature, Gaelic Nationalism and Irish Politics in the 1890s', below. But the current debate on the abandonment of Articles 2 and 3 of the Irish Constitution (claiming the territory of Northern Ireland) has produced some memorable 'impossibilist' rhetoric: see, for instance, a letter from Captain Gibbons to the *Irish Times*, 11 May 1990.

42. Notably Erhard Rumpf, *Nationalism and Socialism in Twentieth-century Ireland* (English translation, edited by A.C. Hepburn, Liverpool, 1977); M.W. Heslinga, *The Irish Border as a Cultural Divide* (Assen, Netherlands, 1962); Charles Townshend, *Political Violence in Ireland: Government and Resistance since 1848* (Oxford, 1983); David Fitzpatrick, *Politics and Irish Life: Provincial Experience of War and Revolution 1913–1921* (Dublin, 1977).
43. *States of Mind: A Study of Anglo-Irish Conflict 1780–1980* (London, 1983).
44. Liam de Paor, *Unfinished Business: Ireland Today and Tomorrow*, pp. 16, 137.
45. Michael Sturmer, *Dissonanzen des Fortschritts*, p. 276, quoted in Geoff Eley, 'Nazism, Politics and the Image of the Past: Thoughts on the West German *Historikerstreit* 1986–1987', *Past and Present*, no. 129 (November 1988), p. 181.

6 The Irishness of Elizabeth Bowen

1. Conversation with Charles Ritchie, 20 August 1983, for a radio programme, 'Life with the Lid Off', transmitted on Radio 4, 28 September 1983.
2. Anne Olivier Bell (ed.), *The Diary of Virginia Woolf. Vol. 5: 1936–1941* (London, 1984), p. 299 (27 June 1940).
3. Elizabeth Bowen interviewed by Jocelyn Brooke, BBC, 1950. She went on to say that she had wanted the action of *The Heat of the Day* to resemble 'the convulsive shaking of a kaleidoscope, a kaleidoscope also of which the inside reflector was cracked' – perhaps a subconscious echo of Stephen Dedalus's 'cracked looking-glass of a servant'. Kaleidoscopes recurred; appearing on BBC's *Desert Island Discs* (11 March 1957), one of her chosen accompanying luxuries was a kaleidoscope.
4. Two biographical treatments which give prominence to her Irish dimension are Victoria Glendinning, *Elizabeth Bowen: Portrait of a Writer* (London, 1977) and Patricia Craig, *Elizabeth Bowen* (London, 1986). Hermione Lee, *Elizabeth Bowen: An Estimation* (London, 1981) is particularly good on Bowen's sense of history and tradition, though not in a specifically Irish sense; she places Bowen perceptively in an Irish historical context in her introduction to the Virago Press edition of *Bowen's Court* (1986). Glendinning has also produced an invaluable edition of *Elizabeth Bowen's Irish Stories* (Dublin, 1978).

5. To Vanessa Bell, 3 May 1934: Nigel Nicolson and Joanne Trautmann (eds.), *The Letters of Virginia Woolf. Vol. 4: A Reflection of the Other Person 1929–1931* (London, 1978), pp. 299–300. Woolf went on to make derisive comments about the 'ramshackle kind of state' kept up there – the sort of attitude which irritated neighbours and friends like Molly Keane (see her comments in 'Life with the Lid Off', as above).
6. Charles Ritchie, 'Life with the Lid Off', as above.
7. 'Origins', pp. 25–6, in Elizabeth Bowen, *Pictures and Conversations* (London, 1975).
8. 'The Bend Back' (first published as 'Once upon a Yesterday', *Saturday Review*, 1950), reprinted in Hermione Lee (ed.), *The Mulberry Tree: Writings of Elizabeth Bowen* (London, 1986), pp. 57–8 (hereafter cited as *The Mulberry Tree*).
9. *The Last September* (London, 1929; Penguin edition, Harmondsworth, 1942), p. 34.
10. Ibid., p. 206. In her 1952 introduction she wrote: 'I *was* the child of the house from which Danielstown derives. Bowen's Court survived – nevertheless, so often in my mind's eye did I see it burning that the terrible last event in *The Last September* is more real than anything I have lived through' (reprinted in *The Mulberry Tree*, pp. 125–6). Both these passages are, for instance, used effectively in Gearóid Cronin, 'The Big House and the Irish Landscape in the Work of Elizabeth Bowen' in Jacqueline Genet (ed.), *The Big House in Ireland: Reality and Representation* (Dingle, 1991) – a perceptive essay that refers almost entirely to *The Last September*.
11. This, for instance, is the way Bowen figures in *The Field Day Anthology of Irish Writing* (Derry, 1991), though the anthology's General Editor Seamus Deane locates Bowen more perceptively in his *Short History of Irish Literature* (London, 1986).
12. *The Last September*, p. 27.
13. Preface to *Castle Rackrent* (1801): the most recent publication, with *Ennui*, is edited by Marilyn Butler (Harmondsworth, 1992).
14. *Pictures and Conversations*, p. 41.
15. *Seven Winters* (Dublin, 1942), quoted in ibid., p. 31.
16. Ibid, pp. 24–5.
17. Introduction to the Cresset Press edition of Joseph Sheridan Le Fanu's *Uncle Silas* (London, 1947), reprinted in *The Mulberry Tree*, pp. 100–113.
18. *Pictures and Conversations*, p. 9.
19. Ibid., pp. 22–3.
20. A recent academic work exploring this territory is Heather Bryant Jordan, *How Will the Heart Endure: Elizabeth Bowen and the Landscape of War* (Ann Arbor, Michigan, 1992).

21. Introduction to *The Demon Lover* (London, 1945).
22. Quoted in Dermot Keogh, *Ireland and Europe 1919–1989: A Diplomatic and Political History* (Cork, 1990), p. 144. Also see Robert Fisk, *In Time of War: Ireland, Ulster and the Price of Neutrality 1939–1945* (London, 1982) and Trevor C. Salmon, *Unneutral Ireland: An Ambivalent and Unique Security Policy* (Oxford, 1989).
23. References FO 800/310 and DO 130/28. I owe thanks to Dr Mary-Lou Legg for help in obtaining copies of these reports.
24. F.S.L. Lyons, *Ireland since the Famine* (London, 1971), p. 551; cf. Ronan Fanning, *Independent Ireland* (Dublin, 1983), pp. 126–7; Dermot Keogh, *Ireland and Europe 1919–1989: A Diplomatic and Political History*, chapters 4–6; Terence Brown, *Ireland: A Cultural and Social History 1922–1979* (London, 1981), pp. 175–6.
25. See '*The Bell*: An Anglo-Irish View' in Hubert Butler, *Escape from the Anthill* (Gigginstown, 1985), pp. 147–52; also Terence Brown, *Ireland: A Cultural and Social History 1922–1979*, pp. 199–206.
26. 22 April 1937; quoted in Heather Bryant Jordan, *How Will the Heart Endure: Elizabeth Bowen and the Landscape of War*, p. 108.
27. Reprinted in *The Mulberry Tree*, pp. 25–30.
28. There is a letter from Lord Cranborne to the Secretary of State for Foreign Affairs, dated 25 November 1940, attached to her 'Notes on Eire', 9 November 1940, sending on this report from the Dominions Office to the Foreign Office. Interestingly, Cranborne remarks that 'previous reports by her to the Ministry of Information have struck us as very sensible and well balanced', but no reports earlier than this one can be found. See FO 800/310.
29. PRO INFI/786, Betjeman to Hope, 15 September 1941: my thanks to Dr Mary-Lou Legg for this piquant reference.
30. 'Eire', *New Statesman and Nation*, 21 April 1941.
31. 'Notes on Eire', Mrs Cameron [Elizabeth Bowen], 9 November 1940: FO 800/310, pp. 253, 255.
32. Ibid., p. 258.
33. Ibid., p. 265. Two years later she described him as

> the *enfant terrible* of the Cosgravites: I notice that in Dail debates his colleagues are at some pains to disassociate themselves from his more positive and dynamic remarks. I have heard, however, on almost all sides (the exception being extreme de Valeraites) expressions of admiration for Mr Dillon's *courage*. If anything, he is seen to err in a too extreme disregard for that general mass of opinion that, in most cases, inhibits Irishmen.

('Notes on Eire', 9 February 1942, DO 130/28, p. 3.)

34. 'Notes on Eire', 9 November 1940, FO 800/310, p. 261.

35. 'Notes on Eire', 9 February 1942, DO 130/28, p. 1.
36. 'Notes on Eire', 20 February 1942, DO 130/28, pp. 1–3.
37. 'Notes from Ireland', 31 July 1942, DO 130/28, p. 2.
38. Ibid, p. 1.
39. See a letter to Virginia Woolf, 1 July 1940. 'I think I told you I had asked the Ministry of Information if I could do any work, which I felt was wanted in Ireland. On Saturday morning I had a letter from them saying yes, they did want me to go. Now it has come to the point I have rather a feeling of dismay and of not wanting to leave this country.' She was to be briefed by Harold Nicolson, and expected to be told to 'move about the place', 'sorting out talk into shape'. 'But Ireland can be dementing, if one's Irish, and may well be so now' (printed in *The Mulberry Tree*, pp. 215–16).
40. Robert Fisk, *In Time of War: Ireland, Ulster and the Price of Neutrality 1939–1945*, p. 366.
41. John Hayward to Frank Morley, June 1942, quoted in Heather Bryant Jordan, *How Will the Heart Endure: Elizabeth Bowen and the Landscape of War*, p. 114.
42. 'Meet Elizabeth Bowen' by 'The Bellman', *Bell*, no. 4 (September 1942).
43. 24 September 1945: reprinted in *The Mulberry Tree*, pp. 266–7.
44. *The Heat of the Day* (London, 1949), pp. 108–9.
45. See 'Protestant Magic: W.B. Yeats and the Spell of Irish History', below.
46. *The Heat of the Day*, pp. 86–7.
47. 'Sundays', reprinted in *Seven Winters*, pp. 49–50.
48. This was an incident in a Wexford village where local Protestants were boycotted, with tacit clerical consent, after the children of a local 'mixed' marriage had been removed by the Protestant parent. See 'Boycott Village' in Hubert Butler, *Escape from the Anthill*, pp. 134–44.
49. *The House in Paris* (London, 1935; Penguin edition, 1976), p. 92.
50. *Pictures and Conversations*, p. 14.
51. Sean O'Faolain, 'A Reading and Remembrance of Elizabeth Bowen', *London Review of Books*, 4–17 March 1982, pp. 15–16.
52. Hubert Butler, 'Elizabeth Bowen', *Escape from the Anthill*, pp. 151, 203; also conversation with Peggy Butler, 1990.

7 Love, Politics and Textual Corruption: Mrs O'Shea's *Parnell*

1. Joseph Hone (ed.), *John Butler Yeats: Letters to His Son W.B. Yeats and Others 1869–1922* (New York, 1946), pp. 184–5, 211.
2. See Michael Steinman, *Yeats's Heroic Figures: Wilde, Parnell, Swift, Casement* (London, 1983), pp. 82–3, 124.

3. Wilfrid Scawen Blunt, *My Diaries, being a Personal Narrative of Events 1888–1914* (London, 1919), vol. 2, pp. 425–6.
4. See, for instance, the *Spectator*, 30 May 1914.
5. Henry Harrison, *Parnell Vindicated: The Lifting of the Veil* (London, 1931), p. 238. Harrison had been the youngest member of the Irish Parliamentary Party, and a favourite of Parnell in his last days.
6. John Butler Yeats to Rosa Butt, 9 January 1915; Yeats–Butt correspondence, letter no. 149, Bodleian Library. My thanks to William Murphy for this transcription.
7. The letter is reprinted in O'Brien's *Evening Memories* (London, 1920), p. 466.
8. *The Times*, 10 September 1913.
9. See *Irish Book Lover*, May 1914, for a round-up of reports, mostly occasioned by the circulation of a publisher's prospectus in April. Most newspapers carried items on 23 April, notably *The Times*, the *Standard* and the *Daily News and Leader*.
10. 19 May 1914.
11. June 1914.
12. *Truth*, 20 May 1914.
13. 19 May 1914.
14. 20 May 1914.
15. *Irish Citizen*, 6 June 1914.
16. 19 May 1914.
17. Daniel J. Murphy (ed.), *Lady Gregory's Journals. Vol. 1: Books 1–29, 10 October 1916 to 24 February 1925* (Gerrards Cross, 1978), 15 April 1922, p. 344.
18. Joyce Marlow, *The Uncrowned Queen of Ireland: The Life of 'Kitty' O'Shea* (London, 1975) and Mary Rose Callaghan, *'Kitty O'Shea': A Life of Katharine Parnell* (London, 1989).
19. This account is based on reports in the *Daily Express*, *Irish Independent*, *Morning Post*, *Standard*, *Daily Mail*, *Daily Telegraph* and *The Times* for 18 May 1914, and the *Cork Examiner* for 19 May.
20. Henry Harrison, *Parnell Vindicated: The Lifting of the Veil*, p. 124.
21. Katharine O'Shea, *Charles Stewart Parnell: His Love Story and Political Life* (London, 1914), vol. 1, p. 190.
22. See Frank Hugh O'Donnell, *A History of the Irish Parliamentary Party* (London, 1910), vol. 2, p. 52; Katharine Tynan, *Memories* (London, 1924), p. 15; Lewis Harcourt's MS diary for 15 November 1882, vol. 352, pp. 66–7, Bodleian Library; and newspaper hints in *Truth* (edited by a famous political gossip, Henry Labouchère), 30 November 1882.
23. Henry Harrison, *Parnell Vindicated: The Lifting of the Veil*, p. 123.
24. Katharine O'Shea, *Charles Stewart Parnell*, vol. 1, p. 247.

25. See a letter from him dated from Eltham on 22 April, in Katharine O'Shea, *Charles Stewart Parnell*, vol. 1, p. 252, and a letter to him from O'Shea, 24 April 1882, O'Shea MSS, National Library of Ireland.
26. T.P. O'Connor, *Memories of an Old Parliamentarian* (London, 1929), vol. 1, p. 228.
27. Katharine O'Shea, *Charles Stewart Parnell*, vol. 1, pp. 204, 244.
28. Ibid., vol. 1, p. 183 (my italics).
29. For example, see Katharine O'Shea, *Charles Stewart Parnell*, vol. 2, pp. 64–7, when Willie was in Ireland, and vol. 2, p. 69, when he was on the Continent.
30. See Mary Rose Callaghan, *'Kitty O'Shea': A Life of Katharine Parnell*, pp. 88–92, and Joyce Marlow, *The Uncrowned Queen of Ireland: The Life of 'Kitty' O'Shea*, pp. 80–83.
31. Alfred Robbins, *Parnell: The Last Five Years* (London, 1926), p. 66.
32. For references to the affair at Galway, where Parnell imposed O'Shea's candidature on a furious local party organization, see F.S.L. Lyons, *Charles Stewart Parnell* (London, 1977), chapter 10; there had been earlier public references from Philip Callan (ibid., pp. 306–7).

    Speeches like that of Churchill at Paddington on 12 February 1886, where he referred to O'Shea as 'repugnant and loathsome . . . politically and from every point of view' are indicators: O'Shea wrote demanding an explanation (15 February 1886, NLI MS 5752). Also see Frank Hugh O'Donnell's letter to *The Times* (16 February 1886), referring to 'the accommodating Captain O'Shea'. Against this background, the famous paragraph in the *Pall Mall Gazette* (31 May 1886) about 'Mr Parnell's Suburban Retreat', identifying O'Shea as the owner of the Eltham house (actually Katharine's), appears as less of a bombshell.
33. Katharine O'Shea, *Charles Stewart Parnell*, vol. 2, p. 165.
34. See my *Charles Stewart Parnell: The Man and His Family* (Hassocks, 1976), *passim*.
35. Katharine O'Shea, *Charles Stewart Parnell*, vol. 2, p. 274.
36. Ibid., vol. 1, pp. 156–7.
37. Ibid., vol. 1, p. 238.
38. *Proceedings of the Special Commission, Reprinted from The Times* (London, 1890), vol. 2, p. 716 (my italics).
39. See Joyce Marlow, *The Uncrowned Queen of Ireland: The Life of 'Kitty' O'Shea*, pp. 216–17, 238; and pp. 235–6 for the jury's doubts.
40. Henry Harrison, *Parnell Vindicated: The Lifting of the Veil*, pp. 149–50; also see Sir Edward Clarke, *The Story of My Life* (London, 1918), p. 289.
41. TS diary, M45/1864 in James Papers, Hereford PRO. Lockwood told a similar story to T.M. Healy (*Letters and Leaders of My Day*, London, 1928, vol, 1, p. 318) and to Alfred Pease (*Elections and Recollections*, London, 1932, p. 276).

42. Justin McCarthy, *Reminiscences* (London, 1899), vol. 2, p. 104.
43. Katharine O'Shea, *Charles Stewart Parnell*, vol. 2, pp. 153–4.
44. Now available in BL Add. MSS 44, 269, with some additions in 44, 503. Her letters to Lord Richard Grosvenor about Willie's political difficulties are in BL Add. MSS 44, 315.
45. Katharine O'Shea, *Charles Stewart Parnell*, vol. 1, p. xi.
46. Herbert Gladstone, *After Thirty Years* (London, 1928) attempted to catch her out on small details. Three years earlier, Peter Wright in *Portraits and Criticisms* (London, 1925) had used her book to claim Gladstone not only knew of the liaison but had a sexual interest in Katharine himself. Herbert Gladstone subsequently provoked a libel case, which Wright lost, and in which Mrs O'Shea's political position was fully discussed: see *The Times*, 28 January to 24 February 1927.
47. J.L. Hammond, *Gladstone and the Irish Nation* (London, 1938), p. 308: Gladstone to Spencer, 26 September 1882. Hammond pointed out that Herbert Gladstone underestimated the number of letters Gladstone wrote to Katharine in 1882–5 (22, not 16); neither knew about their later exchanges concerning O'Shea and the Wood family.
48. By his secretary George Gower (see Wilfrid Scawen Blunt, *My Diaries*, vol. 2, p. 281); by Harcourt at an informal meeting of Cabinet members, 17 May 1882 (recorded in Dilke's diary, quoted by Henry Harrison, *Parnell, Joseph Garvin and Mr Chamberlain*, London, 1938, p. 29); and yet again by Granville on 28 May (J.L. Hammond, *Gladstone and the Irish Nation*, p. 669).
49. See a letter of his in Katharine O'Shea, *Charles Stewart Parnell*, vol. 2, p. 53.
50. In June 1891 Henry Campbell was accused by the *Cork Herald* of 'hiring houses for the immoral purposes of his master'. He sued, saying that letters over his name were forgeries. Parnell wrote a letter stating that Mrs O'Shea had written the letters renting houses, signing them with Campbell's name, which Campbell had given Parnell permission to use. 'I asked Mrs O'Shea to conduct the negotiation because I was shortly going to Ireland, and for the same reasons that I have frequently charged her with the conduct of vastly more important negotiations' (*Spectator*, 27 June 1891). In her book she mentions 'wiring to a London agent of Parnell's (under such a name as he would know the message emanated from him)' during the 1885 election, instructing him to 'beat up' the Irish vote for a certain candidate in Whitechapel – at Willie's request! (*Charles Stewart Parnell*, vol. 2, p. 97).
51. A countering case is quite convincingly asserted in Joyce Marlow, *The Uncrowned Queen of Ireland: The Life of 'Kitty' O'Shea*, p. 73.
52. *Vanity Fair*, 22 November 1890. Also see Afred Robbins, *Parnell: The*

Last Five Years, p. 153; J.L. Hammond, *Gladstone and the Irish Nation*, p. 655; Michael Davitt, *The Fall of Feudalism in Ireland* (London, 1904), p. 642; Maev Sullivan, *No Man's Man* (Dublin [n.d.]), p. 73; T.M. Healy, *Letters and Leaders of My Day*, vol. 1, p. 373; and Wilfrid Scawen Blunt, *My Diaries*, vol. 2, p. 381.

53. Katharine O'Shea, *Charles Stewart Parnell*, vol. 2, p. 184.
54. Ibid., vol. 1, p. 7.
55. Joyce Marlow, *The Uncrowned Queen of Ireland: The Life of 'Kitty' O'Shea*, pp. 298–9, 309.
56. Bertram Maunsell to Denis Gwynn, 22 September 1936, Horgan MSS, NLI n4657 p4645.
57. It was a box-office disaster. Curiously, it was plagued by sexual scandal: while shooting it in England, Gable was sued for paternity by the mother of a thirteen-year-old child.

8 'Fatal Drollery': Parliamentary Novels, Outsiders and Victorian Political History

1. Morris E. Speare, *The Political Novel: Its Development in England and America* (New York, 1924), p. iv.
2. *St Stephen's Review*, 17 April 1886, reviewing Gissing's *Demos*. It continues: 'But three writers of the past half-century have chosen a socialist as hero, and in each case the novel proved unpopular.' The reviewer, however, thought *Demos* might succeed because Gissing appeared unsympathetic to the working class.
3. Christopher Harvie, *The Centre of Things: Political Fiction in Britain from Disraeli to the Present* (London, 1991). Harvie's study engages with some of the themes surveyed here but his survey continues up to the late 1980s, and focuses on regional literature, particularly from Scotland. Moreover, his definition of 'political' is the all-embracing one mentioned at the end of this paragraph, encompassing novels of social critique. And his conclusion for the Victorian period is broadly in line with my own: compared to European novels, he writes, 'the British canvas has been the narrower but hitherto more "realistic" dialectic between the conventions of institutions and those of "personal relationships"; and although the period when the two fused, the epoch of Trollope, Meredith and George Eliot, was only a brief one, roughly from the mid-1860s to the mid-1880s, its influence lasted. But it didn't find crises easy to cope with' (p. 233).
4. Morris E. Speare, *The Political Novel: Its Development in England and America*, p. 14.
5. In *Hard Times* Gradgrind becomes MP for Coketown, an apotheosis

dismissed with Carlylean frenzy: 'one of the respected members for ounce weights and measures, one of the representations of the multiplication table, one of the deaf honourable gentlemen, dumb honourable gentlemen, blind honourable gentlemen, lame honourable gentlemen, dead honourable gentlemen, to every other consideration. Else wherefore live we in a Christian land, eighteen hundred and odd years after our Master?' (Penguin edition, 1988, p. 129). However, if Chancery Court in *Bleak House* may be viewed as a metaphor for Parliament, that novel is 'political' in a more profound and despairing way.

6. Intriguingly discussed by Christopher Harvie, *The Centre of Things: Political Fiction in Britain from Disraeli to the Present*, pp. 33–5.
7. Benedict Anderson, *Imagined Communities* (London, 1983).
8. A case first advanced by D.C. Moore, 'Concession or Cure? The Sociological Premises of the First Reform Act', *Historical Journal*, vol. 9, no. 1 (1966) and *The Politics of Deference: A Study of the Mid-nineteenth Century English Political System* (Hassocks, 1976), and subsequently challenged by E.P. Hennock and Norman Gash.
9. As in A.B. Cooke and J.R. Vincent, *The Governing Passion: Cabinet Government and Party Politics in Britain 1885–1886* (Hassocks, 1974) and M. Barker, *Gladstone and Radicalism: The Reconstruction of Liberal Policy in Britain 1885–1894* (Hassocks, 1975).
10. See John Foster, *Class Struggle and the Industrial Revolution: Early Industrial Capitalism in Three English Towns* (London, 1974).
11. See, for instance, J.P. Parry, *Democracy and Religion: Gladstone and the Liberal Party 1867–1875* (Cambridge, 1986) and T.A. Jenkins, *Gladstone, Whiggery and the Liberal Party 1874–1876* (Oxford, 1988).
12. Anthony Trollope, *Phineas Finn* (World's Classics edition, 1937: first published 1869), vol. 1, p. 439.
13. *Nation*, 12 March 1874, reviewing *Phineas Redux*. For a combative statement of the high-political historian's position, see A. Jones, 'Where "Governing is the Use of Words"', *Historical Journal*, vol. 19, no. 1 (1976), pp. 251–6.
14. Bradford A. Booth, *Anthony Trollope: Aspects of His Life and Art* (London, 1958), pp. 78, 86–7; Leopold Amery, introduction to Oxford University Press edition of *The Prime Minister* (1973).
15. Anthony Trollope, *The New Zealander*, edited and with an introduction by N. John Hall (Oxford, 1972), p. 108.
16. *Can You Forgive Her?* (World's Classics edition, 1938; first published 1864), vol. 1, pp. 302–3.
17. *The Prime Minister* (World's Classics edition, 1938; first published 1876), vol. 2, pp. 186–7.
18. For this and other details of Trollope's work patterns, see T.H.S. Escott,

Anthony Trollope: His Work, Associates and Literary Originals (London, 1913), which remains extremely valuable.

19. *Dublin Review*, vol. 65 (October 1869); Anthony Trollope, *An Autobiography* (1946 edition; first published 1883), p. 260. The best recent treatments of Trollope and politics are John Halperin, *Trollope and Politics: A Study of the Pallisers and Others* (London, 1977); relevant sections of P.D. Edwards, *Anthony Trollope: His Art and Scope* (St Lucia, Queensland, 1977); J.R. Dinwiddy, 'Who's Who in Trollope's Political Novels', *Nineteenth-century Fiction*, vol. 20 (1967), pp. 31ff. More tendentious commentary is to be found in W.L. Burn, 'Anthony Trollope's Politics', *Nineteenth Century and After*, vol. 143 (March 1948), pp. 161–71 and Frank E. Robbins, 'Chronology and History in Trollope's Barset and Parliamentary Novels', *Nineteenth-century Fiction*, vol. 5 (1950–51), pp. 303–16. Since this essay first appeared, two major Trollope biographies have been published: N. John Hall, *Anthony Trollope: A Biography* (London, 1991) and Victoria Glendinning, *Trollope* (London, 1991).
20. See especially R. M. Polhemus, *The Changing World of Anthony Trollope* (Berkeley, 1968).
21. For Trollope and Ireland, see also below, pp. 292–3. Also Christopher Harvie, *The Centre of Things: Political Fiction in Britain from Disraeli to the Present*, pp. 84ff.; Owen Dudley Edwards, 'Anthony Trollope, the Irish Writer', *Nineteenth-century Fiction*, vol. 38, no. 1 (1983–4), pp. 1–42; and Victoria Glendinning, *Trollope*, chapters 6–8.
22. See 'Marginal Men and Micks on the Make: The Uses of Irish Exile, *c.* 1840–1922', below, p. 293.
23. Morris E. Speare, *The Political Novel: Its Development in England and America*, p. 200.
24. *The Warden* (Oxford, 1942 edition), pp. 87–8.
25. *Barchester Towers* (World's Classics edition, 1925; first published 1857), p. 123.
26. Dates given are those in which the complete novel was published. Halperin (pp. 24ff.) discusses fully the question of which novels count as 'political' or as 'Palliser' novels.
27. S.R. Letwin, *The Gentleman in Trollope: Individuality and Moral Conduct* (London, 1982), p. 187.
28. See A.O.J. Cockshut, 'Trollope's Liberalism' in T. Bareham (ed.), *Anthony Trollope* (London, 1980), p. 171.
29. See John Halperin, *Trollope and Politics: A Study of the Pallisers and Others*, pp. 10–11, for Trollope and the Conservative Party. On Trollope and Beverley, see Lance O. Tingay, 'Trollope and the Beverley Election', *Nineteenth-century Fiction*, vol. 5 (1950–51), pp. 23ff., and Halperin, chapter 5. Christopher Harvie, *The Centre of Things: Political Fiction in Britain*

from Disraeli to the Present, p. 61, is perceptive on the use made by novelists of elections, particularly Trollope.

30. *Studies in Contemporary Biography* (London, 1903).
31. Quoted in J. Sutherland, 'Trollope and *St Paul's*' in T. Bareham (ed.), *Anthony Trollope*, p. 171.
32. See P.D. Edwards, *Anthony Trollope: His Art and Scope*, Appendix 1; J.R. Dinwiddy, 'Who's Who in Trollope's Political Novels', pp. 31ff.; Blair G. Kenney, 'Trollope's Ideal Statesman: Plantagenet Palliser and Lord John Russell', *Nineteenth-century Fiction*, vol. 20 (1965), p. 281; T.H.S. Escott, *Anthony Trollope: His Work, Associates and Literary Originals* and John Halperin, *Trollope and Politics: A Study of the Pallisers and Others*, especially chapter 2.
33. B. Curtis Brown, *Anthony Trollope* (London, 1950), p. 84; A.O.J. Cockshut, *Anthony Trollope: A Critical Study* (London, 1955), pp. 241–9.
34. See J.R. Vincent's introduction to *Disraeli, Derby and the Conservative Party: The Political Journals of Lord Stanley 1849–1869* (Hassocks, 1978).
35. See R.B. Martin, *Enter Rumour: Four Early Victorian Scandals* (London, 1962), pp. 86–7.
36. In fact, as Dinwiddy reminds us (and Cockshut missed), Disraeli *had* at one stage of his career supported separation of Church and state; see J.R. Dinwiddy, 'Who's Who in Trollope's Political Novels'.
37. *Phineas Redux* (World's Classics edition, 1937; first published 1874), vol. 2, p. 415.
38. P.D. Edwards, *Anthony Trollope: His Art and Scope*, p. 154.
39. *Phineas Finn*, vol. 1, p. 100.
40. *Phineas Redux*, vol. 1, pp. 358–9.
41. Morris E. Speare, *The Political Novel: Its Development in England and America*, pp. 189–92.
42. *Phineas Redux*, vol. 1, p. 334.
43. *Phineas Finn*, vol. 1, pp. 17–19.
44. 'My friend Frank Tregear . . . is a very good fellow and I hope you'll elect him . . . I have known Frank Tregear ever so long, and I don't think you could find a better member of Parliament anywhere . . . I am sure you feel that he ought to be member for Polpenno . . . I think you'll return Frank Tregear. I was at school with him: – and I tell you, that you can't find a better fellow anywhere than Frank Tregear.'

    This is hailed as 'the speech of the evening'. *The Duke's Children* (World's Classics edition, 1938; first published 1880), vol. 2, pp. 146–7.
45. Quoted in R.S. Churchill, *Winston Spencer Churchill. Vol. 2: Young Statesman 1900–1914* (London, 1966), p. 92.

46. Trollope's usefulness to future historians was forecast by T.H.S. Escott, Nathaniel Hawthorne and Frederic Harrison, among others: Harrison called him the 'photographer' of mid-Victorian England (*Studies in Early Victorian Literature*, London, 1895, p. 208). As specific examples, Asa Briggs in *Victorian People: A Reassessment of Persons and Themes* (Harmondsworth, 1965) has a chapter on Trollope; W.L. Burn, *The Age of Equipoise: A Study of the Mid-Victorian Era* (London, 1964) shows a close reading of his novels; and J.L. Hammond, *Gladstone and the Irish Nation* (London, 1938) used Trollope's description of the Whig attitude towards Mr Bonteen to illuminate Chamberlain's position in Gladstone's Cabinet.
47. A.B. Cooke and J.R. Vincent, *The Governing Passion: Cabinet Government and Party Politics in Britain 1885–1886*, p. 5:

> The deep concern of the politicians as to how the parties should bring parliamentary politics into the life of the people, was partly a concern about laying down terms of reference within which popular political activity could safely be encouraged, and partly a concern about keeping the people out of politics, in the sense of ensuring that the electorate would not want to exercise any initiative in deciding what politicians ought to be doing. These preoccupations could best be sorted out, not by talking directly to electors, but through the medium of clubs, the lobby, the dinner table, the race meeting, the visit to dine and sleep, the morning call, and the stroll in the park. This was where political work was really done. Leading men rarely discussed matters of party machinery: still less commonly did they relate the management of the extra-parliamentary organization to the decisions of parliamentary life or public administration.

48. Anthony Trollope, *An Autobiography*, p. 230.
49. Morris E. Speare, *The Political Novel: Its Development in England and America*, p. 37.
50. Benjamin Disraeli, *Coningsby: or, The New Generation* (London, Gresham Press edition [n.d.]; first published 1844), pp. 59–60.
51. Ibid., p. 217.
52. Christopher Harvie, *The Centre of Things: Political Fiction in Britain from Disraeli to the Present*, p. 41; Harvie's discussion of the trilogy in chapter 3 is the best treatment of Disraeli as political novelist known to me.
53. Liverpool has, however, been rehabilitated in J.E. Cookson, *Lord Liverpool's Administration: The Crucial Years 1815–1822* (Edinburgh, 1975).
54. Longman believed that Goldwin Smith's public complaints about his representation in *Lothair* helped boost a reprint; see Morris E. Speare, *The Political Novel: Its Development in England and America*, p. 20.
55. See R.A. Butler's introduction to the Penguin edition (1980), p. 12.
56. The latter is a wonderfully Masonic ritual of robes, masks and signs; see ibid., pp. 265–71, and, for the Coronation, pp. 66–7.

57. 'The Tory Party ... was held to be literally defunct except by a few old battered cronies of office, crouched round the embers of faction, which they were fanning, and muttering reaction in mystic whispers.' See my *Lord Randolph Churchill: A Political Life* (Oxford, 1981), pp. 59–60, 70, 77, 79, 89–90, 115–16, 149, 182, for Disraeli's influence upon Churchill and the Fourth Party; also my essay 'Tory Democracy and Political Elitism' in A. Cosgrave and J.I. McGuire (eds.), *Parliament and Community* (Belfast, 1983), pp. 147–76.
58. This view is stylishly expounded in J.R. Vincent's essay on Disraeli in H. Van Thal (ed.), *The Prime Ministers*, vol. 2 (London, 1975), pp. 83–108.
59. In the work of H.J. Hanham, *Elections and Party Management: Politics in the Time of Disraeli and Gladstone* (London, 1959); N. Gash, *Politics in the Age of Peel* (London, 1964); and, from a different angle, D.C. Moore, 'Concession or Cure? The Sociological Premises of the First Reform Act'.
60. From George Eliot's 1856 essay on Wilhelm Heinrich von Riehl, 'The Natural History of German Life', in Thomas Pinney (ed.), *The Essays of George Eliot* (New York, 1963).
61. *Felix Holt: The Radical* (1866; Penguin edition, 1972), p. 51.
62. See W. Myers, 'George Eliot: Politics and Personality' in John Lucas (ed.), *Literature and Politics in the Nineteenth Century* (London, 1971), pp. 105–8. Politics in *Felix Holt* have been discussed in Arnold Kettle, 'Felix Holt the Radical' in Barbara Hardy (ed.), *Essays on George Eliot* (London, 1970) and L. Bamber, 'Self-defeating Politics in George Eliot's *Felix Holt*', *Victorian Studies*, vol. 18, no. 41 (1975), pp. 419–35.
63. *Felix Holt*, p. 120.
64. Ibid., pp. 109–111.
65. Ibid., pp. 127–8.
66. Ibid., p. 219.
67. Ibid., p. 275.
68. 'At present, looking back on that day at Treby, it seems to me that the sadder illusion lay with Harold Transome, who was trusting in his own skill to shape the success of his own morrows, ignorant of what many yesterdays had determined for him beforehand' (p. 277).
69. Ibid., p. 363.
70. 'Felix Holt's Address to the Working Men': suggested by Blackwood, and, as Coveney points out, a logical continuation of Felix Holt's views as projected in the novel.
71. George Meredith, *Beauchamp's Career* (1876; World's Classics edition, 1988), p. 361. The speaker is Austin, a 'speculative Tory', who none the less talks sense. Harvie sees Shrapnel as Ruskin rather than Carlyle (*The Centre of Things*, pp. 167–8).
72. This is implied in Romfrey's dream while Beauchamp lies ill.

It was of an interminable procession of that odd lot called The People. All of them were quarrelling under a deluge. One party was for umbrellas, one was against them; and sounding the dispute with a question or two, Everard held it logical that there should be protection from the wet; just as logical on the other hand that so frail a shelter should be discarded, considering the tremendous downpour. But as he himself was dry, save for two or three drops, he deemed them all lunatics. (pp. 502–3)

73. See her letter to Lydiard:

My influence is weak, I suppose, because he finds me constantly leaning to expediency – I am your pupil. It may be quite correct that powder is intended for explosion: we do not therefore apply a spark to the barrel. I ventured on that. He pitied me in the snares of simile and metaphor. He is the same, you perceive. How often have we not discussed what would become of him, with that 'rocket-brain' of his, in less quiet times! Yet, when he was addressing a deputation of workmen the other day, he recommended patience to them as one of the virtues that count under wisdom. He is curiously impatient for knowledge . . . At the risk of your accusing me of 'sententious posing', I would say, that men who do not live in the present chiefly, but hamper themselves with giant tasks in excess of alarm for the future, however devoted and noble they may be – and he is an example of one that is – reduce themselves to the dimensions of pygmies; they have the cry of infants. You reply, Foresight is an element of love of country and mankind. But how often is not the foresight guesswork? (p. 530)

Jenny, like Austin from the Tory side, often seems to speak for Meredith.

74. A point well made in David Howard, 'George Meredith: "Delicate" and "Epical" Fiction' in John Lucas (ed.), *Literature and Politics in the Nineteenth Century*, p. 160.
75. *Beauchamp's Career*, pp. 250–51.
76. Quoted in D. Becquemont, 'Politics in Literature 1874–1875: *The Way We Live Now* and *Beauchamp's Career*' in J. Teissedou (ed.), *Politics in Literature in the Nineteenth Century* (Lille, 1974), p. 248.
77. T.E. Kebbel, 'The Spirit of Party', *Nineteenth Century*, vol. 11, no. 61 (1882), pp. 385–6; Lord Cranborne (later third Marquis of Salisbury) in *Quarterly Review*, vol. 209 (1866), p. 532.
78. See my *Lord Randolph Churchill: A Political Life*, pp. 5–7.
79. See John Lucas, 'Conservatism and Revolution in the 1880s' in *Politics in Literature in the Nineteenth Century*, pp. 173–219, which comprehensively deals with Mallock's novel *The Old Order Changes*. On the whole question of Tory Democracy and the changing nature of Conservatism, see my 'Tory Democracy and Political Elitism'; for Churchill and socialism, see my *Lord Randolph Churchill*, pp. 369–72.

80. See Mrs Humphry Ward, *A Writer's Recollections* (London, 1918), chapters 9–11.
81. In an earlier novel, *Marcella* (1894), she is married to Maxwell as a symbolic union between Labour idealism and Tory paternalism.
82. 'I recognized Fontenoy's jay-like laugh, and was glad that the portrait was not carried out too faithfully,' wrote Lord Rosebery to Mrs Ward on 4 November 1896; see F. Rives, 'Fiction and Politics in *Sir George Tressady*' in J. Teissedou (ed.), *Politics in Literature in the Nineteenth Century*, p. 201, n. 16. Churchill had died the previous year, while the novel was being written. Rosebery used the phrase 'jay-like laugh' in his memoir of his friend ten years later (*Lord Randolph Churchill*, 1906). Personal details of Fontenoy's life mirror Churchill's closely: see *Sir George Tressady* (2-vol. edition in Autography edition of *The Writings of Mrs Humphry Ward*, vols. 7–8, Boston and New York, 1910; first published 1896), vol. 1, pp. 48–9.
83. See above, p. 151.
84. *A Writer's Recollections*, p. 305. But Lord Peel consoled her: 'Of course he was thinking of *us* – the Liberal Unionists.'
85. *Sir George Tressady*, vol. 1, p. 372.
86. *A Writer's Recollections*, p. 307. Beatrice Webb's work as a social investigator – and incidentally her early ideas of becoming a political novelist – are detailed in *My Apprenticeship* (Penguin edition, 1971; first published 1926), chapters 3–5.
87. *A Writer's Recollections*, p. 362.
88. Ibid., p. 361.
89. 'I was born into cowardice and debasement. We all are. Our generation's grimy with hypocrisy. I came to the most beautiful things of life – like Peeping Tom of Coventry. I was never given a light, never given a touch of natural manhood by all this dingy, furtive, canting, humbugging English world' (H.G. Wells, *The New Machiavelli*, London, 1911, p. 516).
90. Ibid., p. 10.
91. Ibid., pp. 329, 335.
92. Ibid., p. 482.
93. Ibid., p. 365.
94. G.K. Chesterton, *The Napoleon of Notting Hill* (Penguin edition, 1946; first published 1904), p. 10.
95. Notably *Natalie Natalia* (1971) and *Imago Bird* (1980). Twentieth-century political novels (in the widest sense) are dealt with in Harvie's last chapters, which are particularly searching on John Buchan and Joyce Cary.

9 Paddy and Mr Punch

1. Ashis Nandy, *The Intimate Enemy: Loss and Recovery of Self under Colonialism* (Oxford, 1983).
2. Francis Eason to M.H. Spielmann, 7 August 1895; I owe this reference to Professor Michael Slater.
3. Vol. 11 (July–December 1846), p. 63.
4. Vol. 13 (July–December 1847), starting p. 56.
5. See vol. 1 (July–December 1841), pp. 117, 125, 153; 11, 29ff. 'Fusbos' was the pseudonym of one H.P. Plunkett, who also wrote as 'Grattan', and was probably Irish. A regular early cartoonist, R.J. Hamerton, was certainly Irish – an ex-drawing-master from Longford. Most of his subjects were Irish, such as the 'Irish Ogre Fattening on the "Finist Pisintry"', and he was particularly severe on O'Connell. See M.H. Spielmann, *The History of* Punch (London, 1895), pp. 282, 453.
6. See ibid., p. 58 for instance.
7. See K.T. Hoppen, *Elections, Politics and Society in Ireland 1832–1885* (Oxford, 1984), pp. 388–408.
8. Vol. 9 (July–December 1845), p. 176.
9. See vol. 8 (January–June 1845), pp. 187, 230; vol. 9 (July–December 1845), p. 102.
10. Vol. 1 (July–December 1841), pp. 47, 133, 226.
11. Ibid., p. 49.
12. See, for instance, ibid., pp. 99, 127; vol. 3 (July–December 1842), p. 183.
13. See, for instance, vol. 2 (January–June 1842), p. 56; vol. 6 (January–June 1844), p. 179.
14. See, for instance, vol. 1 (July–December 1841), p. 177.
15. Vol. 6 (January–June 1844), p. 248.
16. See vol. 8 (January–June 1845), pp. 18–19.
17. See O. MacDonagh, *States of Mind: A Study of Anglo-Irish Conflict 1780–1980* (London, 1983), pp. 56–9.
18. Vol. 2 (January–June 1842), p. 17.
19. Ibid., p. 150.
20. Vol. 6 (January–June 1844), pp. 48–50; vol. 8 (January–June 1845), pp. 38–9.
21. Vol. 6 (January–June 1844), p. 39.
22. R.G.G. Price, *A History of Punch* (London, 1955), chapter 2.
23. Vol. 1 (July–December 1841), pp. 99, 147; vol. 3 (July–December 1842), p. 183.
24. Vol. 8 (January–June 1845), p. 262.
25. Vol. 11 (July–December 1846), p. 79.

26. Vol. 12 (January–June 1847), p. 183.
27. Vol. 9 (July–December 1845), p. 221.
28. Vol. 15 (July–December 1848), p. 228.
29. Vol. 12 (January–June 1847), p. 64.
30. Vol. 9 (July–December 1845), pp. 197, 213, for spoof letter and cartoon; p. 215 for the serious address.
31. Ibid., p. 255.
32. Vol. 10 (January–June 1846), p. 51.
33. Ibid., pp. 156, 181.
34. Ibid., p. 170.
35. Ibid., p. 204.
36. Ibid., p. 208; vol. 14 (January–June 1848), p. 139.
37. Vol. 13 (July–December 1847), p. 213: 'The Lament of Erin'.
38. Vol. 14 (January–June 1848), p. 150.
39. Vol. 11 (July–December 1846), pp. 250–52.
40. Vol. 14 (January–June 1848), pp. 29, 47.
41. Ibid., p. 121; for the historical antecedent, see my *Modern Ireland 1600–1972* (London, 1988), p. 35.
42. Vol. 14 (January–June 1848), p. 239; 'Paddy Redivivus'.
43. Vol. 15 (July–December 1848), p. 77.
44. Ibid., p. 122.
45. Vol. 16 (January–June 1849), p. 79: 'The Irish Old Man of the Mountain'; also see vol. 17 (July–December 1849), p. 48.
46. Vol. 17 (July–December 1849), p. 67.
47. Vol. 22 (January–June 1852), p. 202.
48. Vol. 21 (July–December 1851), p. 223.
49. Vol. 23 (July–December 1852), p. 111.
50. Ibid., p. 23.
51. Ibid., pp. 196–7.
52. Vol. 24 (January–June 1853), *passim*, but especially p. 232, for attacks on Lucas; p. 250 for 'A Week of Irish Wrongs'.
53. Vol. 64 (4 January 1868), p. 5.
54. Vol. 43 (18 March 1862), p. 165.
55. I deal with this phenomenon in the introduction to my *Lord Randolph Churchill: A Political Life* (Oxford, 1981), pp. 2–4.
56. Vol. 80 (26 February 1881), pp. 87–8. Biggar's subsequent appearance in a breach of promise case allowed Toby much gleeful innuendo about his style of life.
57. For Gladstone's surprising estimate of Callan, see J.R. Vincent, 'Gladstone and Ireland', *Proceedings of the British Academy*, vol. 63 (1977), p. 220, n. 2.
58. For Lucy on Parnell, see, for example, vol. 80 (29 January 1881), pp. 39–40.

59. Vol. 78 (14 February 1880), p. 63.
60. See, for instance, vol. 83 (16 December 1882), p. 281.
61. Vol. 77, p. 215. A similar picture is to be found in several contemporary satires, such as Terence McGrath's *Pictures from Ireland* (1880).
62. Vol. 80 (12 March 1881), p. 115.
63. See *Pall Mall Gazette*, 16 June 1881, p. 4.
64. Vol. 78 (17 January 1880), p. 18. Also see vol. 81, for John Bull solacing a beautiful cottager.
65. Vol. 78 (10 April 1880), p. 159. For the Duchess of Marlborough's relief fund, see below, pp. 239–40.
66. Vol. 79 (23 October 1880), p. 187.
67. See also vol. 79 (20 November 1880), p. 234. 'They must first learn to respect *me* [Law]. Your turn comes next [Land Reform].'
68. Tenniel's cartoon appeared on 20 May 1882. Matt Morgan had already used the image in the *Tomahawk* of 18 December 1869, which was in turn cleverly reversed for Irish purposes by Thomas Fitzpatrick, who portrayed Lord Salisbury as 'The Frankenstein of Hatfield', creating the monster of Bigotry (*Weekly Freeman* supplement, 6 May 1893). (The fact that Salisbury actually had a laboratory at Hatfield added to the piquancy.) Tenniel's image of 'The Irish Vampire' (the National League sucking Hibernia's blood as she slept, *Punch*, 24 October 1885) was similarly reversed by an Irish cartoonist in the *Irish Pilot*, within a fortnight. See Perry Curtis, *Apes and Angels: The Irishman in Victorian Caricature*, p. 81.
69. See vol. 84 (24 February and 3 March 1883), for bathetic poetry on the subject, pp. 90, 102.
70. Vol. 84 (24 March 1883), p. 144.
71. Vol. 81 (30 July, 13 August, 24 October 1881), pp. 43, 67, 199.
72. Vol. 81 (29 October 1881), p. 193.
73. Vol. 90 (2 January 1886), p. 12. Cf. the view of Salisbury in A.B. Cooke and J.R. Vincent, *The Governing Passion: Cabinet Government and Party Politics in Britain 1885–1886* (Hassocks, 1974).
74. Vol. 90 (8 May 1886), p. 226.
75. Vol. 90 (24 April 1886), p. 198.
76. Vol. 90 (3 June 1886), p. 271.
77. Vol. 98 (20 December 1890), p. 297.
78. Vol. 98 (13 December 1890), p. 283.
79. Vol. 98 (24 January 1891), p. 43.
80. Vol. 100 (17 October 1891), p. 191.
81. Vol. 85 (8 December 1883), p. 266; vol. 88 (4 April 1885), p. 162.
82. Vol. 90 (24 April 1886), p. 198.
83. See Perry Curtis, *Apes and Angels: The Irishman in Victorian Caricature*, p. 69.

84. Ibid., p. 7.
85. Ibid., pp. 19ff., 30.
86. 'English Attitudes to the Irish in England 1780–1900' in C. Holmes (ed.), *Immigrants and Minorities in British Society* (London, 1978), pp. 81–110.
87. Vol. 85 (22 December 1883), p. 295.

10 Good Behaviour: Yeats, Synge and Anglo-Irish Etiquette

1. See Nicholas Grene, 'Yeats and the Remaking of Synge' in Terence Brown and Nicholas Grene (eds.), *Tradition and Influence in Anglo-Irish Poetry* (Basingstoke, 1989), pp. 47–62; T.R. Henn, *The Lonely Tower* (London, second edition 1965), chapter 5; Ann Saddlemyer, 'Synge and Some Companions, with a Note Concerning a Walk through Connemara with Jack Yeats', *Yeats Studies No. 2* (Shannon, 1972), p. 18 and 'Stars of the Abbey's Ascendancy' in Robert O'Driscoll (ed.), *Theatre and Nationalism in Twentieth-century Ireland* (London, 1971). Chapter 1 of Weldon Thornton, *J.M. Synge and the Western Mind* (Gerrards Cross, 1979) is also relevant.
2. See Ann Saddlemyer (ed.), *The Collected Letters of J.M. Synge* (vol. 1, Oxford, 1983; vol. 2, Oxford, 1984), vol. 2, p. 165, n. 1.
3. See Allan Wade, *The Letters of W.B. Yeats* (London, 1954), p. 18; also J. Hassett, *Yeats and the Poetics of Hate* (Dublin, 1986), p. 151.
4. See Ann Saddlemyer in *Yeats Studies No. 2*, p. 18; the quote comes from Yeats's preface to Synge's *Poems and Translations* (Cuala Press, 1909).
5. Ann Saddlemyer (ed.), *J.M. Synge: Collected Works. Vol. 3: Plays*, Book 1 (Oxford, 1968), p. 63.
6. See Declan Kiberd, *Synge and the Irish Language* (Totowa, NJ, 1979), pp. 36–7.
7. Ann Saddlemyer (ed.), *Theatre Business: The Correspondence of the First Abbey Theatre Directors: W.B. Yeats, Lady Gregory and J.M. Synge* (Gerrards Cross, 1982), p. 27.
8. See Katharine Worth, *The Irish Drama of Europe from Yeats to Beckett* (London, 1978), chapters 5 and 6.
9. See Andrew Carpenter (ed.), *My Uncle John: Edward Stephens's Life of J.M. Synge* (London, 1974), p. 30, for the Synge sense of being in a minority.
10. W.B. Yeats, *Memoirs*, edited by Denis Donoghue (London, 1972), p. 206.
11. Allan Wade (ed.), *The Letters of W.B. Yeats*, p. 278.
12. See ibid., p. 68, for Synge's mystic interests.
13. See 'Protestant Magic: W.B. Yeats and the Spell of Irish History', below, for more detailed consideration of this.
14. George Mills Harper, *The Making of Yeats's 'A Vision': A Study of the Automatic Script* (London, 1987), vol. 2, p. 94.

15. Ibid., p. 108.
16. Ibid., p. 144.
17. See E.H. Mikhail, *Lady Gregory: Interviews and Recollections* (London, 1977), p. 107.
18. Robert Hogan and J. Kilroy, *The Abbey Theatre: The Years of Synge 1905–1909* (Dublin, 1978).
19. See *The Collected Letters of J.M. Synge*, vol. 1, pp. 148ff., 161, 169.
20. Synge to Gregory, 5 January 1906, *The Collected Letters of J.M. Synge*, vol. 1, p. 149.
21. See also Synge to Gregory, 9 June 1906, *The Collected Letters of J.M. Synge*, vol. 1, p. 169: 'I am not writing much to Yeats while he is with Miss Horniman, he is so careless about his letters.'
22. 7 March 1906, *The Collected Letters of J.M. Synge*, vol. 1, p. 161.
23. See Adrian Frazier, *Behind the Scenes: Yeats, Horniman and the Struggle for the Abbey Theatre* (London, 1990).
24. Robert Hogan and J. Kilroy, *The Abbey Theatre: The Years of Synge 1905–1909*, pp. 33, 36.
25. See *United Ireland*, as quoted in ibid., pp. 63–4.
26. Declan Kiberd, *Synge and the Irish Language*, p. 238.
27. Robert Hogan and J. Kilroy, *The Abbey Theatre: The Years of Synge 1905–1909*, pp. 33, 36.
28. *Theatre Business: The Correspondence of the First Abbey Theatre Directors*, p. 205.
29. Robert Hogan and J. Kilroy, *The Abbey Theatre: The Years of Synge 1905–1909*, p. 91.
30. Quoted in *The Collected Letters of J.M. Synge*, vol. 2, p. 135.
31. Synge to MacKenna, 23 February 1908, *The Collected Letters of J.M. Synge*, vol. 2, p. 140.
32. 18 March 1907, *The Collected Letters of J.M. Synge*, vol. 2, p. 316.
33. Synge to Molly Allgood, 21 August 1907, *The Collected Letters of J.M. Synge*, vol. 2, pp. 38–9.
34. *Collected Works. Vol. 1: Poems* (Oxford, 1962), p. 38.
35. See *The Collected Letters of J.M. Synge*, vol. 1, p. 223.
36. For her resentment of Synge on tour, see Robert Hogan and J. Kilroy, *The Abbey Theatre: The Years of Synge 1905–1909*, pp. 73–5.
37. Ibid., pp. 81–8.
38. Ibid., p. 99.
39. Robert Hogan and M.J. O'Neill, *Joseph Holloway's Abbey Theatre* (Carbondale, Ill., 1967), p. 172.
40. See 'Protestant Magic: W.B. Yeats and the Spell of Irish History', below.
41. Andrew Carpenter (ed.), *My Uncle John: Edward Stephens's Life of J.M. Synge*, p. 53.

42. Lily Yeats to John Butler Yeats, 24 October 1909, Yeats Papers. I am indebted to William Michael Murphy for sharing his transcriptions of these and other Yeats letters with me.
43. 13 July 1905, *The Collected Letters of J.M. Synge*, vol. 1, pp. 116–17. 'There are sides of all that western life, the groggy-patriot-publican-general-shop-man who is married to the priest's half-sister and is second cousin once-removed of the dispensary doctor, that are horrible and awful . . .'
44. Yeats to Gregory, 24 March 1909, quoted in *The Collected Letters of J.M. Synge*, vol. 2, p. 55.
45. See Michael Steinman, *Yeats's Heroic Figures: Wilde, Parnell, Swift, Casement* (London, 1983); and note the Synge reference in Yeats's 'In Memory of Major Robert Gregory'.
46. In conversation: Robert Hogan and M.J. O'Neill, *Joseph Holloway's Abbey Theatre*, p. 58 (26 April 1905).
47. 'Introduction' to *Selections from the Writings of Lord Dunsany* (Cuala Press, 1912).
48. See Michael Steinman, *Yeats's Heroic Figures: Wilde, Parnell, Swift, Casement*, p. 71.
49. *Irish Independent*, 24 August 1909, quoted in Robert Hogan and J. Kilroy, *The Abbey Theatre: The Years of Synge 1905–1909*, p. 295.
50. Preface to Oliver St John Gogarty, *Wild Apples* (Cuala Press, 1930).
51. See Jonathan Swift, 'Good Manners and Good Breeding'; it is conveniently printed in J. Gross (ed.), *The Oxford Book of Essays* (Oxford, 1991).
52. 22 May 1907; see *The Collected Letters of J.M. Synge*, vol. 1, p. 351.
53. 9 November 1908, *The Collected Letters of J.M. Synge*, vol. 2, p. 221.
54. See Anna MacBride White and A. Norman Jeffares (eds.), *Always Your Friend: The Gonne–Yeats Letters 1893–1938* (London, 1992), p. 165.
55. *The Collected Letters of J.M. Synge*, vol. 1, p. 84, n. 1.
56. John Morley, *Recollections* (London, 1917), vol. 1, p. 238; see Michael Steinman, *Yeats's Heroic Figures: Wilde, Parnell, Swift, Casement*, p. 79, for a discussion of what this description meant to Yeats.
57. Cf. Nicholas Grene, 'Yeats and the Remaking of Synge', p. 50.
58. Preface to J.M. Synge, *Poems and Translations*.
59. Robert Hogan and J. Kilroy, *The Abbey Theatre: The Years of Synge 1905–1909*, p. 183.
60. Andrew Carpenter (ed.), *My Uncle John: Edward Stephens's Life of J.M. Synge*, pp. 132–3.
61. Denis Donoghue, *Warrenpoint* (London, 1990), pp. 49–50.
62. 'The Three Beggars', *The Variorum Edition of the Poems of W.B. Yeats* (London, 1957), p. 297.

63. Originally dated 4 June 1914, and first published in 1916.
64. *Explorations* (London, 1962), p. 337.

11 Protestant Magic: W.B. Yeats and the Spell of Irish History

1. 'The Poetry of W.B. Yeats' in J. Hall and Michael Steinman (eds.), *The Permanence of Yeats* (New York, 1950), p. 347.
2. 'Passion and Cunning: An Essay on the Politics of W.B. Yeats' in A. Norman Jeffares and K.G.W. Cross (eds.), *In Excited Reverie: A Centenary Tribute to William Butler Yeats 1865–1939* (London, 1965), p. 222. Conor Cruise O'Brien locates this process as beginning in the years after *c.* 1903.
3. *Vale*, chapter 7; text taken from Richard Cave (ed.), *Hail and Farewell: Ave, Salve, Vale* (Gerrards Cross, 1976), p. 540, which reprints Moore's 1933 version of the original 1911 text.
4. Emmet Larkin, *The Making of the Roman Catholic Church in Ireland 1850–1860* (Chapel Hill, NC, 1980), p. 447.
5. In 'The Big House', written for the first number of the *Bell* in 1940 and reprinted in Hermione Lee (ed.), *The Mulberry Tree: Writings of Elizabeth Bowen* (London, 1986), pp. 25–30; see also above, pp. 111–12. The 'affronting' reference is in Antony Coleman, 'The Big House, Yeats and the Irish Context' in Warwick Gould (ed.), *Yeats Annual No. 3* (London, 1985), p. 47.
6. Anthony Trollope, *The Kellys and the O'Kellys* (Oxford, 1982 edition), pp. 491–4.
7. From *On the Boiler*, reprinted in *Explorations* (London, 1962), p. 413.
8. Gifford Lewis (ed.), *The Selected Letters of Somerville and Ross* (London, 1989), p. 294.
9. See her introduction to the 1947 edition, reprinted in Hermione Lee, *The Mulberry Tree: Writings of Elizabeth Bowen*, pp. 100–113, and commented upon above, pp. 108–9, 121.
10. *The Living Novel* (London, 1946), p. 96.
11. Now in the Berg Collection, New York Public Library.
12. See James Longenbach, *Stone Cottage: Pound, Yeats and Modernism* (Oxford, 1988), pp. 108–9. Yeats claimed that the book interested him no more than any other sensational story, but he stayed up all night reading it. Some of these ideas have recently (since this essay was first published in 1989) been explored by W.J. McCormack; see his section called 'Irish Gothic and After' in the *Field Day Anthology of Irish Writing* (Derry, 1991), vol. 2.
13. [After 16 February 1893] in John Kelly and Eric Domville (eds.), *The Collected Letters of W.B. Yeats. Vol. 1: 1865–1895* (Oxford, 1986), pp. 355–6.

14. Denis Donoghue (ed.), *W.B. Yeats: Memoirs* (London, 1972); hereafter cited as *Memoirs*), pp. 195–6.
15. See Steven L. Adams and George Mills Harper (eds.), 'The Manuscript of "Leo Africanus"' in Richard J. Finneran (ed.), *Yeats Annual No. 1* (London, 1982) and 'Swedenborg, Mediums, and the Desolate Places' in W.H. O'Donnell (ed.), *W.B. Yeats: Prefaces and Introductions* (London, 1988), where this idea recurs.
16. Testified to by numerous authorities: see J.H. Parnell, *C.S. Parnell: A Memoir* (London, 1916), p. 263; A. Kettle, *The Material for Victory* (Dublin, 1958), p. 26; T.M. Healy, *Letters and Leaders of My Day* (London, 1928), vol. 2, pp. 169–70; F.S.L. Lyons, *Charles Stewart Parnell* (London, 1977), pp. 24, 183–4, 235, 249, 597, 601, 612.
17. Roger Sawyer, *Casement: The Flawed Hero* (London, 1984). My thanks to Dr Angus Macintyre for this information.
18. *Memoirs*, p. 212.
19. W.B. Yeats, *Autobiographies* (London, 1955; hereafter cited as *Autobiographies*), p. 91.
20. *Memoirs*, p. 147. For Yeats and the arbitrary, see also 'Magic' in *Ideas of Good and Evil* (London, 1903).
21. From 'William Blake and the Imagination' in *Ideas of Good and Evil*, pp. 120–21.
22. Or so he claimed in his dedication to John Quinn's copy of vol. 7 of his *Collected Works*.
23. Violet Martin to Edith Somerville [fragment, 1901] in Gifford Lewis (ed.), *The Selected Letters of Somerville and Ross*, p. 240.
24. *Autobiographies*, p. 14.
25. Jack Yeats to Thomas McGreevy in E.H. Mikhail (ed.), *W.B. Yeats: Interviews and Recollections* (London, 1977), vol. 2, p. 409.
26. John Butler Yeats to Rosa Butt, 31 October 1910, letter no. 111 of a series held at the Bodleian Library, Oxford.
27. *Autobiographies*, p. 83; W.B. Yeats to Augusta Gregory, 1 March 1902, Berg Collection, New York Public Library.
28. Introduction to *The Words upon the Window Pane* reprinted in *Explorations*, p. 345.
29. E.H. Mikhail (ed.), *W.B. Yeats: Interviews and Recollections*, vol. 1, p. 154.
30. James W. Flannery, *W.B. Yeats and the Idea of a Theatre: The Early Abbey Theatre in Theory and Practice* (London, 1976), p. 228 – a generalization based on countless interviews.
31. Augusta Gregory to John Quinn, 3 June 1917, Berg Collection, New York Public Library.
32. John P. Frayne (ed.), *Uncollected Prose by W.B. Yeats*, vol. 1 (London, 1970), pp. 404–5.

33. To Standish O'Grady; reprinted ibid., p. 243.
34. W.B. Yeats, *The Celtic Twilight*, with an introduction by Kathleen Raine (Gerrards Cross, 1981 edition of the 1902 text), p. 65.
35. John P. Frayne (ed.), *Uncollected Prose by W.B. Yeats*, vol. 1, p. 310.
36. These letters of late 1915 and early 1916 are in Allan Wade (ed.), *The Letters of W.B. Yeats* (London, 1954), pp. 603–6; the more accurate transcriptions quoted here may be found in William M. Murphy, *Prodigal Father: The Life of John Butler Yeats 1839–1922* (London, 1978), p. 446.
37. Peter Kuch, *Yeats and AE: 'The Antagonism that Unites Dear Friends'* (Gerrards Cross, 1986), p. 51.
38. See Clive Leatherdale, *The Origins of Dracula: The Background to Bram Stoker's Gothic Masterpiece* (London, 1987).
39. From Major E. Johnson, *On the Track of the Crescent* (London, 1885), pp. 250–51.
40. See Allan Wade, *The Letters of W.B. Yeats*, pp. 297–8. I am grateful to Deirdre Toomey for pointing out that Yeats probably knew the paragraphist was T.P. Gill.
41. 'Ireland and the Arts', first published in *United Irishman*, 31 August 1901, and republished in *Ideas of Good and Evil*, p. 223.
42. W.B. Yeats, *The Speckled Bird*, edited by William H. O'Donnell (Toronto, 1976), p. 33.
43. See her scrapbook TS in the Yeats family papers, p. 13. The Merville servants 'played a big part in our lives. They were so friendly and wise and knew so intimately angels, saints, banshees and fairies.'
44. Reported by Lily Yeats to Ruth Lane-Poole, 23 June 1936, transcript in the possession of William Michael Murphy.
45. *Autobiographies*, p. 183.
46. See 'Thinking from Hand to Mouth: Anglo-Irish Literature, Gaelic Nationalism and Irish Politics in the 1890s', below.
47. '7, Middagh Street' in Paul Muldoon, *Meeting the British* (London, 1987).
48. *Leader*, 27 July 1901.
49. *Memoirs*, pp. 161, 212–13.
50. Ibid., pp. 183–4.
51. John P. Frayne (ed.), *Uncollected Prose by W.B. Yeats*, vol. 7, p. 163.
52. Always denounced by his father as the epitome of *haut bourgeois* solidarity. 'I have no longer any hopes of her [Miss Cox]. A person living in Merrion Square will be as others there. In those magnificent abodes I am as a tainted person . . . [letter to Rosa Butt, 1902]; also: 'One reason why I get irritated with Merrion Square is that it is full of class people' [same to same, 17 July 1908]; Bodleian Library, Oxford.
53. 'He was very quaint when I got to sinistrari he quivered with agitation

and cried out "O this should never be spoken of"': W.B. Yeats to Ezra Pound, 3 February [1919], Beinecke Library, Yale University.

54. Quoted in A. Walton Litz's introduction to T.S. Eliot, 'Tradition and the Practice of Poetry', *Southern Review*, vol. 21, no. 4 (October 1985), p. 873.

12 To the Northern Counties Station: Lord Randolph Churchill and the Orange Card

1. The phrase occurred in a public letter written some time later: W.S. Churchill, *Lord Randolph Churchill* (London, 1906), vol. 2, pp. 64–5.
2. Ibid., p. 59.
3. Marlborough's finances were aired in the *Weekly Irish Times*, 13 January 1877, as well as family papers at Blenheim, D/1/3. Other correspondence there comprises exhortations not to patronize the Belfast Linen Company for political reasons, calls for martial law from the country gentry, Ascendancy sneers about the Dublin bourgeoisie, and frenzied denunciations of the social antecedents of Castle guests, written anonymously by those who had not received invitations.
4. For details, see my *Lord Randolph Churchill: A Political Life* (Oxford, 1981), chapter 2. Fuller footnotes and documentation will be found in the first version of this essay, published in F.S.L. Lyons and R.A.J. Hawkins (eds.), *Ireland under the Union: Varieties of Tension* (Oxford, 1980).
5. See letters from Marlborough to Beach in Blenheim MSS D/1/2 and Glos. RO, St Aldwyn Papers (hereafter D2455) PCC/64–5; also David Thornley, *Isaac Butt and Home Rule* (London, 1964), pp. 350–54; and Lady Victoria Hicks Beach, *Life of Sir Michael Hicks Beach (Earl St Aldwyn)* (London, 1932), vol. 1, pp. 26–7, 467.
6. Bishop Conway of Killala to Beach, 17 January 1877 (Blenheim MSS D/1/19).
7. See for instance Butt to Beach, 28 May 1878 (Glos. RO D2455, PCC/66): 'Since I returned to Ireland, I have been astonished at the number of communications which have been made to me by Roman Catholics in various positions to the effect that a very general feeling is pervading the Roman Catholic body that their true and natural alliance is with the conservative party, and a general wish to be able to support them.' Also see David Thornley, *Isaac Butt and Home Rule*, pp. 350–51, 355, 367.
8. Maud Wynne, *An Irishman and His Family: Lord Morris and Killanin* (London, 1937), p. 98.
9. See editorial in *Weekly Freeman*, 22 March 1879.
10. R.R. James, *Lord Randolph Churchill* (London, 1959), p. 62.

11. Melvyn Fairclough, *The Ripper and the Royals* (London, 1991; second edition, 1992), p. 92.
12. On this group, see Mahaffy's speech at the TCD tercentenary, where he referred to Plunket, Gibson, FitzGibbon, Lecky and Thomas Dudley as 'the most brilliant group of men that ever came together in the [Historical] Society' (J.J. Auchmuty, *Lecky: A Biographical and Critical Essay*, Dublin, 1945, p. 119); also Sir John Ross, *The Years of My Pilgrimage* (London, 1924) on his university days.
13. His father, a master in chancery also named Gerald FitzGibbon, had put himself through law school and produced a series of tracts on the Irish situation, such as *Ireland in 1868* (1868), an argument against Disestablishment; also see J.G. Swift MacNeill, *What I Have Seen and Heard* (London, 1925), p. 132, and above, p. 313.
14. Beach to Gibson, 15 November 1878 (HLRO, Ashbourne Papers, 77/130); for a contemporary comment on his ability, see *Weekly Freeman*, 10 November 1878.
15. He referred disparagingly to the opinions of 'Gibson, Plunket and other *moderates*' (FitzGibbon to Churchill [n.d. but *c.* Christmas 1881]; Churchill College, Lord Randolph Churchill Papers, hereafter RCP, 1/i/62). For comments on his approach to legal questions, see Sir John Ross, *The Years of My Pilgrimage*, p. 201.
16. Same to same, 23 August 1887 (RCP, 1/xxi/2634).
17. Same to same, 20 November 1887 (ibid., 1/xxi/2735).
18. See Wilfrid Scawen Blunt, *The Land War in Ireland* (London, 1912), a diary entry for 10 January 1886, p. 18; Sir Arthur Hardinge, *The Life of H.H. Molyneux Herbert, Fourth Earl of Carnarvon* (Oxford, 1925), vol. 3, pp. 175–6; A.B. Cooke and J.R. Vincent (eds.), *Lord Carlingford's Journal: Reflections of a Cabinet Minister 1885* (Oxford 1971), p. 128, n. 2. For a sensitive treatment of Gibson's career, see A.B. Cooke's introduction to *Calendar of the Ashbourne Papers*; also A.B. Cooke and J.R. Vincent (eds.), 'Ireland and Party Politics 1885–1887: An Unpublished Conservative Memoir', part 2, *Irish Historical Studies*, vol. 16, no. 63 (March 1969), pp. 330–33.
19. He refused to dine with anyone who had broken bread with Parnell, and made a famous retort to Lady Aberdeen when she remarked on the large turn-out of Home Rulers at a Castle function during the Union of Hearts period: 'Not at all, your excellency; barring yourself and the waiters, there's not a home-ruler in the room.' None the less, his cynicism about the English administration of Ireland continued; a family pastime was poking fun at the earnest deputations who visited their home at Spiddal on tours of the Congested Districts (Maud Wynne, *An Irishman and His Family: Lord Morris and Killanin*, p. 90).

20. For Portarlington's relations with his tenants, and his genial view of their Land League activities, see *Weekly Irish Times*, 4 June 1881, and for his views on the Land Bill, a speech of 8 August 1881 reported in ibid., 13 August 1881.
21. Healy's biographer described him as a 'strong conservative': *Memories of Father Healy of Little Bray* (Anon., but actually W.J. Fitzpatrick; Dublin, 1896), p. 160. He was accused of exerting undue influence against Philip Callan in the 1874 Louth election. Also see Emmet Larkin, *The Roman Catholic Church and the Creation of the Modern Irish State 1878–1886* (Dublin and Philadelphia, 1975), pp. 271, 275.
22. An unnecessary precaution; Gladstone confined himself to the country-house circuit and the only sign of disturbance he noted was that somebody had cut down a tree planted by the Prince of Wales. See John Morley, *The Life of William Ewart Gladstone* (London, 1903), vol. 3, p. 571, and Agatha Ramm (ed.), *The Political Correspondence of Mr Gladstone and Lord Granville 1876–1886* (Oxford, 1961), vol. 1, pp. 54, 56.
23. T.P. O'Connor described it as 'moving the small world of Dublin to its depths', *Memories of an Old Parliamentarian* (London, 1929), vol. 1, p. 58. In March 1881 Churchill was still being attacked for having preached Home Rule while his father was Viceroy (see *Weekly Irish Times*, 19 March 1881).
24. *Weekly Freeman*, 22 February 1879.
25. See *Intermediate Education in Ireland: A Letter to Sir Bernard Burke, CB, Ulster, from Lord Randolph Churchill, MP* (Dublin, 1878). (Burke had been closely involved in negotiations between the Castle and the hierarchy; see Glos. RO D2455, PCC/52, 64.) Churchill wanted the Royal Free grammar schools greatly extended into a state system of intermediate education, available to Catholics, with the religion of the schoolmaster in charge of a school being dictated by that of 'the great proportion' of the surrounding population. The scheme also involved precautions like a conscience clause and competitive examinations for gratuitous instruction. In general, the embryonic state of organization of endowed schools was to be rationalized. Inefficient and exclusive foundations like that of Erasmus Smith were to be taken over, and the commission for endowed schools appointed in 1854 dissolved: 'they have never understood the importance of the duties committed to them, and much of the deplorable deficiency in higher education in Ireland must be laid directly at their door' (p. 18).
26. See *Reports from Commissioners, Inspectors and Others 1881, no. 21: Endowed Schools (Ireland)* [c. 2831, 2831–1], HC January–August 1881, xxxv; hereafter cited as *Report*.
27. He was accused of wishing to convert the Erasmus Smith endowment into a Roman Catholic charity (*Weekly Irish Times*, 12 April 1879); and

the whole tenor of his questioning was to condemn the inefficiency and haphazard approach of the 1854 commissioners (see *Report*, vol. 1, pp. 118–19, and vol. 2, pp. 186–7), especially in the management of estates (ibid., vol. 1, pp. 22–3). Many Catholic schools were examined (though many held themselves as not coming under the provenance of the commission); those investigated generally performed impressively, and the thorough, utilitarian nature of the education provided by several of the religious orders obviously appealed to the commissioners (ibid., vol. 1, p. 132); the work of social stabilizing carried out by an institution like St Stanislaus's, Tullamore, was greatly admired. However, the only endowed school which occasioned an unsolicited favourable judgement from Churchill was the Quaker boarding school at Newtown, Waterford: 'it would be fortunate for the Irish people if all their schools were as well managed as yours' (ibid., vol. 2, p. 449).

28. Who recommended nothing more radical than a ladies' charity; see memo of a correspondence between Sir Bernard Burke and Churchill ([n.d.], Blenheim MSS D/1/9); also letters to Duchess from William Gregory and Colonel King-Harman, September–December 1879 (Blenheim MSS D/1/1).
29. Gregory to Duchess of Marlborough, 14 February 1880 (Blenheim MSS D/1/7). For exchanges between the two funds, see newspapers for April–May 1880.
30. See *Weekly Freeman*, 31 January 1880; T.M. Healy, *Letters and Leaders of My Day* (London, 1928), vol. 1, p. 79; William O'Brien, *Recollections* (London, 1905), p. 185.
31. The episode remains preserved in a series of hysterical letters from J.C. Meredith, a trustee of the fund, to the duchess throughout May 1880 (Blenheim MSS D/1/11).
32. See a long memorandum in Churchill's writing ([n.d.], Blenheim MSS D/1).
33. See correspondence with Lord Lytton (Blenheim MSS D/1/8).
34. See for instance Gregory to Duchess of Marlborough, 15 June 1880 (Blenheim MSS D/1/11): 'He – Lord R. – is a very clever fellow, but I wish with all my heart that he would take a higher line than skirmishing . . . Forgive my venturing to interfere, but you know how high is my opinion of his ability, and that opinion was not lightly formed. I like him so much moreover that I want the world to rightly estimate him and to see that he can act as well in heavy armour as in light.'
35. A remark of Wolseley's; *Memories of Father Healy of Little Bray*, p. 216.
36. Maud Wynne, *An Irishman and His Family: Lord Morris and Killanin*, p. 97.
37. FitzGibbon to Churchill, 23 December 1888 (RCP 1/xxiii/3032).

38. As for instance in April 1883, over the debate on the criminal code; see 'Parliamentary Progress' in column in *Weekly Freeman*, 21 April 1883.
39. He was prepared to call for Davitt's arrest in January 1881, to embarrass the government; see *Weekly Freeman*, 17 February 1881.
40. Gorst to Churchill, 2 November 1880 (RCP 1/i/19).
41. Northcote to Gibson, 7 November 1881 (HLRO, Ashbourne Papers B/71/16).
42. For Gorst's general ideas, see a long letter to Churchill, 21 October 1881 (RCP 1/i/52), reporting enthusiastically on the chances for a Conservative initiative in Ireland. On 29 January 1883 (RCP 1/i/105) he wrote a long letter anticipating that the Home Rulers would get their way in the end, and suggesting anticipating them with a scheme of federal devolution. He was also a friend of the shady Philip Callan.
43. See Wolff to Churchill, 28 May 1886 (RCP 1/xii/1514); 'You will see that when the Irish get home rule they will split into two parties and the protestants will have the whip hand.' In October 1885 he sent Churchill (at the latter's request) a long memorandum urging that if Home Rule was taken up 'before it is forced on you, it might be carried out satisfactorily'. He pointed to the Hungarian experiment, and held no fears for the Protestant interest (memorandum dated 9 October 1885, RCP 1/vii/961).
44. For Churchill's remarks about Home Rule at this period, see letter to Morris, 23 October 1884 (Maud Wynne, *An Irishman and His Family: Lord Morris and Killanin*, p. 120), and, more seriously, Healy's statement that Churchill 'spoke vaguely about home rule' to his Irish contacts in 1885 (Algar Thorold, *The Life of Henry Labouchère*, London, 1913, p. 231). Frank Hugh O'Donnell refers to him as an 'ally' (*A History of the Irish Parliamentary Party*, London, 1910, vol. 1, pp. 486–7, vol. 2, p. 186); and William O'Brien recalled the common ground between the Fourth Party and the Irish, and the inability of Liberals to understand the warmth of their relationship, which did not follow the normal course of British party politics (*Evening Memories*, London, 1920, pp. 82–3).
45. T.M. Healy, *Letters and Leaders of My Day*, vol. 1, p. 155.
46. Asking, for instance, why he did not arrest Archbishop Croke as well as Father Sheehy; see *Weekly Irish Times*, 28 May 1881.
47. See Hansard 3, cclxiv, 138–47, reporting debate of 29 July 1881; also W.H. Smith to Churchill, 27 July 1881 (RCP 1/i/45).
48. He spoke for it in 1877, against it in 1879, and supported it again in 1884. His opposition of Brodrick's motion to exclude the Irish from franchise extension was closely connected with his simultaneous dealings with Healy and Parnell over Beach's motion of censure on the Egyptian question (W. St John Brodrick, Earl of Midleton, *Records and Reactions*,

London, 1934, p. 62; also see Andrew Jones, *The Politics of Reform 1884*, Cambridge, 1971, pp. 128–9). It was at this time, Churchill later told Henry James, that Parnell 'came several times to my house' and 'arranged many things . . . the most perfect confidence existing between us' (A.B. Cooke and J.R. Vincent, *Lord Carlingford's Journal: Reflections of a Cabinet Minister 1885*, pp. 129–30, n. 2). For further references to Churchill's constant negotiations with the Irish, see D.W.R. Bahlman (ed.), *The Diary of Sir Edward Walter Hamilton* (Oxford, 1972), vol. 2, pp. 617, 712; and A.B. Cooke and J.R. Vincent, as cited above.

49. See leader in *Weekly Freeman*, 24 May 1884.
50. FitzGibbon to Churchill, 9 September 1885 (RCP 1/vii/883).
51. Molloy had pressed the question on Churchill from late June (Molloy to Churchill, 26 June 1885, RCP 1/v/651). For details of Catholic organization at the time, see Emmet Larkin, *The Roman Catholic Church and the Creation of the Modern Irish State 1878–1886*, pp. 304, 314–15; and for Holmes's part, A.B. Cooke and J.R. Vincent, 'Ireland and Party Politics 1885–1887: An Unpublished Conservative Memoir', part 1, *Irish Historical Studies*, vol. 16, no. 62 (September 1968), pp. 154, 160–61. FitzGibbon had insisted on coming over at once, though Churchill had not been very receptive (see FitzGibbon to Churchill, 5 August 1885, RCP 1/vi/772). Dwyer Gray communicated Catholic discontent to Churchill on 23 August, nine days after the measure passed (RCP 1/vii/825); also Emmet Larkin, pp. 320–22.
52. Walsh objected to the membership of the commission, which he felt under-represented the Catholic interest. See Emmet Larkin, *The Roman Catholic Church and the Creation of the Modern Irish State 1878–1886*, pp. 320–22; FitzGibbon to Churchill, 1 September 1885 (RCP 1/vii/853), 9 September 1885 (RCP 1/vii/883), 11 October 1885 (RCP 1/viii/967), 13 September 1885 (RCP 1/vii/971); also Carnarvon to Churchill, 16 October 1885 (RCP 1/viii/980), Larkin, p. 328 and Labouchère to Chamberlain, 23 December 1885, in Algar Thorold, *The Life of Henry Labouchère*, p. 252.
53. 'It is to the bishops entirely to whom [*sic*] I look in the future to turn, to mitigate, or to postpone the home rule onslaught' (W.S. Churchill, *Lord Randolph Churchill*, vol. 2, p. 4).
54. FitzGibbon to Churchill, 16 January 1886 (RCP 1/xi/1354).
55. 'The existence of the imperialists and Protestants (other than landowners) of Ireland depends on the maintenance of the higher education now offered them in the University of Dublin' (FitzGibbon to Churchill, 16 February 1886, RCP 1/xii/1380). He went on to give instances of lawyers and other professional men leaving Dublin in order to ensure their children an education in England.

56. See Wilfrid Scawen Blunt, *The Land War in Ireland*, p. 183, and Labouchère to Chamberlain, 1 December 1885 (Algar Thorold, *The Life of Henry Labouchère*, p. 244).
57. Callan to Churchill, 19 November 1885 and 27 November 1885 (RCP 1/ix/1070, 1105). Of Parnell he wrote, '*He* has not a few secrets, and they are very well kept.'
58. Manning to Churchill, 15 January 1886 (RCP 1/xi/1277).
59. See Labouchère to Churchill, 31 December 1886 (RCP 1/xviii/2274) and Alfred Rothschild to Churchill, 25 September 1886 (RCP 1/xvi/1842).
60. This conceit appears in a letter from Blunt to Churchill, 19 June 1884 (RCP 1/iii/412). For a characteristic reference to Blunt's *naïveté*, see Gorst to Churchill, 24 December 1883 (RCP 1/ii/230). Blunt was convinced that Churchill had unequivocally declared to him in 1885 his support for Home Rule. Up to January 1886 he believed, and was told by others, that Churchill's intention was to educate his party in this direction (*The Land War in Ireland*, pp. 1, 18, 20, 34, 140, 143). Blunt even believed Churchill had converted a group of Cambridge undergraduates to Home Rule (ibid., p. 24). When Winston Churchill's life of his father appeared in 1906, Blunt's chief criticism was that the book obscured Churchill's initial commitment to Home Rule (Wilfrid Scawen Blunt, *My Diaries, being a Personal Narrative of Events 1888–1914*, London, 1919, vol. 2, p. 128).
61. See A.B. Forwood to Churchill, 11 and 21 May 1884 (RCP 1/iii/377, 395), asking him to stop cultivating Parnell and warning him that the anti-Irish Conservative working men were being alienated.
62. 'Your appointment would be *such* a popular one in Ireland, especially with all the Roman Catholic party . . . The fact is, *you* are the only conservative leader who understands this country. All the others are really in full ignorance of it. They have *never been* over here, and look at all Irish matters from a purely *English* point of view' (Portarlington to Churchill, 'June 1885' (RCP 1/v/629).
63. See Churchill to Salisbury, 16 January 1886 (W.S. Churchill, *Lord Randolph Churchill*, vol. 2, p. 36); also A.B. Cooke and J.R. Vincent, 'Ireland and Party Politics 1885–1887: An Unpublished Conservative Memoir', part 2, p. 329.
64. Morris to Churchill, 5 December 1885 (RCP 1/x/1137) and Churchill to Morris, 7 December 1885 (Maud Wynne, *An Irishman and His Family: Lord Morris and Killanin* and RCP 1/x/445).
65. There remains only the national question – *for heaven's sake don't touch it!* It is red hot. If Parnell takes it up, he must either formulate a demand for total separation, on which whig and tory must join in giving him a facer, or by some recognition

of a continuation of the English connection alienate his extreme followers, who even now are only with difficulty induced to put up with the constitutional method of promoting Irish independence. If Gladstone takes it up he must split with either the Irish or the whigs, whom the counties have returned in force – if an attempt is made to compel you to take it up you can meet it by requiring, as Gladstone did, those who have the mandate to formulate the demand, and at the worst you need only an inquiry, pending which the waste and disintegration which time brings with it will go on, and your university bill with your other measures move on in peace . . .

(FitzGibbon to Churchill, 7 December 1885, RCP 1/x/1149). A postscript warned Churchill against any thought of coalition. See also same to same, 11 December 1885 (RCP 1/x/1161).

66. See, for instance, Gavan Duffy's article in the *National Review*, January 1885, pp. 721–40, urging the Conservatives to take up the Irish question; a similar case was presented by Henry Bellingham in the *St Stephen's Review*, January 1886. MPs such as Justin McCarthy were similarly inclined; and as late as October 1885 Davitt was telling Labouchère of an influential lobby within the Irish Parliamentary Party who would prefer a Conservative Home Rule Bill to a Liberal one, largely because of the Conservatives' record on denominational education (Algar Thorold, *The Life of Henry Labouchère*, p. 234).
67. H. Rochfort to Churchill, 9 July 1885 (RCP 1/vi/681).
68. This incident, so Spencer told many people, led him to accept Home Rule, as an alternative to Irish law and order becoming a party shuttle-cock. See W. St John Brodrick, *Records and Reactions*, p. 63, and Sir John Ross, *The Years of My Pilgrimage*, p. 177. In England, people assumed that it indicated a formal Tory–Parnellite alliance; in Ireland, Carnarvon was inaccurately identified with the action (see Emmet Larkin, *The Roman Catholic Church and the Creation of the Modern Irish State 1878–1886*, p. 318).
69. This is quoted in W.S. Churchill, *Lord Randolph Churchill*, vol. 1, pp. 459–61, and probably came from a letter to the author by Holmes himself.
70. Rather than 'spasms' or 'a dribbling crescendo', he wanted a measure 'unlimited in duration and such as will make trivial overt acts summarily punishable wherever committed and enable serious cases to be tried by special juries' (FitzGibbon to Churchill, 16 and 18 January 1886, RCP 1/xi/1354–5); essentially the view taken by Spencer and his associates a year earlier. At the same time Churchill was writing to Salisbury in much the same vein, but ended by accepting the 'orthodox coercion line' (see A.B. Cooke and J.R. Vincent, 'Ireland and Party Politics 1885–1887: An

Unpublished Conservative Memoir', part 3, *Irish Historical Studies*, vol. 16, no. 64 (September 1969), p. 454. Having come round to Salisbury's way of thinking, Churchill brought pressure to bear on Beach too (see letters between Churchill and Salisbury, 16 January 1886, RCP 1/xi/1302a, 1302b; also Beach to Churchill, 17 January 1886, RCP 1/xi/1305). On 24 January Salisbury told the Queen that Churchill had come round to open coercion 'under party pressure' (*Letters of Queen Victoria*, third series, vol. 1, p. 17); on 26 January, as soon as the government fell, Churchill offered himself to Saunderson for a Belfast trip.

71. See A.B. Cooke and J.R. Vincent, 'Ireland and Party Politics 1885–1887: An Unpublished Conservative Memoir', part 1, pp. 168–9. Churchill had already scandalized Holmes with the notion of arresting the Irish Members on the charge of high treason, and Sir Algernon Bourke had relayed similar ideas to an equally horrified Wilfrid Scawen Blunt five days before the cabinet of 15 January (*The Land War in Ireland*, p. 18). For Carnarvon's reactions to Churchill's 'extraordinary proposals' at the Cabinet meeting, see Sir Arthur Hardinge, *The Life of H.H. Molyneux Herbert, Fourth Earl of Carnarvon*, vol. 3, pp. 211–12.
72. James to Churchill, 30 January 1886 (RCP 1/xi/1349).
73. Justin McCarthy, *Reminiscences* (London, 1899), vol. 1, p. 437.
74. 5 November 1880, HLRO, Ashbourne Papers B/32/1.
75. 'You always will ignore the fact that more than two-thirds the education and *all* the love of England and of law and order, not to mention three-quarters of the property not yet relegated to the laws of Jupiter and Saturn, though probably *en route* thither, belonging to Ireland, is not included in the average Englishman's definition of "the Irish"' (FitzGibbon to Churchill, 11 October 1883, RCP 1/ii/181). Later he argued for a 'local orange university' for Belfast to make her 'the capital of culture, as she claims to be of loyalty' (same to same, 7 December 1885, RCP 1/x/1149).
76. Beach to Churchill, 25 September 1885 (RCP 1/viii/919).
77. Northcote to Ashbourne, 5 September 1883 (HLRO, Ashborne Papers B/71/26).
78. See, for instance, 'Parliamentary Correspondence' in *Weekly Freeman* throughout January 1886, and a widely quoted article by T.M. Healy in *Contemporary Review*, November 1885, pp. 723–31.
79. Churchill to Salisbury, 16 November 1885 (Salisbury MSS, Hatfield House, class E); Salisbury vaguely agreed, but kept clear (Salisbury to Churchill, 16 November 1885, RCP 1/ix/1066a).
80. Wilfrid Scawen Blunt, *The Land War in Ireland*, diary entry for 8 December 1885, p. 6.
81. Saunderson's biographer states that FitzGibbon effected the introduction

(R.V. Lucas, *Colonel Saunderson, MP: A Memoir* (London, 1908), p. 239); Holmes claimed in his unpublished memoir that he arranged the meeting (A.B. Cooke and J.R. Vincent, 'Ireland and Party Politics 1885–1887: An Unpublished Conservative Memoir', part 1, p. 119).

82. See Churchill to John O'Shea, 18 February 1886 (RCP 1/xii/1787). Bound in with his papers of this time are to be found copies of his father's die-hard pronouncements after 1880 (RCP 1/xi/1310).
83. 'He had fought side by side with the Irish party through many a hard battle in the House of Commons. His flippant jeer was almost as much dreaded by the dull Orange wing as the sledgehammer blows of Healy, or the scathing eloquence of Sexton' (*Weekly Freeman*, 20 February 1886).
84. 'That dismissal, of which in my opinion Lord Rossmore may be proud, is but one of many proofs of the strong sympathy which has all along existed between her majesty's advisers and the Irish revolutionary party' (Churchill to Hill, 17 January 1884, RCP 1/ii/259).
85. J. Wallace Taylor, *The Rossmore Incident* (Dublin, 1884), pp. 62, 64, 79, 96, 98, 145, 146, 154.
86. 8 February 1884. This exchange, though reported at length in the *Weekly Irish Times*, 16 February 1884, does not appear in Hansard.
87. *Weekly Freeman*, 28 November 1883. See also *Weekly Examiner and Ulster Weekly News*, 18 January 1886, where he is taken to task for incitement. Also, for a notably anti-Catholic speech delivered at Glaslough on 6 January 1886, see *Belfast Newsletter*, 6 January 1886.
88. Hamilton to Churchill, 17 September 1885 (RCP 1/viii/1898). For Hamilton's association with Churchill, whom he did not personally like, see his *Parliamentary Reminiscences and Reflections* (vol. 1, London, 1916; vol. 2, London, 1922), vol. 1, pp. 204, 279, vol. 2, pp. 20–21.
89. As a child he had had a Jesuit tutor in the South of France (see R.V. Lucas, *Colonel Saunderson, MP: A Memoir*).
90. See ibid., p. 91; Callan is not named, but the circumstantial evidence is overwhelming.
91. Ibid., p. 96. For a detailed analysis of Saunderson's part in these negotiations, see Alvin Jackson, *The Ulster Party: Irish Unionists in the House of Commons 1884–1911* (Oxford, 1989), chapter 2.
92. See a letter from Johnston in *Belfast Newsletter*, 9 February 1886; also comments in *Weekly Examiner and Ulster Weekly News*, 13 February 1886.
93. See Northcote's diary for 6 October 1883 in A.B. Cooke, 'A Conservative Party Leader in Ulster: Sir Stafford Northcote's Diary of a Visit to the Province, October 1883', *Proceedings of the Royal Irish Academy*, vol. 75, sect. C, no. 4 (1975), p. 79.
94. Apropos of his action over the Irish franchise; see *Weekly Examiner and Ulster Weekly News*, 6 February 1886.

95. The details below come from contemporary newspapers, the fullest report being in the *Belfast Newsletter*, 23 February 1886.
96. He emphasized, for instance, that Parnell's party never represented a majority of Irish opinion; but see L.J. Jennings, *The Speeches of Lord Randolph Churchill* (London, 1889), vol. 2, p. 44, for a speech at Hull on 31 October 1881 ('There is only a very small section of the Irish people which does not gladly follow Mr Parnell') and also his speech about Irish education in the House of Commons, 6 August 1884, when he had remarked that 'the Irish gentlemen who sat behind him in that quarter of the House represented entirely and completely the feelings of the whole democratic and Catholic population of the country' (*Weekly Freeman*, 9 August 1884).
97. A.B. Cooke and J.R. Vincent, *The Governing Passion: Cabinet Government and Party Politics in Britain 1885–1886* (Hassocks, 1974), p. 377; for an analysis of the immediate political considerations governing his Belfast visit, see ibid., pp. 76–7.
98. The *Weekly Examiner and Ulster Weekly News* emphasized the lack of Unionist celebrities, describing Rossmore and Johnston as 'a shallow celebrity and a dismissed mackerel inspector' (27 February 1886).
99. William O'Brien recalls a cheery exchange with Churchill about the Belfast visit immediately after his return (*Evening Memories*, London, 1920, p. 113), though elsewhere he subscribed to the orthodox horror at 'the Orangemen, maddened by the guilty incitements of Churchill, drenching the streets of Belfast with blood' (ibid., p. 154). For Blunt's scandalized reaction, see *The Land War in Ireland*, pp. 31–2.
100. See A.T.Q. Stewart, *The Narrow Ground: Aspects of Ulster 1609–1969* (London, 1977), p. 166, and Joseph Lee, *The Modernization of Irish Society 1848–1918* (Dublin, 1973), pp. 132–3.
101. Henry FitzGibbon to Churchill, 22 February 1886 (RCP 1/xii/1386). Gerald's youngest brother, he became President of the Royal College of Surgeons in Ireland and died in 1912.
102. Ibid. At a later stage Gerald FitzGibbon believed that Churchill's disingenuous appeal to loyal Catholics had had the effect of converting numbers of them to Unionism (letter of 26 September 1890, RCP 1/xxvi/3640).
103. Saunderson to Churchill, 10 August 1886 (RCP1/xiv/1653). Also see same to same, 23 June 1886 (RCP 1/xiii/1549), for a commanding letter about electoral matters in Ulster; and Deramore to Churchill, 9 August 1886 (RCP 1/xiv/1648). Churchill's reactions were invariably evasive. He may have exerted some moderating influence; it is interesting to find Kane writing to him about conciliatory ideas on Irish policy to trump the Home Rulers (Kane to Churchill [n.d. but late 1886], RCP 1/xii/

1571). But this was not typical. For Saunderson's reaction to Churchill's attempts to quieten him see R.V. Lucas, *Colonel Saunderson, MP: A Memoir*, pp. 112–13.

104. See Churchill to Gibson, 30 September 1886 (HLRO, Ashbourne Papers B/32/4): 'Those Belfast beggars keep simmering, I wish they would settle down'; and Churchill to Morris, 6 September 1886, complaining about the 'proceedings and manners of Ulster *soi-disant* tories' (Maud Wynne, *An Irishman and His Family: Lord Morris and Killanin*, p. 116).
105. Abercorn to Salisbury, 20 December 1886, Salisbury MSS; for Saunderson's reaction, see Saunderson to Churchill, 12 January 1887 (RCP 1/xix/2333).
106. See Labouchère to Churchill, 'Sunday' (early January 1887) and 19 January 1887 (RCP 1/xviii/2289 and 1/xix/2394).
107. R. Kelly to E. Wilmot, 18 August 1889 (RCP 1/xxiv/3247) and FitzGibbon to Churchill, 10 January 1892 (RCP 1/xxvii/3793). Churchill's Tory Democrat supporters were equally worried, Louis Jennings frequently begging him to concentrate instead upon 'the decent English workman' (Jennings to Churchill, 24 November 1889, RCP 1/xiv/3733).
108. Now in NLI MS 2080; many similar ideas are to be found in FitzGibbon's letters to Churchill throughout 1889.
109. FitzGibbon to Churchill, 3 February 1888 (RCP 1/xxii/2810). This same scene is memorialized, oddly, in *Ulysses*: Bloom remembers climbing a tree in Northumberland Road to view the procession on 2 February 1888.
110. Same to same, 19 February 1888 (RCP 1/xxii/2823).
111. Ibid.
112. Winston Churchill, 'The Dream', in Martin Gilbert, *Winston Spencer Churchill*, vol. 8 (London, 1987), reprinted in J. Gross (ed.), *The Oxford Book of Essays* (Oxford, 1991), pp. 362–71.
113. Ibid., p. 362.
114. Ibid., p. 366.

13 Thinking from Hand to Mouth: Anglo-Irish Literature, Gaelic Nationalism and Irish Politics in the 1890s

1. *History of England* (Albany edition, 1898), chapter 3, p. 425.
2. *The Irish Question* (third edition, London, 1975), pp. 243, 246.
3. John Eglinton, *Irish Literary Portraits* (London, 1935), p. 20.

4. See especially his *Culture and Anarchy in Ireland 1890–1939* (Oxford, 1979), pp. 51ff.
5. See especially O'Brien's brilliant and seminal 'Passion and Cunning: An Essay on the Politics of W.B. Yeats' in A. Norman Jeffares and K.G.W. Cross (eds.), *In Excited Reverie: A Centenary Tribute to William Butler Yeats 1865–1939* (London, 1965). 'In the nineties and in the early years of the new century "the literary side of the movement" was the only side that was moving and its leader was Yeats . . . the politician Yeats was about the poetry business, using for the ends of poetry the political energy diverted by the fall of Parnell' (p. 220). The same theme of diversion is to be found in Richard Ellmann, *Yeats: The Man and the Masks* (second edition, Oxford, 1979), p. 100: 'All the patriotism which Parnell's earlier successes had encouraged was now ready to be diverted elsewhere.' George Dangerfield also adopted it in *The Damnable Question: A Study in Anglo-Irish Relations* (London, 1977), though it is Standish O'Grady's *History of Ireland: Heroic Period* (1878) that Dangerfield places 'somewhere at the heart of the Easter Rising of 1916' (p. 30).
6. Reprinted in *Autobiographies* (London, 1955), p. 559.
7. Hansard 4, viii, 1250–51, 12 February 1893.
8. See Andrew Gailey, 'Unionist Rhetoric and Irish Local Government Reform 1895–1899', *Irish Historical Studies*, vol. 24, no. 93 (1984), pp. 52–68.
9. By James L. McLoughlin; see vol. 5 (1896), no. 1, pp. 26–38; and no. 2, pp. 81–94.
10. Ibid., vol. 6 (October 1896), pp. 109–12.
11. See, for example, vol. 5 (May 1896), pp. 129–41; (August 1896), pp. 729–38.
12. Thus Alfred Webb to J.F.X. O'Brien in 1897: 'What is going on is *talk* about the past and inactivity regarding the present. We went to war for Home Rule and should continue that war each in our way as best we may . . . We have the evicted with us and we are letting them starve . . . in fact Horse Racing, cycling and other amusements is what the country is most eager about at present.' In which he probably also included collecting fairy lore, playing hurley and reviving the Irish language. J.V. O'Brien, *William O'Brien and the Course of Irish Politics 1881–1918* (London, 1976), p. 10.
13. See Paul Bew, *Conflict and Conciliation in Ireland 1890–1910: Parnellites and Radical Agrarians* (Oxford, 1987); Sally Warwick-Haller, *William O'Brien and the Irish Land War* (Dublin, 1990); Philip Bull, 'The Reconstruction of the Irish Parliamentary Movement 1895–1903' (Ph.D., Cambridge, 1977). Also, for the All-for-Ireland League, Brendan Clifford, *Reprints from the Cork Free Press 1910–1916: An Account of Ireland's Only Democratic Anti-Partition Movement* (Cork and Belfast, 1984).

14. J.V. O'Brien, *William O'Brien and the Course of Irish Politics 1881–1918*, p. 112.
15. See Michael D. Higgins and John P. Gibbons, 'Shopkeeper-graziers and Land Agitation in Ireland 1895–1900' in P.J. Drudy (ed.), *Ireland: Land, Politics and People* (Cambridge, 1982), especially pp. 100–101.
16. *Autobiographies*, pp. 358–9.
17. Ibid., p. 195.
18. Ibid., p. 225.
19. R.M. Henry, *The Evolution of Sinn Féin* (Dublin [n.d. but probably 1920]), pp. 36–7.
20. See *Autobiographies*, p. 362. 'I dreaded some wild Fenian movement, and with literature perhaps more in my mind than politics, dreamed of that unity of culture which might begin with some few men controlling some form of administration.'
21. *Ireland in the New Century* (Dublin, second edition, 1905), p. 79. Plunkett, of course, had his reasons for taking this view, as he had to present agricultural and industrial co-operation as unpolitical and therefore unthreatening. Thus he saw the 1890s as repudiating political sterility: 'In practical England the Irish Question became the political issue, while in sentimental Ireland there set in a reaction from politics and an inclination to be practical.'
22. R.V. Comerford, *The Fenians in Context* (Dublin, 1984), p. 194.
23. D.R. Gwynn, *The Life of John Redmond* (London, 1932), p. 152. It should be said that Redmond had to play the nationalist card in order to ensure such support: see Horace Plunkett, *Ireland in the New Century*, pp. 310–11, for Redmond's public letter declaring that Home Rule had to come before the revival of industry and attacking Plunkett's book.
24. According, that is, to Michael Davitt; see J.V. O'Brien, *William O'Brien and the Course of Irish Politics 1881–1918*, p. 111.
25. *New Review*, February 1897.
26. *Celt*, 1 August 1857, p. 5, and leader in ibid., June 1858.
27. As with A.P. Graves, J.H. Cousins, William Larminie, Shane Leslie – and for that matter Standish James O'Grady. A point missed by Martin Williams in his interesting 'Ancient Mythology and Revolutionary Ideology in Ireland 1878–1916', *Historical Journal*, vol. 26, no. 2 (1983), pp. 307–28.
28. *The Revival of Irish Literature: Addresses by Sir Charles Gavan Duffy, KCMG, Dr George Sigerson, and Dr Douglas Hyde* (London, 1894), p. 120.
29. John Kelly and Eric Domville (eds.), *The Collected Letters of W.B. Yeats. Vol. 1: 1865–1895* (Oxford, 1986), p. 338: W.B. Yeats to the editor of *United Ireland*, 17 December 1892.
30. See Michael Tierney, *Eoin MacNeill: Scholar and Man of Action 1876–1945* (Oxford, 1981), p. 19.

31. L. Ó Broin, *Revolutionary Underground: The Story of the Irish Republican Brotherhood 1858–1924* (Dublin, 1976), p. 88.
32. Ibid., p. 49.
33. Ibid., p. 50.
34. R.V. Comerford, *The Fenians in Context*, p. 204.
35. Ibid., pp. 212–13.
36. Michael Tierney, *Eoin MacNeill: Scholar and Man of Action 1876–1945*, pp. 22–3.
37. The nature of Irish Anglophobia has rarely been examined systematically, much as the Catholic confessionalism of Irish nationalism has not often been analysed. Comerford puts it with characteristic forcefulness: 'The creators and custodians of mainstream Irish mythology have succeeded over a period of generations in blurring recognition of a salient fact about Irish nationalism, namely, that since the early nineteenth century at least it has been essentially an expression of the felt needs, social and psychological, of the Irish Catholic body, including their apparent need to challenge other Christians on the island in various ways' (*The Fenians in Context*, p. 30). This is refreshing, but demands some examination of the extent to which this challenge was itself a historical response.
38. L. Ó Broin, *Revolutionary Underground: The Story of the Irish Republican Brotherhood 1858–1924*, p. 117.
39. George Moore, *Hail and Farewell* (1976 edition of the 1933 version, edited by Richard Cave, Gerrards Cross), p. 587.
40. L. Ó Broin, *Revolutionary Underground: The Story of the Irish Republican Brotherhood 1858–1924*, p. 125.
41. *Essays and Introductions* (London, 1961), p. 248.
42. Speech in New York, 1903–4, quoted in E. Cullingford, *Yeats, Ireland and Fascism* (London, 1981), p. 25. Ironically, Parnell would not have agreed; his great ambition was to link the coal mines of Kilkenny with the iron-ore of Wicklow by means of railways, and create something like the 'Black Country' of Pennsylvania, which he greatly admired. See my *Charles Stewart Parnell: The Man and His Family* (Hassocks, 1976), p. 165.
43. *Autobiographies*, p. 233.
44. Referring to a play in Irish in *Samhain*, October 1901, he tempered his judgement: 'although I had not Irish enough to follow it when I saw it played . . .' Subsequently he passed judgement on Father Dineen's *Creideamh agus Gorta* as 'the best Gaelic play after Dr Hyde's'. In a letter to the editor of the *Gael* of November 1899, he remarked how well he was getting on with learning Irish. But it seems to have remained at the level of intention.
45. John Kelly and Eric Domville (eds.), *The Collected Letters of W.B. Yeats*, vol. 1, pp. 455, 399.

46. Richard Ellmann, *Yeats: The Man and the Masks*, p. 97.
47. Malcolm Brown, *The Politics of Irish Literature from Thomas Davis to W.B. Yeats* (London, 1972), pp. 374ff.
48. John Kelly, 'Aesthete among the Athletes: Yeats's Contributions to *The Gael*', in *Yeats: An Annual of Critical and Textual Studies*, vol. 2 (1984), pp. 128–9.
49. *Autobiographies*, p. 199. He wrote at the time, in a letter of 27 January 1899 to the editor of the *Daily Chronicle*, that 'the lull in the political life of Ireland has been followed, among the few, by an intellectual excitement so remarkable that a learned German is writing a book about it; and among the many, by that strange sense of something going to happen which has always in all countries given the few their opportunity.' But the opportunity is an artistic one, and the whole letter is about art, not politics.
50. D.P. Moran, *The Philosophy of Irish Ireland* (Dublin, 1905), p. 11.
51. Ibid., p. 48.
52. Ibid., p. 36.
53. Ibid., p. 57.
54. Cf., ironically, Synge's nationalism as interpreted by Stephen MacKenna:

    I judged Synge intensely, though not practically, national. He couldn't endure the lies that gathered round all the political movement, flamed or rather turned a filthy yellow with rage over them, gently hated Miss Gonne for those she launched or tolerated, loathed the Gaelic League for ever on the score of one pamphlet in which someone, speaking really a half truth, had urged the youth of Ireland to learn modern Irish because it would give them access to the grand old saga literature: I have never forgotten the bale in his eyes when he read this and told me, 'That's a bloody lie: long after they know modern Irish, which they'll never know, they'll still be miles and years from any power over the saga.'

    (E.R. Dodds, ed., *Journals and Letters of Stephen MacKenna*, London, 1936, p. 39.)
55. See R.M. Henry, *The Evolution of Sinn Féin*, p. 86.
56. See Declan Kiberd, 'The Perils of Nostalgia: A Critique of the Revival' in P. Connolly (ed.), *Literature and the Changing Ireland: Irish Literary Studies 9* (Gerrards Cross, 1982), pp. 3–4.
57. 'I have been trying in *An Claidheamh Soluis* to promote a closer comradeship between the Gaelic League and the Irish National Theatre and Anglo-Irish writers generally. After all we are all allies' (S.Ó. Buachalla, *The Letters of P.H. Pearse*, Gerrards Cross, 1980, p. 94). For the earlier references, see his letter to the editor of *An Claidheamh Soluis*, 13 May 1889, ibid., pp. 8–9.
58. Oddly, this vision would have been shared by Parnell, according to his

widow. See interview in *Daily Express*, 18 May 1914, quoted above, p. 128.

59. Cf. R.M. Henry, writing before hindsight in 1920. 'The months before the European War broke out saw Nationalist Ireland practically unanimous in its support of the Home Rule legislation of the Liberal Government, ready to be reckoned as a part of the British Empire, prepared to acknowledge the supremacy of the Imperial Parliament, content with an Irish parliament charged only with the control of a number of matters of domestic concern' (*The Evolution of Sinn Féin*, p. 279).
60. Seanad Éireann Debates, i, 8–20 (12 December 1922); quoted in Margaret O'Callaghan, 'Language, Nationality and Cultural Identity in the Irish Free State 1922–1927: The *Irish Statesman* and the *Catholic Bulletin* Reappraised', *Irish Historical Studies*, vol. 24, no. 94 (1984), p. 231.
61. Letter to the editor of *United Ireland*, 30 December 1893; John Kelly and Eric Domville (eds.), *The Collected Letters of W.B. Yeats*, vol. 1, p. 372.
62. 1978 preface to the second edition of Richard Ellmann's *Yeats: The Man and the Masks*.
63. A point well made in Malcolm Brown, *The Politics of Irish Literature from Thomas Davis to W.B. Yeats*, p. 362.

14 Marginal Men and Micks on the Make: The Uses of Irish Exile, *c.* 1840–1922

1. William Makepeace Thackeray, *The Irish Sketch-Book* (1843; vol. 7 of Smith, Elder & Co. edition of *Collected Works*, London, 1900), p. 264.
2. See especially Seamus Deane, *Heroic Styles: The Tradition of an Idea* in *Ireland's Field Day* (London, 1985), pp. 45–58. In this as in other recent texts the ideas of Franz Fanon and Alberto Memmi are translated to Ireland with deceptive ease; though parallels with the analysis of Ashis Nandy, *The Intimate Enemy: Loss and Recovery of Self under Colonialism* (Oxford, 1983) are perhaps more relevant.
3. See above, pp. 81–5, 90–94.
4. As in Shaun Richards and David Cairns, *Writing Ireland: Colonialism, Nationalism and Culture* (Manchester, 1988).
5. For an interesting survey of Irish careerism in India, see Scott B. Cook, 'The Irish Raj: Social Origins and Careers of Irishmen in the Indian Civil Service 1855–1914', *Journal of Social History*, vol. 20, no. 3 (1987).
6. 'Nuts and Nutcrackers IV', *Dublin University Magazine*, vol. 19, no. 113 (May 1842), pp. 63–4: I owe this reference to Joe Spence.

7. *Tales of the Munster Festivals* (London, 1927), vol. 1, pp. 345–51; my thanks to Tom Dunne for this reference.
8. The *Nation* survey has been edited by Alan O'Day as *A Survey of the Irish in England (1872)* (London, 1990). Also see David Fitzpatrick, 'A Curious Middle Place: The Irish in Britain 1871–1921' in Roger Swift and Sheridan Gilley (eds.), *The Irish in Britain 1815–1939* (London, 1989), pp. 12–13.
9. A good discussion of the recent literature will be found in David Fitzpatrick, 'Was Ireland Special? Recent Writing on Irish Economy and Society in the Nineteenth Century', *Historical Journal*, vol. 33, no. 1 (1990), pp. 169–76.
10. Quoted in David Fitzpatrick, *Irish Emigration 1801–1921*, Studies in Irish Economic and Social History No. 1 (Dundalk, 1984), p. 1.
11. The recent literature is too copious to list here. For guidance, see M. Hartigan, *The History of the Irish in Britain: A Bibliography* (London, 1986); the invaluable essays collected by Roger Swift and Sheridan Gilley in *The Irish in the Victorian City* (London, 1985) and *The Irish in Britain 1815–1939*; and Graham Davis, *The Irish in Britain 1815–1914* (Dublin, 1991).
12. Graham Davis, 'Little Irelands' in Roger Swift and Sheridan Gilley (eds.), *The Irish in Britain 1815–1939*, p. 107.
13. Sheridan Gilley, 'English Attitudes to the Irish in England 1789–1900' in C. Holmes (ed.), *Immigrants and Minorities in British Society* (London, 1978), p. 101.
14. See Jeffrey G. Williamson, 'The Impact of the Irish on British Labour Markets during the Industrial Revolution' in Roger Swift and Sheridan Gilley (eds.), *The Irish in Britain 1815–1939*, pp. 134–62.
15. J.M. Treble, 'The Irish Agitation' in J.T. Ward (ed.), *Popular Movements c. 1830–1850* (London, 1970); and, for a range of local references, Sheridan Gilley, 'English Attitudes to the Irish in England 1789–1900' in C. Holmes (ed.), *Immigrants and Minorities in British Society* (London, 1978), p. 103.
16. See Roger Swift, 'Crime and the Irish' in Roger Swift and Sheridan Gilley (eds.), *The Irish in Britain 1815–1939*, pp. 163–82, and 'The Outcast Irish in the British Victorian City: Problems and Perspectives', *Irish Historical Studies*, vol. 25, no. 99 (1987), p. 267.
17. According to Lyon Playfair in 1845; also see Graham Davis, 'Little Irelands' in Roger Swift and Sheridan Gilley (eds.), *The Irish in Britain 1815–1939*, p. 115.
18. See Colin Pooley, 'Segregation or Integration? The Residential Experience of the Irish in Mid-Victorian Britain' in Roger Swift and Sheridan Gilley, *The Irish in Britain 1815–1939*, pp. 60–83, and Roger Swift, 'The Outcast Irish in the British Victorian City', p. 267.

19. Nelson edition (London [n.d.]), pp. 381–7.
20. See Marx to Augustus Vogt, 9 April 1870 in Karl Marx and Friedrich Engels, *On Ireland and the Irish Question*, edited by Richard Dixon (London, 1971); I. Cummins, *Marx, Engels and National Movements* (London, 1980), p. 109; and W.O. Henderson and W.H. Chaloner's edition of Engels, *The Condition of the Working Class in England* (Oxford, 1971), chapter 5.
21. See above, 'Paddy and Mr Punch', for a consideration of this and reference to important work by L.P. Curtis and Sheridan Gilley.
22. Quoted in Roger Swift, 'The Outcast Irish in the British Victorian City', p. 271.
23. *Emigrants and Exiles: Ireland and the Irish Exodus to North America* (Oxford, 1985). For a critique of this approach, see D.H. Akenson, *Being Had: Historians, Evidence, and the Irish in North America* (Toronto, 1985).
24. Tighe Macmahon, petition to Colonial Office, 1825, quoted in Kerby Miller with Bruce Boling and David N. Doyle, 'Emigrants and Exiles: Irish Cultures and Irish Emigration to North America 1790–1922', *Irish Historical Studies*, vol. 22, no. 86 (1980), p. 107.
25. See Bob Reece (ed.), *Exiles from Erin: Convict Lives in Ireland and Australia* (Dublin, 1991) for a robust view of Irish opportunities in the Antipodes; and Janet Nolan, *Ourselves Alone: Women's Emigration from Ireland 1885–1920* (Lexington, Kentucky, 1989) for a picture of Irish American female emigrants for whom the motif was liberation rather than exile.
26. Of the *Press* and other London journals; there is a useful memoir of him in the *Journal of the Cork Archaeological and Historical Association*, second series, vol. 9 (1903), pp. 249–51.
27. When Gavan Duffy complimented him on the accuracy of the Irish references in *Barry Lyndon*, 'he said he had lived a good deal among Irish people in London and elsewhere'. He also accepted the legitimacy of the Young Ireland rebellion, 'if it had been successful', and admitted that if he had been an Irishman during the Famine, 'I would perhaps have done as you did'. Charles Gavan Duffy, *Conversations with Carlyle* (London, 1892), pp. 194–6.
28. *The Parnell Movement* (London, 1886), p. 100.
29. L.P. Brady, *T.P. O'Connor and the Liverpool Irish* (London, 1983), p. 21.
30. Justin McCarthy, *Reminiscences* (London, 1899), vol. 1, p. 15.
31. 'Fragment of Autobiography', in George Bernard Shaw, *The Matter with Ireland* (London, 1902), p. 10.
32. 'Reminiscences of My Irish Journey in 1849', *Century Illustrated Monthly Magazine*, vol. 24 (May–July 1882), part 3, p. 440. But a more sympathetic attitude towards Ireland is demonstrated in Duffy, *Conversations with Carlyle*: see pp. 45ff. for Duffy's version of the 'Irish Journey'.

33. *The Irish Sketch-Book*, p. 110.
34. Ibid., p. 558.
35. Anthony Trollope, *An Autobiography* (1883; London, 1946 edition), p. 68.
36. Victoria Glendinning, *Trollope* (London, 1991), p. 120.
37. These have been edited by Helen Garlinghouse King and published in the *Princeton University Library Chronicle*, vol. 26 (1964–5), pp. 71–101.
38. For Churchill and Ireland, see above, pp. 233–61.
39. See Sheridan Gilley, 'Frederick Lucas, Forerunner of Liberation Theology' in Stuart Mews (ed.), *Essays Presented to John Kent* (London, 1991). I am indebted to Dr Gilley for showing me an unpublished draft of this engrossing article.
40. W.E. Hughes, *Sophia Sturge: A Memoir* (London, 1940). My thanks to Dr Mary-Lou Legg for this reference.
41. Preface in Constable Collected Edition (London, 1930), p. ix.
42. Ibid., p. viii.
43. For Dowden, see Terence Brown, 'Edward Dowden: Irish Victorian' in *Ireland's Literature: Selected Essays* (Gigginstown, 1988); for Le Fanu, W.J. McCormack, *Sheridan Le Fanu and Victorian Ireland* (Oxford, 1980).
44. The great exception is Tom Garvin, *Nationalist Revolutionaries in Ireland 1858–1928* (Oxford, 1987), to whom much of the following passage is indebted.
45. Ibid., p. 21.
46. *Leader*, vol. 1, no. 1, 1 September 1900, p. 9.
47. M. Waters, 'Peasants and Emigrants: Considerations of the Gaelic League as a Social Movement' in D.J. Casey and R.E. Rhodes (eds.), *Views of the Irish Peasantry 1808–1916* (Hamden, Conn., 1977).
48. Tom Garvin, *Nationalist Revolutionaries in Ireland 1858–1928*, p. 54.
49. Robert Lynd, *Galway of the Races: Selected Essays*, edited by Sean McMahon (Dublin, 1990), p. 13.
50. Quoted in D.G. Boyce, *Nationalism in Ireland* (London, 1982), p. 351.
51. See especially 'Home Sickness' and 'The Wild Goose'.
52. *Remembering Sion* (London, 1934), p. 373.
53. Adrian Frazier, *Behind the Scenes: Yeats, Horniman and the Struggle for the Abbey Theatre* (London, 1990), pp. 164–5.
54. Quoted in ibid., pp. 166–7.
55. Ibid., p. 186.
56. Ibid., pp. 190–91.
57. Ibid., p. 180.
58. Isaiah Berlin, *Russian Thinkers* (Harmondsworth, 1975), p. 187.
59. Dáil Éireann Official Report, *Debate on the Treaty between Great Britain and Ireland* (Dublin, 1922), p. 184.
60. See, for example, Stephen Quinn, 'The Position of W.B. Yeats', *Catholic*

Bulletin, vol. 29, no. 7 (March 1939), pp. 183–4; *idem*, 'Further Placings for W.B. Yeats', ibid., no. 4 (April 1939), pp. 241–4.

61. Edward Callan, *Yeats on Yeats: The Last Introductions and the Dublin Edition*, New Yeats Papers XX (Dublin, 1981), p. 63.
62. T.P. Coogan, *Michael Collins* (London, 1990), p. 9.
63. Desmond Ryan, *Remembering Sion*, p. 249.
64. For an excoriating treatment of this syndrome, see Joseph Lee, *Ireland 1912–1985: Politics and Society* (Cambridge, 1990), *passim*, but especially pp. 380–81.
65. *Nations and Nationalism since 1780: Programme, Myth, Reality* (Cambridge, 1990), p. 134.
66. For a stimulating further example, Terry Eagleton's play *Saint Oscar* (1990) and the accompanying Field Day pamphlet on behalf of 'small nations struggling to be free', as well as his recent audacious essay asserting the Irishness of *Wuthering Heights*: *Irish Review*, no. 12 (Spring–Summer 1992), pp. 108–19.

Index

Names are indexed, but single passing references to places, books or periodicals are not always listed. Titles of works recurrently mentioned in the text are indexed under the author's entry in alphabetical order of title. Names of historians and other commentators are indexed where they occur in the text, but not in the notes – unless the note takes the form of a substantial additional comment rather than a simple reference.